Development Theory

Development Theory
An Introduction

P. W. Preston

Blackwell
Publishing

Reprinted 1997, 2000, 2002
Transferred to digital print 2002

Blackwell Publishers Ltd
108 Cowley Road
Oxford OX4 1JF, UK

Blackwell Publishers Inc
350 Main Street
Malden, Massachusetts 02148, USA

British Library Cataloguing in Publication Data
A CIP catalogue record for this book is available from the British Library

Library of Congress Cataloging in Publication Data
Preston, P. W. (Peter Wallace), 1949–
Development theory / P. W. Preston
p.   cm.
Includes bibliographical references and index.
ISBN 0–631–19554–8 (hbk) — ISBN 0–631–19555–6 (pbk)
1. Economic development. I. Title.
HD75.P734   1996   95–52581
338.9—dc20   CIP

Typeset in 11 on 12.5pt Sabon
by Graphicraft Typesetters Limited, Hong Kong
Printed in Great Britain by
Marston Lindsay Ross International Ltd, Oxford

Contents

List of Figures

Abbreviations and Acronyms

APEC	Asia Pacific Economic Cooperation
DC	developed country
ECLA	Economic Commission for Latin America
ERP	European Recovery Programme
GATT	General Agreement on Tariffs and Trade
IBRD	International Bank for Reconstruction and Development (World Bank)
ILO	International Labour Office
IMF	International Monetary Fund
IPE	international political-economy
ISI	import-substituting industrialization
ITO	international trade organization
LIC	low-intensity conflict
MNC	multi-national corporation
NAFTA	North American Free Trade Agreement
NGO	non-governmental organization
NIC	newly industrialized country
NIEO	new international economic order
ODA	official development aid
OPEC	Organization of Petroleum Exporting Countries
TNC	trans-national corporation
UDC	underdeveloped country
UNCTAD	United Nations Conference on Trade and Development
UNDP	United Nations Development Programme
WTO	World Trade Organization

Preface

In this book I have attempted to sketch the outline of the intellectual resources open to those scholars concerned with development who are working within, or with reference to, the classical European tradition of social theorizing. It seems to me that it is only on the basis of a critical appreciation of the scope and possibilities of received sets of ideas that more particular dialogic arguments and proposals for development can be made. An earlier treatment of the issues dealt with in this book appeared as *Making Sense of Development* (1986) and the present text builds on those discussions coupled to the more recent reflections presented in *Discourses of Development* (1994). The overall structure of the argument of this book can be reviewed as a series of related claims about the nature of social theorizing and the business of theorizing development.

1

Human beings are inhabitants of language-carried patterns of meaning which are conjoined with practical action. Human beings can be taken to be inhabitants of culture. The cognitive resources of a culture will be made available to the inhabitants of that culture in practical action, explanation and tradition.

One use to which these resources will be put is the business of making sense of the culture or form-of-life.

Human beings can be taken to be inhabitants of discrete forms-of-life.

Making sense of a discrete form-of-life can be understood generically to encompass the business of reading, interpreting, explaining or constituting the social world.

Making sense of the social world in this generic sense is thus hugely diverse and embraces a series of realms: common sense and routine practice; the technical knowledges and procedures of formally constituted organizations; the traditional knowledges of institutions; and the formal reflections created within the narrow and particular spheres of the arts and sciences.

2

Social science can be understood as a series of particular ways of making sense of the social world. The practices of social science can be taken to revolve around a core tradition.

In the classical European tradition, social theorists were concerned with the political-economic, social-institutional and cultural analysis of patterns of complex change. It can be said that they were concerned with making sense of the shift from agrarian feudal societies to industrial capitalist societies. The work was engaged, prospective and oriented to the pursuit of the modernist project.

3

As the industrial-capitalist system expanded it drew in a series of Third World territories. In each case the existing pattern of life was more or less extensively reconstructed so that the territory could fit within the increasingly integrated industrial-capitalist system.

It is possible to identify a series of contexts within which the nature of the Third World and its relationship to the industrial-capitalist system have been theorized: (a) readings from the pre-colonial period of early and limited trading contacts; (b) readings from the colonial period; (c) readings from the post-colonial period following decolonization; and (d) readings which treat the dynamics of the present tripolar global system.

If we simplify the debates in each period, we can say that all these episodes of involvement and theorizing express particular sets of concerns on the part of the First World countries in respect of the countries of the Third World.

All these episodes of theorizing are attempts to make sense of complex change within the increasing territory of the form-of-life of industrial-capitalism.

4

Any specific and restricted episode of theorizing in respect of the dynamics of complex change within the Third World must be understood as a discrete exercise in making sense and can be analysed schematically in terms of the following sequence: (a) occasion; (b) theory; (c) institutional base; and (d) results and aftermath.

In other words theorists have occasions to join in the debates about complex change and do so by proposing theories on behalf of a particular audience with a particular institutional power base in the hope of contributing to the efforts of that audience to effect change.

In the post-Second World War period a series of theories have been proposed: growth, modernization, dependency, institutional, marxist, global interdependence, and market liberal. Today, new work continues in both structural and agent-centred analysis.

The results and aftermaths of such complex political exercises in theoretically informed intervention in the dynamics of complex change are likely to be restricted and ambiguous.

It will not be easy to disentangle the particular contribution of formal theory to episodes of complex change.

5

Social theorists are only one group involved in the political-economic, social-institutional and cultural processes which make up the overall dynamic of the industrial-capitalist system. The theories which they have proposed can be taken to be contributions to particular debates within and about the processes of ongoing complex change within industrial-capitalism.

The arguments which social scientists have made have typically been addressed to audiences working in one of three main spheres: (a) policy advice; (b) political action; and (c) scholarship.

The post-colonial social scientific debate about development has generated substantive arguments which stress either the role of the state, or of the market, or of the polity.

The post-colonial social scientific debate about development has been dominated by the expectation of the recapitulation by the Third World of the historical experience of the First World.

At the present time the industrial-capitalist system is taking on the form of an interdependent tripolar global system. It seems clear that any simple export of the model of the West in either its state or market version can no longer be accepted as intellectually plausible.

In this book it will be argued that the immediate theoretical task for social scientists arguing on behalf of scholarship in the sphere of development work is the elucidation of a dialogic discourse of development oriented to the pursuit of democracy.

Such a discourse would express the core of the received tradition within which First World scholars necessarily work, and would be the basis for dialogic exchanges with members of other cultural traditions in respect of the sceptical elucidation of patterns of complex change.

In all, it would be a contemporary sceptical scholarly variant of the modernist project.

Acknowledgements

The arguments presented in this book have been pursued over a number of years and in that time I have accumulated intellectual debts to friends, colleagues and students in several universities in Europe and Asia. I am happy to acknowledge these debts as it seems to me that the pursuit of scholarship is a collective endeavour and the contribution of one person is heavily dependent upon the help of others. In respect of financial or institutional support I should like to thank The Research Committee of the University of Aberdeen, Scotland; Professor Hairi Abdullah, National University of Malaysia; Mr Richard Burke, The Canon Foundation in Europe; The Carnegie Trust for the Universities of Scotland; Professor Chan Heng Chee, Institute for Southeast Asian Studies, Singapore; Professor John Clammer, Sophia University, Japan; Professor Hans-Dieter Evers, University of Bielefeld, Germany; The Humboldt Foundation, Germany; Professor Ben Kerkvliet, Australian National University; Professor Richard Robison, Asia Research Center, Murdoch University, Australia; and The Research Committee of the University of Strathclyde, Scotland.

PART I
The Nature of Social Theorizing

1

Arguments and Actions in Social Theorizing

Overview of the General Nature of Social Theorizing

It is clear that development theorizing is a creative, complex and problematical exercise rather than a narrowly technical one, and that a measure of sensitivity to the inherent difficulties of social theorizing is important for development theorists. All exercises in social theorizing can be taken to involve ontological, epistemological, methodological and practical commitments on the part of the theorist. We can order these matters around the particular epistemological commitments made by social theorists. In their treatments of the formal nature of knowledge, philosophers have distinguished between empiricism and rationalism. The former view sees knowledge as essentially a product of experience; the latter sees knowledge as essentially a product of thought. This distinction reappears in social science. There are those who think that social science is or ought to be like natural science, and thus essentially concerned with describing how things are in fact. And there are those who think that social science is a variety of social philosophy, and thus concerned with the interpretive understanding of patterns of culture. The adherents of both approaches make characteristic claims for the strengths of their views and vigorously criticize the other. These debates continue. It can be noted that the key substantive concern of the classical European social scientific tradition is with the analysis of complex change. Ernest Gellner and Peter Worsley offer examples of prospective social theorizing and in each case a sophisticated substantive theory of the nature of change within the contemporary global system is presented.

Approaches to Theorizing

The business of social theorizing encompasses a wide variety of activities.[1] All these activities have it in common that they are attempts to make sense of the social world. Thus we can say that the term 'social theorizing' is a generic, or very general, one and that social theorizing is essentially about making sense of social situations. So we may instance, by way of examples, the following: literature and the arts; political and ethical schemes; the world of common sense; and the realm of formal social sciences, and so on. Each of these very diverse ways of making sense has its own procedures and goals, and inevitably there has been dispute about precisely how these various strategies of making sense should proceed (see figure 1).

In the sphere of the social sciences there is a series of ways of making sense of the social world and these can be analysed formally in terms of the complex set of claims they embody. In this sense all social theorizing can be understood to comprise complex 'package deals' which combine inter-linked claims in respect of the nature of the social world itself (ontology), the nature of the knowledge in respect of that social world which might be obtained (epistemology), the manner in which such knowledge might be secured (methodology), and finally, the use to which that knowledge might be expected to be put by particular agents in practical action within the social world (practice).[2]

The matter of the ontology of the social world has often been cast in terms of the distinction between the realm of material causes on the one hand and the realm of meanings and understandings on the other. The former sphere is taken to characterize the natural world, the sphere of operation of the natural sciences, and it is argued by some that the realm of the social can be approached in a similar way. The fundamental task of the social sciences then becomes one of naturalistically describing and explaining observable human behaviour – and the realm of meanings and understandings are pushed to one side as somehow derivative of the basic-ally material social world. On the other hand, in opposition to this view, it can be suggested that the central characteristic of the human world which is the sphere of concern of the social sciences is the extensive patterns of mean-ings and understandings which enfold human life. It is argued by some that such meanings and understandings are a matter of social beings inhabiting language-carried culture. In this case it is clear that the sphere of the social

1   On this see P. W. Preston 1985 *New Trends in Development Theory*, London, Routledge, especially ch. 2 which deals with these issues – how to characterize different 'modes of social theoretic engagement' and how to relate them to one another. Academic social theorizing is characterized by its 'pursuit of the truth (science)' and other modes (politics, policy, media and so on) may be ordered around this core scholarly mode.
2   There is a large literature dealing with these issues. See R. J. Anderson et al. 1985 *The Sociology Game*, London, Longman; R. J. Anderson et al. 1986 *Philosophy and the Human Sciences*, London, Croom Helm; Z. Bauman 1987 *Legislators and Interpreters*, Cambridge, Polity; M. Root 1993 *Philosophy of Social Science*, Oxford, Blackwell.

Figure 1 Making social science arguments

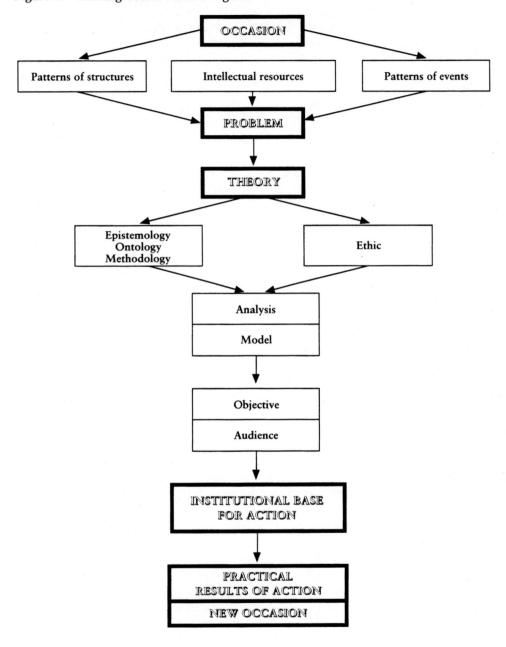

cannot be approached in a naturalistic fashion and that the matter of meanings and understandings must be directly acknowledged.

The fundamental ontological commitments in respect of the social world which are made by social theorists have clear epistemological implications. If the social world is construed as essentially a realm of material facts then enquiry can appropriately be descriptive and explanatory. The role of the social scientific observer is detached from enquiry and technical value-neutral reports on social mechanisms may be presented. If, on the other hand, the social world is construed as essentially a realm of cultural meanings and understandings then enquiry can appropriately be interpretive and critical. The role of the observer is not detached from enquiry and all social scientific results are seen to be value-suffused interventions in ongoing social processes.

In turn, the particular commitments which are made in respect of epistemology feed through into methodological strategies. In the case of those who argue for the fundamental materiality of the social world, and its consequent amenability to natural-science-style measurement and thereafter theory building so as to offer explanations of the descriptions made, the central methodological problem is one of securing accurate description of the given material social realm. In this perspective matters of valuation and the involvement of the researcher appear as so many potential sources of error. Again, in the contrasting perspective which views the social world as essentially a realm of meanings which might appropriately be addressed in an interpretive and critical fashion, the procedural problems revolve around interpretation and include reflection on premises and chains of reasoning.

The matter of the relationship of social theorizing to practical activity in the social world has been discussed at length within the social sciences. A range of views are available which for present purposes we can simplify by reporting that social scientists typically argue for one of three main audiences: scholarship, policy analysis and political life (see figure 2). In the first case an overriding commitment to the dispassionate display of the truth is affirmed. In the second case a concern for bureaucratically useful formulations comes to the fore. And in the last noted case a concern for the pursuit of particular political projects is central. In respect of this issue there has been a sharp debate between those who are concerned with policy analysis on the one hand and those who are concerned with political life on the other. The former have tended to see the latter as intellectually irresponsible whilst the latter have tended to see the former as intellectually blinkered. Of course, each group has made appeal to the sphere of scholarship. However, the ways in which scholarship has been construed have differed, with those disposed to policy science tending to assimilate scholarship to fact-based enquiry whereas those disposed to politics have tended to assimilate scholarship to the broad needs of the community. A recent variant of this debate cast matters in terms of a distinction between 'legislators' and 'interpreters' but there is little sign of any final agreement.[3]

3   See Bauman 1987 op. cit.

Figure 2   Social science arguments and actions

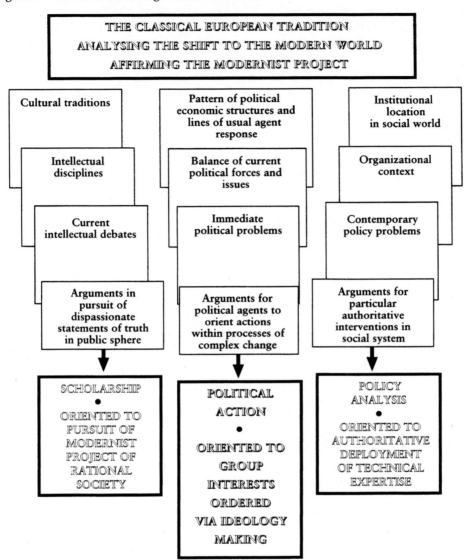

Overall, it is clear that within the sphere of the social sciences there is a series of ways in which these four elements can be combined. However, to simplify matters I will identify two different views of the nature of theorizing. The two views can be regarded as complex 'package deals' and each has different ideas about the nature, possibilities and problems of social science. Each view is informed by a particular view about knowledge in general and I will use these epistemological commitments as a way of distinguishing the two broad approaches. These positions can be called 'empiricism' and 'rationalism' and I will look at three points: first, the dispute between the proponents of the two positions as it appears within philosophy; second, the problems that typically associate with each position as they appear in social science; and, third, I will look at the positive claims made for each position within the social sciences.

Empiricism and rationalism

Within treatments of the history of philosophy authors sometimes find it convenient to identify two lines of thinking as to the basis of knowledge. On the one hand, there are those who argue that fundamentally knowledge comes primarily from experience, and that if we would be wise then we had best go out and look at the world. On the other hand, there are those who argue that knowledge comes primarily from thought, and that if we would be wise then we had better sit down to some serious thinking about the world. This is a bit of a caricature and usually in any one philosophical treatment of knowledge there is a mix of these elements. Nonetheless, they have been used as general labels for particular dispositions: the one designating those who look to experience (empiricism), the other those who look to thought (rationalism).

With the construction of modern social science through the nineteenth century these very general epistemological (theory of knowledge) views found expression, as one would expect, in the formulations of the new discipline. The presently identifiable divergent 'schools' within social science came into being at the same time as the discipline and they reflect, in some small measure, the disputes within philosophy. For my purposes I present these two schools of social science as follows: on the one hand we have those who think that social science is, or ought to be, like natural science (where this is conceived in an empiricist way); and, on the other, we have those who think that social science is best read as a variety of social philosophy (where this is taken as tending to the rationalistic).[4]

Natural science as it is conceived by the proponents of the orthodoxy of social science, and in 'lay' or commonsense notions, presents itself as the collection of facts, the preparation of descriptive generalizations, and finally, the presentation of summary theoretical statements. Few theorists in social science would offer quite such a crude scheme today; nonetheless, it represents the unspoken commonsense of social science. And it is this model that is invoked by those who would make social science like natural science.

Thus they confront the problem of collecting facts. In the natural sciences this seems to be straightforward; observation may require high technology but it is basically a matter of the measurement of the real world. Not so in social science: where are the equivalent 'facts' in the web of human relationships that is the subject-matter of social science? Taking measurements of

4   Often over the post-Second World War period this distinction empiricism/rationalism has been close to a distinction Anglo-Saxon/European.

the social world looks to be a difficult task even after you have decided that it is possible.

Similar problems confront the proponents of the orthodoxy when it comes to presenting the 'results' of observation. The detail of the social world does not lend itself, in the way detail of natural scientific enquiry does, to quantification and statistical analysis. People in groups typically inhabit a realm of meanings, hopes and fears, intentions and so on, whereas natural science deals with physical causes and effects. Translating the substance of social life into quantified and manipulable data is not just technically difficult, it is philosophically problematical. The orthodox either ignore all this or resolve to try very hard to be 'objective'.

This brings us to a major related worry: that of the extirpation of value-seepage. The orthodox take natural science to be value-free, which is to say that the results of natural science are ethically and politically neutral. Clearly this is a plausible claim – even if it looks rather strained when one thinks of, say, research into weapons technology – but can the same claim be made in social science? The results of social science work evidently do have ethical and political relevance; so how can the social scientist be sure that values are not creeping into the research and biasing it this way or that? The orthodox worry about being 'objective' and value neutral and they draw a clear distinction between science and ideology. It is ideology that lies at the foot of that slippery slope which opens up if the unwary social scientist becomes embroiled in value-laden work.

The issue which summarizes, for the orthodox, all these various insecurities in respect of their intellectual status, is that of the maturity (or immaturity) of social science. Taking note of the continuing argument within social science as to how it ought properly to proceed, the orthodox suggest that this squabble will subside when social science attains scientific maturity. This is a matter, it is said, of methodological, procedural and conceptual refinement. The continuing debate is evidence of immaturity, and in particular of a failure to off-load political and ethical concerns.

So much for the problems of those who would make social science like natural science. Let us now turn to those who would make social science a variety of social philosophy: they rather tend to affirm a rationalist epistemology. The active, creative contribution of thought to knowledge is stressed. Additionally, it is claimed that the advocates of the orthodoxy have a very restricted idea of science. It is suggested that they place far too much emphasis on scientific experimental procedure: their epistemology is swamped by considerations of a particular method. The rationalists affirm a notion of science as 'disciplined enquiry' and the split between science and ideology is denied. This creates the intellectual space for various disciplines, including social science, to lay claim to be producing knowledge without having to apologize for the manner of the production of their work – without, that is, feeling that the absence of an experimental procedure entails a reduced intellectual status.

In social science, conceived as a variety of social philosophy, the typical problems are these: starting points, theoretical frameworks, criteria of truth and validity (relativism) and, in the background, the business of ranking competing schemes. Those who make social science a variety of social philosophy see the business of social theorizing as, centrally, making sense of the social world so as to be able to act in it. The discipline aspires to an interpretive (and sometimes critical) knowledge rather than, as with orthodox schemes and natural science, a descriptive knowledge.

An initial problem for this (central) view concerns starting points: what premises are arguments which interpret the world to be based upon? Premises have to be appropriate to given circumstances and problems. This seems to entail, generally, providing a set of premises that are both coherent and explanatorily rich enough to accomplish interpretation. More particularly, this might involve: intelligible accommodation to the facts as they are ordinarily understood; and the illumination of the possibilities for the future in a way relevant to present practice.

A related problem concerns the matter of theoretical frameworks, ordered sets of premises. In this school, theory is not a summary statement; it is, rather, the set of premises deployed in order to make sense of the world. Theoretical frameworks tell us what sort of world we have, what sort of explanations to provide, of which particular problems. Consequently, this school is very concerned with theoretical frameworks, for once you accept the premises of an argument you are bound, if it is valid in form, to accept the conclusions.

A central issue for those who affirm a notion of social philosophy is that of the use of the concept of ideology. The term can be used in a variety of ways: one of these is to designate those general, interpretive arguments designed to make politically relevant sense of the world. An issue that flows out of this area is that of rationally adjudicating between competing schemes.

In sum, for the orthodox the production of knowledge is essentially a matter of reporting how things are, and problems tend to cluster around accuracy of reports. For the social philosophers the production of knowledge is essentially a matter of generating interpretive understanding and the business has many guises, and problems cluster around the making of sense (by whom, how, when and what for?). Turning to my final point it may be asked: what do the proponents of these two 'tendencies' claim as the strengths of their positions? Here the orthodoxy, those who invoke the natural sciences, tell us that they produce a scientific-type knowledge that enables the social world to be organized in an authoritative way. Knowledge is the possession of the expert. In Western industrial societies much social scientific work, conceived in this fashion, feeds into the state planning machines, or corporations. And, on the other hand, the counter-tradition, who invoke social philosophy, see academic social theorizing as one activity amongst many which are concerned to make sense of the world. As academics, they are concerned to display the truth – and when they deal with society they often discover an interpretive role: making the actions of one group intelligible to themselves and to other groups.

The two approaches of rationalism and empiricism, and their associated social science approaches, are not sharply exclusive. They are 'tendencies' and both elements will be found in some proportion in the work of any one theorist. Most do lean clearly one way or the other – few inhabit the middle ground. In this text I will understand social science in this rationalist or social philosophical style. Academic social science is interpretive and concerned to display the truth disinterestedly. My view is that orthodox empiricist social science is too narrow in conception. The detailed descriptive work offered by these theorists is valuable but the claim that is often made to the effect that empirical social science is the only legitimate social science is false. However, let us now look at the business of social theorizing from another perspective by considering the work of the theorists Ernest Gellner and Peter Worsley.

Ernest Gellner's Theorizing

Gellner's book *Thought and Change*[5] is an example of the social-philosophical approach to social science that I have spoken of above and although his work is interesting for a number of reasons I am interested not so much in what he says, but in how he says it. It is clear that Gellner's work is prospective, multi-disciplinary and engaged. Gellner's major concern is to display the nature of a politics relevant to the industrializing and industrial present. Clearly this is an interpretive rather than descriptive role, and in the text models, morals and methods of ordering change are all explicitly invoked and intermingled. This explicitness makes the total process self-conscious, or reflexive. Gellner argues that sociology is the heir of political philosophy because it now asks those questions which are central to both conceptualizing and legitimating modern society. So far as Gellner is concerned, sociology seeks to elucidate the nature of industrialism. This is an interesting claim and it lodges Gellner firmly within the classical European tradition of social theory. However, for our immediate purposes Gellner's text is of interest because: (a) he declares his goal, his intention, which is to rework political philosophy (which now embraces sociology) for the tasks of the present day; (b) he openly reviews and plunders the intellectual resources of his discipline, reworking available ideas to suit his declared intention; (c) he explicitly discusses how to theorize his problem once he has sketched its outline; and finally (d) he goes on to identify some of the more obvious consequences of his newly constructed position. In the text an argument is presented which is designed to interpret the world so as to guide action and the addressees, those to whom the remarks are primarily aimed, are the intellectuals, planners and bureaucrats of complex modern industrial society.

Gellner is an anthropologist, political philosopher and sociologist. Writing in the mid-1960s, before the optimism in respect of change which characterized the period had declined, he attempts to redraw the boundaries

5 E. Gellner 1964 *Thought and Change*, London, Weidenfeld.

of political philosophy to accommodate the contemporary debate about industrialism, convergence and modernization. The aim is to offer a general statement which presents the key ideas of the relatively new theory. Gellner reviews existing philosophical and sociological theories of change and having indicated their respective strengths and weaknesses goes on to advocate a scientifically informed politics of 'the transition': the shift to the modern world. The process of industrializing can be understood as a species of scientific problem and can be ordered as a species of social-science-informed practical political work. A key role is therefore given to those experts with knowledge of the relevant social processes. For the industrializing Third World nations political power must rest with an industrializing elite which will be Western trained and/or Western oriented. For the West, coming perhaps towards the later phases of the transition, this elitist corporatist model of politics is somewhat muted. Gellner's overall vision is revealed in his expectation of the future character of ideology when there will be a dual system of explanations of the social world: (a) broad, vague, legitimating slogans for the masses; and (b) detailed scientific knowledge (natural and social) as the actual basis for ordering society which will be the property of the elite.

Gellner begins his argument with the claim that any society has a scheme which will render that society's form and apparent historical direction both coherent and legitimate in the eyes of its inhabitants. An explanatory ideology in other words. In the Western world this has, since the Renaissance's reworking of mystical religious ideals of perfectibility, typically been a notion of social progress. Often these matters have been discussed historically,[6] but Gellner presents another route through this material: he offers a schematic reconstruction. There are three forms of the idea of progress. Each has a philosophical and historical character, each has explanatory benefits and disbenefits. Gellner wants a scheme for the present. He identifies the following.

1   The episodic view: there is in world history one move from a bad state of affairs to a good state; for example the making of the 'social contract'. Sociologically, these schemes are unsophisticated. It is, historically, typically Enlightenment material.

2   The evolutionist view: there is in world history an all-embracing and permanent process of cumulative progressive change. This is typically a nineteenth-century line and it tends to be associated with Darwin, even though the extent of his contribution to the social sciences is problematic. Gellner identifies three defects with the evolutionist strategy: (a) locating an event in a series does not explain it; (b) a moral judgement has to be more than affirming a trend otherwise you run into the problem of the incoherence of affirming determinism; and (c) the scheme does not fit the experience of the Third World, and this for Gellner is important as it is the experience of debates on the Third World that provides a learning experience for everyone.

3   The neo-episodic view: Gellner offers this as the outline of a new

6   See, for example, S. Pollard 1971 The Idea of Progress, Harmondsworth, Penguin.

legitimating myth of progress. It is constructed by selectively reworking the above noted schemes. From the episodic theory he takes the idea of progress as an event and from the evolutionist scheme the idea of progress as a pervasive continuing process. The two are run together in his neo-episodic stance which affirms that the politics of today must focus on the episode of progress, that is, industrialism. Gellner calls this a politics of the transition. The episode of progress, which is conceived by Gellner as a pervasive and continuing process, has the twin virtues of plausibility and manageability. The neo-episodic scheme posits an event in world history: it is empirically plausible and intellectually it does not expand to fill all available explanatory space.

Having thus far described the general character of the required new myth or legitimating theorem of modern industrial society, Gellner now proceeds to consider the business of how to theorize the new scheme. He begins by reflecting upon the nature of a moral problem. It is characterized as being a dilemma where the appropriate rules of judgement, as well as judgements of detail, are problematic. We neither know what to think nor how to think. Gellner sees the business of theorizing the transition as being a similar sort of task. The transition will have to be grasped from the inside by the use of scientific thought. Scientific thought, for Gellner, is a qualitatively different sort of thinking from any other because it is routinely self-critical. The transition is science-based and thus potentially self-conscious. It is science that is the key to grasping its character and the key to a new morality.

Gellner reviews established ethical theories and rejects them all. Thus he looks at the following: (a) the Platonic, where concepts give standards as they classify the world; thus the notions 'gentleman', 'bride', 'court of law', and so on, both designate the character of phenomena and set limits to variation; (b) the Hidden Prince, which suggests that inside every man is a good man trying to get out, and that it is society which, as the young Marx argued, is alienating; (c) the Dream of the Bureaucrat, where life is conceived as exemplifying rules, and ethics are rules; (d) the Way of Residue, which is complementary to (b) except that the goal is not specified – rather the obstacles to its realization are, so remove the obstacles; (e) the Supreme Target, which takes behaviour to be purposeful, so a supreme target and ranked intermediate steps can be specified, as with, for example, utilitarianism; and (f) the Rail, which suggests that freedom is the recognition of necessity, as with historicist schemes. Gellner then presents his own ethic which centres on industrialism. In the short term we can discern the future in very broad outline and it will be an industrial society free from want. A mixture of the Supreme Target and the Rail are finally appropriated to support the idea of industrialism. We have an outline of our future and can take sensible steps towards that future goal.

Gellner then turns to matters of method and looks to the philosophy of science. Gellner starts by noting that social arrangements have often been legitimated in a dualistic fashion, by invoking parallel worlds, as with religion.

But these strategies are now out of fashion and there are two favoured replacements: (a) centring explanatory theories on the social totality; and (b) centring theories on the individual. Gellner rejects the first strategy as it is liable to slide into general evolutionist nonsense and affirms a variant of the second strategy. It is Popperian critical rationalism with a central celebration of the method of science. In scientific enquiry the work proceeds by the systematic elimination of error. The programme is limited in its formal claims about the world but is hugely optimistic in respect of its possibilities. This science encompasses both natural and social scientific concerns.[7]

In the wake of the transition Gellner expects ideology to wither away. He points to the fact of affluence which reduces social tension, and to the character of scientific thinking. Gellner sees a social system comprising for presently relevant purposes two sorts of thinking. On the one hand, there will be very general and vague legitimating ideas and the implication is that these ideas will be virtually mere noise. On the other hand, there will be scientific thinking and here the implication is that technical rationality will encompass not merely the natural sciences, but also the social and in particular policy science. The model of Gellner's future industrial world is of a rational order, functionally and hierarchically organized.

This all establishes the core of his stance, and he now turns to some related issues. Gellner acknowledges, firstly, that there is one social philosophy that actually does look at the transition, namely marxism. The approach taken in marxist analysis, with the focus on social structure and conflict in the process of the development of the division of labour, is correct. However, the particular concepts chosen which revolve around the idea of capitalism are wrong, and they should be replaced by those which centre upon the notion of industrialism. Then, secondly, Gellner goes on to look at nationalism which is the familiar locus of legitimating social myths in the modern period and argues that nationalist sentiment is a functional requisite of the establishment of autonomous capitalisms within the world economy. Just as nationalism was needed first time around to aid the bourgeoisie in establishing itself both internationally and domestically, so new nationalist industrializing elites find the doctrine of assistance. Nationalism is the culture of otherwise fragmented polities. So far as Gellner is concerned, it can be 'nice' or 'nasty' – it is the politics of the philosopher kings, the modernizing elite.

Gellner's final remarks look to the manner of production of social knowledge. It is science that is 'the mode of cognition of industrial society, and industry is the ecology of science'[8] and given this it is the scientist who

---

7   Gellner, having borrowed Popper's 'critical rationalism', wants to adopt an idea of science which combines, so to say, the two traditions of rationalism and empiricism where enquiry is driven by theory and guaranteed by the facts. Unfortunately it cannot be done in this fashion and, in the event, Gellner's position ends up close to the empiricist position. His overall argument is thus ambiguous and unpersuasive as his calls for an authoritative planning rest upon this unsatisfactory notion of science.
8   Gellner 1964 op. cit. p. 179.

moves centre stage. The scientist displaces the man of letters. Gellner sees a conflict between the sophisticated common sense of humanist culture and the non-obvious conflicting science. Gellner takes this conflict to be profound for at base these are conflicting views of humankind. Gellner confidently reports that the humanist image of humankind will be replaced by the scientific–industrial image.

Overall, Gellner presents a theory-driven interpretive analysis of the present dynamic of the social world which is addressed to a particular group in the expectation that it will inform their practical action in the world. The substantive argument presented is a variant of the industrial society theory which looks to the expert elucidation of the inherent logic of the industrial system. The expectation is that the global system will slowly converge on the model of the modern exemplified by the developed West. However, the key lesson for the present is that the work is multi-disciplinary, prospective and engaged.

Peter Worsley's Theorizing

The work of Peter Worsley is a further example of the social philosophical strategy of enquiry and is concerned with analysing the historical development of the industrial capitalist form-of-life.[9] Worsley analyses the situation of the countries of the Third World in terms of the dynamic of expansion of the global system and the process of absorption experienced by the countries of the Third World. The absorption within the expanding global capitalist system can be understood as an episode of complex change which ushered in the slowly changing systems of colonialism. The collapse of the colonial system ushered in a new phase of complex change as territorial areas which had been elements of wide Europe-centred empire trading blocks reconstituted themselves as sovereign nation states within the global system with its transient bipolar character. At the present time the processes of further global extension are presenting the peoples of the Third World with new structural demands to which they must fashion a reply in the form of an apposite political project. The approach adopted by Worsley combines material from cultural anthropology, the humanist–marxist tradition, modern development theory, and makes routine reference to contemporary political discussions and events in order to produce a dense substantive statement in respect of the development experience of the countries of the Third World. Overall, the argument is that what we are trying to grasp under the heading of 'development' is in fact the large scale historical process of the development of the world capitalist industrial system. Worsley is interested in how this system has developed over time in the First and Second Worlds, and how it now bears down upon the Third World.

The modern world can be understood as a particular cultural form which

9 P. Worsley 1984 *The Three Worlds: Culture and World Development*, London, Weidenfeld; P. Worsley 1964 *The Third World*, London, Weidenfeld.

originated in Europe and has slowly spread to cover much of the world. Existing local cultures have been slowly drawn into the modern system and their patterns of life variously altered. The modern world is dominated by industrial capitalist culture. This cultural form comprises the general celebration of the power of human reason, the extensive development of natural science, and a political-economic system dedicated to material progress via industry. This cultural form developed in Europe over the period 1500–1900. And over this period it both refined itself internally (that is, it became better organized and penetrated through the social world) and expanded externally (that is, it grew geographically). This expansion has slowly absorbed new territories. In these territories there were usually existing cultures. However, these cultures have been extensively modified in the process of absorption into the European-centred system. Geographically the expansion took this form: (a) 1550–1800 Latin America (Portugal, Spain); (b) 1550–1800 North America (France, UK); (c) 1700–1900 Asia (France, Netherlands, UK, Russia, USA); and (d) 1800–1935 Africa (France, Portugal, Spain, Belgium, UK, Italy). Then economically the expansion took this form: (a) by 1550 precious metals traded, or seized; (b) by 1700 spices and other luxury goods traded; (c) by 1800 agricultural goods produced for developing industrial capitalist system; and (d) by 1900 plantation agricultural goods and minerals produced for developing industrial scientific capitalist system. Relatedly, politically the expansion took this form: (a) by 1550 there were occasional trade visits; (b) by 1700 there was routine trading plus local agents (factory); (c) by 1800 there was extensive trading plus growing political influence; and by 1900 trade was conducted within the frame of imposed colonial rule. The process of the expansion of the industrial capitalist form-of-life means that present patterns of underdevelopment are the outcome of long historical processes, with the Third World usually having been on the receiving end of European pressures. It also means that the present attempts by Third World countries to achieve development are undertaken within a world system that is dominated by the industrial capitalism of the USA, East Asia, and Europe.

Worsley begins his detailed analysis by noting that most of the people of the world have organized and continue to organize their livelihoods with small-scale farming. If we consider the peasantry it is clear that their fates in the developed West, the old Second World, and the Third World have been shaped by the rise of industrial capitalism. Worsley notes that it is typical of the broad shift to the modern world that there are large population shifts from rural-agricultural patterns of life to urban-industrial patterns of life.

Peasant forms-of-life revolve around subsistence agricultural production and whilst peasants are difficult to define the key seems to be that the basic economic and social unit is the household: (a) economic activity centres on the household (production and consumption); and (b) the household is the crucial unit for most social matters (marriage, residence, kin networks). The key resource is land which is typically viewed as held in trust so it is not a commodity and it cannot be bought and sold. The exchange of peasant households with the wider political-economic world was usually asymmetric and peasants were the weaker players who were often exploited either directly via tithes, rents, taxes, or theft, or indirectly via credit/debt relations.

In Europe the system of feudalism develops in the post-Roman period and is characterized by large estates with subordinate peasantries subject to weak states. It was a hierarchical society centred on agriculture/land and had many fissures and conflicts (peasant revolts, vagabonds, use of marginal land, running away et cetera). The feudal system declines as modern capitalism develops with the rise of the towns, the decline of the political power of estate holders as the central state becomes powerful, and rise of trade, travel and science. As industrial capitalism develops there is shift of population to the industrial towns and agriculture slowly becomes the commercial agribusiness of today. In a similar way in the USSR the legacy of the Russian peasant feudalism is taken up by the Bolsheviks and the system of the collective farm is instituted. In China after 1948 the pattern is repeated. Both have seen mixes of state and regional direction of large collective farms coupled to local level or individual household private holdings. The peasantry resist and are absorbed. Overall no-one starved but nor did production flourish. And certainly the utopian dreams came to nothing. In contrast, in the Third World peasant communities have survived. Peasant life in colonial territories recalls the experience of the European peasantry: the pattern of life centred on the household; the economic basis was subsistence farming; a new system gradually encroached; culminating in formal colonialism (officials, laws, taxes); economic life remained largely on the land (as subsistence or plantation) but the wider world of market capitalism increasingly impacted upon the peasantry. The episode of decolonization bequeathed subsistence plus plantation agriculture to the replacement elites and they have pursued rural development. In many Third World countries the larger part of the populations still subsist as peasant farmers. However this is rapidly changing as the modern world impinges upon even the most remote communities. And all the time capitalist relations continue to invade the sphere of peasant life. The World Bank and the IMF actively encourage cash-cropping with the result that hunger increases as agricultural products are exported to the First World. Worsley sees a world agribusiness system in the making and the demise of the peasantry.

Worsley argues that the shift to the modern world which will destroy the peasantry began with the rise of urban-industrial patterns of life. This has been taking place down through history with the rise and decline of civilizations. In nineteenth-century Europe there was a massive shift from the land to the cities. The shift now taking place in the Third World is even greater in terms of numbers. The shift began with the colonial period, as the global system reached into these areas and made them elements in the wider system. There were migrations to serve the needs of mines and plantations and the cities that acted to link system and locality. The pull-factors were those of an economically active centre. The push-factors were hardship. In the First World the historical record involves urbanization coupled to industrialization. Today in the Third World there seems to be urbanization with only partial industrialization. The conditions of cities are bad, and look as though they might remain so for a long period. What we find in Third World cities is a very mixed pattern: areas of prosperity, linked to state-machinery or branch offices of MNCs; areas of relative security, linked to the established production and service activities of the city; and areas of relative insecurity, found in the extensive marginal patterns of life (some speak of urban petty subsistence on the analogy of rural peasant subsistence). Worsley details eleven patterns of poor living in Third World cities: urban poor in industrial jobs; sweat-shops; homeworkers; self-employed artisans; domestic labour; street vendors; personal service sector; casual labour; petty traders; criminals and deviant groups; beggars and unemployed. What is noticeable is that these patterns are active and coherent, and that many of these forms are not marginal to the wider system, they are fully integrated, but poor. They are active economically and rely on kin networks for support. And the closer to the core of the local economy the better the livelihood. The patterns of life of the poor are varied. Yet they have it in common that they are active in their engagement with the structures that enfold them. Life in a shanty town is still therefore life in a town. And for those with jobs near the core of the economy the usual global consumerism can be available.

The classical nineteenth-century European tradition of social science concerned itself with the political-economic, social institutional and cultural analysis of complex change: in general, the attempt to make sense of the shift from agrarian feudal to industrial capitalist societies. The development theory of today inherits this tradition and concerns itself with the particular experience of the countries of the Third World. The nature of economy and society in Third World countries was altered very extensively by this process of absorption into the European system, and we can identify the following patterns: (a) settler colonialism with the local populations displaced, and occasionally exterminated (USA, Canada, Australia); (b) settlers plus intermarriage plus marginalized locals (Latin America); (c) transplanted populations with local populations displaced (Caribbean, East Africa, parts of Asia); (d) colonial regimes replacing existing ruling groups and only slowly changing political-economic systems and then withdrawing (most of Asia); and (e) colonial regimes replacing existing rulers and disrupting radically existing cultures and then withdrawing (Africa). It was on the basis of these legacies that in the post-Second World War period the new countries of the Third World became participants in a sustained drive to reconstruct their societies as integral parts of the global industrial capitalist system. The key was the pursuit of effective nationstatehood. Worsley picks up this theme in terms of the demands of nationalism and the construction of identity, and to this are added notions of race and ethnicity. Worsley discusses the complex and situationally relative allocation of groups into categories having stereotyped characteristics and specific patterns of social superiority and subordination within the overall pursuit of new national identities.

Overall, Worsley analyses the situation of the countries of the Third World in terms of the dynamic of expansion of the global system and the process of absorption experienced by the countries of the Third World. The absorption within the expanding global capitalist system can be understood as an episode of complex change which ushered in the slowly changing systems of colonialism. The collapse of the colonial system ushered in a new phase of complex change as territorial areas which had been elements of wide Europe-centred empire trading blocks reconstituted themselves as sovereign nationstates within the global system with its transient bipolar character. At the present time the processes of further global extension are presenting the peoples of the Third World with new structural demands to which they must fashion a reply in the form of an apposite political project.

Analysing Change

The work of Gellner and Worsley like all prospective social theorizing involves models, morals and methods of ordering change. The substantive core concern of the classical European tradition of social theorizing has been with the analysis of complex change. This means that the elements of models, morals and methods have been extensively discussed in the literature and it will be useful for us to take note of some of these broader discussions.

Models of change[10]

It is generally true that many areas of concern within social science are made more difficult than they might otherwise be by the fact that the issues looked at are, at the same time, issues upon which the commonsense of society has a view. In discussing change in society we immediately confront the commonsense view that change is all-pervasive and accelerating. This pervasive and accelerating rate of social change is often both contrasted with a more stable past ('the good old days'), and held to be responsible for many present social ills ('disruption and the loss of surety'). In social science we need to be aware of both (a) the subtle role of metaphor within social theorizing and (b) the need for social scientists to uncover the crucial axes of underlying social change.

It can be argued that many people, including social scientists, are bemused by changes of a superficial kind and arguably by the continuing

10 See A. D. Smith 1976 *Social Change: Social Theory and Historical Process*, London, Routledge; E. Etzioni-Halevy 1981 *Social Change: The Advent and Maturation of Modern Society*, London, Routledge; P. Sztompka 1993 *The Sociology of Social Change*, Oxford, Blackwell.

implications of the undoubted major change of the coming of industrial capitalism. It is possible to be misled into thinking that rapid and continuing change is essential to all social systems. However, if we turn to consider the broad sweep of human life then it is possible to argue for long periods of stability. The matter cannot be resolved empirically because what is at issue in this area of debate – change versus stability – is the choice of basic metaphors. The decision made by the social theorists to construe change as either inevitable or unusual has wider implications for the explanations which will thereafter be offered. The change versus stability debate echoes a series of related debates: (a) political radicalism versus political conservatism; (b) optimism versus pessimism; (c) the necessity of social scientific engagement versus the possibility of social scientific general description, and so on.

An issue that follows on from the matter of the role of the metaphors lodged within the common sense of society, and running into the thinking of social theorists, is the importance of social scientists' distinguishing between significant social change and superficial changes in style. As I have said above, in social science we are concerned to grasp underlying or significant social change. Social theorists select amongst the variety of surface social phenomena according to sets of assumptions, or theoretical frameworks, which identify crucial axes of social change. This, of course, was precisely the strategy adopted by the classical nineteenth-century theorists of complex change. In the work of Adam Smith, significant social change was taken to flow from the marketplace-regulated changes generated by technological improvements in the division of labour. In the work of Marx, significant social change is taken to flow from class conflict within the context of the progressive development of the overall mode of production. In the case of Durkheim, significant social change was evidenced in the growing complexity of the evolving division of labour. In a related way, Weber saw significant social change being evidenced in the growing disenchantment of the world which was the cultural counterpart to increasingly rational patterns of social order.

Social theorizing is full of the use of metaphor and we inherit these metaphors from earlier generations of thinkers and often their thought comes to us as wholly unremarked commonsense, be it the commonsense of society or the commonsense of the discipline of learning we follow. In talking about social change there are two basic metaphors: continuity and rupture. Social change is seen as either cumulative, slow, ceaseless, and so on, or as violent, discontinuous and periodic.

In respect of continuity we can note that in the nineteenth century evolutionary explanations of social change were frequently presented. It is often said that Darwin was the great influence here but this is rather misleading as schemes of social evolution had been produced before the ideas of biological evolution. Indeed, it has been said recently that Darwin borrowed from the social theorists whilst thereafter lending them greater superficial credibility. In the early twentieth century, for example, the social evolutionist

Herbert Spencer was welcomed in the USA by business circles as they felt that his theories legitimated their unrestrained pursuit of wealth and it is clear that notions of natural selection and the survival of the fittest sat easily with doctrines of economic *laissez-faire*.

The logic of evolutionism can be summarized in five points:[11] (a) the idea of holism, where the object of enquiry is the whole and not the parts (and thus the broadest possible approach is taken – 'civilization' or 'culture'); (b) the idea of cumulative change, which insists that there are no sharp discontinuities; (c) the idea of endogenous change, which suggests that the impetus for change arises from within the system; (d) the idea of increasing complexity, which suggests that there is a shift from simple social forms (traditional) to complex ones (modern); and (e) the idea of a unitary direction to change, which suggests that the whole process has a fixed direction. However, evolutionism fell into disrepute in the early years of the twentieth century. It was attacked by anthropologists of the diffusionist and functionalist schools: the former looking to external sources of change, and the latter pointing to the internal complexity and stability of societies. A little later in the 1940s and 1950s, neo-evolutionary approaches were presented. In these schemes we find that elements of evolutionism, diffusionism and especially functionalism are run together in a general approach that claims to be able to explain stable, ordered, change as societies evolve and mature. These neo-evolutionist explanations of social change have been very influential. They have claimed to explain change and identify an overall pattern which leads in the direction of modern society. However it seems more plausible to see the evolutionist argument of recent years as little more than a celebration of the history of the West, and the USA in particular.

In respect of the notion of rupture we find a very different view. Here we have schemes of social change which stress the role of social tensions and group conflict. Change is seen as discontinuous and periodic. Most importantly. we have the marxist school. In place of the pursuit of a theory of ordered and stable change, we have the presentation of a theory which postulates the existence of groups in society having conflicting interests. The interplay of these interests – the historical pattern of conflict – provides the motor for change. The historical world of industrial capitalism is seen as a dynamic expansionist system riven by class conflict.

The classical marxian expectations of the future of capitalism involved its gradual spread across the globe as capitalist entrepreneurs destroyed local historically outmoded social forms and created in their place new centres of capitalist society. This optimistic scheme was modified around the turn of the century when the marxian notion of imperialism was presented. It came to be thought that the capitalist system might be longer lived than originally anticipated and that peripheral areas might have their development hindered by the interests of the centres. In the post-Second World War period a new analysis of capitalism has been presented and the neo-marxists

11   Smith 1976 op. cit. pp. 34–6.

see an essentially static and stagnating capitalist heartland surrounded by a deformed and dependent periphery.

In summary it can be noted that when we consider social change it is not enough merely to aim to describe changes. The attempt to make sense of social change is central to social science. Social change is grasped via a social theory which specifies the crucial elements of change. Ankie Hoogvelt,[12] dealing with approaches to theorizing development, remarks that what is crucial is the choice between the acceptance of historical change and the pursuit of timeless ahistorical formulae.

Ethics of change[13]

Discussions of change within the literature of social science have been, in the main, couched in terms of approval. There are some social theorists who have regretted the rise of industrial society, but these figures are in a minority. The most familiar ethical term associated with discussions of changes is 'progress'. This term can be elucidated by identifying the two principal eighteenth- and nineteenth-century versions of it, and from there we can turn to post-Second World War theories of development and identify a series of versions of the idea of progress. All the major theories of development are informed by Western ethics and this raises an obvious question. What have other ethical systems to say about development?

The idea of progress was given recognizably modern formulation in the eighteenth and nineteenth centuries. There are two main positions: their political labels would be liberal-democratic and (radical) democratic. The first position analyses society by invoking the specialist social sciences within a general evolutionary framework. The model of man invoked is 'man as consumer'. The ethic is thus not optimistic, seeing humankind acting in the light of selfish wants, and the general scheme of historical change is implausible and the whole process is seen as only restrictedly intelligible. In contrast, the second position analyses society by invoking an historical materialist approach. The model of man invoked is 'man as doer'. The ethic is thus optimistic, seeing humankind acting in the light of social goals which advance over time, and the analysis of historical change is plausible, and the whole process is taken as amenable to interdisciplinary enquiry and extensively intelligible. It is these two positions which form the background to post-Second World War theories of development. Three types of theories can be identified, each having a different idea of what actually counts as progress or development: liberal market, social market and radical democratic.

The earliest group of theorists were those labelled liberal market and their work falls into three parts: an early UK/UN line which was heavily influenced by economics; a subsequent line which was a distinctly US product and mixed in rather more sociology with the economics; and finally an

12   A. Hoogvelt 1982 *The Third World in Global Development*, London, Macmillan.
13   This is pursued further in Preston 1985 op. cit.

atavistic neo-classicism which emphatically asserted the priority of the marketplace in human affairs and the subordination of the state thereto. All three versions have it in common that progress is equated with economic growth, which is evidenced in statistical indices of growth. The goal of development, or progress, is understood to be amenable to technical characterization and taken as elicited by authoritative social-science-informed intervention in the social world. The ideological function of this scheme is quite clear: a relationship of super- and sub-ordination is legitimated whereby the development of the presently underdeveloped is ordered by the experts of the developed countries and their agents.

The social market theorists have it in common that they reject orthodox economics and substitute a 'sociologized economics'. The goal of development, or progress, is no longer associated with economic growth called forth by the application of the technical expertise of the economists, but is conceived much more broadly: it becomes equated with planned, ordered, social reform. It is arguably the case that this position – progress as ordered social reform – represents the commonsense of much work in development studies, particularly that produced by theorists other than economists: it is pragmatic, humane and plausible.

The radical democrats affirm a democratic ethic and an historical materialist strategy of analysis. The radical democrats within development studies attempt to recover what is a rather submerged countertradition to the liberal-democratic schemes noted above. The model of humankind affirmed, the ethic, is that of 'man as doer' and development, or progress, is understood to be coterminous with the pursuit of (radical) democracy.

Within social sciences the phenomenon of social change has been, in the main, viewed with approval and such approval has been expressed in terms taken from Western ethical schemes. Given that social science was constructed in the West during the period of the industrial revolution, this bias should not surprise us. For our present interests in theorizing development there are two matters to note: one concerns the orthodox view of development and the other raises more general questions in respect of ethical systems.

The orthodox (both liberal and social market) rather tend to take the whole business of development as being technical or obvious, and usually both. In the former case development is conceived as a matter of building appropriate physical, social and economic structures – largely a matter of accumulating a set of characteristics familiar in the experience of the developed nations. In the latter case development is taken to be the fundamentally uncontentious business of organizing decent lives for the presently disadvantaged people of the Third World. Both these views are products of particular episodes in the post-Second World War career of development studies and both are wrongheaded. In opposition to these familiar views I would argue that the notion of development is not technical and certainly not obvious; it is an ethico-political notion and what is going to count as development, in a practical and engaged sense, will inevitably depend upon circumstance-sensitive and problem-specific analyses. What is going to count as development will have to be locally determined; and such schemes can then be ranked in scholarly commentary against the criteria specified above.

The foregoing remarks have indicated that most social theorists regard change with approval, and that most post-Second World War theories of development have been informed by Western ethics. It is also the case that patterns of ethical commitment are threaded through analyses in a subtle and diffuse fashion: sets of values cannot be extracted and changed in a mechanical fashion. More broadly, ethics are embedded in patterns of social life, and just as social change is a complex phenomenon, so too must be the interaction between formalized ethical notions and wider pressures for change (economic, political, cultural and so on) within any society.

Methods of change

One of the major preoccupations of the classical European tradition of social science has been with understanding mechanisms of social change. It is a fairly short step to a concern for methods of securing change. In a recent text Giddens has discussed the theoretical ground of any proposal for action to secure change, and argued that this centres on the extent to which social change is actively secured rather than experienced passively as the outcome of either structural change or chance events.[14] Giddens talks about this in terms of the exchange between agency and structure.

So when we discuss change one major question is the extent to which identified changes, or desired changes, are to be conceived in terms of willed human actions (active) or social structural forces (passive). What is at issue is how structure and agency mutually interact. The analysis of any particular set of circumstances will involve some mix of the two explanatory strategies, thus for example we could discuss national development strategies in terms of effective action within the bounds of a particular colonial legacy.

So, in speaking of methods of change, we are obliged to take up a position on the matter of agency and structure. Any willed action will inevitably be context-dependent. Setting this issue to one side we can turn to look at the familiar patterns of active pursuit of change within the social world. We can also note that there is one method of securing change that is often discussed within development theory and that is planned change.

First, we can look at political action which is the most obviously active mode of securing change. Such action can be pursued by a range of agents moving from national states and thereafter formally constituted parties in a variety of contexts – some relatively open and some highly restricted – down through to local-level actions. Some forms of political action might include kin groups acting for mutual interest, and pressure groups acting for some particular material interest. Also there are groups dissenting from

14   A. Giddens 1979 'Agency, structure' in idem *Central Problems in Social Theory*, London, Macmillan.

the established order for a variety of reasons and such dissent can take the form of mild protest through to violent rebellion. Evidently, history is littered with examples of these active modes.

In addition to these familiar political patterns, development theory has had a major preoccupation with deliberately engineered social change oriented to specific goals. The literature of development theory is suffused with the planning imperative – Gellner's work is one such presentation – and this should be noted at the outset as it is a theme that will recur throughout this text. There is now a major strand within the literature of development theory which challenges the assumptions of the evident superiority of planned change in contrast to change secured through open political debate.

Overall, in respect of methods of change we must first establish the scope for active change and thereafter the particular social strategy for securing effective change and these are highly context-specific considerations. In this text I will be looking at the proposals of a series of major theorists. And in this case we can usually pick out the method of change a theorist has in mind fairly easily because any theory must have an agent of theory-execution, otherwise there is no way in which the theory can be translated into practice.

Arguments and actions about change

It is clear that the business of analysing social change is not a simple descriptive task. In grasping the underlying logics of social change the social theorist must actively deploy complex social theories in order to uncover crucial axes of social change. The social theories which are deployed will be constructed by the theorist with reference to the available intellectual resources of the discipline. The material produced by the social theorist will be addressed to a particular audience so as to assist their practical activity in the social world. In the material following, which deals with the classical theorists of the nineteenth century and the contemporary theorists of development, the trio of models, morals and methods of change will recur in many guises. In other words, social theory is an active and engaged business.

Arguments and Actions about Development

The rich and diverse material of social theory has been put to work in the drive to secure 'development' in the Third World. Over the post-Second World War period as the colonial powers withdrew and new nationstates were formed there has been a series of quite distinct approaches to the issue of development. The available social theoretical approaches have found practical expression in the work of a variety of agencies of social intervention and reform. These approaches can be grouped, for preliminary expository purposes, around three paradigms of the business of characterizing and securing development: arguments which look to state-engendered order; arguments which look to the spontaneous order of the marketplace; and arguments which look to political debate within the community to achieve order.[15]

Arguments for state action to secure order

The basic set of ideas invoked in this context relate to intervention by the state to secure ordered change. A set of claims are made to relevant knowledge, expertise and ethic. It is the approach of agencies committed to planning in pursuit of the development goal of effective nationstatehood. It has been pursued by international agencies linked to the United Nations, by the governments of the new nations and by multi-lateral linkages with the departing colonial powers. It was an influential approach during the early phases of decolonization but it has been heavily criticized in respect of its core claims and the results secured, which are taken by critics to be somewhat meagre. Nonetheless, the approach which centres on agencies of planned change retains extensive intellectual support and relevant institutional vehicles.

Arguments for the spontaneous order of the marketplace

The basic set of ideas invoked in this context relate to the spontaneous order and development generated by free market systems. A set of claims are made which offer a characterization of the self-regulating market and from which a series of policy proposals in respect of the minimum rule-setting state are derived. The goal of the proponents of the free market is the maximization of economic, social, political and cultural benefits for the populations concerned. The institutional vehicles of this approach to development have been the monetary institutions of the post-Second World War settlement, the IMF and the World Bank. The approach was influential in the 1980s as doubts grew about the essentially Keynesian-inspired celebration of the power of the state. However, critics have pointed to intellectual incoherence and practical failure. In the Third World the poor have become poorer and there is little sign of the promised realization of maximum benefits for their populations. However, the approach retains strong intellectual backing and a very strong institutional base.

Arguments for the polity in achieving order and development

The basic set of ideas invoked in this context relate to the power of the political community to secure rational goals in respect of order and development.

15   See P. W. Preston 1994 *Discourses of Development: State, Market and Polity in the Analysis of Complex Change*, Aldershot, Avebury.

A central role is allocated to the public sphere within which rational dialogue can find its role. The approach is oriented to securing formal and substantive democracy and has an institutional vehicle in the realm of NGOs, charities and dissenting social movements. In the European context much support has been found in the overlapping worlds of media, political activism and academe. However, critics have pointed to an alleged impractical idealism coupled to a tendency to generate conflicts with powerful groups in the peripheries and the metropolitan centres which often has the effect of making the situation of the poor worse. Nonetheless, the approach retains strong intellectual support and still finds a variety of institutional vehicles. It should be noted that this text is constructed from a position which finds much to support in the work of the proponents of formal and substantive democracy.

Chapter Summary

It has been argued that social theorizing is an activity central to human life. It is the business of making sense and it presents itself in diverse guises. In the sphere of the social sciences we can distinguish between social philosophical and empiricist positivist approaches. The familiar invocation of the model of the natural sciences has been rejected. The social philosophical line has been affirmed as the basis of this text. The social philosophical line takes social theorizing to revolve around the theory-based interpretation of particular sets of social circumstances and the possibility of a natural science of the social is taken as illusory. Two examples of prospective interpretive theorizing were presented in the writings of Ernest Gellner and Peter Worsley whose work involved the self-conscious mixing of models, morals and methods of change in pursuit of presently relevant understandings of the dynamics of the modern world. The business of models, morals and methods of change was noted to reveal the typical ways in which these matters have been approached. Taking note of the Western ethics built into theories of development it was suggested that other ethics might be available and that consequently what was to count as development would have to be locally determined.

PART II
Classical Social Theory

2

The Rise of a Social Science of Humankind

Overview of the History of the Social Sciences

The scientific analysis of the social world with its key concern with analysing complex change is a product of definite historical processes. The rise of the natural and social sciences was closely bound up with the rise of the modern world. The shift from agrarian feudalism to industrial capitalism in Europe was fostered crucially by the commercial-industrial bourgeoisie and they were the enthusiasts for natural and social science. The rise of social science has three stages, which together express the project of modernity: (a) seventeenth-century natural science with Newton as the exemplar; (b) the eighteenth-century social and political theorists of the Enlightenment who applied the model of science to the human sphere; and (c) the early-nineteenth-century social theorists of republican democratic industrial society who offer the first formulations of modern social scientific work. Together this sequence of historically embedded argument bequeaths to us our familiar ideas in respect of the nature and possibilities of social science. In the classical tradition of social science the central substantive concern was with the analysis of complex change in the making of the modern world.

The Rise of a Science of Humankind

The rise of the social sciences is one aspect of that broad set of changes to which we refer as the rise of the modern world. The work of social scientists was concerned with understanding and ordering the extensive sets of changes which were in progress. I will present the material of social science as comprising national schools, but the episode transcended national boundaries both intellectually and as a 'movement'.[1] We are dealing with a broad period of European history.

All history is written from the perspective of the present. In the case of the rise of social science we could write two histories: an empiricist's history and a rationalist's history. I will present a general history which records the slow advance of the claims of reason.[2] The disputes between the proponents of empiricism and rationalism will be noted briefly and I will indicate, as in the previous chapter, a preference for the tale told by the rationalists. In this perspective, the core concern of the classical tradition of social science is with making practical sense of complex social change and the work is necessarily multi-disciplinary, prospective and engaged (see figure 3).

The English Enlightenment[3]

The major figure in natural science was Newton (1643–1727) who, in the late seventeenth and early eighteenth century, offered statements in respect of natural science and mathematics that proved influential to the French and Scottish Enlightenments. It is clear that his ideas were 'circulated in many popular accounts published in England and throughout the continent'[4] and that by '1784 there were forty books on Newton in English, seventeen in French, three in German, eleven in Latin, and one each in Portuguese and Italian'.[5]

The crucial change is from Aristotelian metaphysics to modern physics; roughly, Copernicus, Galileo, Newton. The key areas of work were physics, astronomy and mathematics. In all this there is a movement from long established religious and Aristotelian *a priori* reasoning about the world and the nature of humankind, to a recognizably modern stress on attention to the mundane detail of the natural world as a route to knowledge. It is a complex shift: ontological (the nature of existence, from theistic to materialistic schemes); epistemological (the nature of knowledge, from medieval scholasticism to modern rationalism and empiricism); methodological (from abstract theoretical reflection to the use of the experimental

1   S. Pollard 1971 *The Idea of Progress*, Harmondsworth, Penguin.
2   F. Gellner 1991 *Plough, Sword and Book: The Structure of Human History*, London, Paladin; F. Gellner 1992 *Reason and Culture*, Oxford, Blackwell.
3   My expression – I wish to gesture to the overall process of the shift to the modern world and this term lets us link up the English experience with later episodes.
4   T. L. Hankins 1985 *Science and the Enlightenment*, Cambridge University Press, p. 9.
5   Ibid. p. 9.

Figure 3   The rise of social science in the shift to the modern world

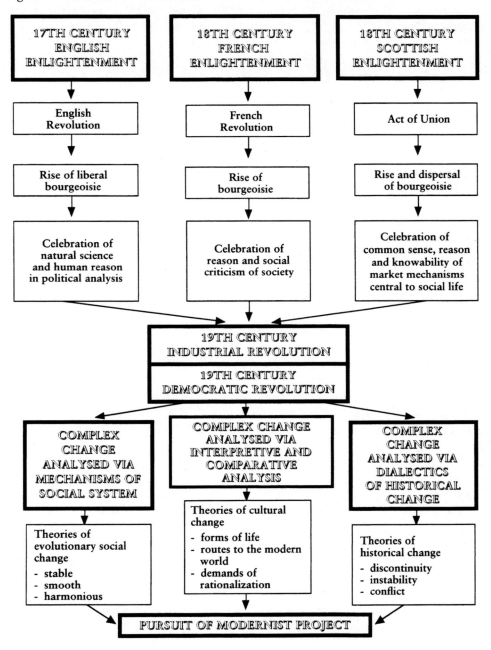

method);[6] and practical (such that contemplative acquiescence gives way to the notion that effective action flows from the deployment of practical reasoning).

This was all bound up with the rise of bourgeois mercantile capitalism: the new rising bourgeoisie needed and supported natural science against the church-led feudal status quo. In the seventeenth century this was all presented in the established language of reflection, and it was called natural theology. It was left to the French Enlightenment to shrug off religion explicitly.

The English Enlightenment also includes Hobbes and Locke[7] offering political philosophy, inspired in part by the work of natural scientists, in response to the English civil war. On Barrington Moore's argument the civil war was the first bourgeois revolution.[8] However English politics in the seventeenth century established a commercial, trading, mercantile bourgeoisie in power. It was not a republican democracy of the sort established in the USA and France. Benedict Anderson talks of this imagined community – nationalist, democratic, sovereign – appearing first in the USA and then France.[9] Only thereafter did it spread to the rest of Europe, and it did so in various forms. Again, the implication is that the seventeenth-century English Enlightenment was in a significant sense pre-modern as it pre-dated the historical invention of the notion of nationstate.[10]

Hobbes and Locke are key figures in the philosophy of liberalism. MacIntyre suggests that Hobbes drew on Galileo for his method and followed a strategy of analysis designed to identify logically primitive ideas followed by a reconstruction of complex reality.[11] The influence of a natural scientist is thus present early in liberal philosophy. Reducing society to its elements, in the hands of Hobbes, gives us individuals who are discrete social atoms pursuing their own wants. In the pre-social state of nature there is war of all against all. Here, famously, life is poor, mean, brutish and short. The social is constructed because it is prudent. By the contractual constitution of a sovereign power the effects of individualism can be mitigated.

Individuals are bound by natural and social laws: the former govern our pursuit of satisfactions in the context of there being other persons pursuing their satisfactions (power relations basically), whilst the latter are both convenient and backed by the power of the sovereign. A discussion of Hobbesian liberalism is not necessary to our purposes, however. In general, political philosophers seem to be either firmly committed to the approach

6   See A. F. Chalmers 1978 *What Is This Thing Called Science?* Milton Keynes, Open University Press, pp. 67–75.

7   My understanding of these figures is largely taken from the work of C. B. Macpherson.

8   See B. Moore 1966 *The Social Origins of Dictatorship and Democracy*, Boston, Massachusetts, Beacon Press.

9   B. Anderson 1983 *Imagined Communities*, London, Verso.

10   On this see T. Nairn 1988 *Enchanted Glass*, London, Radius, and L. Colley 1992 *Britons: Forging the Nation 1707–1837*, Yale University Press, both of whom make it clear that the emergent modern bourgeoisie looked backwards to the model of Venice.

11   A. MacIntyre 1967 *A Short History of Ethics*, London, Routledge.

or find the effort both hugely impressive and hopelessly flawed.[12] But we can note, with MacIntyre, that Hobbes linked morals to models of man (an issue that recurs today as different models are tried in political theories and ideologies), and opened up the issue of authority. He also introduced the role of education, in a broad sense, in the socializing of man (original sin was denied – in the state of nature men are asocial).

Locke's political philosophy is a variant of Hobbesian themes and the same issues are addressed in respect of the nature of sovereignty, persons, and rights. Locke's state of nature is not a war of all against all because men live in families. Thus Locke builds in a minimum sociology and politics because natural law now encompassed property. Social law centrally acts to safeguard (natural) property: hence a sovereign to protect natural rights (especially property) empowered by the consent of the governed. The politics we can set aside; it is the ideas of education that give a link to the French Enlightenment. Locke presents a sensationalist psychology and a theory of the mind as *tabula rasa*. The key to social life and progress is education.

A series of key ideas can be associated with seventeenth-century natural science: (a) an affirmation of a mechanical philosophy which presents an ontology of matter and causes, thus shifting from theism to materialism; (b) an affirmation of the idea that the natural world can be taken as a sphere for the deployment of human reason and understood; (c) an affirmation of the idea that the way to do this is via attention to mundane detail coupled to experimental method; (d) and finally an affirmation of the idea that use of reason can enable mankind to progress.

The French Enlightenment

The French Enlightenment produced a series of thinkers who, broadly, had it in common that they were inspired by Newton, the rise of a science of humankind, and by the English bourgeois revolution which offered them the model of a modern polity. These theorists, the *philosophes*, were committed to political change in France and they saw themselves as a new class in alliance with the rising bourgeoisie. They were the ideologues and they adopted an educative role to aid progress, via clubs, societies, pamphlets and books. They took the view that progress was evident in both thought and society. The shift to the modern world was partially visible, so to say, and progress could be argued for inductively. They took themselves to be applying the new experimental method to the sphere of the social, and they affirmed the scientific strategy of paying attention to mundane detail in order to discover laws rather than relying solely on abstract philosophical reflection. They focused on economic and social history and constructed universal histories of the process of the rise of civilization, usually in the form of stage theories.

12 A recent review of the territory which finally comes down on the side of the second position is R. Plant 1991 *Modern Political Thought*, Oxford, Blackwell.

Montesquieu (1689–1755) is noted for his text *The Spirit of the Laws* (1748) where the key aim is to make history intelligible by reducing observable diversity in socio-political life to the operation of a few underlying factors, thus enabling effective political practice.[13] What we have in today's terms is a social structural analysis. The intellectual project unpacks as follows: (a) from Aristotelian political philosophy three types of government are sketched (republican, monarchy, despotism); (b) the material and social causes of all three are indicated (and here, size, climate, land holdings, and trade patterns, for example, are invoked); and (c) on the basis of these analyses the example of Great Britain and the pursuit of material progress via the establishment of liberal democracy were presented as routes to the future for France.

Rousseau (1712–78) affirms determinism and a general rationalism, and argues that human freedom depends on a clear understanding of the laws of nature and society. Any society can diverge from these laws and such a divergence would have a negative impact on the individual – a notion of alienation is being offered. Rousseau looks for an ideal moral/social order, one that fits closest to natural laws of man and society. With this ideal we can shape remedies for the distorted present. A notion of critique is being presented. The ideal is the state of nature, an idea of pre-social innocence. If we remove social factors, which are taken to distort humankind, then we are left with natural man, and this natural man is good. In present society, argues Rousseau, the social contract, which was originally designed to establish a minimum state/society so as to protect members, has become twisted into inegalitarian forms. Social reform for citizenship in republican democratic polities is needed to solve the problems of the day. It is not too difficult to see why Rousseau is often taken to have been the theorist of the French Revolution.

The legacy of Montesquieu for social science is threefold: (a) the affirmation of determinism (thus chance does not rule the world, rather it is structured by underlying laws); (b) the rationalism in the general sense (thus the human intellect can discover these laws); and (c) the social structural analysis (thus characterizing and explaining the causal structuring of distinct polities). In a similar fashion the legacy of Rousseau is very rich, with a notion of alienation, a scheme of moral critique, notions of equality and inequality and ideas of republican democracy.

The Scottish Enlightenment

The Scottish Enlightenment represents a remarkable cultural flowering in the relatively brief and transitional period of 1745 to 1790.[14] The background

13   This short discussion of the French Enlightenment derives from in particular Pollard 1971, MacIntyre 1967.
14   For overviews see Jane Rendall 1978 *The Origins of the Scottish Enlightenment*, London, Macmillan; A. C. Chitnis 1976 *The Scottish Enlightenment: A Social History*, London, Croom Helm; and D. Daiches ed. 1986 *A Hotbed of Genius: The Scottish Enlightenment 1730–1790*, Edinburgh University Press.

to the period involves the Act of Union of 1707 which saw the Scottish parliament removed from Edinburgh, thereby removing the principal focus of intellectual and political life. At the same time Scotland was experiencing a period of improvements in agricultural production, and commerce was burgeoning in the towns: in brief, it was the heyday of an agrarian Scotland. In this period, bereft of their natural political and cultural centre, and living in a period of economic prosperity and expansion, the Scottish bourgeoisie and intelligentsia, with the clergy, teachers and lawyers figuring strongly, channelled their energies into the realm of ideas. This brief cultural flowering declined as industrial capitalism grew up south of the border in England and as the class divisions and politics associated with this spilled over into Scotland. The Scottish bourgeoisie and intelligentsia came to look to London and the political-cultural project of 'Britain'.[15]

The Scottish Enlightenment thus addressed the issues of political, social and economic change. Its key preoccupations were history and moral philosophy, the former concern flowing from the troubled run-up to the Act of Union, the latter flowing from associated attempts in a period of change to characterize the nature of humankind. The broad contribution of Scottish Enlightenment figures to social scientific and political thought (morals) is rather lost to view at the present. The figures we do recall are picked out as specifically a philosopher and an economist: Hume and Smith.

David Hume (1711–76) is a key figure in philosophy as a major contributor to the notion of empiricism: he gives us typical notions of cause and the distinction between facts and values; he advances experience as the basis for knowledge; he offers a view of the relationship of thought to action by saying that reason is the slave of the passions; and, rather differently, he stresses the role of custom or habit in buttressing knowledge claims. Hume's philosophical ideas run through to the present day as the taken-for-granted underpinning of much of the orthodox idea of empiricism. A more directly social scientific figure is Adam Smith who, routinely, is taken to have opened the way to the science of economics.

Smith (1723–90) wrote on morals and like the other Scottish moralists he spoke of self-interest, sympathy and benevolence. And like the other Scottish moralists he tended to introduce morals, sympathy particularly, after he had characterized human beings in essentially liberal terms. Its not very clear how morals can function as an addendum to otherwise characterized persons, nor is it very clear, of course, how one can characterize human beings apart from the social worlds they inhabit. And specifically it is none too obvious how the proposed ethics fit with the proposed economics.[16] The whole we may briefly regard as the political ideology of the rising Scottish bourgeoisie presented as if it were general to mankind.[17] However, it is Smith's economics that are remembered. Smith's *Wealth of Nations*

15 See Colley 1992 op. cit.
16 Commentators on Smith's work sometimes speak of the problem of their being two Adam Smith's and then go on to pick the one that suits their particular arguments.
17 See Pollard 1971 op. cit.

(1776) affirmed the Newtonian method of proceeding from first principles to reconstruct the complexity of the observed world. Simplifying greatly, we can say that Smith presents a model of the economy as a developing system, including the following key ideas: (a) the division of labour, where specialization in production coupled with technical innovation allows vastly increased production and economic growth; (b) the notion of the market, an institutional structure which allows buyers and sellers to meet; (c) the postulate of economic rationality, the idea that all buyers and sellers are rational agents; and (d) the notion of spontaneous order whereby the pursuit of individual satisfactions generates via the mechanism of the invisible hand optimal societal benefit.

The social scientific aspects can be picked out of all this as follows: (a) the sphere of the market can be investigated naturalistically because it is a realm of economic causes and effects; (b) the technical knowledge of economic science will enable actors to order their activities better; (c) the notion of the invisible hand is hinting at the dialectic of structure and agency; and (d) Smith's rational economic man is still used in economics as an ideal type whereby economic activity can be analyzed. Overall, we may note that Smith's work dates from before the industrial revolution and does not anticipate industrial society. Yet Smith's work inspired nineteenth-century political-economy in the shape of Ricardo, Marx and Mill. In the late nineteenth century this tradition of political-economy declined as neo-classicism was established. This scheme is understood by its proponents as a positive scientific economics. At the present time Smith is taken, professionally, as the bridge across the great divide to scientificity for economics, and by neo-liberal conservatives as a major inspiration for their ideological schemes.[18]

The early nineteenth century

Early nineteenth-century social science represents the first material that could be said to be distinctively modern. Whereas in the period of the French Enlightenment there was much optimism amongst the major figures for the power of human reason, it is the case that these contributions were made before the advent of industrial capitalism and before the episode of the French Revolution. These two episodes occasioned a revision of intellectual theorems. It is within the period of the early French Enlightenment that subsequent theorists have located the divergence in thinking which comes to be expressed in the conflicting traditions of empiricism and rationalism.[19]

The French Revolution saw the political optimism of the Enlightenment advocates of the power of human reason to order human affairs take a

18   It may well be that this is an error, see Heinz Lubasz 'Adam Smith and the Invisible Hand of the Market?' in R. Dilley ed. 1992 *Contesting Markets*, Edinburgh University Press.
19   See Z. Bauman 1987 *Legislators and Interpreters*, Cambridge, Polity.

severe knock. The French Revolution was both self-conscious (the first revolution to discuss itself routinely via newspapers, pamphlets and so on) and violent. The upshot of all this was to create a widespread measure of doubt about the political project of the French Revolution and thus the Enlightenment which had provided the ideas.[20] At the same time the industrial revolution of the UK also provided Europe with a new model of economic activity, with factory production using powered machines – a sharp move away from typically home-based production using craft skills. Many reacted against this model as here was Smith's division of labour with a vengeance. Overall, the two revolutions provoked extensive change in Europe and America. In France the revolution gave way to Napoleon and eventually the bourgeoisie came to power, and there is a slow shift to an industrial liberal-democracy through the nineteenth century. In the UK the Chartists were defeated and as industry burgeoned the slow shift to liberal-democracy began. In the USA, with a polity inspired by the Enlightenment, and with an open continent to develop, both economic growth and liberal-democracy went straight into practice.[21] Elsewhere in Europe, away from the core territories of the northwest, nationstate creation and the establishment of liberal-democratic industrial societies proceeded rather more slowly.[22]

In social science all these issues were picked up by Saint-Simon and taken into his social scientific scheme – a scheme often taken as the first recognizably contemporary social science. Saint-Simon (1760–1825) was a nobleman, revolutionary, man about town and social theorist. He published a series of social science texts which were innovative, original, scattered, vague, and mad. He died in penury. In summary we can pick out these broad points.

In the first place, Saint-Simon affirmed the power of human reason and stressed positive science, especially applied science. Eventually it would generate a scheme of social engineering. Secondly, he stressed the role of intellectual scientific elites. These are the people who should rule because it is ideas that move history. This is a significant change from earlier *philosophes*, whose work tended to centre on education (construed broadly – books, pamphlets, the *Encyclopédie*) and by implication to expect a broad social take-up of theorists' ideas, to an idea of expert direction of society. As Saint-Simon went on to characterize industrial society, it is also anti-*laissez-faire* in the sense of being socialistic. Thirdly, he analysed society in terms of classes – merchants, bureaucracy, scientists, and industrials. The last group are seen as vital to society, but it is not entirely clear whom this

20 In Europe throughout the nineteenth century to declare oneself a democrat was to declare that one had blood on one's hands. See A. Rosenberg 1938 *Democracy and Socialism*, London.

21 On the distinctiveness of national experiences for intellectual development, in particular in respect of sociology, see G. Hawthorn 1976 *Enlightenment and Despair*, Cambridge University Press.

22 See B. Anderson 1983 *Imagined Communities*, London, Verso; E. Gellner 1983 *Nations and Nationalism*, Cambridge University Press.

grouping encompassed and he seems to have meant all those who contributed productively to social wealth. Fourthly, he firmly believed in progress, because history was moving forward and with the use of science, including social science, this movement was becoming self-conscious and rapid. Fifthly, progress was seen as involving phases with 'organic periods' of stable development (classical Hellenic, medieval Catholic, and a third organic period, scientific, which was in the offing) and 'critical periods' which were transitions from one organic period to another and were necessary, destructive and confused episodes. The nineteenth century, so far as Saint-Simon was concerned, was lodged in a critical period which had started about the time of the Renaissance and had seen the slow rise of scientific industrial society.

Saint-Simon offered the first recognizably modern discussion of a range of social scientific concerns, including the role of intellectuals, the nature of socialist reforms to unfettered markets, class, industrialism, the dialectics of history, plus the growth of bureaucracy, professionals, finance, and the spread of the European industrial system. Saint-Simonian theory was translated into practice via clubs and societies and he had adherents spread around the world. Auguste Comte was his secretary, co-worker and successor.

Comte took his master's ideas and expanded them into a systematic and general theory. Comte was introduced to English theorists and proved influential with J. S. Mill.[23] Mill takes the idea of inverse deduction from Comte where empirical generalizations are tested against the twin assumptions of human nature and given circumstances. The upshot, says Mill, are rules of ethology, the science of human behaviour. We also find that Mill acknowledges the notion of the hierarchy of the sciences such that in principle sociological explanations could be reduced to the physio-chemical sciences. Mill also liked Comte's history: the rise of science. Yet Mill differed from Comte because there were differences between France (with the bourgeoisie still embroiled in establishing themselves) and England (where the bourgeoisie had won its battles). Mill was wedded to liberalism as a political philosophy but Comte shifted abruptly from the establishment of social science to its authoritative deployment. Mill's work was never as emphatically elaborate as that of Comte precisely because of his circumstances. Mill never doubted UK arrangements in any fundamental way, nor did he posses the intellectual drive for theoretical closure of Comte for his was a modest, pragmatic, reforming English social theory.

The later nineteenth century

In the middle and late nineteenth century there are two major names: Darwin and Marx – respectively standing for ideas of social evolution and historical materialist analysis.

---

23 Hawthorn 1976. On this see also R. Swedberg 1987 'Economic Sociology Past and Present', *Current Sociology*, 35, who suggests that Comte's intemperate attempts to appropriate political-economy to his schemes contributed to the reaction which ushered in marginalism, which later figured in the institutional split of economics/sociology.

Notions of evolution were used widely in the nineteenth century: there was extant work in the areas of palaeontology and biology especially. Also as a result of European capitalist expansion there were evolutionary theories available within anthropology and social philosophy. Darwin accomplishes two tasks: he constitutes biology as an empirical natural science by identifying mechanisms of speciation where previously the stress had been on categorization of types of organisms; and he extends the approach to human beings. However ideas of evolution were widespread and the exchange between ideas of biological evolution and social evolution was not one of the latter taking from the former: it was a distinctly two-way exchange.[24]

Herbert Spencer advanced a complex scheme of philosophical evolution. It was quickly simplified by his followers into social darwinism: a celebration of late-nineteenth-century market capitalism. There were three replies to Spencer:[25] the defensive reaction of biologists who disliked the extension of evolution into ethics; the favourable reaction of eugenicists, like Galton, who saw a route to the improvement of humankind; and the reformist response.[26]

The reformist response turned evolution back against Spencer and argued that to the extent that we could comprehend evolution we could act to assist its longer-run tendencies. Thus sensible social reform and not *laissez-faire* could usher in the future.[27] This line gives us both the Fabian Socialist tradition, and L. T. Hobhouse and the British sociology of the first half of the twentieth century.[28] The ideas of social Darwinism continue down to the present in residual and ever resurgent eugenics ideas, and lately with sociobiology.[29] More broadly, evolutionism has become submerged within functionalism: they are both linked yet separable but it is arguably the case that the latter is preeminent.

Completing this broad sweep through the early history of social theory we should mention Marx. It is here that we find notions of historical materialist analysis. Marx argued that the nature of human social life revolved around the collective deployment of creative labour. The materialist conception of history claims that people make their own lives in their productive activity. This activity is the central business of human social life and around it other more abstract concerns cluster. Marx uses the distinction between economic base and social superstructure. Any society can be analysed in

24   See G. Jones 1980 *Social Darwinism and English Thought*, Brighton, Harvester; J. W. Burrow 1966 *Evolution and Society*, Cambridge University Press.

25   Hawthorn 1976 op. cit., ch. 5.

26   S. Hughes 1959 *Consciousness and Society*, London, MacGibbon and Kee, makes the point that reaction against Comtean and Spencerian positivism by fin-de-siècle thinkers fed into revival of hermeneutics.

27   All detailed by S. Collini 1979 *Liberalism and Sociology*, Cambridge University Press.

28   See P. Abrams 1968 *The Origins of British Sociology*, Chicago University Press, who characterizes the effort as a 'sickly child'.

29   Jones 1980 op. cit.

terms of its characteristic economic base and associated superstructure. Marx analyses bourgeois capitalism in line with this ethic and method and looks to uncover the dynamic of the system via a critical reconstruction of English political-economy. The trend of history is towards the radical reconstruction of the industrial capitalist system with the abolition of class society and the overcoming of the division of labour and thus of alienation.

Later debates, claims and counterclaims

In contrast to the empiricist's elaboration of a natural scientific type study of the social world as an observable system, the theorists of the rationalist counter-tradition offer an historical, interpretive and critical approach oriented to diagnosing extant trends so as to inform social practice construed broadly rather than in terms of expertise. The proponents of these two approaches offer different versions of the history of the rise of social science.[30] The history of social science is a contested history.

In the familiar tale of the empiricist, the history of the rise of the social sciences is one which involves the slow excision of extraneous social philosophical issues in order to reveal and order the hard empirical scientific core of the endeavour. It is suggested that the maturation of the social sciences into fully fledged sciences is slow precisely because of the persistence of ideological confusions. However, the proponents of empiricism remain confident that a social science constructed on the model of the existing natural sciences is possible and will eventually be achieved.

In the rationalist's version of this history the relationship of enquiry, valuation and practice is construed differently. In place of the neutral pursuit of technical knowledge the entire history of social science is relocated within the social world which it tries to grasp. In other words, social science is taken to be routinely practical and concerned with the dynamics of complex change in the shift to the modern world.

It is my view in this book that a sceptical, critical and reflexive social science can encompass both the empirical material considered by the orthodox and the routinely multi-disciplinary, prospective and engaged enquiry advocated by the rationalists.

Theoretical Issues

A broad historical and cultural review cannot go very far in establishing clear sets of theoretical ideas. However we can sketch out a cluster of matters that have continued to exercise social scientists. We can also pick out the key themes. There are five broad areas: (a) the scientific approach; (b) the role of enquiry, (c) the characterization of second nature; and (d) the matter of politico-ethical schemes; and (e) the analysis of complex change.

---

30   See Bauman 1987 op. cit.

The scientific approach

The key legacy of the English Enlightenment was a notion of science which was quite distinct from Aristotelian schemes and the influence of theological material. Over the early modern period in Europe the proponents of natural science were engaged in a long-drawn-out debate with those disposed to defend the intellectual status quo, in particular within the Church. On Pollard's tale the rise of natural science was bound up with the rise of the commercial and trading power of the towns.[31] An alliance of nascent capitalist enterprise and newly successful natural science grew up: the one group supported the activities of the other. And in respect of both partners, success was a great help in securing further advance.

The nature of a scientific approach has subsequently become a major issue within philosophy and the social sciences. The most widely accepted line of reflection in this area points to the success of the natural sciences and argues that the social sciences should look to their procedures. The result is a familiarly empiricist positivist version of the nature of social science. On the other hand there is a series of critical replies which claim either that the notion of natural science affirmed by empiricists is too narrow or that the realm of the social is simply different from the realm of material forces, and that social science should be constituted independently. In other words, the precise status of science is now contested.

However, overall, the key elements of this part of the story are these: (a) the influence of the rise of Newtonian natural science with its stress on the experimental method, the attention to mundane detail and the pursuit of general laws; (b) the rise of an ontology of matter and cause (from theism to materialism), and sometimes with persons/ideas seen as odd varieties of matter/cause; and (c) the rise of the view of the social world that sees it as accessible to deciphering by human reason deployed scientifically.

The role of enquiry

The shift to the modern world entailed new ideas about the role within society of both the ideas themselves and the groups who produced the ideas. It is in the late eighteenth century that the familiar role of the intellectual begins to be discernible. In the early period of the French Enlightenment the intellectuals involved in theorizing both a new role for reason (against the received ideas of theology) and a new role for politically progressive groups (against the *ancien régime*) held to a view of their role which saw it as facilitating the growth of reason in the sphere of the social. Pollard speaks of both a strong sense of solidarity amongst intellectuals and their alliance with the rising commercial and industrial bourgeoisie.[32] It has recently been argued that this role modulated slowly into a more restricted celebration of the power of the expert in possession of relevant technical

31 S. Pollard 1971 *The Idea of Progress*, Harmondsworth, Penguin.
32 Ibid.

knowledge.[33] This debate points to one aspect of the history of the early modern period which is adduced by those who would argue that the radical democratic tradition of the Enlightenment was in a sense subverted in the drawn-out process of the rise of the restricted set of positivist social sciences with which we have become familiar. However, it is perfectly clear that the role of reason deployed to deal with matters social does become widely accepted, and however the matter is debated this central role for reason, and thus the producers of ideas, has remained intact.

The key elements of this matter are: (a) the rise of contemporary views about the role of ideas and by extension of intellectuals in society from education broadly conceived to narrow schemes of technical expertise; and (b) the use of the power of reason to effect progressive change by identifying laws and bringing action into line.

The characterization of second nature

As the social sciences developed throughout the nineteenth century, attaining their familiar form in the early years of the twentieth, a crucial shift in thinking occurred as the critical work of the early years of the Enlightenment gave way to a more familiar positive approach.

The matter can be pursued in a number of ways. On the argument of Bauman what we have is the invention of a 'second nature', on the analogy of the natural sphere which was the object sphere of the natural sciences.[34] The sphere of second nature, the realm of the social, was taken by positivist thinkers to be a systematically interrelated sphere which was amenable to lines of enquiry which were in essentials like those of the natural sciences. In other words, we have the slow construction of strategies of enquiry which can be called empiricist positivist. The corollary is that the negative critical line of enquiry, also a descendant of the Enlightenment, is marginalized. Indeed, when the social role of social science is considered, the debates amongst social scientists and the wider community of users in the nineteenth and early twentieth century can be seen to be between those who preferred the modest advances apparently available to empiricist positive science and those who preferred the more speculative possibilities afforded by negative critical thinking oriented to public discourse.

The debate recurs in a second way in which the rise of a second nature can be considered. On the arguments of Passmore, the nineteenth-century social philosophers shifted the early Enlightenment debate about progress away from defective voluntaristic schemes (where it was never clear how the possibilities of reason would in fact be translated into practice) into the realm of structural arguments (where progress was tendentially guaranteed by the logic of the system).[35] The nature of the social system and the possibilities of action remain central concerns for contemporary social scientists.

33   Z. Bauman 1988 *Legislators and Interpreters*, Cambridge, Polity.
34   Z. Bauman 1976 *Towards a Critical Sociology*, London, Routledge.
35   J. Passmore 1970 *The Perfectibility of Man*, London, Duckworth.

In either case, it remains central that the social system now comes to be seen as a realm of both research and practical activity. And we can summarize the key ideas in these terms: (a) social actions are seen as together generating the social system; (b) the necessity of historical enquiry is stressed by critical thinkers as the business of change is identified as crucial; and (c) at the same time conservative counter-Enlightenment ideas of tradition and order are promulgated and come to be linked with empiricist positivist lines of argument, and these find expression in the rise of the ideas of the evolution/function of stable social systems.

Politico-ethical schemes

As the nineteenth century progresses the proponents of social science become increasingly clear about the problematical nature of valuation within social science argument. A long-drawn-out debate begins, which takes different forms within the different national schools of social science, but which, to simplify, issues in a dominant scheme which stresses the value-neutrality of social scientific enquiry. In the dominant sphere of orthodox empiricist positivism a general view is affirmed which insists that the social sciences are essentially technical exercises which are neutral as between competing ethical or political positions.

Against this dominant, and still widely influential view, the proponents of the critical counter-tradition insist that valuation is central to and inherent within social scientific argument-making. The proponents of the counter-tradition insist that matters of valuation must be addressed directly, and a notion of the dialogic nature of social science is often presented, and moreover the critical thinkers suggest that the orthodox aspiration to value-neutrality serves only to disguise a liberal ideological position which is eminently open to critical inspection.[36] This dispute in respect of the nature of the relationship of social scientific work to ethically informed practice has continued to the present day.

In these debates the key ethically substantive issues are these: (a) the issue of the relationship of models of man to moral stances (liberalism, democracy, liberal-democracy); (b) the issue of the nature of authority, in particular the matters of concentration versus diffuseness, imposition versus consent, and legitimation by tradition versus legitimation by reason; and overall the slow rise of the familiar notion of industrial society.

The idea of complex change

The classical tradition of social theorizing was concerned with the dynamics of complex change within the political-economic, social-institutional and cultural spheres in the overall process of the shift to the modern world. The task of the classical theorists was with the elucidation of the details of these

36 See M. Root 1993 *Philosophy of Social Science*, Oxford, Blackwell.

complex and intermingled processes. It was a problem which had to be attempted in a multi-disciplinary, prospective and engaged fashion. The work was practical. The work was an attempt to elucidate patterns of change which were ongoing and which enfolded the theorist. The analyses which were produced were, in consequence, typically open textured, and there was none of the concern for theoretical closure which typifies contemporary discipline-bound technical professional social scientific work. The latter style of work can only be pursued when the social world is taken to be essentially unproblematic and ordered such that external-style empirical descriptions can be made.

In the nineteenth century the theorists of the classical tradition offered a series of ways of making substantive analyses of complex change: from Smith, the evolution of the division of labour; from Marx, the dialectics of historical change; and from Durkheim, the evolution of the social world. In analyzing complex change in the global system today all these materials are available to be put to use. It is possible to speak of the political-economic structures of power which order the global system, and thereafter of the particular social-institutional arrangements which join particular territories to the overarching global structures, and finally, the ways in which these patterns are expressed within the sphere of culture may be noted.

As regards the formal element of theorizing, in the nineteenth century the theorists of the classical tradition confronted problems of great scale, complexity and demanding urgency and these theorists typically argued on behalf of a particular audience, a group who might be taken to be likely to act in line with the prescriptions contained within the theories. In this way Smith argued for the rising commercial bourgeoisie, Marx for the working classes, and Durkheim for the rational-minded reformist bourgeoisie. At the present time it has been argued that scholarship must be oriented to the development of the public sphere of open democratic debate.

In this way, scholarly analyses of complex change can be given ethical direction and substantive focus and the prospective efforts of other theorists ordered and judged in relation to this continuing core tradition.[37]

Theoretical issues and lines of argument

All the issues which I have noted here were part and parcel of eighteenth- and nineteenth-century social scientific work. The ideas noted did not fall into clearly separate and distinct sets. Debate in social science is always a drawing down on available stocks of ideas. Thus we can say an empiricist-line is identifiable in the work of theorists who have thus understood themselves. Also a critical line is identifiable in the work of theorists who have

37   A schematic way of using the notion of change is found in S. Strange 1988 *States and Markets*, London, Pinter. A fuller statement of contemporary debates on the nature of change can be found in P. Sztompka 1993 *The Sociology of Social Change*. See also J. A. Scholte 1993 *International Relations of Social Change*, Milton Keynes, Open University Press.

thus understood themselves. And today debate about social science is a drawing down on received tradition where this embraces commentary on earlier debates. However, so far as I am concerned in this book, the classical social scientific tradition is rationalist and centers upon a critical concern for the elucidation of the dynamics of complex change.

Chapter Summary

The scientific analysis of the social world, with its key concern for analysing complex change, is a product of definite historical processes. The rise of the natural and social sciences was closely bound up with the rise of the modern world. The shift from agrarian feudalism to industrial capitalism in Europe was fostered crucially by the commercial-industrial bourgeoisie and they were the enthusiasts for natural and social science. The rise of social science has three stages, which together express the project of modernity: (i) seventeenth-century natural science with Newton as the exemplar; (ii) the eighteenth-century social and political theorists of the Enlightenment who applied the model of science to the human sphere; and (iii) the early-nineteenth-century social theorists of republican democratic industrial society who offer the first formulations of modern social scientific work.

3

Adam Smith and the Spontaneous Order of the Marketplace

Overview of the Work of Adam Smith

The European Enlightenment of the eighteenth century, which celebrated the power of human reason, had a number of centres including England (where natural scientific and political philosophical work was produced), France (where noted work relating to politics and society was produced) and Scotland (where noted work relating to philosophy and economics was produced). A key figure in the Scottish Enlightenment was Adam Smith who took his strategy of enquiry from Newton and offered a scheme of the gradual evolution of society. The key ideas were of the division of labour driven by technical innovation which via the regulation of the invisible hand of the marketplace generated material and moral advance. Smith's work inspired the preeminent nineteenth-century social science of political-economy. Yet at the end of the nineteenth century political-economy gave way to the familiar spread of social science disciplines. However, in the twentieth century economics has become a key social science and presents itself in several technical forms. In the post-Second World War period the neo-classical liberal free market approach has been influential.

The Historical Context of Smith's Work

Smith's work is an integral part of the Scottish Enlightenment.[1] We may note two matters: (a) the occasion and character of the Scottish Enlightenment; and (b) the role of Smith's economics in theorizing the circumstances of the established bourgeoisie. In respect of the economics it should be noted that Smith's work predates the industrial revolution and also the French revolution. There is little sign that Smith's work anticipates industrial society. However, his work did inspire nineteenth-century political-economy (see figure 4).

The occasion and character of the Scottish Enlightenment

The Scottish Enlightenment represents a remarkable cultural flowering in the relatively brief and transitional period of 1745 to 1790. The background to the period involves the Act of Union of 1707 which saw the Scottish parliament removed from Edinburgh, thereby removing the principal focus of intellectual and political life. At the same time Scotland was experiencing a period of improvements in agricultural production, and commerce was burgeoning in the towns: in brief, it was the heyday of an agrarian Scotland.

The period of the eighteenth century was the last phase of the old pre-industrial order and it saw growth in commerce, improvements in technology, and a concern for schooling and learning.[2] The eighteenth-century elite of Scotland was aware of the country's backwardness in contrast to England; so they were both cut-off and aspiring to an improved economic, social and cultural condition. In this period, bereft of their natural political and cultural centre, and living in a period of economic prosperity and expansion, the Scottish bourgeoisie and intelligentsia channelled their energies into the realm of ideas as a precursor to the exercise of modernizing.[3] As it happened the modernization took the form of the industrial revolution and as this was located in England it drew away the talent of Scotland and absorbed it within the burgeoning project of 'Britain'.[4] However, in the middle years of the eighteenth century Scotland saw a cultural flowering. The Church, the law, the universities and a series of popular clubs and societies were the institutional vehicles of the Scottish Enlightenment.

1 For overviews see J. Rendall 1978 *The Origins of the Scottish Enlightenment*, London, Macmillan; A. C. Chitnis 1976 *The Scottish Enlightenment: A Social History*, London, Croom Helm; and D. Daiches ed. 1986 *A Hotbed of Genius: The Scottish Enlightenment 1730–1790*, Edinburgh University Press. Most of the notes here are taken from these sources.
2 Rendall 1978 op. cit.
3 A magisterial review of the intellectual work of the Enlightenment is provided by A. MacIntyre 1988 *Whose Justice? Which Rationality?*, London, Duckworth, chs. 12–16.
4 See L. Colley 1992 *Britons: Forging the Nation 1707–1837*, London, Yale University Press.

50

Figure 4   Adam Smith and the spontaneous order of the marketplace

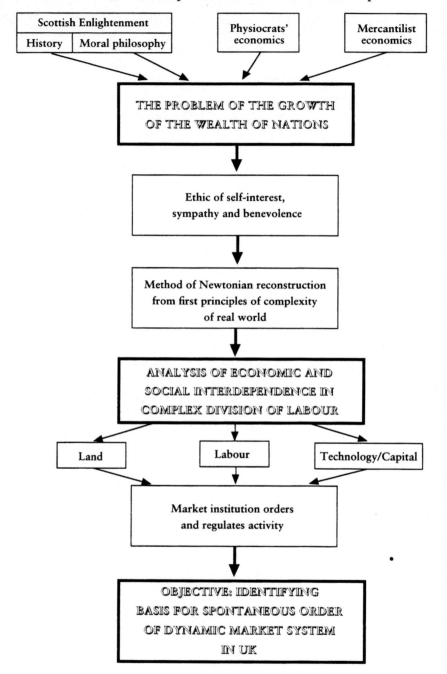

In the Church a radical libertarian group called the moderates won control and influence over more reactionary groups, the evangelicals, and this set the scene for the pursuit/acceptance of new ideas.[5] The Church was a major career route for thinkers and a labyrinthine, complex, internal debate sprang up. Relatedly, the law in Scotland was based on European rather than English law and there were many routine links to the continent, especially for training. This class of professionals provided a reservoir of supporters and participants for Enlightenment ideas and activities and a linkage to the European debates. The third grouping were the universities which in the period experienced major reform and expansion and they became important centres for Enlightenment thinking. In Scotland the tradition of education was well established with extensive secondary schooling, across a broad range, feeding into the university system. In additional to the above trio there were popular clubs, societies, journals and publishing. All served as vehicles for Enlightenment thinking. This brief cultural flowering declined as industrial capitalism grew up south of the border in England and as the class divisions and politics associated with this spilled over into Scotland. The Scottish bourgeoisie and intelligentsia came to look to London and the political-cultural project of Britain.[6]

The Scottish Enlightenment thus addressed the issues of political, social and economic change. Its preoccupations were with history and moral philosophy, the former concern flowing from the troubled run-up to the Act of Union, the latter from associated attempts in a period of change to characterize the nature of humankind. The substance of Enlightenment thought focused on humankind as social animals.[7] There was an intellectual shift away from theology towards the social sciences. In this vein Francis Hutcheson advanced an early philosophy and sociology focusing on human nature and proper social behaviour. Hume picks up from Hutcheson and pursues the empirical study, after Newton, of the nature of human beings, their claims to knowledge and their proper social behaviour. The empirical method was widely applied, after the inspiration of Newton, and historical and comparative sociology was produced.[8] An overriding concern was with the correct behaviour of government in respect of the economy.

An economic theory of the bourgeoisie

Adam Smith (1723–90) wrote first on ethics in his *Theory of Moral Sentiments* (1759) and like the other Scottish moral philosophers he spoke of self-interest, sympathy and benevolence. Smith can be understood to be attempting to give a 'psychological explanation of moral judgements'.[9] The

5 Chitnis 1976 op. cit., see chs. 3, 4, 6, 7.
6 See Colley 1992 op. cit.
7 Chitnis 1976 op. cit., see ch. 5.
8 Rendall 1978 op. cit., see chs. 2, 3, 4.
9 D. D. Raphael 1986 'Adam Smith' in Daiches ed. op. cit. p. 86.

substance of the scheme revolves around the sentiments with which we judge the practical actions of others, both in terms of the intentions they embody and the results they realize. And like the other Scottish moral thinkers he tended to introduce moral ideas after he had characterized human beings in essentially liberal terms. It is not very clear how the proposed ethics fit with the proposed economics.[10]

Turning to the economics, Smith's *Wealth of Nations* (1776) affirmed the Newtonian method of proceeding from first principles to reconstruct the complexity of the observed world. Smith presents a model of the economy as a developing system centred on the market-carried refinement of the division of labour which ensures, in the absence of interference, the evolutionary growth of the wealth of the nation. The whole we may briefly regard as the political ideology of the rising Scottish bourgeoisie presented as if it were general to mankind.[11] However, it is Smith's economics that are remembered.

The Practical Theory of Adam Smith

The shift to the modern world in Europe was a long-drawn-out episode of complex change extending from the sixteenth through to the nineteenth century which attracted the engaged attention of a series of major theorists, including Adam Smith. His work can be understood to comprise an inter-related series of claims in respect of the economy, society and government of eighteenth-century Britain. Cole and others discuss the shift to the modern world in terms of the slow development of capitalism within the overall framework of agrarian feudalism.[12] In the early phases of this complex change two approaches to analysing economics were presented.

In England the theorists of mercantilism argued that economic activity centred on trade and exchange. It was the theory of the early commercial bourgeoisie. The conclusion which was drawn from this view of the nature of economic activity was that the state should be strong enough to break down feudal patterns of restriction to trade and that thereafter the state should exercise regulation of internal trade via guilds and monopolies in order to avoid damaging competition. In respect of external trade the mercantilists took the view that the state should assist them as much as possible in competition with the merchants of other countries as the role of external trade was primarily to accumulate wealth in the form of precious metals. In the early years of the expansion of the European powers, major trading companies were established. They were powerful and influential at home and acted as surrogate governments in the slowly accumulated overseas possessions. As mercantile theory found expression in practice in the early years of the expansion of European mercantile capitalism there

---

10   Commentators on Smith's work sometimes speak of the problem of there being two Adam Smiths and then go on to pick the one that suits their particular arguments.
11   See S. Pollard 1971 *The Idea of Progress*, Harmondsworth, Penguin.
12   K. Cole et al. 1991 *Why Economists Disagree*, London, Longman.

were conflicts between trading nations which looked to protect exclusive spheres of activity.

In France in the eighteenth century the king had established an absolute monarchy and ruled via an elaborate bureaucracy. The old landowning nobility were assimilated to this power structure but lacked independent power. The pattern of rule was expensive (in terms of the tax demands it placed on many sectors of society) and inefficient (insofar as it failed to encourage new productive activity). The system slowly became untenable as the resentments of the peasants began to coincide with the irritations of the emergent commercial bourgeoisie. A respite was sought in the theory of economics proposed by the physiocrats who argued the case for the French landowning nobility and suggested that economic activity centred on the production of goods and this in turn derived from a strong agriculture. The theory also opposed the interests of the mercantile traders and it rejected the strategy of monopoly privileges in favour of an open trading system. In this way the core activity of the landowning classes was presented as the productive core of the society in general. However, in eighteenth-century France the efforts of the physiocrats to guide the state foundered as the protection of the landowning nobility had the effect of damaging the interests of almost all of the rest of the population.

It is clear from these cases that economic analysis in the period of the rise of European capitalism was routinely practical in orientation. The concern of theorists was with elucidating the dynamics of the system as it developed so as to inform the actions of particular groups. It is also clear that around the economic aspects of the analyses which were presented there were an elaborate set of commitments in respect of the nature of enquiry and the general make-up of the social world. The theories were complex intellectual exercises in which ethics, politics and economic analyses were all intermingled.

It is on the basis of these early movements towards liberal trading capitalism that the slow shift to the fully fledged industrial capitalism of the nineteenth century began. At first the development takes place within the towns which were relatively free of the restrictions imposed by the state on economic activity. In the early periods of the shift towards liberal capitalism the patterns of new activity took place at the margins of established society. However, as the economic activities of the merchants and manufacturers develop so too does their political power and as they begin to move towards the centre of the social and political sphere this, in turn, demands new social theory to articulate these interests. It is on the basis of commercial liberal capitalism that industrial capitalism subsequently develops.

The work of Adam Smith articulates this new commercial liberal capitalist interest in the period of late eighteenth-century Britain. The group against whom Smith made his arguments were the now less influential proponents of mercantile capitalism. Smith's work is concerned to show how the free pursuit of private gain can act to raise the levels of living of the entire community. In the work on ethics Smith shows how self-interest can be linked to an appreciation of the role of the community in supporting and disciplining individual activities. In the work on economics Smith goes on to show how individual activities can be pursued within the community to the mutual benefit of both individuals and community.

The method used for making analyses follows the Enlightenment stress on the active deployment of human reason, as against the elucidation of sets of ideas derived from received authoritative sources (traditional theology and philosophy), and is expressed in terms of the contemporary celebration of Newton. A mixture of simple explanatory principles on the one hand and attention to the empirical detail of the world on the other are advocated as the bases for making arguments.

The practical ethics of Smith

In Smith the ethic revolves around the practical business of the members of a community securing their livelihoods. It is a mixture of self-assertion in respect of material concerns and acknowledgement of the demands and support of the community. The scheme is summarized by Cole et al.:

> Smith argued that for people to live in society as free individuals, there must be an element of perceived common interest in order to make social life tolerable and possible . . . In common with the physiocrats . . . Smith believed in a system of natural law through which the individual was reconciled to society. The hand of God was present in the world and could be discovered through empirical regularities which were the expression of these natural laws. And these laws acted as a ladder between the reflecting individual . . . and the punishing society . . . The first step on the ladder is self-judgement . . . [and the] second step is when the judgement of other people is brought to bear on us . . . the [third is] the perception by all individuals that it is in their own interests to conform . . . [and the fourth] is the power to punish . . . The argument runs from the individual to society and ideas of morality . . . are the products of the experience of active people pursuing their own ends.[13]

It is an ethic of practical action in the material world which is guided by the more or less enlightened appreciation attained by individuals of the natural laws governing human life. It is an ethic of the modest actions and modest aspirations of the respectable Scottish bourgeoisie presented as a general model.[14]

The practical economics of Smith

The ethic of individual action within the community was represented in Smith's *Wealth of Nations* (1776) which offers a political-economy of the

13 Ibid. p. 28.
14 A. MacIntyre 1988 *Whose Justice? Which Rationality?*, London, Duckworth, ch. 13.

growth in the wealth of nations which is built around the observation of the increasing interdependence of people within society as the underlying productive system advances. In Smith's analysis wealth was derived from creative human labour working on available natural materials in order to produce useful objects. The key to the increase in the wealth of nations is the rise in labour productivity associated with the increasing division of labour. As the tasks of production are broken down into specialist parts on the basis of advances in productive techniques and machinery then both the overall output of the economy increases and the interdependence of the various elements of the economy also increases. The interdependence and productivity which Smith identified thereafter generated a further question in respect of the manner of ordering these individual actions so as to generate general wealth harmoniously. The answer which Smith gave was that the mechanism of the marketplace acted to regulate economic exchanges, and Smith went on to analyse the workings of the marketplace in terms of the contributions and rewards of land, labour and capital to the productive process.

The conclusions which Smith drew from these analyses in respect of the proper role of government were in favour of the pragmatic and sensible removing of privileges so that the market could operate. Cole and others comment that Smith was in favour of capitalism but rather suspicious of capitalists and that accordingly his recommendations to government were not dogmatic but measured and sceptical.[15]

If we summarize the work in more contemporary terms we can say that Smith affirmed the Newtonian method of proceeding from first principles to reconstruct the complexity of the observed world. Simplifying greatly, we can say that Smith presents a model of the economy as a developing system, including the following key ideas: (a) the division of labour, where specialization in production coupled with technical innovation allows vastly increased production and economic growth; (b) the notion of the market, an institutional structure which allows products to be offered to consumers; it is the sphere of exchange where buyers and sellers meet and agreements on price signal to all parts of the economic system how future economic behaviour can be rationally ordered – the key variables being land, labour and capital, earning respectively rent, wages and profit in a self-regulating system that rewards all its participants; (c) the postulate of economic rationality, the idea that all buyers and sellers are rational agents who know their own wants; (d) the notion of spontaneous order, the idea that the pursuit of individual satisfactions generates via the mechanism of the invisible hand optimal societal benefit – and here in the invisible hand is Smith's theory of social structure; and (e) the idea of economic progress over time as the market freed of mercantilist restriction worked to secure the growing wealth of the nation.

15   Cole et al. 1991 op. cit. p. 32.

Subsequent Commentaries on Smith

The work of Adam Smith, like that of all major social theorists, has been routinely and vigorously contested with the upshot that there are now on offer a variety of 'Adam Smiths'. We can review a series of these lines of commentary in order both to grasp the spread of such commentaries, which together display the richness of Smith's work and the inventiveness of the tradition of social science, and to identify the way in which Smith has been read as the progenitor of contemporary positive economics.

Smith the progenitor of a generally scientific economics

A familiar version of Smith suggests that his work was the earliest version of what has subsequently become the preeminent social science of economics. William Barber argues that Smith's 'work deserves to be remembered primarily as a highly ingenious contribution to economic theory'.[16] However, Smith's work had a precursor in the work of ethics which offered a statement of the ethical bases of action in society in terms of self-love, sympathy and labour. The actions of individuals together generated a harmonious society, a theme which was to reappear in the economics. The book *The Wealth of Nations* (1776) is divided into five books and the economics are found in the first two.

Smith was concerned with economic development over the long term. The subtitle of his book was *An enquiry into the nature and causes of the wealth of nations*. The core idea was that of the advancing division of labour which was regulated by the institution of the market. Within the institutional framework of the market the refinement of the division of labour would issue in higher levels of production. The concept of the division of labour had two senses: specialization within the labour force; and the sectoral division of the economy into productive and non-productive sectors, such that the former helped the economy develop whilst the latter (which included services, professions and government) did not. Here Smith is giving a fresh twist to the distinction made by the French physiocrats who had stressed the productive nature of agriculture as against other sectors in the economy.[17] In Smith's view, the sum total of the activities of the productive sectors advanced the total of national wealth.

Smith's concern with the productive power of the marketplace required that attention be paid to the matter of economic value.[18] This was what the system generated. Smith like all classical economists drew a distinction between value and price, and a key theoretical issue was how these two were established and how they were related. A basic position was that the notion of value was taken to underpin and discipline the more fluid market-determined price. It was clear that prices in the marketplace

16 W. J. Barber 1967 *A History of Economic Thought*, Harmondsworth, Penguin, p. 24.
17 Ibid. p. 28.
18 Ibid. pp. 30–8.

varied for all sorts of reasons. However, if value was determined essentially from outside the market then it would be more stable over time. The notion of value allowed the performance of an economy over time to be measured. And given Smith's focus on economic development this was crucial.

Smith adopted the labour theory of value. The fundamental basis of the value of goods traded in the marketplace derived from the quantity of labour embodied in them. On this basis it was possible to speak of a 'natural price' (derived from the labour embodied in the land, labour and capital involved in producing the goods). The convergence of natural price and market price implied a satisfactory economic situation. The notion of a natural price, set by the marketplace-mediated deployment of land, labour and capital to produce a particular good, implied that interference in the marketplace was likely to hinder production. A preference for the free market is thus lodged in Smith's analysis.[19] The idea of the labour theory of value was both familiar to classical economists and has been widely ignored by economists schooled in marginalist techniques which focus only on market price.

The natural price of a good derived from the components of land, labour and capital which earned, in turn, rent, wages and profit. Smith thereafter had to address the issue of the mechanisms whereby these types of income were determined at their natural rates. Smith uses two general lines of argument to deal with the determination of rent incomes, wage levels and profits. The first is an institutional analysis which looks at the social circumstances of the actors in question. The second looks to the overall condition of the economy – growing, static or declining. In general Smith is here dividing the population into broad class groupings and analysing their position within the overall economy. This is quite different from orthodox marginalist economics which treats factors of production, not classes. It is also quite clear that orthodox economics does not use institutional analyses or analyses dealing with the system as a whole.

The final element of Smith's scheme was a notion of economic growth and this was secured via a distinction between gross and net income of a society: the former was the sum total of the economy's output whilst the latter was the surplus available for productive investment after all the needs of reproducing society at present levels of living had been deducted.[20] Smith considered the situation of the three classes, the landowners, wage-earners and capitalists. Smith argued that the wage-earners would not have any surplus available to invest. In contrast the landowners and capitalists would. However, the former were disposed to consumption so that left the capitalists as the dynamic force for future investment and the growth of the wealth of the nation.

Finally, Smith put these analytical machineries to work in respect of

19 Ibid. p. 33.
20 Ibid. pp. 45–7.

proposals for government policy.[21] Smith took the view that the prevailing mercantilist preference for self-sufficiency at home coupled to trading-company-vehicled overseas trade amounted to an unhelpful restriction of the natural vigour of the marketplace. As Smith was also aware that merchants would seek collusively to secure their own immediate advantage if left to their own devices, he took the view that an economy which was expanding overall would foster competition as there would be chances for all. Smith thus looked optimistically to an expanding competitive market.

Overall, it could be said that the novelty of Smith's work lay in its synthesis of much available work such that the economy was presented as an integrated system which could be analysed in order that policy might better accommodate to the system's inherent logic.[22]

Smith as the proponent of a specific economic discourse

A rather more structuralist reading of Smith would first lodge his work in an historical context and thereafter insist that it should be read as a coherent self-contained text, in which case the work of Smith displays certain preoccupations and strategies of argument-making. In sum his work constitutes a particular economic discourse. A series of ways of making such an analysis are available: one line would draw on notions of ideology and lodge economic discourses within social and political debates, which in turn might be related to changes within the underlying contextualizing political-economy, society and culture;[23] and a rather more austere line would look at the texts as self-contained statements, as amenable to reading and re-reading.[24] I will follow the former line of analysis.

It can be argued that there is no unitary economic science and that consequently there is no simple history of the development of that science.[25] Instead the body of work of economics must be seen to fall into a series of epochs, where the work of the economists is shaped by the questions which they asked, and these in turn can be seen to have been shaped by real world circumstances. A trio of approaches can be identified. In the first place, the work of classical political-economy, with Adam Smith conventionally taken as its key instigator, was concerned with innovation, accumulation and progress, on the one hand, and exploitation, distribution and poverty on the other. Secondly, the work of the marginalists of the late nineteenth and early twentieth century who reacted against the social philosophy of classical political-economy, which was seen to be latently socialistic, and focused instead on the business of price setting and resource allocation

21   Ibid. pp. 47–50.
22   Ibid.
23   See A. K. Dasgupta 1985 *Epochs of Economic Theory*, Oxford, Blackwell.
24   V. Brown 1994 *Adam Smith's Discourse: Canonicity, Commerce and Conscience*, London, Routledge.
25   Dasgupta 1985 op. cit.

within a competitive marketplace. Thirdly, the work of J. M. Keynes addressed the question of depression equilibrium and mass unemployment and in the process identified a strategic regulative role for the state.

It is made clear that these various schools are not to be taken to be different versions of a single unitary economic science, nor are they to be seen as different perspectives on a single coherent economic system; rather, these economic theories do different jobs. We can say that these theories 'slice up the world differently'.[26] They handle different strategies of economic argument and the package deals carried by the argument machineries propose quite different lines of action, to quite different audiences. These are, respectively: the theories of economic development oriented to the newly victorious bourgeoisie; the theories of market stability oriented to the established bourgeoisie; and the theories of state intervention oriented to the reformist technocrats.

In this fashion it can be argued that classical political-economy is concerned with grasping the structural dynamics underlying surface market phenomena. The typical intellectual focus is on human social production and the familiar spread of concerns would include: the primacy of capital accumulation; an aggregative approach; a concern for value as a measure; and a sensitivity to class. The strategy of classical political-economy centres its concerns on growth and distribution, and Adam Smith took the view that competitive capitalism would ensure the ongoing development of the market-sustained division of labour, and this in turn would ensure general benefit in the long run.[27]

Smith as the theorist of the bourgeoisie

An equally familiar version of Smith lodges him within his historical context and reads his work as argument on behalf of the rising, and indeed largely successful, UK bourgeoisie. Sidney Pollard notes that the theorists of the European Enlightenment experienced a cross-cutting process of mutual learning.[28] In this context the French Enlightenment owed a significant debt both to the work of the English Enlightenment, with Newton, Hobbes and Locke, and to the Scottish in the form of the work of Hume.

26   J. Culler 1976 *Saussure*, London, Fontana.
27   This is a fairly familiar story in the literature. See also K. Tribe 1978 *Land, Labour and Economic Discourse*, London, Routledge, who argues that the assimilation of all previous economics to the prehistory of positive neo-classical economics, the standard position in orthodox work, is hugely misleading and against this view characterizes a series of discourses; see also M. Dobb 1973 *Theories of Value and Distribution Since Adam Smith*, Cambridge University Press.
28   Pollard 1971 op. cit. pp. 60–77 also usefully links the work of the theorists of the Scottish Enlightenment, in particular Hume and Smith, to the recently influential work of development economics. In other words, we might say that this version of Smith sees the issue of analyzing complex change so that its direction could be comprehended and made subject to human will come to the fore.

Hume shifts the focus of epistemological concerns away from a Newtonian mechanical universe towards the sphere of the social production of knowledge.[29] Relatedly, in respect of human social life, Hume noted a recurrent tension between conflict and reason and unreservedly affirmed the role of reason. Hume, unlike the *philosophes* at the same period, inhabited a country where the bourgeoisie had already come to power. The intellectual concerns of the successful bourgeoisie were quite particular. The shift is from the circumstance where capitalism was historically progressive to the circumstance where capitalism was historically conservative. The confident bourgeoisie could turn away from abstract reasoning in the natural sciences and equally abstract reasoning in the sphere of the social sciences or philosophy in order to open up a sphere of commentary upon matters of government policy. It was this sphere that came to be pursued in terms of the science of economics.

The nature of eighteenth-century economics in Scotland, as in Britain more generally, revolved around the established intellectual and political preference for a national self-sufficiency coupled to overseas trading, the whole oriented to building up the surplus of an economy as the basis for the polity's strength: in brief, mercantilism. It was against the claims of mercantilism, and the established class groupings which it served, including the old landed powers, that the new economics of free trade and the market were deployed. In terms of the debates of today, the shift is from surplus derived from exchange to surplus derived from production (and this in turn was located essentially in agriculture by the French theorists and in emergent urban-manufacturing production by those in the UK).[30]

The work of Smith argued the case for the newly established bourgeoisie.[31] Smith could take the idea of progress for granted as Scotland at the time was prosperous. And as the UK had had its bourgeois revolution, Smith could take the political and social arrangements for granted. All that remained was to manipulate the relevant economic variables. The upshot was a theory of economic development which centred on the market. And Smith could argue plausibly that the key to the prosperity was the activity of the merchant. This was both the strength and weakness of Smith's work. It was a strength because Smith was arguing for the rising historical class and could do so in a direct policy-focused fashion; debates about humankind and the necessary political arrangements needed to secure progress, all of which troubled the French Enlightenment economists, could all be set aside. It was a weakness in that Smith, like those who followed him, culminating in the work of neo-classicism, was disposed to argue that the model of economics which he presented was not merely appropriate to Scotland (and Britain) at that time, but was rather true in a general fashion. Pollard sees Smith as having taken the first step on the slippery slope which

29   Pollard 1971 op. cit. pp. 60–70.
30   See Barber 1967 op. cit. pp. 17–22.
31   Pollard 1971 op. cit. pp. 71–7.

culminates in the intellectually impoverished, yet ideologically useful, ahistorical and formalistic economics of the marketplace-in-general.

The Influence of Adam Smith in the Work of the New Right

As the post-Second World War liberal-democratic contested compromise in the West began to be seriously challenged by the New Right in the period of the 1980s, the work of Adam Smith was invoked as the original inspiration for the economic analysis of the free-market system. It is clear that this is a misleading treatment of Smith. The work of Smith was firmly lodged within classical political-economy, which in turn addressed quite particular issues in respect of the historical growth of capitalism and few of the concerns which were later to animate the theorists of marginalism who are the recent and direct antecedents of the New Right. However, the work of Adam Smith has come to be associated with the claims of the New Right celebrants of the free market and it is thus appropriate to take some note. I will look at the ideological package deal on offer, and then briefly note the practical record of the New Right over the period of the 1980s.

The ideological claims made

Smith's work has been claimed for the tradition of economic liberalism which centres its analyses on the notion of a free market system. The theorists of the New Right advance a set of arguments. An overarching claim is made that free markets maximise human welfare, and in turn this unpacks as a series of interlinked claims: (a) economically, the claim is that as free markets act efficiently to distribute knowledge and resources around the economic system, then material welfare will be maximized; (b) socially, the claim is that as action and responsibility for action reside with the person of the individual, then liberal, individualistic, social systems will ensure that moral worth is maximized; (c) politically, the claim is that as liberalism offers a balanced solution to problems of deploying, distributing and controlling power, then liberal polities ensure that political freedom is maximized; and (d) epistemologically, the claim is that as the whole package is grounded in genuine positive scientific knowledge, then in such systems the effective deployment of positive knowledge is maximized.

The substantive core of the package is made up of the claims in respect of the functioning of the 'free market'. The free market comprises atomistic individuals who know their own autonomously arising needs and wants and who make contracts with other individuals through the mechanism of the marketplace to satisfy these needs and wants. The market is a neutral mechanism for transmitting information about needs and wants, and goods which might satisfy them, around the system.

All this economics work revolves around the model of the pure market economic system. Todaro summarizes the core elements which make up this model of a satisfaction-maximizing automatic asocial mechanism: (a) in respect of goods and services there is a fundamental underlying naturally given situation of scarcity; (b) there is legally guaranteed private ownership of the means of production; (c) there is pervasive perfect competition amongst suppliers who operate in a complex division of labour; (d) who are aiming to meet the demands of sovereign consumers; (e) all ordered via the market; and (f) there is a definite politics is attached to this model, thus the free market is taken to underpin human freedom in general.[32] So far as the New Right are concerned this model represents the essential character of all human economic and social activity in society.

However, this pure market model is a sophisticated intellectual construct, and 'the market' is not a natural given of human life. When the pure market model is examined it rapidly disintegrates: scarcity is created, not given;[33] individuals are created in society, they are not prior to it;[34] economic competition is always imperfect;[35] the division of labour is political, not technical;[36] sovereign consumers are a myth;[37] the market-price mechanism cannot fulfil the information-transmission role given to it;[38] and the political philosophical position linked to ideas of the free market is liberalism, not democracy which is the current locus of our thinking about freedom.[39]

The recent track record noted

The 1980s have seen the New Right experiments in the USA, UK[40] and Australia[41] fail. The experiment has produced unemployment, reductions in general welfare, declining manufacturing production, and mountains of debt. Against these ideas, European commentators now look to the model of Germany,[42] that is to a social market system where this is a variety of consensus-centred corporatism. In development theory circles the work of the New Right, in particular as it has been vehicled through the IMF and World Bank, has been regarded as less than helpful.[43] Against the claims of the proponents of the sovereign joys of the marketplace the

32   M. P. Todaro 1982 *Economics for a Developing World*, London, Longman.
33   M. Sahlins 1972 *Stoneage Economics*, London, Tavistock.
34   It seems to me that this is commonplace amongst all but a handful of sociological and anthropological positions.
35   G. M. Hodgson 1988 *Economics and Institutions*, Cambridge, Polity.
36   D. Reuschemeyer 1986 *Power and the Division of Labour*, Cambridge, Polity.
37   J. K. Galbraith 1958 *The Affluent Society*, Harmondsworth, Penguin.
38   Reuschemeyer 1986 op. cit.
39   C. B. Macpherson 1973 *Democratic Theory: Essays in Retrieval*, Oxford University Press.
40   J. Krieger 1986 *Reagan, Thatcher and the Politics of Decline*, Cambridge, Polity.
41   D. Horne ed. 1992 *The Trouble with Economic Rationalism*, Newham, Scribe.
42   D. Marquand 1988 *The Unprincipled Society*, London, Fontana.
43   See J. Toye 1987 *Dilemmas of Development*, Oxford, Blackwell.

models of Japan and East Asia are widely cited as examples of state-assisted development.[44]

In the context of the present development of the global system with its movement towards tri-polarity, the arguments of the New Right can be seen to have been addressed to and to be influential within the American liberal market sphere. In this sphere the economy is competitive, the social-institutional sphere is fragmented and the culture individualistic. If the New Right package makes any sense at all, then it makes sense in respect of this part of the global system. However, the other spheres of the tri-polar system work differently. In mainland Europe there is a social-democratic welfare capitalist system which now centres on the Northwest European countries around Germany. In this model of industrial-capitalism there is a state-regulated economic core associated with a social-institutional sphere oriented to enlightened cooperation and finally buttressed by a subtle civic culture. And, similarly, in the Pacific Asian sphere the economy is state-regulated, the social-institutional structures are dominated by expectations of cooperative work within the community and the culture is hierarchical and communitarian.[45]

The experience of the Third World

In respect of the Third World the dominant post-Second World War First World theories of development have tended to grant the claims of neo-classical theory and to argue for the priority where possible of market solutions to development policy problems. Over much of this same period of time however the preference for markets was ameliorated by a strong appreciation of the general political-economic, social-institutional and cultural weaknesses of the countries of the Third World. Nonetheless, the radical ideology of the free marketeers has governed the major institutions of capitalist development efforts since the early 1980s.

The IMF and World Bank have pressed for economic liberalization and proposals have involved: (a) the elimination of market imperfections, thus the removal of controls on private sector, the privatization of state assets, the liberalization of foreign investment regulations and so on; (b) the elimination of market-inhibitory social institutions and practices, thus curbing trades unions and professions, abolishing various subsidies, liberalizing employment regulation and so on; (c) the elimination of surplus government intervention, thus the imposition of restrictions on government spending, the reduction in government regulative activity, the reduction of government planning activity, the abolition of tariff regimes and so on; and, (d) it might

44 Indeed the World Bank and IMF are even now presenting their ideological counter-offensives on behalf of their fantasy model of the market. See, for example, World Bank 1993 *The East Asian Miracle*, Oxford University Press.
45 L. Thurow 1992 *Head to Head: The Coming Economic Battle Among Japan, Europe, and America*, New York, Morrow; E. Vogel 1980 *Japan as Number One*, Tokyo, Tutle.

be noted that such programmes of liberalization have usually required parallel programmes of political repression.

In all, the affirmation of the role of the marketplace has led to untold damage to fragile economies and societies in the Third World. Susan George, for example, has traced the links between US agricultural problems and the World Bank's preference for market-oriented agricultural development programmes, and the consequent inability of African nations to feed their populations.[46] George argues that the machineries of the IMF and World Bank can be taken to be concerned with the business of making the world safe for business.[47] Such strong claims are familiar.[48]

Chapter Summary

The European Enlightenment of the seventeenth and eighteenth century which celebrated the power of human reason had a number of centres including England and France. In Scotland influential work relating to economics was produced. The key figure was Adam Smith who took his strategy of enquiry from Newton and working from abstract principles to the detail of the social world offered a scheme of the gradual evolution of the economic system of society. Smith's work inspired the pre-eminent nineteenth-century social science of political-economy which was the main vehicle whereby theorists attempted to grasp the dynamics of complex change. However, at the end of the nineteenth century political-economy fell out of favour as the successful established industrial capitalist bourgeoisie grew wary of its critical and progressive dispositions. The approach gave way to the familiar spread of social science disciplines. In the twentieth century economics has become a key social science and presents itself in several technical forms (neo-classical, institutional and Keynesian). All these lines of enquiry have found expression in various strands of development theory. In particular the work of the New Right has emphatically stressed the progressive power of the free market for First, Second and Third Worlds, and has lodged claims to be the direct legatee of Adam Smith.

---

46   S. George 1984 *Ill Fares the Land*, Washington, Institute for Policy Science.
47   S. George 1988 *A Fate Worse than Debt*, Harmondsworth, Penguin; and in this vein see also W. Sachs ed. 1992 *The Development Dictionary*, London, Zed.
48   P. Korner et al. 1984 *The IMF and the Debt Crisis*, London, Zed.

4

Marx and the Dialectics of Historical Change

Overview of the Work of Karl Marx

In the mid-nineteenth century it became clear that the French and industrial revolutions had together ushered in a new phase in the overall development experience of Europe. In place of essentially agrarian, hierarchical and deferential societies a new pattern of industrial, liberal and individualistic societies was taking shape. In this context the prospective, multi-disciplinary and engaged arguments of Marx are important. The key to the ethic of Marx can be found in the idea that humankind has become alienated from its true nature but might now overcome this condition. Human beings are taken to create themselves and their societies in and through their creative labour, and consequently a just and rational society is one that acknowledges this and is organized accordingly. A productive system that degrades human labour into mere work is a system of alienated labour. Relatedly, Marx's method rests upon the materialist conception of history which claims that people make their own lives in their productive activity. This activity is the central business of human social life and around it other more abstract concerns cluster. Marx uses the distinction between economic base and social superstructure. Any society can be analysed in terms of its characteristic economic base and associated superstructure. Marx analyses bourgeois capitalism in line with this ethic and method and looks to uncover the dynamic of the system via a critical reconstruction of English political-economy. The trend of history is towards the radical reconstruction of the industrial capitalist system with the abolition of class society and the overcoming of the division of labour and thus of alienation.

Ethic and Method in Marx

Marx was concerned with analysing complex change in industrial capitalist society. He drew on a rich and broad stock of intellectual resources in order to argue on behalf of the proletariat whom he took to be the inevitable agents of further general social progress. There are three broad areas of influence in the work of Marx: the tradition of German idealist philosophy, exemplified by G. W. F. Hegel; the tradition of English political-economy, in particular the work of Adam Smith and David Ricardo; and the work of the nineteenth-century socialist movement in France.[1] It is from these materials that Marx[2] in cooperation with his collaborator Friedrich Engels[3] fashioned his general analysis of the dynamics of industrial capitalism (see figure 5).

The concept of alienation

The key to understanding Marx's ethic is to be found in his discussion of the notion of alienation. There are two ways in which this idea can be approached: (a) via a critical reworking of the idealist philosophy of Hegel; (b) via a critical review of the assumptions of the English political-economists.

In mid-nineteenth-century Germany philosophy was a central academic discipline and it was the work of Hegel that was most influential.[4] Hegel's philosophy was idealist and the 'centrality of thought – of the power of ideas, or as Hegel reified it, the Idea – was the centerpiece in this conception of the world'.[5] In this scheme human history was interpreted as the gradual extension of the power of reason: 'The successive stages in the emergence and maturation of Mind – the human spirit – began with the perception of the immediate situation; then progressed to consciousness of the self; and finally, with the full flowering of Reason, permitted understanding of the world as a whole, its laws of motion, and the place of humanity in that world'.[6]

Hegel's idea of the dynamic self-development of the Idea is essentially progressive but in his later years, as he became an establishment figure, he adjusted his views. The evolution of the Idea, the extension of reason, had reached its culmination, he argued, in his philosophy and in the Prussian rational state. The German state was seen as an embodiment of the Idea and from it order was taken to flow. It is the state which orders society and it is the state which identifies the general interest.

Marx thought that Hegel's notions of the dynamism and creativity of

1 For a good discussion of Marx, Durkheim and Weber, see A. Giddens 1971 *Capitalism and Modern Social Theory*, Cambridge University Press.
2 See D. McLellan 1973 *Karl Marx: His Life and Thought*, London, Macmillan.
3 See T. Carver 1981 *Engels*, Oxford University Press.
4 P. Worsley 1982 *Marx and Marxism*, Milton Keynes, Open University Press, pp. 22–34.
5 Ibid. p. 22.
6 Ibid. p. 25.

Figure 5   Karl Marx and the dialectics of historical change

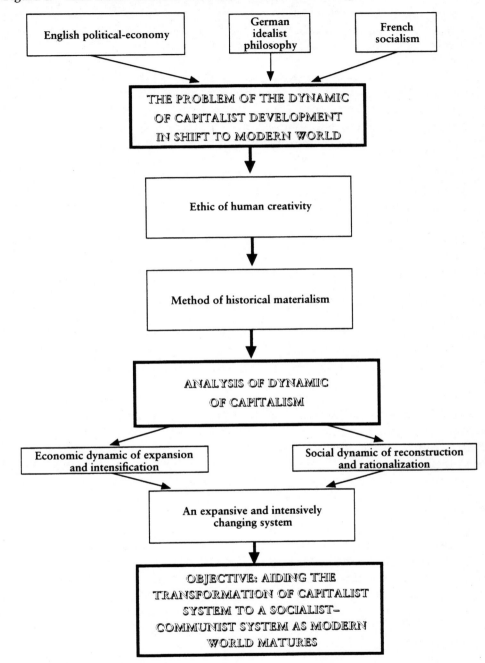

thinking were correct but he did not accept the idealism or the political conservatism. Marx reworked Hegel around two issues: (a) the issue of religion and the consequent denial of idealism; (b) the issue of the state and the consequent denial of conservative authoritarianism.

Hegel's general philosophical system is essentially religious and if we substitute the word 'God' for the word 'Idea' then world history is the story of God's self-loss and subsequent rediscovery via the extension of reason. In the Hegelian schema, the Idea migrates into the material (the ideal becomes base). The internal dynamic of the material issues in the rediscovery of the Idea (thinking human beings extend rationality until it culminates in the rediscovery of the Idea). In German idealist philosophical terms the process can be formally characterized as follows: reification, where thought becomes thing-like; estrangement, where the original thought becomes lost; alienation, where the original is now wholly other; and the supersession of alienation, as self-loss is overcome in rediscovery.

The remarkable general idealist system of Hegel was attacked by a group, of which Marx was a member, called the 'young Hegelians' or 'left Hegelians'. One line of attack focused upon religion, and thus idealism. The philosopher Feuerbach argued that far from the world and humankind having been created by God (or being emanations of the Idea) it was, in fact, humankind that made the gods: 'the gods, far from creating humanity and determining its fate, were themselves idealised creations of human thought, but of erroneous human thought'.[7] Feuerbach's critique was very influential as he substituted human beings for God, or the Idea, and he proposed that his philosophical system replace that of Hegel.

Marx found Feuerbach's strategy of 'inverting Hegel' fruitful, but he did not accept Feuerbach's solution and he went further. For Feuerbach all this alienation of self was the result of the operation of mind – the minds of human beings in general. In Feuerbach's scheme human beings were only thinking, but Marx points out that prior to thinking comes existing. Marx wants to start from the person in all his/her complexity. It is the totality of human existence in society that has to be looked at because alienation is a social and an historical phenomenon.

At this point we can introduce the element of the discussion of the state. In Hegel's scheme the state is understood to be prior to society and acts to order society. Marx argues that this is an inversion of the truth because human beings are political animals as soon as ever they are social animals. Hegel's scheme extracts one aspect of human life and lodges that aspect, and its functions, in the state. For Marx, the modern state is 'an alienated form of political activity'.[8] In the political sphere radical democratization represents the overcoming of alienation. Later Marx will argue that alienation in the productive sphere is the key to all forms of alienation and so democratization will have to begin in the productive sphere.

7   Ibid. p. 26.
8   Ibid. p. 5.

This sequence of initial revisions is complex. Marx rejects Hegelian ideal-ism whilst affirming the dialectical strategy of enquiry. Feuerbach's mater-ialism is critically appropriated and materialism is preferred to idealism, but Feuerbach's rather static understanding of materialism which saw ideas as reflections of the material world is rejected. Marx also rejects the restrictedly philosophical character of Feuerbach's critique in favour of calls for practical action in the real world. At this point we should note the influence upon Marx of French socialist ideas and in concert with Engels his increasing concern for political-economy. By this stage Marx was begin-ning to establish the idea of the practical centre of human life – the active creation and recreation in social life of humanity – and the nature of its present distortions.

In the period 1843–6 Marx wrote a series of texts which established the basis for all his subsequent work. Chief amongst these are *The Economic and Philosophical Manuscripts* (1844 – sometimes also called *The Paris Manuscripts*) and with Engels *The German Ideology* (1846). In these texts all the complex movements alluded to above reached a first approximation of the position which Marx was to hold for the rest of his life. In the latter text we find the first general outline of the idea of historical materialism (this we will look at later). It is in *The Economic and Philosophical Manu-scripts* that Marx discusses, in the context of a critique of political-economy, the notion of alienation.

Marx's criticisms of the work of the political-economists rest on the charge that they take for granted the characteristics of the economic, social and political system of their day – crucially, the existence of private prop-erty. Their work rests in part upon their treating human beings as essen-tially egotistical. The political-economists in fact use English utilitarianism to inform their analyses. The individual enters political-economic theorizing as an abstract insatiable appetite in pursuit of satisfactions: consumption is taken as the key to human character. Marx thinks this is a preposterous procedure. The political-economists are accused of merely abstracting and generalizing from the society they inhabited and of failing to offer an explanation of labour in any fundamental sense. Human beings, for Marx, create themselves and their societies in social production. Bourgeois creeds of individualism are simply the ridiculous justifications for an historically progressive yet humanly degrading system. Marx then uses the notion of alienation to analyse the way in which modern industrial capitalism acts to distort this basic human characteristic via the degradation of creative human labour into mere work.

At this point we can introduce a familiar summary of Marx's discussions in *The Economic and Philosophical Manuscripts* which suggests that ali-enation presents itself in four ways.[9] In the first place, the worker is alien-ated from the product of his labour because in industrial capitalist society

9   See Giddens 1971 op. cit.; or S. Lukes 1967 'Alienation and Anomie' in P. Laslett and W. G. Runciman eds. *Philosophy, Politics and Society Third Series*, Oxford, Blackwell.

work is specialized, routinized and controlled by others. The worker's product exists apart from him and it confronts him as the wealth of the capitalist, or abstractly as capital. Then, secondly, the worker is alienated from the act of production because routinization, specialization and submission to external control effectively destroy the typically human creativity of labour. In his work the worker denies his creativity and reduces himself to the status of an element in a wider process. Labour is not voluntary in capitalist society, rather it is coerced. Thirdly, human beings are alienated from their 'species being' as capitalistic social relations degrade the collective human creation of self and society by reducing the social world to a vehicle for the satisfaction of private wants. Capitalistic social forms deny the social character of labour. Then, fourthly, human beings are alienated from their fellows as capitalistic social relations are typically fragmentary, because individual human beings do not confront each other: role-incumbents do, and so lives become fragmented.

This is the ethical core of the work of Marx. Human beings, he argues, create themselves and their societies through their labour. A productive system that degrades labour into mere work is thus a deformed system inhabited by deformed people. The recovery of human creativity requires the reconstruction of the productive system. The fundamental contradiction of capitalist society is the private control of social production. The abolition of private property is the necessary condition of the establishment of a system of free, creative labour. In *The German Ideology* Marx and Engels look forward to the effective overcoming of the present division of labour so that human beings would not be restricted to a particular sphere of activity.

The strategy of historical materialism

Historical materialism is best regarded as an approach to social scientific enquiry. It is not an elaborated evolutionist-style general theory. The key to the whole is the claim that people make their own lives in their routine productive activity. This productive activity is taken to be the central business of human social life and around it more abstract concerns cluster – law, religion, art and so on. Any existing or historical or future envisioned society should be analysed in terms of its pattern of economic activities and the associated cluster of cultural factors. History on this scheme is regarded as the largely unconscious creation of human beings who are in turn subject to definite historically inherited constraints. In the famous preface to *A Contribution to the Critique of Political Economy* (1859) we find the following summary formulation of the 'materialist conception of history':

> In the social production of their life, men enter into definite relations that are indispensable and independent of their will, relations of production which correspond to a definite stage of the development of their material productive forces. The sum total of these relations of

production constitutes the economic structure of society, the real foundation, on which rise a legal and political superstructure and to which correspond definite forms of social consciousness. The mode of production of material life conditions the social, political and intellectual life processes in general. It is not the consciousness of men that determines their being, but, on the contrary, their social being that determines their consciousness.[10]

In his formulation of the materialist conception of history Marx made human productive activity the key to analysis of human life. Marx also made use of the metaphor of economic base and cultural superstructure and this has been the focus of much of the subsequent debate. The metaphor can be read as revealing a latent economic determinism in the work of Marx. Worsley takes the view that Marx's work is indeed overly economic in tone.[11] A similar view is advanced by Raymond Williams.[12] Worsley concludes that the use of economic determinist versions of the approach must be avoided:

> It seems simpler and more scientific to conclude that Marx and Engels were right in insisting that it is necessary for people to produce, that social life cannot be sustained unless production is organized, and that both production and exchange entail crucial patterns of relationships. Other institutions, too, have to be compatible with the economy. But the 'fit' can be quite loose; cultural forms, from art forms to forms of religion or family codes, can persist and be made compatible with quite different 'modes of production', and need only be slightly altered in the process, not totally reconstituted or replaced.[13]

Overall, Marx is arguing that human beings make their own patterns of life and themselves in creative and cooperative human labour. It is true that the simplified metaphorical expressions of this profound insight can be reworked into a mechanical economistic scheme, but in general it seems safe to conclude that the 'materialist thesis' is now widely and routinely accepted within the classical tradition of social science.

The Substantive Analysis of Capitalism

The analysis of the capitalist mode of production begins from the position noted above: all societies must reproduce themselves from year to year and this requires that they engage in material production. A law of social reproduction can be posited which identifies a movement from production to consumption to further production. This law is the base of all economic

10   K. Marx and F. Engels 1968 *Selected Works*, London, Lawrence and Wishart, p. 181.
11   Worsley 1982 op. cit. pp. 47–56.
12   R. Williams 1973 'Base and Superstructure in Marxist Cultural Theory', *New Left Review*, 82.
13   Worsley 1982 op. cit. p. 52.

systems. In capitalism this law is hidden in a complex division of labour where the link between production and consumption is mediated by the mechanisms of the market. Supply and demand rather than production and consumption seem to be basic, but the market is actually secondary. Marx aims to uncover and display the underlying laws of social production in capitalism.

Marx's economic analyses are complex and may be sketched via the ideas of commodities, use value, exchange value, surplus value, labour power and the labour theory of value, exploitation, centralization and concentration, and contradiction.[14]

The economic dynamic of capitalism

Marx's discussion of the economic anatomy of capitalism centres on the analysis of commodity production. The capitalist system is historically novel in that production is oriented not to the satisfaction of social or human needs but to the requirements of the market exchange of commodities. In respect of any commodity we can distinguish between use value (the function of the commodity) and exchange value (the value of the commodity in the marketplace). Marx tackles the problem of value in a typically nineteenth-century fashion and affirms the position adopted by political-economists called the labour theory of value. The key claim is that all value is created by the expenditure of human labour. This notion of value is further explicated in terms of the idea of the socially necessary labour time (which will depend on local circumstances) expended in creating the commodity and giving it its value.[15]

Marx argues that commodities are exchanged in the market at their true values according to the socially necessary labour time embodied in them. The capitalist buys and sells labour and other necessary inputs at their value and he sells the finished commodities at their true value. The system does not run on any sort of 'theft' and so we might ask how the capitalist makes profits. Marx explains that in capitalist society human labour power is a commodity. The labour power of human beings can be bought and sold on the market just like any other commodity. Capitalism has free labourers who are able to sell their labour power. It is also clear that modern industry is very productive. In a day the labourer selling his labour power at the market price produces a surplus over his replacement needs (the value of his labour power). Marx speaks of necessary labour, which is the time taken to provide the labourer's conditions of existence (food, housing, basic welfare and so on), and surplus labour, which is the time during which the

---

14 The exposition here draws on the work of Giddens 1971 op. cit.
15 On the labour theory of value, see J. Robinson 1962 *Economic Philosophy*, Harmonds-worth, Penguin; R. L. Meek 1956 *Studies in the Labour Theory of Value*, London, Lawrence and Wishart.

labourer produces goods over and above his replacement needs, over and above the value of his labour power. It is this surplus labour which is the source of surplus value, the basis of profit in the marketplace. The ratio between necessary and surplus labour is called the rate of exploitation.

The foregoing is a summary of the abstract model of the capitalist system. Marx went on to devote a considerable amount of effort in attempting to display how this fundamental logic manifested itself at the level of the market – in price movements, the point where orthodox marginalist economics begins. There has been much debate about these issues. The orthodox criticism centres on the difficulty of predicting prices using Marx's analysis but these criticisms are really rather beside the point as Marx wished to uncover the fundamentals of the system.[16]

Having established the mechanism of exploitation there remains the issue of the immanent dynamic of the system. The capitalist system is competitive and thus technically innovative.[17] Over time there is a shift to 'capital-intensive' industry: thus the organic composition of capital, the ratio of constant to variable capital, rises and necessarily the average rate of profit falls.[18] The economy as a whole may very well generate more profit – but the individual firms find that the rate declines. They respond by increasing the pressure of exploitation: longer hours, lower wages, an increased membership of the 'reserve army' of the unemployed. Each firm strives to cut costs and to protect its own position. The system is thus anarchic: there is no overall regulation. The system is able to contrive crises of overproduction. But it is overproduction of exchange values rather than use values. Crisis is endemic to the system and the periodic crises serve to purge the system. Wages fall, factories close, production declines until at the bottom of the business cycle profitable opportunities are once again available to the capitalist. Crises thus serve a regulatory function for an anarchic and irrational system and they also serve to encourage centralization and concentration of firms (bankrupt firms are taken over, ailing firms merge).

Marx did not anticipate the disappearance of capitalism in one final revolution-triggering mega-crisis. Economic crises are regulatory but they do cause misery for the proletariat and thus foster class consciousness. Relatedly, within the capitalist system production units become larger. The individual capitalist becomes redundant as the social nature of production

16 Giddens 1971 op. cit. pp. 50–2.
17 On this, see R. Brenner 1977 'The Origins of Capitalist Development: A Critique of Neo-Smithian Marxism' in *New Left Review*, 104.
18 Surplus value is the basis of profit. Surplus value is generated in productive enterprise and this productive enterprise has two elements: constant and variable capital. The former includes plant, machines, buildings and so on, whilst the latter is the human labour employed. Only variable capital creates value – according to the tenets of the labour theory of value – and the ratio of constant to variable capital is called the organic composition of capital. As profit derives from surplus value, the greater the organic composition (the higher the capital intensiveness) then the lower the average rate of profit. Absolute profit does not fall, only the rate of return declines.

is obviously displayed and increasingly acknowledged as firms become internally more complex. The concentration of power in giant firms is similarly underscored. The economic dynamic of capitalism tends in the direction of its replacement and at the same time engenders in the proletariat a consciousness of its position in the system which in turn is the basis of proletarian political insistence upon the realization of these immanent tendencies. The basic contradiction of the capitalist system is the private ownership or control of social production and it is overcome in the process of establishing socialism.

The social dynamic of capitalism

Turning now to Marx's analysis of the social dynamic of the capitalist system we find material which is more sociological and political but which is also comparatively underdeveloped. This has meant that subsequent commentators and political activists have had to try to divine the outline of Marx's analysis of the social anatomy of the system from scattered writings. Nonetheless, the key areas of concern are fairly clear and we have the following issues: class, ideology, base/superstructure, the state, and the party and revolutionary change. Like the terms dealing with the economic anatomy, these are closely associated with each other. They do not represent a list of discrete elements and they are separated for exegetical convenience.

It is a basic claim in Marx's materialist approach to history that what is crucial to comprehending human social life is the fact of productive activity. This involves two elements: (a) an exchange with the natural world upon which humankind works; (b) a related exchange between the people involved in this work. Human creative labour is social labour. As Giddens puts it: 'Every kind of productive system entails a definite set of social relationships between individuals involved in the productive process'.[19]

Productive activity is Marx's starting point for examining industrial capitalist society and he investigates via a critique of its principal theorists, the classical political-economists.[20] A key error on their part is their individualism. Marx calls them the 'Robinsonades' as their model saw human beings as isolated and non-social, like poor Robinson Crusoe.[21] The economics of the political-economists reflected this assumption with contracts struck in the marketplace in pursuit of egocentric gratifications. Against this model,

19   Giddens 1971 op. cit. p. 35.
20   T. Carver 1975 *Karl Marx: Texts on Method* explains in his Editor's Preface (pp. 3–45) that Marx undertook the critique of political-economy because it was the premier social science of nineteenth-century capitalism, and, with the ideological facade set aside, could provide the basis of a scientific grasp of the dynamics of that society. Carver also usefully characterizes the style of enquiry of political-economy (catholic in its intellectual scope and self-critical, pp. 6–9) and Marx's idea of scientificity (interpretive and prospective, pp. 40–1).
21   K. Marx 1973 *Grundrisse*, Harmondsworth, Penguin, p. 83.

Marx insisted that production be regarded as a social practice. With the development of industrial productive enterprise there grows up a complex division of labour and within this antagonistic classes can emerge as one group gains a privileged position. Class is not established by source of income, it is not an income group. Class is not a functional position within the division of labour. The notion of class points to the existence of groups identified by the position occupied in relation to the social means of production. Specifically, in bourgeois society, class position is a matter of the ownership of private property in the means of production.[22]

Marx focused upon nineteenth-century capitalist society and it is this specific historical period that comes closest to his abstract model of the two antagonistic classes of bourgeoisie and proletariat. In addition to these we can identify other class groups, including: residues from earlier social productive formations (for example, the peasantry which were leftover from feudalism in the nineteenth century or similarly the English landed aristocracy);[23] or marginal groups possibly forming new classes (for example, in recent years theorists have looked at youth, white-collar technocrats, a consumption-oriented working class, consumers, and yuppies);[24] or functionally dependent strata whose futures are bound up with the fortunes of a particular class (for example, modern senior management).

However, the key antagonistic class relations within capitalist society in Marx's scheme are those between bourgeoisie and proletariat. The extent to which and the way in which class engenders class consciousness will depend on local circumstances. The result of class-conscious political action is similarly context-dependent: 'Class relationships are the main axis around which political power is distributed, and upon which political organisation depends'.[25] Thus when we look at modern industrialized societies we see that the existing pattern of relationships and state form will depend on the deals struck between bourgeoisie, landed aristocracy and proletariat in the various states. It is wrong to ascribe to Marx any scheme of mechanical movement based on economic and class forces of social forms through history. The specific concrete social formations have to be deciphered and their historical conditions grasped. Thus may we understand their present dynamics.[26]

22   Class position is first a structural matter (class-in-itself) and thereafter may become a matter of consciousness as class members act in the light of collective goals (class-for-itself).
23   Although here the story is a little more complex, but see for example T. Nairn 1988 *The Enchanged Glass*, London, Radius.
24   See respectively: H. Marcuse 1969 *An Essay on Liberation*, Harmondsworth, Penguin; J. K. Galbraith 1967 *The New Industrial State*, Harmondsworth, Penguin; C. Kerr et al. 1960 *Industrialism and Industrial Man*, Harmondsworth, Penguin; and D. Bell 1973 *The Coming of Post-Industrial Society*, Harmondsworth, Penguin. On postmodernism see D. Harvey 1989 *The Condition of Postmodernity*, Oxford, Blackwell.
25   Giddens 1971 op. cit. p. 39.
26   For an example of the diversity of the historical experiences of countries in the shift to the modern world see B. Moore 1966 *Social Origins of Dictatorship and Democracy*, Boston, Mass., Beacon.

It is within the realm of political struggle that we most often encounter the notion of ideology. In a class-fissured society the ideas of the dominant group are presented in terms designed to legitimate the group's position. Social arrangements which are specific to times and places are explained or explained away as natural and proper. Disadvantaged groups on the other hand attempt to propound alternative visions of society.

The notion of ideology has had a rather chequered career. It originated with the French philosopher Destutt de Tracy in the late eighteenth century and he intended the term to designate the 'science of ideas'. It was no less a historical figure than Napoleon who gave the term its familiar pejorative sense: he speaks of 'ideologues'. Thus ideology becomes the province of the dreamer or the charlatan. In the work of Marx a range of meanings is given to the term. In *The German Ideology* Marx and Engels criticize the left Hegelians for abstracting from history and focusing on ideas. It is the failure to see the link between material relationships and ideal statements which produces ideology, the world seen upside down. Ideology in this sense flows from errors of conceptualization and analysis. Marx and Engels later extend this usage to include the products of apologists for particular social forms. However, there is another sense given to the notion of ideology in the work of Marx and Engels. Ideology is the way in which people became conscious of conflicts in their societies. In this sense ideology means the set of ideas which arise from a given set of material interests/circumstances. Ideology is thus 'making sense'[27] – and this sense reflects particular circumstances. Here we have the notions of class ideologies; we do not have error, rather we have particular cases argued from a particular point of view. But that point of view could be a restricted one leading to misconception and error. Thus the two versions are rather tangled. Ideology has to be deciphered. This means that explanations of the social world have to be set in their historical location and thereafter investigated so as to disentangle sense and nonsense. This was Marx's approach to the critique of political-economy.[28]

Closely related to the matter of the nature of ideology is the debate around the relationship of base and superstructure. If social productive activity is central to human life, just how does it fashion or shape cultural forms such as law, religion, art and political formulations (ideologies), and so on? We touched on this issue above and saw then how complicated discussion of this issue had become. The marxist faces a dilemma. On the one hand, a strong determinism can be affirmed which is useful for political purposes – thus we can speak of, say, class law (one law for the rich and another for the poor). But such determinism is intellectually difficult to sustain. On the other hand, a looser more subtly articulated relationship can

---

27   This is close to my own favoured usage: ideologies are thus self-conscious strategies for interpreting the world so as to guide action in it.
28   See A. Giddens 1979 'Ideology and Consciousness' in *Central Problems in Social Theory*, London, Macmillan.

be affirmed which is more intellectually plausible but which also has its polemical edge dulled. And in mentioning polemic we shift our attention into the realm of the political. To complete this sketch of Marx's analysis of the social anatomy of capitalism we can add a few brief remarks on marxian politics: state, party and revolution.

There is little systematic exegesis in the work of Marx and Engels on the subject of politics. Milliband takes the view that the political was so pervasive in their work and lives that they simply took it for granted.[29] It can be argued that the state occupied a fairly central position as it is the key political institution of modern industrial society. In the *Manifesto of the Communist Party* Marx and Engels observe: 'the bourgeoisie has, at last, since the establishment of Modern Industry and of the world market, conquered for itself, in the modern representative state, exclusive political sway. The executive of the modern state is but a committee for managing the common affairs of the whole bourgeoisie'.[30] This represents the classical marxian view. Yet Marx himself did not pay a great deal of attention to analysing the state and this task, like others in respect of the social anatomy of change, has fallen to subsequent marxist theorists.[31] Much orthodox communist thinking on this and related matters derives from Lenin's work and the experience of the Russian revolution, and the subsequent struggles within the infant USSR to secure the success of the revolution. Lenin's 1917 text *The State and Revolution* argues for the inevitability of violent revolution and the necessity of destroying the state machine.[32] To this familiar image is to be added Lenin's conception of the role of the Communist Party as the revolutionary vanguard of the proletariat. There is a shift from the comparative open-endedness of Marx and Engels on these issues towards a distinctly more specifically articulated view on the part of Lenin. However, the final (intellectual) descent into the rigid and mechanical formulations of official Marxism-Leninism was only effected in the period of Stalin's rule. In the late 1930s in the USSR Marxism-Leninism became an official state ideology and marxist social theorists have been trying to escape from this suffocating deformation of the work of Marx and Engels ever since.

Scope and Role of Marx's Work

It is useful to discuss Marx at some length so as to illustrate the claims made about social theorizing in the earlier chapters of the text. After Gellner, it is clear that social theorizing has been since its inception in modern guise

29 See R. Milliband 1977 *Marxism and Politics*, Oxford University Press.
30 K. Marx and F. Engels 1968 *Selected Works*, London, Lawrence and Wishart, p. 37.
31 For a simple summary of Marx's scattered writings on the state, see R. Milliband 1965 'Marx and the State' in R. Milliband and J. Saville eds. 1965 *The Socialist Register*, London, Merlin.
32 His work on this book was, in fact, interrupted – by the Russian revolution!

in the late eighteenth century centrally concerned with the attempt to render intelligible the transition to the modern industrial world. This is not to say that all social theorists have operated at a broad scale because clearly they have not. Much social scientific work has been addressed to particular elements of the transition as the task is so complex that any grasp of detail across a broad range of elements eludes all but the discipline's geniuses. Again, it could be noted that much social scientific effort at present is less concerned with offering an ethically based, argued case or with pursuing any intellectually pure (or academic) interpretation than with the provision of policy-scientific formulations designed to meet the information or interpretation needs of planners. This is true for First, Second and Third Worlds. Further than this we could observe that social science is also at the disposal of the industrial-commercial economic base of modern societies, and could point to the work of management, market research, opinion testing, advertising, design work, the output of the media and so on which is all informed to a greater or lesser degree by the work of the social sciences. Clearly in this realm we are far removed from the concerns of Marx or the other figures lodged within the classical tradition of social theorizing. Yet it is on the basis of these last two areas – applied social science and policy science – that claims are made for the technical scientificity of the social sciences. It is here that we find the naive celebration of the received model of the natural sciences and the eschewal of concern for and involvement with ethical and political issues. It is here that we find Gellner's 'jejune official textbook definitions of sociology'[33] and equally jejune definitions of economics and politics. The truth is both more exciting and distinctly more intimidating as the central tradition of social scientific enquiry has been with making sense of the transition to the modern industrial world. And it is Marx who offers the first well-grounded, richly elaborated, intellectually coherent and thoroughly engaged interpretation.

However, it is clear that the work of Marx is not merely a matter of intellectual discussion for the work of Marx spawned marxism – and this political application of Marx has its own very complex history. The work of Marx thus encompasses a body of social scientific ideas and a related subsequent social movement. As Hobsbawm has argued, the social movement is central to the history of the twentieth century.[34] Intellectually Marx is central to social science. Irving Zeitlin prefaces a discussion of Weber and Durkheim[35] with the subtitle *The Debate with Marx's Ghost*.[36] He also remarks that 'in the twentieth century much of social science took shape in a critical encounter with the theories of Karl Marx'.[37] Since Marx's

33   Gellner 1964 op. cit. p. 34.
34   E. Hobsbawm 1994 *Age of Extremes: The Short Twentieth Century*, London, Michael Joseph.
35   I. Zeitlin 1968 *Ideology and the Development of Sociological Theory*, New York, Prentice Hall.
36   Ibid. p. 109.
37   Ibid. p. 108.

death his work has been used to fashion a series of quite distinct versions of marxism. The core material of his work has been deployed by particular groups (of both political actors and more academic theorists), in particular contexts, to illuminate particular problems. We can take note here of the major European schools of marxism which have been developed over the last hundred years or so.

In the closing years of the nineteenth century and in the pre-First World War period a marxist political party in Germany secured widespread support amongst the working classes and the party's leaders/intellectuals advanced a particular reading of the marxist legacy. In brief, they argued that with the maturation of the capitalist system and the organizational successes of the working classes a reformist route to a communist future had become possible. Such theories, advanced by Eduard Bernstein, expressed the circumstance and programme of the German Social Democratic Party.[38]

The most significant version of marxism in the period after Marx's death has been associated with the experience of the Soviet Union.[39] The Russian revolution issued in the first avowedly 'workers' state'. Its premier theorist was Lenin who advanced a theory of imperialism to grasp the expansive nature of capitalism and a theory of the vanguard role of the party in regard to the proletariat. However, in intellectual terms the development of marxism was quite odd. A critical social-scientific strategy of analysis was put to use to order the industrial development of what was at the time an underdeveloped country on the periphery of Europe. In other words, a social scientific approach was turned into official state ideology. In broad outline this took the form of reading Marx in a positivistic fashion, as having identified an inevitable set of causal laws of social development, and conjoining this with the political vanguardism of Lenin, issued in an official ideology which accorded all power to the experts and elite, official Marxism–Leninism. Althought the Soviet Communist Party was taken seriously in the West, as was the industrialization drive of the inter-war period (when Stalin's activities were not widely known), few thinkers ever took the Soviet version of marxism very seriously, and it degenerated completely in the dictatorial episode of Stalin. However, the Soviet experiment caused considerable consternation in the developed West throughout the 1930s and 1940s. After the Second World War the hostile stance was resumed under the umbrella of the Cold War. This marxist tradition came to an end in 1991.

After the First World War and the abolition of the monarchy there was a period of upheaval in Germany. One aspect of this was the attempt of the German Communist Party to echo the successes of the Russian revolution. This revolution was defeated but the particular brand of internationalism and the stress on spontaneous action propounded by Karl Liebknecht and

38   See G. Lichtheim 1961 *Marxism: An Historical and Critical Study*, London, Routledge.
39   Hobsbawm 1994 op. cit.

Rosa Luxemburg are now seen as significant in the history of marxism. At the time their revolution failed and they met their deaths at the hands of the subsequently powerful political right. Then in the late 1920s and early 1930s a group of intellectuals came together to form a school for social research in Frankfurt.[40] They opposed both the prevailing positivism of western European social science and what they saw as the sterility of official Soviet Marxism–Leninism and advocated a return to a 'humanist marxism' based on the more philosophical material produced by the young Marx. They fled Germany in the period of the rise of fascism and after a sojourn in the USA returned to West Germany after the Second World War. The work of the Frankfurt School was influential in the social and political upheavals of the 1960s. At this time there was a widespread rediscovery of the marxian tradition amongst Western scholars and political activists. It was argued by Euro-Communists that the analytical machineries of Marx could be put to work in the context of western Europe directly; that is, without reference to the experience of the Soviet Union.[41] The example of the French, Spanish and Italian communist parties was acknowledged. However, the political enthusiasm waned as the 1970s turned into the 1980s. Yet the intellectual legacy of the period is strong. The critical theorist Jürgen Habermas is regarded as one of Europe's foremost theorists, and there is a continuing interest in the work of the Frankfurt School and the Italian theorist Antonio Gramsci, as in Italy in the inter-war period a particular version of marxism developed which stressed the need to analyse patterns of culture and ideas. This work has given us the idea of hegemony and culture-criticism. We might note that a similar concern for the detail of ordinary life and culture has been evidenced by a group of British marxist historians – E. P. Thompson, Eric Hobsbawm, Rodney Hilton and Christopher Hill.[42] Finally, we should note that in France in the post-Second World War period a briefly influential school of marxism grew up around the philosophical work of Louis Althusser, a logically rigorous version of Marx which insisted, against the humanist adherents of Gramsci or the Frankfurt School, that Marx had indeed founded a hard science of society.

The work of Marx and his followers constitutes such a rich body of social scientific analysis that most contemporary social scientists use parts of the material in their own work. Most social scientists who offer general theories of society feel obliged to state where they stand in relation to Marx. Most social scientists would grant the central insight of his materialist conception of history, that is that humankind is ineluctably social in nature. Many social scientists would grant that the whole business of theorizing is somehow or other grounded in ethics (even if it is not clear how, or what precisely this implies for objectivity). Marx's claim that social life

40   M. Jay 1973 *The Dialectical Imagination*, Boston, Mass., Little Brown.
41   P. Anderson 1983 *In The Tracks of Historical Materialism*, London, Verso.
42   H. Kaye 1984 *The British Marxist Historians*, Cambridge, Polity.

centres on the production of the material necessities of human life would also probably be widely granted (although there is much debate as to how to characterize the sphere of economic activity).

Overall, the following points can be made. First, Marx offers a set of fundamental conceptions of the nature of social scientific analysis, and these include the notion of humankind's self-creation through routine social action and the affirmation of the radical democratic ethic of collective and individual self-realization. Secondly, Marx offers a set of analytic strategies (most importantly, political-economic structural analysis and the culture-critical elucidation of patterns of meaning). Thirdly, Marx offers a major substantive theory of the analysis of complex social change which, although no longer wholly accepted, is still routinely cited in debate. Fourthly, Marx offers a body of work which is routinely plundered for useful concepts which can be put to work on this or that problem (class, alienation, bourgeoisie, proletariat, revolution, capitalism, exploitation, conflict, state, civil society and so on).

Marx and Third World Development

The legacy of Marx in the particular areas of concern for development can be noted briefly as this will let us see how present-day marxist work follows on from the work of Marx.[43] We can do this by making use of the work of Gabriel Palma whose work is concerned with analysing the relations between the metropolitan centres of the First World and the peripheral territories of the Third World.[44] Palma identifies a series of ways in which theorists have dealt with these issues: the work of Marx and Engels; the work of the theorists of classical imperialism; and the recent work of the neo-marxists.

The first of the attempts made within the marxian tradition to analyse the relations of centres and peripheries was that of Marx and Engels themselves. However, there is a problem in elucidating this early position as the discussion of the Third World is restricted to scattered remarks in scholarly texts and journalism. Marx and Engels seem to have supposed that the dynamism which they diagnosed as utterly essential to the capitalist system would manifest itself in both intensification within the established system and expansion of that system. They expected the capitalist system to become more intensively developed within its central territories and they expected it to spread geographically. Indeed, so confident was this early position in respect of the dynamic of capitalism that existing non-Western and non-capitalist modes of production tended to be dismissed as moribund

43   A excellent survey is made by A. Brewer 1980 *Marxist Theories of Imperialism*, London, Routledge; see also R. Peet 1991 *Global Capitalism*, London, Routledge.
44   G. Palma 1978 'Dependency: A Formal Theory of Underdevelopment or a Methodology for the Analysis of Concrete Situations of Underdevelopment?' in *World Development*, 6.

and unprogressive historically. However, Marx and Engels were optimistic about the future and they anticipated the spread of autonomous centres of capitalism wherever colonialism had broken down moribund social forms and introduced the seed of capitalistic change.

The second set of marxian attempts to grasp the relationship of centres and peripheries is to be found in the classical statements of imperialism. Theorists in this area were preoccupied by the situation in Russia and argued that whilst capitalism was a progressive force the situation of Russia as a late industrializer made the whole process problematical. As regards the industrialization of the Third World, the theorists of classical imperialism began by taking up an optimistic position. The dynamism of the capitalist mode of production when implanted via colonial rule, as Marx and Engels argued, is granted. However, the rise of monopoly capitalism within the First World was seen as a potential brake on industrialization in the peripheries as new patterns of industrialization fashioned to the interests of monopoly-capitalist enterprises were established. It came to be argued that monopoly capitalism could sustain a less developed peripheral capitalism perhaps indefinitely. It was suggested that a solution could be found in political reform and decolonization seemed to be a sufficient remedy. The theorists argued that with the removal of monopoly-capitalist distortions the local capitalist centre could proceed to industrialize and, eventually, to usher in a socialist system. In time, this optimistic position came to be revised and what was stressed was the power of local elites to secure mutually beneficial alliances with monopoly capitalism thereby arresting the historical dynamic of the capitalist system in the Third World.

The third set of marxian analyses of the exchange of centres and peripheries is usually taken to have been generated by the work of Paul Baran. His work represented the notion of monopoly capitalism such that the world capitalist economic system becomes split into a non-progressive capitalist core and a deformed periphery. A programme of political action via disengagement from this world system is for Baran the prerequisite of any progressive change. Other related lines include a reformist position associated with ECLA (Economic Commission for Latin America), and a line which stresses the political-economic analyses of the social and economic dynamics internal to the nations of the Third World and which may be taken to be a corrective to the overstated and sometimes polemical work of Baran and A. G. Frank.

The work of this last noted marxian approach to analysing the relations of centres and peripheries has been influential within post-Second World War development theorizing. Palma's argument neatly illustrates the way in which the work of Marx has been both handed down and revised. We will discover later that the matter of the application of Marx to development issues has become a contentious one and there has been much debate as to what counts as a marxian analysis of development. In this self-critical climate the work of Marx himself is of direct relevance and is explicitly treated.

Chapter Summary

In his analyses of the patterns of complex change attendant upon the dramatic mid-nineteenth-century development of the modern industrial world, Marx advances a theory of capitalism via a critique of nineteenth-century political-economy. The ethic is radical democratic and finds expression in the notion of alienation, and the method is the historical materialist analysis of change. The objective of the theoretical analyses is to inform the practical activity of the progressive forces of society. Marx attempts to uncover the fundamental dynamic of the social world in the interconnection of the political-economic, social-institutional and political-cultural logics of development. Marx's work is an emphatic celebration of the project of modernity. Although he had little to say about the Third World, his work has been extensively used by development theorists.

5

Durkheim and the Evolution of the Division of Labour

Overview of the Work of Emile Durkheim

The major nineteenth-century social theorists were concerned to analyse the complex change from agrarian feudalism to industrial capitalism. In this vein we can look at Durkheim and consider the ideas about social morality, the notions of sociological method and the substantive analysis of *The Division of Labour*. Durkheim's ethic can be approached via the distinction between what was normal and abnormal in society. The normal state of affairs in a complex division of labour is one of organic solidarity secured by the moral code of individualism. In the late nineteenth century the pressures of rapid change had fostered conflict. The ethic of social solidarity should be reinforced by the establishment of guilds which will both regulate the behaviour of individuals and simultaneously make evident to them the nature of their contribution to the social whole. It is a corporatist strategy. Relatedly, Durkheim's method involves identifying social facts, looking for their antecedent social causes characterizing their social function within the social whole which may thereafter be studied in terms of its social evolution. In Durkheim's major substantive analysis he addressed the issue of complex change in late nineteenth-century European capitalist society in terms of the evolutionary development of the division of labour in the broad historical process of the shift from traditional to modern societies. Durkheim is concerned to argue that the moral order of contemporary society is changing. It is moving away from traditional ties of community towards the more informal ties of a society committed to notions of individualism (see figure 6).

Figure 6   Emile Durkheim and the evolution of the division of labour

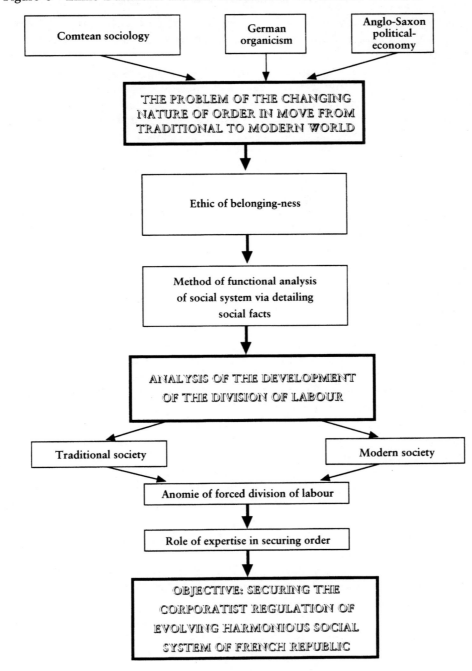

Durkheim's Ethic

Durkheim argues that formal ethical schemes tend to revolve around a few simple ideas which are then unpacked and applied to a variety of situations. The problem identified by Durkheim is that such moralists never study the social processes which create the rules the moralists speculate upon. A scientific study must look at actual social rules. These social moral rules are characterized by being obligatory and we can identify moral rules by the sanctions called forth by them. It is society that constitutes the moral world: 'morality consists in being solidary with a group and varies with this solidarity'.[1] As moral rules are generated by the social whole and express the conditions for the reproduction and development of the social whole then for an individual moral action is self-conscious practical action oriented to sustaining the social whole.

Durkheim's ethic finds particular expression in his ideas of normal and pathological social development. Durkheim declares that his definitions will be based on observable phenomena. The normal will be the average and the pathological that which deviates from it. This formulation is refined somewhat by lodging normality/pathology within a group and historical context. Normality will be that which is necessary to that society. In essence patterns of behaviour which support the ordered development of the social whole can be judged normal. In the case of societies in transition the normal may be difficult to identify. In periods of rapid change the social rules can break down and individuals can become unsure what is expected of them. Durkheim calls this condition anomie. Durkheim concludes that it is the business of 'every science of life . . . to define and explain the normal and to distinguish it from its opposite'.[2]

In *The Elementary Forms of Religious Life* (1912) Durkheim pursues the matter of moral authority and the particular character of moral rules. Religion, for Durkheim, presents the source of all abstract thinking. In the area of moral ideas, Durkheim argues that religious precepts are the symbolic representations of the society itself. So by breaking moral rules the deviant is denying the society. The response of the society is the use of retributive sanctions. Durkheim elucidates the character of moral authority with reference to the religious distinction between the sacred and the profane.

These brief remarks indicate how Durkheim 'was . . . concerned with . . . the problem of the "changing nature of order" in the context of a definite conception of social development'.[3] In the key early text *The Division of Labour* (1893) Durkheim offers an attempt to characterize the nature of changing forms of social solidarity and to distinguish normality and

1   Durkheim, in A. Giddens 1972a *Emile Durkheim: Selected Writings*, Cambridge University Press, p. 101.
2   Ibid. p. 105.
3   A. Giddens 1971 *Capitalism and Modern Social Theory*, Cambridge University Press, p. ix.

pathology in novel patterns of behaviour. This enquiry was itself subject to definite conceptions of scientificity.

Durkheim's Sociological Method

Durkheim argues that sociology must be clear about its procedures and field of enquiry. This entails separating out of the complex real world a specified area and Durkheim wants to identify social facts and take them as expressive of the social wholes of which they are the elements. Durkheim also insists that sociology must be distinct from other social sciences and this implied a need for clarity in respect of the study of social facts.

A social fact must be studied as if it were a thing in nature. A social fact would express the character of the social whole within which it was embedded. A social fact could be identified via its property of constraint because as the facts of nature constrain action so the social facts which comprise the social world constrain action. A social fact can be described via empirical research. It cannot be accessed via introspection. Durkheim points out that laws, duties, and social mores all exist externally to the actor. Such formal and informal rules are given and coercive (if we disobey we suffer sanctions). A social fact may be recognized by its power of external coercion. The focus of sociological analysis is therefore the complex web of social rules which shape the behaviour of individuals, and thereafter the sequence of causes of social facts (which must be sought in antecedent social states of affairs), the function of social institutions within the social whole, and finally the way in which social wholes change and develop over time.

In *The Rules of Sociological Method* (1895) Durkheim attempts to elucidate the notion of the social with the ideas of externality and constraint. Humankind is seen as being born into an established social world and the web of rules constituting society simply confronts the individual as given. In this sense society constitutes a set of rules, a moral order. These matters are pursued further and it is pointed out that law, duty, established social practices and so on all exist externally to the actor. Moreover, patterns of action are not only externally given, they are also imperative and coercive. A social fact is to be recognized by its power of external coercion. External coercion or social constraint is the key to identifying social facts and the crucial social facts for the sociologist centre upon the web of rules which social beings inhabit. Thus, says Durkheim, sociology can be regarded as the science of social institutions. So, generally, it is the character of the historically unfolding succession of social states of affairs that must be grasped.

Much of *The Rules of Sociological Method* is given over to distinguishing between normality and pathology in given social situations. Durkheim searches for normality/pathology in society on the analogy of normality/pathology in biological systems. The outcome is a conception of normality which identifies the normal as that which is a functional requisite of the type of society in question. In response to the suggestion that this scheme looks rather conservative, Durkheim says not; rather sociologists just see clearly how things work.

In *Suicide* (1887) Durkheim is concerned to investigate what he takes to be a symptom of the moral failings of society. The issue of suicide was often used as a vehicle for moral speculation at this time. Durkheim looks to challenge extant debate with his positive scientific approach which looks at social facts and produces what we would now call a social-structural explanation. Suicide he takes to be occasioned by upheaval in the organic condition of society. It is a matter of failures in the integrative moral codes of society. Durkheim distinguishes between suicide rates and the aetiology of particular cases. It is the former which he looks at. The suicide rate is seen as patterned and the issue is how to explain this patterning. Durkheim considers and rejects geographical and biological explanations and looks to social reasons. Thus he finds, for example, that there is a correlation between suicide rate and religion (many more Protestants than Catholics) – both prohibit suicide but the two churches have very different social characters. The Catholic Church displays greater integration. It is this matter of social integration that Durkheim fastens on – thus, for example, unmarried people commit suicide more than married people. Conversely, suicide rates decline at times of national crisis. So there is a basic relationship: integration is inversely related to suicide. Durkheim presents a tripartite categorization: anomic suicide, which is linked to the loosening of the bonds in the division of labour; egoistic suicide, which is a spin-off of the modern cult of the individual; and altruistic suicide, where the individual submits to the demands of a strong collective conscience, for example, suttee.

Durkheim's Substantive Analysis

The Franco–Prussian war of 1870–1 saw the defeat of France and a move towards establishing a republican form of state in France which was finally accomplished in 1877. The support for the new republic was somewhat uncertain and the discipline of sociology which was newly established in the universities came to be associated with the republican cause. The clear political task in the face of monarchical reaction was the offer a theoretical model of a route towards a rational modern future for France and this formed a key element in the work of Durkheim.[4]

Durkheim's general interest was with trying to comprehend the nature of industrial capitalism and he accomplished this via a comparison of traditional and modern societies. Durkheim offered a characterization of traditional agrarian small-scale rural society in terms of its typically strong sense of community. The moral web of rules binds people tightly together. If the rules are broken the law will act to expiate the offence given to society, and penal codes are typically retributive. Durkheim contrasted this with modern

---

4   G. Hawthorn 1976 *Enlightenment and Despair*, Cambridge University Press, ch. 6.

industrial large-scale urban society with its stress on individualism. The moral web of rules leaves much scope for individual action. If the rules are broken the law will act to compensate for any loss suffered, and penal codes are typically restitutive. Durkheim argued that this shift from traditional to modern society (a matter of social differentiation) was driven by an increase in the dynamic density of society, by which he meant the extent and character of interaction (itself further driven by population growth and the advance of technology). It is a matter of the naturally given evolution of the progressively more differentiated division of labour. As the underlying social form changed and developed the social world was reintegrated via a new social ethic. Durkheim's concern with the moral regulation of the social world is central to his work and it is a theme that is addressed in several of his major works.

The intellectual context of the work on the division of labour

The Division of Labour introduced Durkheim's central concern with the moral nature of the social world. As we saw in the discussion of Marx the process of the intellectual crystallization of a novel theoretical perspective upon society is very complex. It is also true of Durkheim's views. Durkheim produces his analysis in debate with others: (a) the legacy of Saint-Simon and Comte; (b) the work of the German 'organicist' social philosophers; and (c) the work of marxists who stressed conflict.

The general intellectual milieu of the turn of the century included the widespread popularity of sociology. The claim is made by Lukes, who goes on to say that a major reason for this was the work of the English philosopher and social theorist Herbert Spencer.[5] The scheme proposed by Spencer was an evolutionist one where societies move from simple (and savage) social forms to complex (and civilized) forms. The mechanism of change is a sort of cultural Lamarckianism with a social struggle and survival of the culturally fittest.

Spencer was very popular with the US bourgeoisie around the turn of the century. They saw in his social Darwinism a legitimating theory for their own pursuit of wealth. In Darwin's theory it is the fittest who survive yet that they are the fittest is evidenced solely by their survival. In Darwin's theory 'fittest' does not mean 'best', yet when misapplied to the social world fittest tends to be equated with 'socially most deserving'. A further refinement can be introduced from Lamarck, another biologist, who suggested that learned behaviour could be passed on in addition to inherited genetic characteristics. If this idea is presented in a social context, then it can be read as meaning that those who acquire social skills can pass them on to the next generation (and may have inherited earlier learned characteristics from their parents). Thus it is the culturally best who survive and

5   S. Lukes 1973 *Emile Durkheim*, London, Macmillan, ch. 20.

transmit their advantages in competitive society because they are the fittest
– and now fittest does mean best or socially most deserving.

Spencer was not the only social philosopher and sociologist writing at the
time. In Germany, Georg Simmel was working at Berlin, and Ferdinand
Tonnies was at Kiel. In the USA, too, there was a widespread development
of sociology departments in the universities.[6] Nonetheless, Durkheim saw
France as the place where social science had received its most important
elaboration.

Against the backdrop of this milieu we can identify two major areas of
intellectual debt: Saint-Simon (via Comte); and a group of German organicist
social theorists. And to this we can add the major negative influences of
socialism in general and marxism in particular.[7]

As regards the German thinkers, two areas of their concerns were con-
genial to Durkheim: the first is their organicism, the second their concern
for the moral regulation of society.[8] The former point entails the use of an
organic metaphor to characterize society: thus the social whole is made up
of functionally interdependent elements. This metaphor reflects the pervasive influence of Darwin whose thought had an 'extraordinary impact . . .
upon social thought, in the concluding decades of the nineteenth century'.[9]
The second point relates to the stress these theorists placed upon the idea
of society as a moral community that can be studied scientifically.

The second positive contributory source used by Durkheim is to be found
in Saint-Simon mediated by the work of Comte. Both are French theorists.
Saint-Simon is said to have 'straddled two epochs: the Revolution, on the
one hand, and the conservative Reaction on the other'.[10] Durkheim follows
Comte in developing the conservative aspects.[11] And, crucially, what we
find is the idea that the modern world is an industrial system which has
evolved out of earlier social forms and is to be understood as a comprising
a set of functionally interdependent parts. Conflict within the system is
either irrational or temporary and integration will be enhanced by fostering
appropriate moral ideals and these are amenable to identification by positive social science.

Turning now to the third contributory element to Durkheim's position
we find the negative influence of socialism and marxism. Durkheim's characterizations and proposals in *The Division of Labour* differed sharply
from those of contemporary socialists. Where the latter saw social conflict
and the necessity of social reconstruction before the benefits of industrial
production could be enjoyed by the majority, Durkheim urged the necessity

6   See Hawthorn 1976 op. cit. for a history of sociology which identifies how national
sociologies were formed.
7   I. Zeitlin 1968 *Ideology and the Development of Sociological Theory*, New York,
Prentice Hall.
8   Giddens 1971 op. cit. ch. 2.
9   Ibid. p. 66.
10   Zeitlin 1968 op. cit. p. 235.
11   Marx, it is sometimes argued, developed the radical elements.

of acknowledging the social harmony engendered by the new social form with its new integrative pattern of solidarity. Any social science predicated upon the assumption of inevitable conflict was wrong and social action based upon it futile.

The division of labour analysed

The central claim of *The Division of Labour* was that social life in contemporary Europe was not suffering a breakdown with the passing of traditional society, but on the contrary was moving to a new style of integration centred on the social ethic of individualism which expresses the requirements of a complex industrial society. As the new form of society emerges it relies on a new form of social solidarity. A new pattern of interdependent social relations and appropriate moral rules has emerged such that it can be said that the normal state of a complex division of labour is one of organic solidarity. The role of sociological analysis is to identify the problems occasioned by rapid complex change to those in society who are able to effect reform. It is a corporatist strategy.

The argument has three elements: to begin with, Durkheim follows what was a familiar nineteenth-century strategy of attempting to grasp the nature of the present day by comparing it with the past. Thus we have before and after characterizations. These could then be slotted into a series of such characterizations which expanded upon the basic dichotomy. Durkheim identified the two ideal-types of mechanical and organic solidarity by considering the nature of the moral order in traditional and modern societies. The enquiry continues by positing a mechanism to account for the shift from before (traditional society) to after (modern society): thus Durkheim speaks of increases in the moral density of society underpinning the evident increase in complexity of the division of labour. Finally, having offered his interpretive scheme Durkheim adds a tailpiece by way of a discussion of normal and pathological forms of the modern division of labour. The strategy of enquiry is thus in essence a straightforward elucidation of the evolution of the division of labour.

The first part of Durkheim's project attempts to grasp the nature of the present by noting (and taking as being of salient importance) the increase in social differentiation. This way of grasping the present is informed by organicist ideas. The social organism, like the natural organism, becomes more complex as it becomes more highly evolved. The nature of the present can be elucidated in a comparative fashion focusing upon the nature of moral order in traditional and modern societies. These are ideal-types and are constructed with reference to types of legal codes. A legal code is an 'index'[12] of the moral character of a society. And as in a legal code the Durkheimian-style social facts have indeed become things, it is an apposite starting point for ideal-typification. So Durkheim distinguishes between

12 Giddens 1971 op. cit. p. 74.

repressive and restitutive legal codes: the former is characteristic of traditional society and the latter of modern society (and these ideal-types are characterized in familiar terms: the former, small-scale, rural, intimate, close knit; the latter, large-scale, urban, anonymous, diffuse and so on).[13]

Repressive law is penal law and its presence in society presupposes a strong collective conscience. The moral web binds people tightly and punishment is expiatory. All this is typical of the mechanical solidarity of traditional societies. It is to be contrasted to restitutive law which presupposes a complex division of labour and functional interdependence. The law is concerned to compensate for broken contracts. And this is typical of organic solidarity. The collective conscience declines in terms of its pervasive insistence upon adherence to general rules. The moral web is no longer tightly binding – it cannot be when individuals are engaged not in roughly similar tasks (as in traditional societies), but in dissimilar tasks. Social solidarity is organic and expressed in the doctrines of individualism associated with the complex division of labour.

The new moral code of individualism is seen as a socially integrative ethic. This rather paradoxical claim is made intelligible if we take note that, for Durkheim, this term was not that of English political-economy (where it had come to mean a political and social ideology predicated upon natural egoism), nor was it that of marxian humanism (where each individual was seen as uniquely creative in his/her socially located work). Durkheim's notion designates an ethic of 'recognition of proper social niche', an acknowledgement of unity in ordered individual diversity.

The growth of the division of labour is the second issue dealt with by Durkheim. This growth is a function of the dynamic density of society (the extent and character of social interaction). This increasing dynamic density is in turn underpinned by population growth and technological progress. The shift from traditional medieval European society to modern industrial Western European society is a matter of population growth, technological advance and the rise of the power and importance of the cities. And if we push this explanation back one more stage and ask why did this increase in dynamic density produce an increasingly complex division of labour rather than some other social form we can see in Durkheim an appeal to Darwin's notions of competition and survival.[14] Darwin's mechanism of evolutionary change is once again invoked and (mis)applied.

If we now recall Durkheim's original concern – the nature of the moral regulation of industrial society – we can see an interpretation proffered that identifies a progressive evolutionary shift. Movement is away from tight-knit communities whose web of moral rules is religious in character and tightly binds the individual into society, and towards loosely ordered social interaction in the increasingly differentiated division of labour with

13   See I. Roxborough 1979 *Theories of Underdevelopment*, London, Macmillan, ch. 1; see also Robert Nisbet 1966 *The Sociological Tradition*, New York, Basic Books, ch. 3.
14   Lukes 1973 op. cit. ch. 7.

its reintegrative ethic of individualism. The image presented is of essentially smooth change and of a harmonious self-regulating system. And this creates a problem for Durkheim.

Durkheim's problem was that his scheme did not allow for the conflict that was clearly discernible in society. Durkheim responds with an ad hoc adjustment to his theory so as to make it at least minimally plausible: thus he grants that there is conflict, but argues that it is temporary. The extant state of social affairs was pathological because the growth in complexity of the division of labour had been so rapid that moral regulatory codes had been outstripped – they had not adjusted quickly enough. Durkheim argues that the extant division of labour is anomic; that is, the present situation of society approximates to the model of the English political-economists. A direct way of tackling this problem would be via the introduction of workplace associations which would offer support to the workers and identify to them – and to managers – their crucial functional roles. In short, Durkheim here proposes a corporatist and managerialist strategy. However, Durkheim also notes that society is rapidly changing and a programme of social reforms can also be used to tackle this problem of conflict. The removal of systemic inequality, of inherited wealth in particular, will permit individuals to discover and occupy positions within the division of labour appropriate to their skills. The diminution of inequality tends towards the dissolution of the anomic division of labour but for the present Durkheim acknowledges that there is a forced division of labour.

However critics have argued that having acknowledged the gross facts of conflict Durkheim's work could have moved in two possible directions.[15] The one choice would have focused on the forced division of labour and characterizations of inequality. Strategies of alleviation would have been in order; that is, Durkheim would have moved in the direction of Marx. The other choice, the one Durkheim in fact made, was to look at anomie. Problems of social integration came to the fore and the workplace organizations are increasingly central to his prescriptions. Overall it has been suggested by critics that the key to Durkheim's work was a conservative commitment to social order.[16]

Durkheim Today

The work of Durkheim has been very influential and this encompasses both the strategies of analysis which he proposed (which have been pursued in functionalism and structuralism) and the substantive discussions which he offered (leading into ideas of industrial society). In France Durkheim's work has influenced the *Annales* School of historians[17] and the more recent school

15 Zeitlin 1968 op. cit.
16 Ibid.
17 S. Clark 1985 'The Annales Historians' in O. Skinner ed. *The Return of Grand Theory in the Human Sciences*, Cambridge University Press.

of structuralist social theorists, as well as the work of sociologists. In the Anglo-Saxon world his work has been influential via the work of Talcott Parsons[18] and the whole package known as the structural-functionalist analysis of the logic of industrial society.

The rise of structural functionalism

In the USA many universities established sociology courses very early in the twentieth century. These courses were established, however, only after those in economics. The familiar division between the subjects was very sharp, with economics taking itself as the 'hard' social science, leaving sociology with what were regarded as the less important and distinctly intellectually softer social studies leftovers. In the USA early work was done on rural life, community studies and urban sociology by the Chicago School. Important work was done in social psychology by C. H. Cooley and G. H. Mead. However, the intellectual giant of US work was the structural-functionalist theorist Talcott Parsons whose work, along with that of his many followers, dominated American and European work in the early years after the Second World War.

Parsons was preoccupied with the nature of social action and his theoretical reflections found more substantive expression in the familiar functionalist theory of society, which in turn played a significant role in the overall ideological package of the 'free world'. Parsons offered a very complex general theory of social action. We can note four aspects (which are in turn subdivided).

First, the analysis of social action which is taken to comprise four elements: (a) a subject or actor (individual, group or collectivity); (b) a situation (physical and social to which the actor relates); (c) a set of symbols (carrying meaning, which allow the actor to read this situation); and (d) a schedule of rules, norms and values (which guide the orientation of action).

Second, the scheme of the pattern variables which govern the orientation of action of the particular actor (i.e., cultural resources): (a) ascription versus achievement; (b) diffuseness versus specificity; (c) particularism versus universalism; (d) affectivity versus affective neutrality; and (e) collective orientation versus self orientation.

Third, it is clear that systems of action have functional requisites so that the particular system of action and interaction can be coherently maintained over time. There are four such functional requirements of systems of action: (a) adaptation, which links up system and environment; (b) goal-attainment, which moves the system to achieve targets; (c) integration, which expresses the requirement that the system should remain coherent over time; and (d) latency, whereby the system draws upon stocks of symbols to motivate actors within the system.

Then, fourth, an idea of equilibrium is introduced as the endpoint to

18   G. Rocher 1974 *Talcott Parsons and American Sociology*, London, Nelson.

which all systems tend when disturbed. Systems are in complex exchange with their environment, and this often requires internal adjustments, but the whole is governed by the notion of equilibrium. The business of disturbance and restoration of equilibrium generates system learning. The system as a whole can be said to experience differentiation, reintegration and evolution.

Parsons then used this general theory of action to analyse society. The general social system comprises a set of sub-systems which are dealt with by the various social sciences (economics, sociology, politics and psychology). From the perspective of the general theory of action it is the job of sociology to study the integrative function and Parsons produced along with his co-workers the functionalist theory of society. From this point Parsons' general work can be developed with the usual repertoire of concepts: self, role, role-set, socialization, groups, class, organization, institution and values.

It is on the basis of this work, both in general action theory and in the restricted area of sociological concepts, that the familiar version of functionalism is constructed. What we have is a model of the social world as a self-regulating harmonious whole held together by common values. It developed through the post-Second World War period into a broad approach to the analysis of contemporary society. Here we can speak of the modernization, industrialism, convergence, end-of-ideology package deal. Essentially it is the celebration of the model of the 'Free West': (a) modernization was the process whereby the less developed countries would shift from traditional patterns of life to become developed; (b) industrial society was the goal, where society was driven by the demanding 'logic of industrialism'; (c) and this logic would lead to the convergence of Western and Eastern political economic systems; and (d) the achievement of prosperity, as with the USA in the 1960s, would mean that ideological debate would wither away.

Functionalism presented a view of the social world as essentially harmonious and stable yet in the 1960s it came under severe pressure as the USA, and the Western world, went through a phase of violent conflict. In the USA the Civil Rights movement, the Vietnam War and the student movement all combined to render a theory premised on stability irrelevant. In addition intellectual criticism abounded and functionalism retreated. We can identify two broad sorts of criticism: the focused sociological and the broader social philosophical.

Sociological critics objected to the teleological nature of the scheme which suggested that the system had goals. It was further suggested that Parsons' work was deeply conservative because it did not admit the possibility of alternative ways of organizing society. Critics also said that characterizing the social world as fundamentally harmonious was again conservative, and wrong, and against this Parsonian position they argued that conflict had to be acknowledged and addressed. Other critics looked at the way in which systems seemed to absorb actors, and they wondered if the theory of action did not paradoxically have very little action in it. Similar objections were made to the notions of system learning and evolution when it was suggested that they offered no real way of analysing social change or the mechanisms which underlay it.

Very many critics objected to the wider package deal of which functionalist sociology seemed to be a part. The theory of modernization was widely regarded as an excuse for the USA to pursue its interests in the Third World like any other imperial power in history. And the doctrine of convergence seemed to be an implausible way of dismissing the historical experience of the USSR. Relatedly, the notion of industrialism seemed to be a straightforwardly ideologically motivated avoidance of the notion of capitalism, and the intellectual legacy of Marx. And the related idea of the end-of-ideology seemed like an excuse for the mass consumer culture of the USA, which was often taken by critics as degraded and degrading.

On the social philosophical level strong attacks were made on the fundamental epistemology affirmed by such work which was characterized as technical-interventionist. These theorists were taken to be attempting to copy the model of the natural sciences in order to produce the same sort of causal knowledge. Critics pointed out that this was either impossible or immoral or both. Developing this argument social philosophical critics spoke of 'Durksonian sociology', a mix of Durkheim and Parsons who were together taken to have invented the intellectual machineries of essentially arbitrary bureaucratic control.[19] Other critics went further and argued that this type of interventionist social science functioned as a legitimating myth which acted to disguise the true nature of arbitrary power in society.[20]

The science of unfreedom

The contemporary social theorist who coined the word 'Durksonian' to characterize orthodox social science reviews the issues around the fundamental distinction between positive-constructive and negative-critical strategies of enquiry.[21] The first noted strategy is that of Durkheim and subsequently Parsons and seeks to prepare descriptive and general explanations of a determinist, causal character. Society is taken to admit of ordered enquiry on the analogy of the natural sciences. The heart of this explanatory mode is the equation of explanation with prediction.[22] The model of political activity this strategy of enquiry affirms centres on what has been called technical-rational, or instrumental-rational, action; that is, politics is reduced to rational administration where the administrators lay claim to specialist, expert, knowledge. Put directly, what we have here is the ideology of the (authoritarian) bureaucrat-planner of a corporatist political system.

19   Z. Bauman 1976 *Towards a Critical Sociology*, London, Routledge.
20   A. MacIntyre 1981 *After Virtue*, London, Duckworth.
21   Bauman 1976 op. cit.
22   See B. Fay 1975 *Social Theory and Political Practice*, London, Allen and Unwin, chs. 1, 2.

The second mode of enquiry follows the tradition of the humanist Marx of the early *Economic and Philosophical Manuscripts*.[23] The contemporary theorist Jürgen Habermas has been at pains to rescue the notion of social scientific enquiry from the narrow and restricted vision of the positive-constructive theorists, with their associated politics of the expert, in order to insist that social science can rationally and legitimately offer interpretive-critical schemes.[24] Bauman following Habermas's central affirmation of radical democracy offers sociology a particular role in the critique of commonsense patterns of thinking, where this task is taken as a prerequisite of social change. Social theorizing for this school is inevitably engaged. It does not aspire to the production of technical-rational descriptions of the social world; nor does it accept the self-legitimations of the orthodox, whose work is neither intellectually nor politically neutral as it is oriented to the needs of the technocratic politics of the bureaucrat-planner. The critical theorists seek to fracture the commonsense of society and display the possibilities for the future lodged in the present. Bauman argues that when set against this schema of two distinct modes of social scientific enquiry, the Durksonian approach presents itself as a science of unfreedom.

The modernization of the Third World

Contemporary theories of modernization follow Durkheim in stressing the stable evolutionary change of social systems conceived as essentially harmonious and self-regulating. Thus the contemporary theorists first define traditional society, much as Durkheim would do, and then modern society, again much as Durkheim would do, and modernization is then introduced as the process whereby societies make the designated before-to-after move. This scheme was presented in one very influential form by W. W. Rostow in his text *The Stages of Economic Growth* (1960). Rostow took the basic dichotomy of traditional and modern and expanded it to a five-element stage theory. Rostow argued from the experience of Britain in the eighteenth and nineteenth centuries to the conclusion that every country had to pass through five stages in the shift from the traditional world to the modern. In the optimistic climate of the times, Rostow's work was well received. It not only seemed to give every country a chance of achieving development but even suggested that once begun the process was more or less automatic. However, as the decade of the 1960s progressed the work of Rostow and modernization theory slowly fell out of favour.

23 It seems to me that Marx was not 'scientistic' in approach. However, his economic work was turned into a rather wooden and implausible scheme by Soviet ideologists. The rediscovery of an early or young Marx made by theorists in the 1920s was thus set against the prevailing orthodox version of Marx.
24 See A. Giddens 1982 *Profiles and Critiques in Social Theory*, London, Macmillan, for a brief introduction to Habermas. For a fuller study see R. C. Holub 1991 *Jurgen Habermas: Critic in the Public Sphere*, London, Routledge.

Chapter Summary

Durkheim is overwhelmingly preoccupied with the moral order of society, which he conceived in terms of a dense network of external coercive rules, and he analyses nineteenth-century society in terms of the notion of the evolutionary development of the division of labour where he is concerned to argue that the moral order of society is changing away from tradition ties of community towards the more informal ties of a society committed to notions of individualism. The normal state of affairs of a complex division of labour is one of organic solidarity secured by the new moral code of individualism. Transitional problems of maladjustment, or anomie, can be addressed via guilds which order the individual's contribution to the social whole. It is a corporatist position.

Durkheim's work has been very influential, both the strategies of analysis which he proposed, leading into functionalism and structuralism, and the substantive discussion which he offered, leading into ideas of industrial society. In turn this has generated modernization theory which has been one of the most influential theories of Third World development in the post-Second World War period.

6

The Transitional Work of Weber

Overview of the Work of Max Weber

The work of Max Weber is difficult to present in any simple fashion because his work lacks the obvious intellectual coherence of Smith, Marx or Durkheim. Weber was a committed German nationalist and from the outset he was preoccupied with the analysis of capitalism and in particular with the nature of its development in Germany. Weber is a transitional figure whose work links the classical tradition with the concerns of the short twentieth century.[1] Weber not only continues the concerns of the classical nineteenth-century social theorists with the analysis of complex change but also begins to operate within the emerging patterns of discipline-bound enquiry. In addition there is within the work an element of the deep scepticism in respect of the modernist project which was subsequently voiced in the 1980s by the theorists of postmodernity. Indeed, Weber is reported as having indicated that the key intellectual influences on his work were Marx and Nietzsche.

1   E. Hobsbawm 1994 *Age of Extremes: The Short Twentieth Century*, London, Michael Joseph.

Ethic and Method in Weber's Work

Max Weber's approach to social theorizing is quite distinct from the approaches of other theorists of the classical nineteenth-century tradition. The overriding concern with analysing complex change remains in place but the intellectual machineries deployed to deal with the problems owe more to the materials of the emerging specialist social science disciplines of the short twentieth century. The overall package has often been summarized as an 'interpretive social science'[2] (see figure 7).

Weber contrasted with Durkheim and Marx

Weber's thought is to be contrasted with the tradition inhabited by Durkheim. The French sociology of the period, to some extent as a result of Durkheim's influence, conceptualized society as an organic whole, a system in itself, which was morally and logically prior to the individual and which could be studied in a formal scientific fashion. Subsequent commentators have spoken of Durkheim's deification of society.[3] Weber stands in complete opposition to this view and it is the individual who is the starting point of Weberian theory building.

Stuart Hughes speaks of the generation of 1890–1920 as effecting a revolt against positivism.[4] Weber's opposition to scientific positivism reflected this widespread reaction. In this period a number of major intellectual figures – historians, sociologists, philosophers and psychologists – embarked upon studies of the social world which had it in common that they denied the possibility of any simple methodological borrowings from the natural sciences. The social world was human (and thus meaningful and intentional), historical (and thus constituted by specifics rather than laws), and had to be analysed in appropriate terms (though what these terms were was not obvious). A final complexity derived from the recent discovery of the power of the unconscious. These elements constituted the bones of the 'revolt against positivism'.[5] Not only did Weber inhabit this intellectual milieu, but he moved in the same circles as those presenting these complex reworkings of social analysis and he was a friend of Georg Simmel and Ferdinand Tonnies and he knew György Lukács whose work is often characterized as

2 A good introduction is D. G. MacRae 1974 *Weber*, London, Fontana.
3 See for example Z. Bauman 1976 *Towards a Critical Sociology*, London, Routledge.
4 S. Hughes 1959 *Consciousness and Society*, London, McGibbon.
5 There is one further point to note: these thinkers accepted positivistic interpretations of natural science. Their revolt was thus partial and some contemporary thinkers have suggested that this was an error of some magnitude – see, for example, A. Giddens 1979 *Central Problems in Social Theory*, London, Macmillan, ch. 7, or T. Benton 1977 *The Philosophical Foundations of the Three Sociologies*, London, Routledge, pp. 46–7. I do not agree with these critics as it is not the business of social theorists to put theories of the nature of natural science to rights.

Figure 7   The transitional work of Max Weber

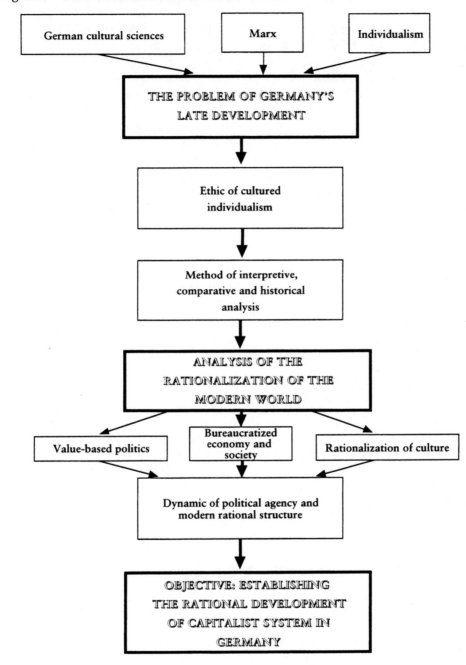

a reconstruction of the early Marx before the rediscovery of the relevant texts.[6]

If we pursue the vexed issue of the relationship of Marx and Weber we find a rather closer agreement on strategies of enquiry than is usually supposed. Once we set aside the vulgar idea that Weber refuted Marx by identifying the role of ideas in history[7] we open up the more fruitful viewpoint which suggests that the whole of Weber's work can be seen as a sustained debate with Marx in respect of the nature of capitalism. There is however the complication of the question of the real Marx: the young humanistic Marx of *The Economic and Philosophical Manuscripts* (1844) or the later Marx of *Capital* (1867). This matter arises simply because the work of the young Marx was not rediscovered until the 1930s – after Weber's death. There was no young Marx for Max Weber. The criticisms which Weber makes of the work of Marx and marxist schemes generally are focused upon the positivistic readings of Marx which were then current. In the generations after Marx's death, the keepers of his work, the Social Democratic Party of Germany (SPD), became increasingly cautious and reformist. A mechanistic marxism suited their immediate organizational and political needs. And as regards subsequent claims that Weber refuted Marx, it is the material of official versions of Marxism–Leninism that adherents of Weber have in mind. A modest conclusion to these matters is that Weber's work 'must not be read as a repudiation of Marx's methodological principles but rather as a "rounding out" and supplementing of his method'.[8]

The spread of Weber's concerns

The breadth of Weber's concerns is reflected in the intellectual biography of the man. Weber was an economic historian, a historian of culture, a student of law and then a sociologist. And to this complexity we must also add his political controversiality both at the time and since. Weber was always interested in politics but save for a brief involvement late in his life never fully involved in political life.[9] Some commentators have seen him as a forerunner of post-First World War liberal-democracy, and he did assist in the preparation of the constitution of the Weimar Republic. But others have seen his work as an anticipatory version of the Führer (leader–dictator) principle.[10] One thing is clear, he was a passionate German nationalist.

6   W. J. Mommsen and J. Osterhammel eds. 1987 *Max Weber and his Contemporaries*, London, Unwin.
7   This is precisely the claim that is found in textbooks informed by structural-functionalist approaches.
8   I. Zeitlin 1968 *Ideology and the Development of Sociological Theory*, New York, Prentice Hall, p. 112.
9   D. Beetham 1985 *Max Weber and the Theory of Modern Politics*, Cambridge, Polity.
10   C. Antoni 1959 *From History to Sociology*, Detroit, Wayne State University Press, pp. 132–4.

Weber contributed to both the general reworking of the nature of social theorizing and the debates about the future of the German state. The cultural historian Stuart Hughes characterizes his contribution to social science in terms of an inspiring and ambiguous attempt at a synthesis of the divergent materials of (natural) scientific and cultural enquiry, thus he says:

> [Weber] stands at more decisive meeting points than any other thinker. To begin to list these contributions is to suggest his range and the ambiguous nature of his achievement: idealism and scientific method; economics and religion; Marxism and nationalism; political commitment and an insistence on 'objectivity' in social science . . . Even in his contributions to the terminology of social science his contradictions and ambivalences are mirrored.[11]

An interpretive social science

Weber's methodological writings have been variously described. Some have claimed to see in his work anticipations of much of contemporary sociology's concerns,[12] and some have seen his methodological work anticipating all the central concerns of twentieth-century philosophy.[13] Others have presented him as the arch-priest of value-free sociology.[14] For Antoni, Weber is one stage in the decline of historicism into sociology;[15] and in this vein both Giddens[16] and Hughes[17] focus their attention upon the complexity of the issues he addressed and the confusions of the period. In respect of the methodological commitments made by Weber I will pick out four elements: (a) Weber grants that social science is concerned with ideal phenomena (meanings, intentions and so on) but insists that objectivity and causal analysis must also be retained; (b) Weber further insists upon the absolute separation of matters of fact from matters of value and so scientific enquiry can provide the means but it cannot identify the ends; (c) the human world for Weber is composed of persons and this entails an anti-holistic anti-organicist voluntarist-stance methodologically, and it also denies the possibility of a universal ethics as the social world comprises a realm of competing ideals; and thereafter (d) these views inform his political theory where politics can be oriented either to ultimate ends (and thus it is essentially religious) or to pragmatic calculation (where social science is of use).

---

11   Hughes 1959 op. cit. p. 288.
12   See, for example, J. E. T. Eldridge 1971 *Max Weber: The Interpretation of Social Reality*, London, Michael Joseph, 'Introductory Essay' and pp. 69–71.
13   G. Runciman 1972 *Critique of Weber's Philosophy of Social Science*, Cambridge University Press.
14   This is the textbook structural-functionalist position: see Alan Dawe 1971 'The Relevance of Value' in A. Sahay ed. *Max Weber and Modern Sociology*, London, Routledge.
15   Antoni 1959 op. cit.
16   A. Giddens 1971 *Capitalism and Modern Social Theory*, Cambridge University Press.
17   Hughes 1959 op. cit.

The particular mode of enquiry associated with Weber is often called interpretive sociology and the crucial procedural novelty is that of ideal-typical analysis. The ideal-type serves to resolve the dilemma for social scientific enquiry posed by Weber's disjunctions between fact and value, causes and meanings, and practical means and ethical ends.[18] Positive science cannot interpret the realm of human meaning for us, nor can it tell us what we ought to do. The social world is a complex of partial views, themselves embedded in a web of historical causes. The social world must be presented as a realm of meanings (interpreted) which are themselves subject to complex patterns of historical causation. Any social scientific enquiry involves choosing both a point of view and an area of enquiry. The tension between the factual description of a situation and its interpretive evaluation is resolved via the notion of an ideal-type. The ideal-type is an intellectual construct – a model, so to say – which accentuates particular elements of the social world in the light of some value orientation. The ideal-type represents a reference point in enquiry, so to speak, where the theorist presents some sort of fusion of empirical descriptive enquiry (the realm of causes) and interpretive evaluation (the realm of meanings) where this fusion will be patterned by the theorist's own commitments as to values and useful explanations.

The text *Economy and Society* which was published after Weber's death was intended as the introductory volume to a collaborative series of texts on society. Weber is concerned with elucidating concepts adequate to the analysis of society – that is, with presenting the key concepts of a systematic sociology. The method presented is designated interpretive sociology. Weber speaks of explanations which are adequate at the level of meaning and causally adequate. One theme that lies at the back of these ideas is the distinction between sociological generalization and historical specificity – as before, Weber is trying to bridge the gap between positivism and idealism.

Step number one in analysis involves interpretive understanding. The key to plotting the patterns of meaning inhabited by social actors is via ideal-typical analysis. Weber, confronted by the bewildering fluidity of human meanings, found it convenient to use rational ideal-types in the first place – non-rational behaviour could then be treated as deviations from the rational. We might note that Weber was impressed by the apparent successes of economics achieved by using a notion of 'rational economic man' as an ideal-type. The second step of Weber's method looks to causal adequacy of explanation and when we try to pin down this notion we find that Weber seems to be pointing to an explanation that invokes empirical generalization: that pattern of meaning 'x' will tend to issue in behaviour pattern 'y'. In sum, we could say that Weber takes interpretive sociology to be concerned with elucidating the relatively stable patterns of meaning inhabited by given actors or groups and this elucidation both interprets and identifies

18   See J. Rex 1971 'Typology and Objectivity: A Comment on Weber's Four Sociological Methods' in Sahay ed. op. cit.

antecedent social (or, more broadly, historical) causes and possible future patterns.

There has been much discussion about Weber's methodological ideas – and also over the years much discussion about the nature of social science generally. Recent work in the philosophy of social science has rejected the positivist model of explanation in natural science and its extension into the sphere of the social.[19] Putting matters simply, Weber's problem is that having begun by affirming the methodological priority of meanings, and having at the same time affirmed an essentially orthodox descriptive notion of science, he has to contrive some link between the two. From this point we enter the confusing realm of explanations at the levels of meaning and cause. Yet fortunately Weber's focus on politics was so central that it imposes coherence upon what otherwise would be an impossible swirl of competing and irreconcilable philosophical and methodological commitments.[20]

We can now look at the substance of *Economy and Society* and take note of the fundamental ideal-types of social action, and Weber's discussions of political sociology. As Weber has insisted that sociological analysis must begin with persons, he is obliged to begin with generic patterns of social action: four ideal-types of social action are presented. First, we have purposive-rational action, which is action based upon rational calculation designed to secure some desired end or goal. Second, we have value-rational action, which is behaviour oriented to some ultimate ideal, an ethical commitment for example. Third, we have affective action, which is action informed by emotional commitments. Fourth, we have traditional action, which is action governed by custom or habit. Weber thereafter looks to the use of these four ideal-types of human action in the world to analyse particular substantive patterns of behaviour.

These ideal-types form the basis of Weber's enquiries and they are represented in his political sociology. Patterns of social relationship are seen by Weber to be stable to the extent that they are informed by beliefs that the social order structuring these relationships is a legitimate order. Weber identifies three ideal-types of legitimate order which can structure social relationships. That a social order is seen as legitimate entails that power relationships within the social complex in question are accepted: the power of superiors is accepted by subordinates as legitimate authority. The three types of legitimacy are: (a) traditional authority, where patterns of social order are legitimated by custom; (b) legal authority, where patterns of social order are legitimated by rational bodies of rules; and (c) charismatic authority, where patterns of social order are legitimated by the person of the ruler.

The notion of traditional authority has its principal application in examining

19   A. F. Chalmers 1980 *What Is This Thing Called Science*, Milton Keynes, Open University Press; R. Bernstein 1976 *The Restructuring of Social and Political Theory*, London, Methuen.
20   See M. Root 1993 *Philosophy of Social Science*, Oxford, Blackwell.

pre-capitalist social formations. The notions of legal and charismatic authority are both crucial to the analysis of capitalism – and to Weber's political
evaluation of the situation in Germany. Weber argues that modern capitalism
is governed by legal-rational authority. The social institution which embodies
such legal-rational authority is the modern bureaucracy. Contemporary capitalism on Weber's view could not function without bureaucratic organization. Weber also thinks bureaucratic authority tends to be conservative and
expansionary. In the modern capitalist world ever greater areas of social life
are subject to legal-rational rules. This is the key so far as Weber is concerned to understanding capitalism – the spread throughout social life of
rationality. In political life he speaks of the 'iron cage of bureaucracy' and,
more generally, of the 'disenchantment of the world'. As a historical process
Weber viewed it with distaste and his own self-definitions seem to have
involved notions of a cultured European individualism. In very direct political terms he did not trust the German bureaucracy with its alliance to the
Prussian officer corps because he saw them as incompetent and blind to the
needs of the German nationstate.

At this point we can introduce Weber's notion of charismatic authority
which points to legitimations of social order which flow from the person
of the ruler, from his or her special qualities. Weber's analysis of capitalism saw a process of bureaucratic rationalization periodically upset and
revivified by the appearance of a charismatic political figure. Weber's individualism, with his disjunction between fact and value, presents itself in
the context of the politics of capitalism in the view that the contemporary
legal-rational bureaucratic capitalist system requires periodic inputs of non-
rational value positions. The modern capitalist state is typically a plebiscitary
democracy and at periodic intervals the mass of the people elect a leader,
who necessarily will have charismatic qualities (in order, first, to get elected
and thereafter to lead). At this point we can see why Antoni identifies in
Weber the basis of the Führer principle.[21] It is also fairly clear how this
analysis was shaped by Weber's judgements in respect of the situation in
Germany because it is from the ranks of the bourgeoisie that there must
spring a charismatic political figure capable of leading the nationstate in the
post-Bismarckian era.

The Substantive Analysis of Capitalism

It is in the substantive work which deals with the historical development
of capitalism that we see most clearly the legacy of the nineteenth-century
classical tradition of social theorizing. Weber was concerned to elucidate the
dynamics of complex change in order to argue for the political role of the
nationalist bourgeoisie in Germany. The key issue for Weber was whether
the German bourgeoisie were mature enough to assume the leadership of
Germany. The concern with the development of capitalism in Germany was

21   Antoni 1959 op. cit. See also Zeitlin 1968 op. cit. p. 158.

subsumed within a series of broader enquiries into the nature of capitalism in general.[22]

The early work on capitalism in Germany

In the study of the development of the Prussian landed estates, *Die Verhältnisse der Landarbeiter im ostelbischen Deutschland* (The Conditions of Rural Labourers in Germany East of the Elbe, 1892),[23] and the incipient conflict between landowners and free labourers, where these conflicts in turn generated problems of national policy, Weber offered a strong statement in favour of the interests of the German state.

The problems, as analysed by Weber, revolved around the changing economic and social character of the great Prussian landed estates. These changes involved, first, a steady flow of German workers from the agrarian feudal east towards the more advanced west. The shortfall in labour for the estates was met by the eastern Slavic nations who provided a supply of cheap labour. In this way there was a slow change in the demographic character of the eastern lands, with Germans being replaced by Slavs. The second aspect of these changes concerned the character of the labour force where there was a clear shift away from the bonded labour characteristic of medieval times towards the free day labourer characteristic of industrialism. The shift towards a commercial-type agriculture accentuated conflict between employer and employee. It is clear that the labourers moving to western Germany are affirming the importance of political freedom over economic security because their life situations in the western markets are more precarious. More generally, Weber took the view that the economic rationality of the Junker landowners – employing cheap imported labour – threatened the integrity of the German state.

Weber's answer was simple and revealing because Weber argued that Germany's eastern frontier must be closed. In adopting this stance Weber is declaring in opposition to economic deterministic social analyses that invoking economic rationality was not sufficient to secure conclusions in socio-political argument. Indeed, it was clear that invoking economic rationality was not explanatorily rich enough to cope with the observed behaviour of the labourers on the landed estates as the free labourers were often economically worse-off than the bonded labourers. Weber insists that the tendency to capitalistic relations and patterns of life was not an iron law of economics. And the solution proposed by Weber to the problem of the eastern frontier is political. Weber here reveals his intellectual background (with all its concerns for human meanings and history) and declares his own ultimate value position (and here we see the acceptance of the irrational in human life and history) which is the necessity of maintaining the integrity of the German nationstate. If it is to survive then it must act as a power state, as political activity is in the end simply a struggle for power.

22   B. S. Turner 1992 *Max Weber: From History to Modernity*, London, Routledge.
23   Text cited in Giddens 1971 op. cit. p. 122ff.

This area of enquiry is developed further in his 1895 professorial inau-
gural lecture. Weber advocates the centrality of the interests of the power
state in German politics and in this context identifies as crucial the question
of the leadership of the state. Weber argues that the German state was
constructed in a top-down manner by Otto von Bismarck (first chancellor
of the German Empire, 1871–90). The power of Bismarck was based on the
power of Prussia and thus upon the power of the Junker landowners, the
civil service bureaucracy and the officer corps. The problem now, thought
Weber, was of transferring political power. The issue was whether or not
the economically prosperous bourgeoisie could develop a political consciousness adequate to the task of leadership of the nation. Weber did not
consider the claims of the proletariat as he felt that their future lay within
capitalism. On the other hand, the economically declining landowning class
is dangerous if it retains the political power which should pass to the
hitherto supine bourgeoisie.[24]

These early works centre Weber's attention upon the dynamic of capitalism, especially in Germany, and they reveal a complex set of commitments
about political values, economics, social change, the nature of motivation,
and the character and role of sociological analysis (objective characterizations of means to irrational value-prescribed ends). The central problems
for Weber are the nature of the consciousness of the historically progressive
bourgeoisie, and the task of identifying for the German bourgeoisie its
historical leadership role. Weber's text *The Protestant Ethic and the Spirit of
Capitalism* (1904–5) is his first general treatment of this complex of issues.

The logic of capitalism in the protestant ethic

Weber broadens his interest in the development of capitalism in *The Protestant Ethic* and against the mechanistic marxists Weber argues for the
effective if restricted role of ideas in history. Again, the disjunction is made
as in the earlier works between economics and politics. Weber feels no
inclination to bow to economic forces and he insists on the effectiveness of
political action. Relatedly, Weber's comparative analysis of major world
religions finds quietist cultures of acceptance in the East in contrast to the
religions of the West with their roots in Judaism which evidence a streak
of rationality which in the particular guise of protestantism helped fuel the
rise of capitalism.

In *The Protestant Ethic* Weber discusses the role which certain religious doctrines played in facilitating the emergence of capitalistic social
forms. Weber rejects the then current marxian view that protestantism was
simply the ideological consequence of earlier economic changes and instead
advances the claim that ascetic protestantism actually aided the emergence
of capitalism.

---

24 These matters are discussed at length in A. Giddens 1972b *Politics and Sociology in
the Thought of Max Weber*, London, Macmillan; see also D. Beetham 1985 *Max Weber and
the Theory of Modern Politics*, Cambridge, Polity.

The analysis begins by noting the apparent anomaly that whereas it is usually said that those with a strong religious faith are comparatively indifferent, or hostile, to material advancement, it is also true that protestants are disproportionately overrepresented in modern industrial enterprise. Weber then goes on to analyse, in an ideal-typical way, both the spirit of modern capitalism and the particular belief system of protestantism. Reduced to its bare bones Weber's argument points to an elective affinity between the protestant (in particular, calvinist) notion of a calling – which has been transposed from a monastic reflective form into an outwards-directed active form – and the requirement of capitalistic material accumulation which requires, amongst other things, the habit of delayed gratification. As a historical phenomenon, then, the rise of capitalism can be seen to have been assisted by particular sets of religious ideas. The belief system of the calvinists led them to act in such a way that they served as the catalyst for widespread changes in the economic character of society.

Weber seeks to demonstrate that the rationalization characteristic of capitalism is derived, in a sense, from irrational value commitments. Weber does this in order to create a space within the historical process[25] for human-willed action and to identify the role of ultimate value commitments. In this way the work serves as an exhortation for the German bourgeoisie. Weber also takes his work to refute decisively the naive mechanical schemes of historical materialism which were prevalent at that time. This is the basis of the claims since made that Weber refuted Marx. The point is that not only is this claim nonsense, but it is also a claim which Weber would not have made. Indeed, he was at some pains to disavow any intention of replacing a mechanistic marxian unicausal (economic) explanation – reducing social life to economics – with another unicausal explanation which reduced social life to the play of ideas.

The Protestant Ethic combines and generalizes the conclusions that Weber had reached in studying both the situation of eastern Germany and German politics in general. The disjunction between economics and politics made in 1892 remains, because human-willed action, political action, can decisively impact upon the massively complex and powerful logic of history and economic events. That the German bourgeoisie can and should act to take over the direction of the German nationstate from the faltering hands of the declining landowning aristocracy is the practical lesson of Weber's scholarship. Carlo Antoni argues: 'All of his activities centred around the nature of Bismarck's succession, that is, around the life-possibilities of the Bismarckian empire as a modern state. Weber himself could never forgive Bismarck for having refused to allow the formation around him of a group of political talents capable of assuming the burden of his legacy ... Above all, his

---

25 That 'process' he characterized in terms of the increasing rationalization of the world: and if we recall Zeitlin's comments on Weber's 'rounding out' of Marx's method, then this rationalization of the world just looks like the dynamic of capitalist development written in an ideal and generalized fashion.

sociology is a theory of the political class, the absence of which in Germany appeared to him to be the gravest menace of all to the future of his father-land'.[26] However, it should be noted that the exchanges between political and scholarly concerns in the body of Weber's work are complex for he was not merely a sophisticated ideologue. Gerth and Mills observe:

> In many ways Weber's life and thought are expressions of political events and concerns. His political stands, which must be understood in terms of private contexts as well as public happenings, make up a theme inextricably interwoven with Weber the man and the intellec-tual. For he was a political man and a political intellectual . . . To judge politics and rhetoric in terms of consequences and to measure the motives of men in terms of the intended or unintended results of their actions remained a constant principle of his political thinking. In this fundamental sense, Weber the scholar always wrote from the point of view of the active politician.[27]

The logic of capitalist civilization

The matter of the exchange between the abstract sets of ideas which com-prise religious doctrines and the dynamics of capitalist development which Weber addressed in *The Protestant Ethic* were pursued in his extensive cultural analyses of the religions of ancient Israel, China and India. In these studies we find the histories of the peoples reviewed, with a particular concern being the extent to which religious doctrines with their impact upon social structure tended to assist or inhibit the rise of capitalism. Weber's preoccupation with capitalism and the effective role of ideas in history is pursued in these studies. At the same time, more broadly still, the civilizations of the East and West come to be seen as fundamentally differ-ent. In the West there had been demystification and the culturally pervasive extension of rationality, whereas in the East this demystification has not occurred.

The religion of China, revolving around Confucianism and linking to Taoist mysticism and ancestor worship, is diagnosed by Weber as essen-tially quietist and myth-ridden. The pattern of religious ideals sits neatly with the society in which it was embedded. The vast empire of the Chinese emperors was ruled via a network of officials owing allegiance to the centre – which appointed them on the basis of examination – and drawing tax revenues from their sphere of authority. The aspirations of the educated, the literati, are to the ethical, aesthetic and social model of the Confucian gentleman who represents a figure in harmony with his environment. The arrangement was thoroughly conservative. Related to it is the myth-ridden mentality of the peasantry with its additional handicaps of ancestor wor-ship and thus geographical limitation to the ancestral village. China had no

26 Antoni 1959 op. cit. pp. 123–4.
27 H. H. Gerth and C. W. Mills eds. 1948 *From Max Weber*, London, Routledge, p. 32.

equivalents of the self-governing medieval European towns, it never had Western ideas of private property, and it never had a capitalistic bourgeoisie.

A similar tale is told for India in respect of the development of the caste system and the ascendancy of the Brahmins – the equivalent of the literati – with a vested interest in the maintenance of their privilege. Acquiescence and magic again rule the culture and there is no shift towards that disenchantment which Weber diagnosed as the crucial element of Western culture. This element he traced to Judaism, the source of the rationality he saw in the West's culture.

The detail in these studies is beyond my scope, but we can take note of the way in which Weber's understanding of capitalism became subtly broadened – a manifestation of the rationalization of the world – such that later (mis)interpreters could see an evolutionary tendency against which the belief systems of traditional societies could be characterized as obstacles to development. At the same time there are signs of an uncertainty of focus in his work such that the complexity of historical causation upon which he insisted is elided in favour of an exclusive focus upon the contribution of religious ideas. Again, this allows the (mis)interpretation of Weber as having proved the key role of ideas in history to be deployed. The overall drift of Weber's writing on the religions and cultures of China and India can be summarized as follows:

> Ultimately . . . what he sees as really crucial is that despite the rational, scientific elements in the East, and the existence there of economic strata and forms seemingly conducive to the emergence of a modern rational economy, the East remained an enchanted garden. This meant that all aspects and institutions of Oriental civilisation were permeated and even dominated by the magical mentality – which became a brake on economic developments in particular and on rationalisation of the culture as a whole. On the other hand, Occidental civilisation, already in its early stages of development, had undergone significant disenchantment . . . This disenchantment began with the scriptural Judaic prophets . . . and generated the process which has made Western civilisation as a whole fundamentally different from that of the East.[28]

The pessimism of Max Weber

Unlike Smith, Marx and Durkheim, Weber sees no progressive trend in history. The slow inevitable spread of technical rationality threatens his own ethic of cultured western liberal individualism and his social theorizing is in part an attempt to reconcile these two incompatible patterns. Weber centres his enquiries upon the nature of capitalism and he characterizes it in terms of the spread of a technical rationality which he comes increasingly to regard as characterizing the cultural processes of history itself. It is clear

28 Zeitlin 1968 op. cit. p. 145.

that this is a tendency to which Weber reluctantly acquiesces. Weber is not an optimist. Weber once remarked that the two most important figures in contemporary culture were Marx, with his elaborate social science, and Nietzsche, who was a somewhat mystically inclined anticipator of existentialism and postmodernism. It is little wonder that Anthony Giddens speaks of Weber's analyses as a 'brittle synthesis'.[29]

Weber and development studies

Turning now finally to the subsequent use of the work of Max Weber in contemporary development studies we find two imporatant areas of work: (a) a familiar area of debate in respect of the role of (religious) ideas in development; and (b) a less often remarked concern for empirical economic sociology.

The material on economic sociology can be taken to be an element of the work of the inter-war period on the nature of economic life. It is an influential tradition of enquiry which offers a sharply different discussion of the nature of economic activity from that which is familiar in either the guise of neo-classicism or Keynesianism.[30]

However, the more familiar way in which Weberian ideas have been used in development studies is discussed by R. I. Rhodes. Thus he notes: 'Two closely related approaches to development have emerged as a result of Weber's influence, the cultural and the psychological'.[31] In the first case Rhodes points to the way in which theorists speak of traditional patterns of thought and belief which severely inhibit the spread of economic rationality. The characterization of Third World societies as traditional is typical of modernization theory approaches and Weber's work is drawn on to help characterize the cultural schemes of these traditional societies. All the work on comparative culture and history from *The Protestant Ethic* onwards is drawn on so as to enable the refractory nature of non-Western cultures to the prerequisites of capitalism to be discussed. This misuse of Weber involves taking what he said was one element of the complex histories of these regions and making it a simple necessary condition of change. In the second case, Rhodes has a series of specific targets: McLelland, Hagen and Lerner,[32] all of whom attempt to characterize the psychology of the people in the underdeveloped countries and try to identify ways of encouraging those with the right psychologies. Rhodes comments: 'The weakness characteristic of the cultural and psychological approaches . . . are not

29 A. Giddens 1972 op. cit. – see the concluding remarks.
30 We can pursue this in the next chapter, but see R. Swedberg 1987 'Economic Sociology Past and Present', *Current Sociology*, 35.
31 R. I. Rhodes 1968 'The Disguised Conservatism in Evolutionary Development Theory' in *Science and Society*, 32.
32 D. C. McClelland 1961 *The Achieving Society*, New York, Van Nostrand; E. Hagen 1962 *On The Theory of Social Change*, Homewood, Dorsey; D. Lerner 1958 *The Passing of Traditional Society*, New York, Free Press.

empirical . . . One of the most serious problems is simply that of omission. When these findings are not placed in a proper historical context they lead to misleading conclusions'.[33] In particular the history of colonialism is simply omitted and along with it the historical record of the active suppression of local industries where they conflicted with the interests of the colonizers. These theorists thus: (a) vulgarize Weber with the Weber thesis; (b) proceed in a cultural/psychological reductionist fashion; and (c) neglect actual histories, colonialism in particular.

Chapter Summary

Weber was preoccupied with the nature of capitalism in general and its condition in Germany in particular where he was concerned to argue for a political role for the German bourgeoisie. Weber wanted the bourgeoisie to take control from the Prussian aristocracy and order Germany's development according to political objectives. Weber's general sociology reflected these concerns and included: the role of ideas in history; the nature of power; the influence of historically specific cultures upon development; and the necessity to counteract the tendency to bureaucratic rationality in modern societies with charismatic infusions of values. Weber's work has inspired social scientists in a number of areas and the key issues would include: the study of comparative and historical sociology; the study of religion; the study of the role of ideas in social and historical processes; the construction of a methodology for sociology with the scheme of ideal-types and the notion of value-freedom; the study of bureaucracy; the study of the process of rationalization; and the study of economic sociology.

---

33 Rhodes 1968 op. cit. p. 392.

7

The Divisions of Intellectual Labour of the Short Twentieth Century, 1914–1991

Overview of the Divisions of Intellectual Labour

The theorists of the nineteenth century pursued the modernist project of the rational apprehension of the social world and for much of the century the key strategy was political-economic analysis. However, towards the end of the century this objective fell into disrepute and the social science disciplines with which we are now familiar emerged. Each area of enquiry lays claim to a particular object sphere, a relevant method, a body of accumulated wisdom and the status of a professional discipline. The professional expertise of discrete disciplines can be deployed within the knowledge marketplace. However, it is characteristic of development theory that from a post-Second World War starting-point conceived in technical terms it returns to the concerns of the classical nineteenth-century theorists. At the same time, in recent years, the end of the short twentieth century has presented the general task of analysing patterns of complex change within the interdependent tripolar global industrial-capitalist system. Overall, we can point to a renewed relevance for the classical tradition of social theorizing with its prospective and engaged attempts to grasp the logic of complex change within political-economic, institutional and cultural systems.

Grasping the Logic of the Period

The industrial-capitalist form-of-life developed in Europe. It was from this relatively small geographical area that the patterns of political-economic activity, social arrangements and cultural understandings typical of industrial capitalism were spread ambiguously around the globe. It was in this period of expansion that the nineteenth-century European classical tradition of social theorizing was elaborated. It was this tradition that fed into the spread of work subsequently pursued in the twentieth century (see figure 8).

The patterns of intellectual enquiry and practice established over this recent twentieth-century period form the most immediate backdrop to contemporary social theorizing in respect of the matter of complex change in First, Second and Third Worlds. Yet the detail of the period can only be grasped in terms of an overarching series of themes. In this way we return in this final chapter of the section to the general style of the opening chapter which dealt with the broad pattern of the Enlightenment. Hobsbawm's notion of the history of the short twentieth century[1] offers a way in which we can capture in a brief synoptic way the manner in which the intellectual legacies of the classical social scientific work of the nineteenth century found routine intellectual and practical expression.

Hobsbawm's notion of the short twentieth century sees it running from 1914 to 1991. Over the period 1914 to 1945 the European world sees war, revolution, depression and further war. In 1914 the European world of the nineteenth century collapsed with the outbreak of the Great War. In 1917 the Russian empire collapses and is replaced by the influential model of the USSR. In the 1930s the Western world experiences a profound economic depression and one consequence of these dislocations in mainland Europe is the rise of fascism. Eventually, a second major war breaks out. In the Second World War the overseas empires of the Europeans are fatally undermined and thereafter quickly dissolved. However, in the post-Second World War period from 1945 to 1970 there is a wholly unanticipated golden age with high economic growth, social welfare reform and political consensus. Thereafter, with the impact of the oil crises and the decline in vigour of the social-democratic compromise there is a long period of decline and drift which finds an unexpected conclusion in the collapse of the USSR, the end of the Cold War, and the rapid acknowledgement thereafter of the development of a tripolar interdependent global system which is no longer dominated by the model of the European modernist project.

The short twentieth century has seen the eclipse of the European influence within the world and its replacement by the influence of the USA. As the industrial-capitalist system developed the centre of gravity of what was becoming a global system shifted across the Atlantic and it was in the USA that the new advances in technology, social organization and modern cultural

---

1   E. Hobsbawm 1994 *Age of Extremes: The Short Twentieth Century, 1914–1991*, London, Michael Joseph.

116

Figure 8   Divisions of intellectual labour, 1914–91

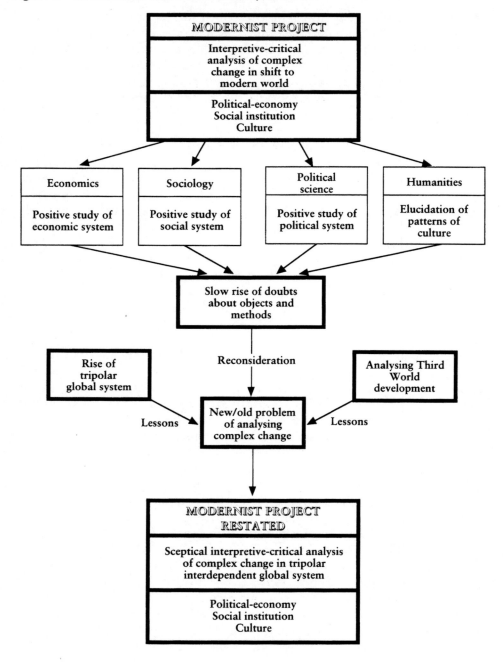

forms were made. However, the dominance of the model of the USA did not go unchallenged and for much of the period there was considerable tension between the proponents of liberal capitalism and the proponents of the marxist-inspired criticism of that model which came to find expression in the rise of the USSR.

The end of the short twentieth century was announced by the practical dissolution of the post-Second World War Cold War competition between liberal capitalism and its socialist critic which was occasioned by the actual collapse of the USSR. However, the decline of the USA had proceeded apace over the same period and the new global circumstance of tripolarity was quickly acknowledged. In the tripolar global system the discussions of the nature of humankind and its possible futures is no longer bound by the European modernist project whose restatement in an appropriate contemporary guise now seems to be a necessary condition of dialogue with denizens of other cultural traditions.

We might argue therefore that the twentieth century has seen a particular treatment of the legacies of nineteenth-century classical social theory, and in this chapter we will take note of the various strands of debate in order both to offer a provisional conclusion to our discussions of the nature of social theorizing and to sketch out the backdrop to the efforts of the theorists of today to grasp the business of complex change. In order to keep the potentially vast amount of material under control the centre of gravity of the review will be Anglo-American. This is appropriate as the development of liberal capitalism in the short twentieth century has been centred on the Anglo-American sphere. However, it is quite clear at the end of the short twentieth century that the dominance of the global system by the USA is now over and a new pattern with a tripolar interdependent global system is emerging. We can posit an overall sequence moving from European unipolarity to US-dominated bi-polarity to a recently identified tri-polarity within the global system. The intellectual sequence follows the practical sequence as the interest in analysing complex change gives way to the specialist technical disciplines oriented to analysing the functioning of US-centred industrial capitalism, which in turn is now giving way to an interest in analysing complex change within a newly tripolar global system.

Overall, within the intellectual sphere of the First World, the period sees an initial intellectual relocation of effort away from the political-economic, social-institutional and culture-critical analysis of the dynamics of complex change and towards the specialist economic, sociological, political-scientific and cultural analysis of industrial society. But as the tri-polar global system emerges the issue of analysing complex change also reemerges as the legacy of the nineteenth-century theorists is reaffirmed in contemporary guise as the basis for dialogic exchange with other cultures.

Expansion, Fragmentation and Consolidation

The theorists of the Enlightenment supposed that the social world could be understood and brought under rational human control. In turn, the classical nineteenth-century social theorists pursued the modernist project of the rational apprehension of the social world. The key strategy was that of political-economy which encompassed the political-economic analysis of structures, the social-institutional analysis of patterns of social life and the culture-critical elucidation of forms of understanding. However, towards the end of the nineteenth century this typical concern and strategy fell into disrepute. Over the period from the marginalist revolution in economics of the 1870s through to the Great War the familiar specialist social science disciplines emerged. As the disciplines develop each lays claim to a particular object sphere, a relevant method, a body of accumulated wisdom, and on the basis of these three to the status of a professional discipline. In terms of the fundamental trio of strategies whereby the relationship of theory and practice can be conceived – scholarship, policy and politics – it is the second sphere that comes to the fore.

Overall, the story of the development of the legacy of classical nineteenth-century social science in the First World over the period of the short twentieth century is one of expansion (as the formal institutionalized pursuit of social science burgeons), fragmentation (as separate disciplines form and define themselves one against the other), consolidation (as disciplines develop their technical expertise and build up their stocks of knowledge), and eventual stagnation (as originally engaged scholarship slowly subsides into mere professional technical expertise). This broad characterization can be pursued in terms of a simple sequential agenda: (a) the nature of the work of the nineteenth-century theorists of modernity can be recalled; (b) along with the process of its eclipse with the early-twentieth-century emergence of the familiar spread of professionalized specialist social sciences; (c) the new work of the inter-war period can be noted; and (d) the process of incipient post-war stagnation can be indicated.

The rational comprehension of the nature of the social world

The modernist project of the European intellectual tradition comprises a deep-seated set of assumptions about how the world might be understood and rationally ordered. It can be viewed as a cultural project centred upon the celebration of the cognitive mode of science and the demystification and rationalization of the world. Or, again, it can be viewed as a social scientific project which centres on the deployment of strategies of political-economic, social-institutional and culture-critical analysis oriented to the rational comprehension of patterns of complex change. Or, relatedly, it may be viewed as a political project which entails the affirmation of the formal and substantive democratic project.

The modernist project is bound up with the rise of European capitalism as alliances of intellectuals and commercial groups first brought together the agents, ideas and interests necessary to set the project in motion. Subsequently the bourgeoisie drew back from the more radical implications and sought a new status quo built around the self-regulation of the market. The modernist project appears in various guises as agent groups read structural circumstances and promulgate their views. It is a contested tradition. The best advocate for the modernist project has been the success of natural science. Gellner argues that science is the mode of cognition of industrial societies and that industrial society is the ecology of natural science.[2]

The classical nineteenth-century modernist project centres on the affirmation of the cognitive power of human reason and the proposal that reason be deployed in regard to both the natural and the human worlds. An ideal of material and ethical progress is affirmed. So overall, we can grasp the dynamics of the system that enfolds us and having deciphered it render it amenable to rationally specified control (celebration of science). Relatedly the project affirms that the capitalist system is dynamic and inherently progressive (future-optimism). The political-ethical project of formal and substantive democracy can be seen as advancing/affirming the modernist project via the celebration of social agency.

The emergence of professionalized specialist social sciences

In general there are two aspects of the shift from classical nineteenth-century social theory to the familiar intellectual patterns of the short twentieth century: (a) the movement towards discrete social science disciplines; and (b) the coloration given to this movement by the existence of distinct national intellectual traditions. An additional matter is the relative eclipse of the British and European positions and the rise of the USA to a hegemonic status within the First World in the period of the short twentieth century.

In the UK the intellectual scene underwent an extensive change when around 1870 the strategy of political-economy was superseded by marginalist economics. Pollard argues that this meant that a key social science 'became a mathematics, irrefutable as long as it was internally consistent, but utterly lacking in a historical dimension' and he adds that it 'was a mark of triumph ... of the new liberal capitalist order ... The important thing was ... that by making economics ahistorical, the economists made social conservatism orthodox. To advocate further progress by basic social change, as had occurred in the past, was not only politically deplorable, but economically nonsensical'.[3] Pollard records that by the 1870s political-economy had become both intellectually moribund and overtaken by the success of the liberal bourgeoisie in Western Europe.[4] In the period from 1870 through to the outbreak of the Great War, a period of high bourgeois optimism, and labour-based counter-optimism, political-economy dissolves: (a) marginalism is constructed to serve as an economic science which celebrates and

2 E. Gellner 1964 *Thought and Change*, London, Weidenfeld.
3 S. Pollard 1971 *The Idea of Progress*, Harmondsworth, Penguin, p. 139.
4 Ibid. pp. 138–150.

theorizes the activities of the entrepreneurs and the city financiers; (b) the work of Charles Darwin inspires both Herbert Spencer who gives us social Darwinism and L. T. Hobhouse who gives us social evolutionist gradual-ism and thereby sets the tone for subsequent ameliorist sociology; (c) the notion of competition is picked up by Walter Bagehot who presents a celeb-ration of the political model of the advanced countries and bequeathes an approach to the study of politics which focuses narrowly on government;[5] and (d) the expansion of colonial holdings generates the stock of com-parative material inaugurating anthropology. In general, a similar story could be told for the intellectual scene in mainland Europe. In this case also there are specific intellectual traditions available, and in the French and German traditions the contributions of history and philosophy remained more prominent.

In France after the 1870 Prussian-led German invasion the work of Durkheim and his followers became influential and as the university sys-tem developed the position of sociology was assured as a practical reform-ing discipline oriented to the political project of the Third Republic. The optimistic, prospective and holistic text entitled *The Division of Labour* expressed the practical and political commitments of Durkheim.[6] However, after the experience of the Great War the confidence of French intellectuals became dissipated and in the inter-war period a series of dispersed enquiries were pursued.[7]

In Germany the period from 1848 to 1919 sees a rapid modernization and then unification from above achieved by Bismarck and a failure of the bourgeoisie to take power. A parallel intellectual debate revolved around the nature of knowledge of the social and the way in which such know-ledge might inform action. The traditional view looked to the humanities and the arts as vehicles of personal cultivation and any arguments in favour of a more practical social science were regarded as positivistic. However, as Germany shifted decisively into the modern world in the later years of the century the practical demands of the period became pressing. It was here that Max Weber made his ambiguous contribution to the illumination of the interests of the bourgeoisie and the German powerstate.[8] However, the debacle of the Great War, a failed revolution and the emergence of the fragile Weimar Republic had the effect of reducing the influence of practical social science as the majority of intellectuals withdrew to the old traditions of the humanities.[9]

In the USA the shift to the modern world had taken place within the material circumstances given by a rich and largely uninhabited continent

---

5 In regard to the UK D. Marquand 1988 *The Unprincipled Society*, London, Fontana, speaks of the 'Westminster Model' within which politics is reduced to the narrow focus of that which happens within Westminster/Whitehall.
6 G. Hawthorn 1976 *Enlightenment and Despair*, Cambridge University Press, ch. 6.
7 Ibid. ch. 10.
8 Ibid. ch. 7.
9 Ibid. ch. 8.

and the intellectual framework of an ostensibly radical but in practice profoundly conservative individualistic social philosophy.[10] The notion of progress familiar to Europeans was not available to American thinkers except in the guise of material advance. In the absence of any percieved need to reflect upon the possibility of structural reforms the work of American social theorists turned to the pragmatic pursuit of a multiplicity of more particular reforms.[11] However, it was in the inter-war period that the influential general theoretical work of Talcott Parsons took shape. And in the period of unquestioned US hegemony in the wake of the Second World War it was the theories of industrial society inspired in part by Parsons which came to dominate the social science of the First World.

In general, the elaboration of the familiar spread of technical social scientific disciplines was different in different countries as the shift from the early modern period to the developed modernity of the years of the short twentieth century proceeded. The relative decline of the European theorists saw a rise in the influence of US social scientists. In the USA the divisions of intellectual labour were particularly clearly drawn within a cultural context well disposed to the practice of deploying expert knowledge in the knowledge marketplace. In the shift from the broad prospective analysis of complex change oriented to dialogue in the public sphere, which was the typical concern of classical nineteenth-century social science, to the pursuit of discipline-bound technical expert knowledge oriented to the professionally delimited knowledge marketplace, much of the critical edge of nineteenth-century work was lost. As Bauman puts it, in place of negative-critical work we have positive-constructive work.[12] It is characteristic of discrete disciplines of learning that they lay claim to privilege in respect of methodologies, areas of concern and accumulated bodies of knowledge. On the basis of these positions they claim privileged expert knowledge. In the knowledge marketplace of contemporary capitalism the claim to expert knowledge is the basis of a further claim to an exclusive possession of this expertise within the knowledge marketplace, that is to the status of a profession. The result is clear and in terms of the schematic trio of practice noted earlier – scholarship, policy and politics – the balance shifts away from scholarship conjoined to politics and towards a policy sphere that expands to embrace the political. In Habermasian terms,[13] the fragmentation of the classical nineteenth-century modernist project allows the substitution of claims to technical expertise to displace the imperative of democracy. In the contemporary modern world an ever broadening spread of experts of one sort or another lay claim to the technical expert professional knowlege necessary to legislate for the broad mass of the population.

10   Ibid. ch. 9; see also R. Swedberg 1987 'Economic Sociology Past and Present', *Current Sociology*, 35.
11   Hawthorn 1976 op. cit. ch. 9.
12   Z. Bauman 1976 *Towards a Critical Sociology*, London, Routledge.
13   On the work of Habermas see R. C. Holub 1991 *Jürgen Habermas: Critic in the Public Sphere*, London, Routledge.

The new work of the inter-war period

As the legacy of classical nineteenth-century social theory with its concern to analyse complex change in terms of political-economic, social-institutional and cultural processes slowly declined into the familiar spread of discipline-bound social sciences a series of new intellectual departures were made. The new work produced in the inter-war period can be taken to have contributed significantly both to the elaboration of narrowly discipline-bound work but also to the subsequent possibility of restating in contemporary guise the concerns of the classical nineteenth-century tradition. Out of a wealth of material we can point to the following significant economic, social and political analyses: (a) the elaboration of neo-classical economics and their partial eclipse by Keynesianism; (b) the pursuit of economic sociology; (c) the collapse of marxist work into official Marxism–Leninism; (d) the work of the Frankfurt School; (e) the first statements of structural-functionalist sociology; (f) the pursuit of anthropology; and (g) the rise of nationalist developmentalism in the colonies.

(a) Keynes and neo-classicism

The collapse of political-economy was followed within technical economics by the development of neo-classical marginalist analyses.[14] The substantive core of the neo-classical economic package is made up of claims in respect of the functioning of the free market. The free market comprises atomistic individuals who know their own autonomously arising needs and wants and who make contracts with other individuals through the mechanism of the marketplace to satisfy those needs and wants. The market is a neutral mechanism for transmitting information about needs and wants, and goods which might satisfy them, around the system. A minimum state machine provides a basic legal and security system to underpin the individual contractual pursuit of private goals.

The theorists of neo-classical economics claim that free markets maximize human welfare and in turn this unpacks as a series of interlinked claims. First, economically, the claim is that as free markets act efficiently to distribute knowledge and resources around the economic system, then material welfare will be maximized. On this basis the neo-classical theorists attended closely to the construction of formal models of the market system. The extent of the value of these analytical machineries is in some doubt.[15] Second, socially, the claim is that as action and responsibility for action reside with the person of the individual, then liberal individualistic social systems will ensure that moral worth is maximized. In this claim the fundamental ontological commitment of neo-classicism to the priority of the individual is affirmed. It would be reasonable to say that most of the

---

14 A. K. Dasgupta 1985 *Epochs of Economic Thought*, Oxford, Blackwell.
15 P. Ormerod 1994 *The Death of Economics*, London, Faber.

theorists of the classical nineteenth-century tradition of social science would offer a more social notion of humankind. At the present time the profoundly social nature of humankind would be a commonplace for most social sciences. Third, politically, the claim is that as liberalism offers a balanced solution to problems of deploying, distributing and controlling power, then liberal polities ensure that political freedom is maximized. In this simple claim the tradition of philosophical liberalism is affirmed. However, the fundamental incoherence of the position has been widely advertised.[16] And, four, epistemologically, the claim is that as the whole package is grounded in genuine positive scientific knowledge then in such systems the effective deployment of positive knowledge is maximized. However, the great discovery of twentieth-century philosophy has been human language and the simplicities of naturalistic positivism are not now widely taken seriously.[17]

The work of the neo-classical theorists was pursued in the early part of the short twentieth century but when the system collapsed into depression in the 1930s the approach fell out of favour.[18] In the First World a series of sharply contested interventionist approaches were pursued. In the USA the institutionalist approach was influential in the New Deal. In the UK the work of Keynes came to underpin the welfare state and in mainland Europe similar work was accomplished. The long post-war economic boom is credited to the interventionist machineries of the Bretton Woods system which was inaugurated in 1944 in order to regulate the global economy and ensure that the pre-war depression did not recur. However the collapse of the Bretton Woods system in the early 1970s led to disequilibrium within the global system. In the American sphere of the tripolar global system a restatement of neo-classicism was made by the New Right in the 1980s.

(b) The work of economic sociology

In the late nineteenth and early twentieth centuries there were a series of conflicts between proponents of what were to emerge as economics and sociology, conflicts that were methodological, political and institutional.[19] In the first, the debate turned on the scope of sociology and its relation to economics. Comte launched a series of attacks on political-economy and urged the priority of sociology. A sharp reaction amongst economists in the UK followed and contributed to the formation of neo-classicism. As for the second conflict, around the beginning of the twentieth century there was a debate in respect of the claims of individualism and collectivism which had both intellectual and political implications and sociology was taken to be

16   C. B. Macpherson 1971 *Democratic Theory: Essays in Retrieval*, Oxford University Press; R. Plant 1991 *Modern Political Thought*, Oxford, Blackwell.
17   R. J. Bernstein 1976 *The Restructuring of Social and Political Theory*, London, Methuen; M. Root 1993 *Philosophy of Social Science*, Oxford, Blackwell.
18   Hobsbawm 1994 op. cit. ch. 3.
19   R. Swedberg 1987 'Economic Sociology Past and Present', *Current Sociology*, 35.

unreliably collectivistic in contrast to economics.[20] Finally, in the USA economics was established within the institutional sphere of the university world first and was in a position to oversee the later establishment of sociology and the upshot was that in the Anglo-Saxon world economics became the hard social science and sociology became a vague soft study of leftovers.[21]

As the early sociologists established themselves, economic sociology was sketched out as a distinct sub-field, and one key inheritance was German. An aspect of the intellectual debates amongst German scholars in the late nineteenth century was the method appropriate to economic enquiry. In this debate the German Historical School lost out to the proponents of the Austrian variant of emergent neo-classicism. However the empirical, historical, comparative and evolutionary approach favoured by the now rejected Historical School fed into the first generation of economic sociology. The early work on economic sociology involved Weber, Simmel, Pareto and Durkheim. However this early work was never developed because in the period 1930–60 it was overshadowed by the work associated with Keynes. Yet important work was done in this period by J. A. Schumpeter, Michael Polanyi, Karl Mannheim and Parsons. It is a strong group of theorists.[22] The key positive claims of an economic sociology would seem to be that: (a) economic activity is social activity; (b) which needs must be studied as such; (c) which means rejecting extant disciplinary knowledge-claims and boundaries; (d) in pursuit of the direct social scientific apprehension of the social processes constituting the sphere of the economic. Commentators have spoken of the strategic tasks of arguing against the naturalizing habit of orthodox economics in favour of the contextualizing strategy of economic sociology.[23]

(c) The fate of marxian enquiry

The history of the fate of the marxist tradition in the period of the short twentieth century is one of slow decay. At the outset of the period the theorists concerned were part of the wider European intellectual scene. However, the emergence of the USSR as a nominally revolutionary state fostered an intellectual divide which mirrored the divide which would subsequently become routinized as the Cold War system. Within the ambit of

20   S. Collini 1979 *Liberalism and Sociology*, Cambridge University Press.
21   In a similar way it has been argued that the key to the contemporary self-understanding of orthodox economists derives from the late-nineteen-century model of physics, long overthrown within physics but still deforming any direct acknowledgment that economics is a social science: see P. Mirowski 1988 *Against Mechanism: Protecting Economics from Science*, New Jersey, Rowman and Littlefield.
22   Swedberg 1987 op. cit. p. 25ff, p. 42ff.
23   F. Block 1990 *Post Industrial Possibilities: A Critique of Economic Discourse*, Berkeley and Los Angeles, University of California Press.

the USSR the vitality of the marxian tradition slowly faded away in the face of the demands of the state for the formulation and maintenance of an official marxist ideology oriented to the needs of a developmental state. In the First World the marxist tradition was pursued at the margins of society. Whilst the work was often hugely influential within intellectual spheres, the efforts of theorists were routinely assimilated by conservative critics to the official products of the ideologists of the USSR and were thereby generally dismissed.[24]

(d) The work of the Frankfurt School

If we compress the history of the development of marxist theorizing within the First World we can say that following the failure of the socialist revolutions in Hungary and Germany after the Great War a strand of marxian theorizing emerged in the work of the Frankfurt School, which called attention to the cultural pre-conditions of effective socialist revolution.[25] The Frankfurt School identified an irrational and stable monopoly capitalist system. The sphere of culture was seen to be increasingly commodified as the capitalist market extended its scope into the realms of symbols which previously had been apart from the system. The cultural products of monopoly capitalism were understood to encourage an unthinking conformism, as with the Hollywood dream machine. The work of the Frankfurt School has been developed by Jürgen Habermas who argues that the increasing rationalization of the life world by the demands of the productive sphere of modern capitalism, where this includes economic and administrative (including state) spheres, must be resisted in the reaffirmation of the role of the public sphere of democratic discourse and communal goal-setting.

(e) The structural-functionalist approach

In the USA Talcott Parsons was responsible for the construction of an elaborate theory of social action which both drew upon European social theory and rejected the political left. As the work developed, Parsons came to elaborate the core of what came to be expressed in the post-Second World War period as the structural-functionalist orthodoxy of social science, which in turn played a significant role in the ideological package of the free world.

The general theory of social action can be taken to have four aspects (which are in turn subdivided). First, the analysis of social action which is

24 G. Lichtheim 1967 *Marxism: An Historical and Critical Study*, London, Routledge; P. Anderson 1976 *Considerations on Western Marxism*, London, New Left Books; P. Anderson 1983 *In the Tracks of Historical Materialism*, London, Verso; C. W. Mills 1963 *The Marxists*, Harmondsworth, Penguin.
25 See M. Jay 1973 *The Dialectical Imagination*, Boston, Mass., Little, Brown and generally D. Held 1980 *Introduction to Critical Theory*, London, Hutchinson.

taken to comprise four elements: (a) a subject or actor (individual, group or collectivity); (b) a situation (physical and social to which the actor relates); (c) a set of symbols (carrying meaning which allow the actor to read this situation); and (d) a schedule of rules, norms and values (which guide the orientation of action). Second, the scheme of the pattern variables which govern the orientation of action of the particular actor, they are cultural resources: (a) ascription versus achievement; (b) diffuseness versus specificity; (c) particularism versus universalism; (d) affectivity versus affective neutrality; and (e) collective orientation versus self-orientation. Third, it is clear that systems of action have functional requisites so that the particular system of action and interaction can be coherently maintained over time. There are four such functional requirements of systems of action: (a) adaptation, which links up system and environment; (b) goal-attainment, which moves the system to achieve targets; (c) integration, which expresses the requirement that the system remains coherent over time; and (d) latency, whereby the system draws upon stocks of symbols to motivate actors within the system. Then, fourth, an idea of equilibrium is introduced as the endpoint to which all systems tend when disturbed. Systems are in complex exchange with their environment, and this often requires internal adjustments, and the whole is governed by the notion of equilibrium. The business of disturbance and restoration of equilibrium generates system learning. The system as a whole can be said to experience differentiation, reintegration and evolution.

Parsons used this general theory of action to analyse society. The general social system comprises a set of sub-systems which are dealt with by the various social sciences (economics, sociology, politics and psychology). From the perspective of the general theory of action it is the job of sociology to study the integrative function and he produced along with his co-workers the structural-functionalist theory of society. What we have is a model of the social world as a self-regulating harmonious unit held together by common values.

The approach was developed through the post-Second World War period into the broad modernization, industrialism, convergence, and end-of-ideology package. It was essentially a celebration of the model of the free West: (a) modernization was the process whereby the less developed countries would shift from traditional patterns of life to become developed; (b) industrial society was the goal, where society was driven by the demanding logic of industrialism; (c) and this logic would lead to the convergence of Western and Eastern political economic systems; and (d) the achievement of prosperity as in the USA in the 1960s would mean that ideological debate would wither away. In general, structural-functionalism presented a view of the social world as essentially harmonious and stable yet in the 1960s it came under severe pressure as the USA went through a phase of violent conflict. The Civil Rights movement, the Vietnam War and the student movement all combined to render a theory premised on stability irrelevant.

(f) The work of anthropology

The industrial capitalist form-of-life which originated in Europe was inherently dynamic and expanded to draw large areas of the rest of the globe into a dependent periphery. In the early phases of the expansion the European traders, missionaries and travellers operated at the margins of available knowledge and technology and their impact upon other cultures was relatively slight. However, as the European industrial capitalist system continued to develop, the exchanges with other forms-of-life became much more extensive until by the late nineteenth century large areas of the world had been brought under direct or indirect metropolitan rule. It was alongside this process of expansion that the present discipline of anthropology developed in the later part of the nineteenth century.[26] It began with the reports of the traders, missionaries and other travellers over the long period of the seventeenth and eighteenth centuries in America, Asia and Africa. In the early years of the Enlightenment in Europe the materials of the travellers had been taken optimistically to indicate how people shorn of the ills of civilization could make coherent lives.[27] However, as the demands of the metropolitan core upon the newly incorporated periphery deepened and became more disruptive of existing forms-of-life there was a move towards more self-consciously systematic empirical study of non-European cultures. The traders and travellers provided the raw material which was to form the basis of the major works of anthropology in the late nineteenth century.

The early statements of nineteenth-century anthropology were influenced by the evolutionary theory of Darwin and identified lines of progress from primitive to civilized societies. The enquiries of anthropologists were cast in terms of the historical evolution of society and available ethnographic material was read in the light of these overriding preoccupations. Thus, the American scholar Lewis Morgan discussed the movement to the modern world in terms of the three stages of savagery, barbarism and civilization.[28] The approach was revised in the late nineteenth century and the role of the influence of one culture upon another was acknowledged in the similarly rather speculative diffusionist approach. Subsequently, an overarching approach to the subject was found in functionalist analysis.

The late nineteenth century habit of data accumulation meant that by the early twentieth century the stock of available ethnographic material had become very large.[29] It had also begun to be of considerable interest to the colonial administrators of the various European empires. Around the turn of the century a series of important anthropological studies were undertaken. The work of social anthropology came to centre formally upon the comparative analysis of the social institution structures of discrete pre-industrial

26 J. Beattie 1966 *Other Cultures*, London, Routledge.
27 I. Sachs 1976 *The Discovery of the Third World*, London, MIT Press.
28 L. Morgan 1877 *Ancient Society*, London.
29 As with the study of religions made by J. Frazer 1922 *The Golden Bough*, London, Macmillan.

cultures.[30] The related study of the sets of ideas which both sustained and interpreted the institutional structures to those people who lived with reference to them came to be known as cultural anthropology.[31] In both cases, what is at issue is the general study of the multiplicity of ways in which humankind constitutes its social world. The substantive concerns of anthropology were in significant measure bound up with the colonial episode and the needs of colonial administration. It was the colonial sphere within which anthropologists worked – whether or not they affirmed or criticized the arrangement.

The subsequent formal development of the discipline of anthropology can be taken to parallel the patterns of change in the other critical social sciences. As the discipline advanced the early assumptions in respect of the priority of the model of the modern embodied in the West and the simple assumptions in respect of the scientificity of enquiry lodged in the recieved model both began to fall away. The consequence has been that anthropology has not merely presented itself in diverse theoretical guises,[32] but also participated generally in the slow shift towards theoretical scepticism which characterizes the broad spread of critical social sciences. Relatedly, the substantive concerns of anthropologists have also changed as the colonial period has given way to the post-colonial period. The nature of the anthropologists' role within the colonial period has been reproduced in the context of talk about development.[33] Again, the debate is complex, but it has been suggested that just as other social sciences can manifest a positive-constructive or negative-critical approach to an area of concern, so too can anthropology. In recent years the precise contribution of anthropology to the broad social sciences has come under critical question and it has been suggested that a return to the Enlightenment concern for human emancipation might be a route to the future for the discipline.

(g) The scholarship of nationalism

The situation in respect of intellectual and practical activity in the Third World itself over this long inter-war period is rather different and three broad points can be made: (a) that intellectuals educated within the institutional structures of the colonizers brought back the critical ideas of the West and turned them against the colonial;[34] and (b) that the early example of Japan, the USSR and later still the People's Republic of China all exemplified to thinkers in the colonial territories the power of the rational pursuit

30   As with B. Malinowski and A. R. Radcliffe-Brown, or E. E. Evans-Pritchard, or E. Leach.
31   As with Margaret Mead or Ruth Benedict.
32   As with the structuralist work of Claude Levi-Strauss, or the work produced in the marxist tradition; see M. Bloch 1983 *Marxism and Anthropology*, Oxford University Press.
33   P. Grillo ed. 1985 *Social Anthropology and Development Policy*, London, Tavistock, or M. Hobart ed. 1993 *An Anthropological Critique of Development*, London, Routledge.
34   B. Anderson 1983 *Imagined Communities*, London, Verso.

of national strategies of industrialization;[35] and (c) in the wake of the epis-ode of decolonization there has been concern to recover indigenous cultures and to indigenize intellectual imports.[36]

Consolidation, stagnation and reactions to uncertainty in the post-war period

In the post-Second World War period the discipline-bound social sciences found expression in the complex package deal of theories of industrial-ism which for a time attained the status of a more or less unchallenged orthodoxy. The critical traditions of the nineteenth century and the more recent work within the marxist tradition were consigned to the sidelines as structural-functionalism offered its naturalistic analyses of industrial society. The central image was of the social world as a self-regulating harmonious whole which was held together by common values. The social system could be analysed in terms of a series of functional sub-systems each of which was the concern of a particular discipline (economy, polity, society, culture). The central image is unpacked in a series of related areas: (a) the model of industrial society which is the goal to which the logic of industrialism is driving all societies; (b) the process of modernization whereby the less developed countries shift from traditional to modern societies; (c) the pro-cess of the convergence of East and West as both are driven by the logic of industrialism; and (d) the realization of the end of ideology as scarcity is overcome and conflict disappears. The critics objected that this was little more than the generalized model of the post-Second World War USA and it began to fall out of favour as the USA experienced social problems in the 1960s and 1970s. However, the intellectual doubts quickly came to tran-scend any restrictedly local context and over the next few years there was a return to themes within social philosophy which were related to the con-cerns of the classical tradition of social theorizing.

The Post-war Phase of New Debate

In the early 1970s a series of overlapping doubts began to assail the the-orists, policy analysts and political agents of the First World: (a) amongst intellectuals the project of modernity in its short twentieth-century guise came into question from the liberal right and the democratic left, and in the intellectual confusion of the end of the short twentieth century a denial of the project of modernity in the form of ideas of postmodernity was offered; (b) amongst policy analysts confidence in respect of the post-Second World War settlement which involved state-sponsored welfare to stabilize mono-poly capitalism faltered as confidence in strategies of intervenion dipped in

---

35 G. Barraclough 1964 *An Introduction to Contemporary History*, Harmondsworth, Penguin; Hobsbawm 1994 op. cit.
36 E. Said 1993 *Culture and Imperialism*, London, Chatto.

the face of accumulating failures; and (c) amongst political agents confidence in the progressive nature of the polity splintered as the post-Second World War settlement dissolved into a disputatious market-obsessed interregnum that was overtaken by the end of the short twentieth century and the establishment of a phase of general confusion.

The intellectuals' debate about goals

In the early 1970s the multiple crises of the post-war settlement between capital and labour in the metropolitan heartlands of capitalism deepened. The confusions began with severe upheavals within the economies of the First World. There was a rising preoccupation with both inflation and the apparent inability of established national and international mechanisms to deal with the problems.[37] Relatedly, there were political problems in that the post-war bipolar system of the USA and the USSR was coming under pressure. In particular the USA, having become embroiled in a futile war designed to contain communism in Vietnam, was entering a period of decline.[38] Relatedly we may note the rise of new economic and political powers in Japan and the European Union. The relative eclipse of the post-Second World War settlement with its liberal-democratic compromise has seen a trio of replies: the progressive reaffirmation of the notion of democracy; the regressive reaffirmation of the sovereign power of the marketplace; and a radical version of the celebration of the marketplace which suggests not merely that it will secure progress but that it has already generated a new postmodern pattern of consumption-centred life.

The progressive reply has been presented by theorists of formal and substantive democracy, for example, Alasdair MacIntyre, C. B. Macpherson and Jürgen Habermas. However, as the post-Second World War settlement dissolved the immediate advantage was seized by the right. It was European democratic reformism plus the active promulgation of emerging US hegemony that acted to structure the post-Second World War compromise in Europe, yet there were irreconcilable opponents. Amongst the early intellectual critics were Friedrich von Hayek, Karl Popper and Milton Friedman. In the early post-war period the rewriting of history proceeded apace and soon the European fascists were linked to Soviet communism under the umbrella label of totalitarianism. The culpability of the Western powers in regard to the pre-war rise of European fascism and the aggressive US drive against the left after the war were rapidly and actively forgotten. An extensive vocabulary of legitimation was developed and free enterprise was equated with free economies, which were equated with the free West, which in turn was equated with freedom. The further development of the celebration of the market is much wider than the ideologists of the New Right. In the guise of notions of postmodernity we now have celebrations of the global

37   E. A. Brett 1985 *The World Economy Since the War*, London, Macmillan.
38   P. Kennedy 1988 *The Rise and Fall of the Great Powers*, London, Fontana.

knowledge-based marketplace which offers consumers an opportunity to assemble their own life-styles from the goods and services on offer. The strong claim is lodged that all the ideas of progress which were integral to modernity have now been superseded. In the new postmodernist world there are no metadiscourses.

The policy analysts' debate about intervention

One theme of the attack made by the political right had concerned the role of state intervention within the market. It was argued by these theorists that state intervention almost always generated results which were worse than those which the market, left to its own devices, would contrive. This attack was addressed to the central point of the Keynesian intellectual machineries of the welfare state. And there were other lines of criticism. On the political left Jürgen Habermas identified the ever widening spheres of social life that were subject to authoritative regulation of one sort or another and spoke of the technocratic invasion of the lifeworld. These themes have been picked up by others within the broad democratic tradition. The diagnoses of right and left are different and so are their prescriptions. However the two lines of attack have it in common that they resist both the claims to success of the interveners and the slow collapse of personal autonomy within the social world.

In the sphere of development theory a similar debate began as development theorists called attention to the lack of any very obvious successes. At the same time critics pointed out that the reliance on expert-provided structural analysis acted to block the voice of the ordinary people of the Third World.

In both First and Third Worlds critics have looked for ways in which the power of ordinary people could be acknowledged. The right have claimed to see the marketplace as an appropriate institutional vehicle whilst the left have preferred to speak of the political life of the community vehicled through the public sphere.

The political agents' debate about liberal-democracy

The short twentieth century has seen a period of catastrophe followed by a golden age followed by a renewed phase of drift. The catastrophic period ran from 1914 through to 1945 when the liberal capitalist system experienced war, revolution, depression and further war. The post-Second World War economic boom was a golden age which was largely unexpected. In recent years the machineries of economic prosperity have faltered and a general unease has been compounded by the collapse of the USSR which had at the very least provided the capitalist world with a useful 'other' against which it could define itself. The elaborate theories of the market enshrined in postmodernism have had a brief influence but the end of the short twentieth century has seen confusion in respect of the political philo-sophies of contemporary First World societies.[39]

Development theory and the analysis of complex change

In the post-Second World War period a series of approaches to develop-ment have been advanced. The theories presented have had different real-world occasions and have drawn upon different intellectual and cultural traditions in order to make their arguments. However, a common theme amongst the diverse theories offered has been their preoccupation with the analysis of complex change. This common preoccupation has called forth a second common factor in the routinely multi-disciplinary, prospective and engaged nature of the work. In the post-Second World War period devel-opment theorists have been concerned with the ways in which dynamic global structures have placed demands on local agents in the process of drawing these territories into the global industrial-capitalist system. In this way development theory has recalled the work of the nineteenth-century classical social theorists.[40]

The short twentieth century in retrospect and prospect

The notion of the short twentieth century bridges the gap in this text between the work of the classical nineteenth-century social theorists of complex change and the materials of development theory. The short twen-tieth century has seen the rise to hegemonic status of the USA and this has been paralleled by a dispersal of the work of First World social scientists amongst a spread of interests bounded by disciplines and the aspiration to professional status. However, the end of the short twentieth century has represented in contemporary guise the key issue which was addressed by the classical theorist of the nineteenth. Once again social theorists must grapple with the business of complex change. However, the task must now be accomplished both within a changed environment comprising new struc-tural patterns in the global system and new sets of intellectual assumptions within the sphere of social theorizing. These two revisions constitute a significant change from the assumptions and concerns of the nineteenth-century classical social theorists whose work focused on the metropolitan heartlands of global capitalism whilst deploying a straightforwardly Euro-centric strategy of analysis. The focus and the strategy are now untenable and both must be revised. We now inhabit an interdependent tripolar global industrial-capitalist system which presents new challenges to analysis. And an intellectually plausible vehicle for enquiry requires a restatement of the modernist project in order to provide the basis for a sceptical, tentative, piecemeal and dialogic strategy of enquiry.

39   F. Fukuyama 1992 *The End of History and the Last Man*, London, Hamish Hamilton; R. Robertson 1992 *Globalization: Social Theory and Global Culture*, London, Sage.
40   A point made clearly by Gellner 1964 op. cit.

Chapter Summary

The major theorists of the nineteenth century all pursued the modernist project of the rational comprehension of the nature of the social world. This was conceived as a broad, prospective and engaged intellectual strategy and for much of the nineteenth century the key was political-economic analysis. However, towards the end of the century this typical concern and strategy fell into disrepute and in the period of the US-centred short twentieth century we find the emergence of specific social science disciplines. In this context each discipline lays claim to a particular object sphere, a relevant method and a body of accumulated wisdom, and on the basis of these to the status of a professional discipline. The professional expertise of discrete disciplines can be deployed within the knowledge marketplace. In the post-Second World War period this situation finds expression in the US-inspired inter-disciplinary package of the structural-functionalist analysis of industrial society. However, as the short twentieth century comes to a close and a new tripolar global system emerges a return to the classical nineteenth-century concerns with analysing complex change seems inevitable. It is characteristic of development theory that from a post-Second World War starting-point that was conceived in technical terms it turns away from narrow specialization and inter-disciplinarity and returns to the concerns and procedures of the nineteenth-century theorists with their prospective and engaged attempts to grasp the logic of complex change.

PART III

Contemporary Theories of Development

8

The Legacies of the Colonial Era: Structures, Institutions and Images

Overview of the Colonial Project

The expansion of the European capitalist system involved a long-drawn-out exchange with non-European peoples and pre-contact forms-of-life were extensively remade. The long period of colonialism left in place a series of structures, institutions and images which have shaped the subsequent pursuit of development by the replacement elites of the new nationstates. The images of the non-European world which were established over the period of these exchanges have continued to influence the ways in which social scientists, policy analysts and political agents in the First World have comprehended the situation of the Third World. The ways in which the non-European world was understood and approached by Europeans varied. In the period of the Enlightenment non-Europeans were taken to represent an ideal innocence. However, as the European empires expanded the imagery shifts to uncivilized savages. In the period of formal colonialism the ruling elites adopt a posture of taking responsibility for civilizing the less advanced peoples. In the years before the Second World War there was an acknowledgement of a responsibility to organize development so that colonial territories could eventually become independent. The various colonial powers adopted different schemes and most advanced very slowly until the Second World War fatally undermined the European empires and ushered in the post-war phase of decolonization. The sets of structures, institutions and images generated over this long-drawn-out period form an ambiguous legacy. This chapter will consider the sets of ideas, the images and the ideologies of colonialism, as these form the received wisdom with which subsequent development theorists have worked.

The Nature of the Colonial Legacy

The sets of ideas which were produced over the period of the eighteenth and nineteenth centuries were fed into the theories which explained and ordered the expansion of Europe. In turn the experience of expansion provided material which fed into the sets of ideas current within European social theorizing (scholarly, policy analytic and political). It is clear that within the ambit of the European exchange with the non-European world there is both a wealth of practical experience and an extensive stock of social scientific ideas in respect of the nature of these non-European peoples.

The preoccupation with the development of the countries of the Third World has its particular occasion in the post-Second World War period of decolonization which marked a significant moment in the history of the relationship of metropolitan capitalist powers and the peoples of the periphery. In turn there is a longer history reaching back to the early years of the modern period. The European capitalist system expanded slowly from the fifteenth century. As the system developed, the ways in which the non-European worlds were understood by European traders, missionaries, soldiers, settlers and home populations (scholars, policy-makers, political agents and publics) varied considerably.

At the outset in the earliest periods of European trade non-European peoples were regarded as exotic cultural equals. Later, in the period of the Enlightenment as trade and commerce grew, non-Europeans are taken to represent innocence, and ideas of the noble savage are presented. Later in the nineteenth century, as European colonial holdings in the Third World start to become extensive and increasingly integrated into metropolitan patterns of production, trade and finance, the imagery shifts and ideas of uncivilized savages are presented. Subsequently, in the period of formal colonial empires the ruling elites slowly move away from treating the territories as abstract general responsibilities of the civilized which might presently be exploited towards a posture of taking a more direct and practical responsibility for the less advanced people.

In the inter-war period of Hobsbawm's short twentieth century[1] the nascent concern for the peoples of the colonial territories slowly modulates into a series of initial commitments to order the development of these territories with a view to their becoming self-governing members of the community of liberal capitalist nationstates. It was granted that it was the responsibility of the colonial powers to bring colonial territories to the condition of independence. The colonial powers advanced slowly along this path until the upheaval of the Second World War destroyed the colonial systems and ushered in the post-war phase of rapid decolonization. Finally, in the most recent phase of the post-colonial period, the exchange of First and Third World has been construed in terms of the notion of development which has

---

1   E. Hobsbawm 1994 *Age of Extremes: The Short Twentieth Century, 1914–1991*, London, Michael Joseph.

looked to the First World-assisted pursuit of effective nationstatehood on the part of the replacement elites of the new nations of the Third World.

Overall, the broad business of the expansion of European capitalism to encompass large areas of the globe can be understood in terms of the expansion of one form-of-life at the expense of other long established local forms-of-life. As the European capitalist system became ever more global in its reach the structures of that economic, social and political system drew in and reordered a series of extant forms-of-life. In this invasive process the indigenous patterns of economic, social, political and cultural life were radically remade. The expansion of capitalism absorbed forms-of-life and recast them in system-friendly forms. The overall process of the expansion of the system was accomplished via a diverse spread of agents who ordered/understood their activities with reference to a diversity of motives and understandings. As the relationship of the elements within the global system altered along with the overall development of the system, the ways in which the various groups who both constituted and were subject to this system construed each other also changed.

In considering contemporary development theory the sets of ideas promulgated over the long period of the involvement of Europeans with the peoples of the Third World constitute a set of available ideas upon which theorists can draw. However, cultural studies work has recently called attention to the deep-seated sets of prejudices which are lodged within European thought and which can find expression in development theorizing.[2] It is true that misunderstanding and prejudice were not the province solely of Europeans. However, the asymmetries of power inherent within the colonial system mean that the colonized suffered rather more than the colonizers. Overall, it is clear that the long colonial period constitutes an ambiguous legacy which must be approached critically.

The European capitalist system and the patterns of action and understanding that went along with it can be taken to have engaged with the non-European world in three broad phases: (a) the drive for expansion; (b) the episode of colonization and decolonization; and (c) the pursuit of development (see figure 9).

The Expansion of European Capitalism

The expansion of European capitalism involved a series of elements, including: (a) the establishment of the material base of the extant modern system in patterns of industry, trade and finance; (b) the construction of the administrative machineries of the colonial state, with its base in the new cities; and (c) the elaboration of the complex sets of the ideas whereby the expansion was understood and ordered and which are the basis of the ways in which we presently read this phase of expansion and the extant global system.

2   R. Kabbani 1986 *Imperial Fictions: Europe's Myths of Orient*, London, Pandora; E. Said 1993 *Culture and Imperialism*, London, Chatto; E. Wilkinson 1990 *Japan Versus The West: Image and Reality*, Harmondsworth, Penguin.

Figure 9   Legacies of the colonial era

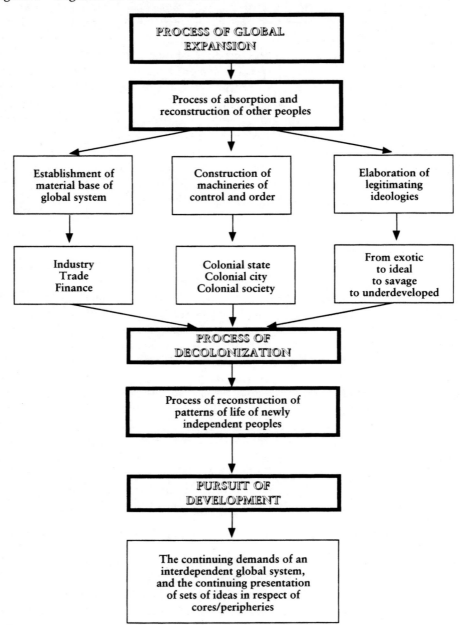

System, agent and theory

The European capitalist system underwent a dual process of expansion and intensification from its inception in the fifteenth century (taking the Italian city states of the Renaissance as a nominal start point) through to its apogee in the early years of the short twentieth century. The expansion was geographical, firstly within Europe and thereafter across the globe. The intensification process has been characterized by many social theorists in terms of the ongoing development of the rationality of the system. In the modern world the demands of the capitalist system extend to many areas of human life.[3]

The geographical expansion of the European capitalist system which began in the sixteenth century and continued through to a high point in the years before the Great War took place in a series of phases, and with multiple conflicts between the European powers and between European powers and indigenous peoples: firstly, the Americas; secondly, Asia; and thirdly, Africa.

The expansion of the capitalist system took place via a series of agents: traders, soldiers, missionaries, settlers and so on. All these agents would have had particular reasons for becoming involved with non-European peoples. The range of agents involved in the particular case of the expansion of the British into the Far East involved the following:[4] (a) traders, who would have travelled out as mariners in very small numbers, enduring long voyages, who set up factories with very small staffs, and who acted routinely in complex and shifting alliances/relationships with indigenous groups and other European and non-European traders; (b) mariners, running sailing ships prior to the 1840s over long distances and with many risks, who were an elite whose technology was superior to that of indigenous groups, and who could make handsome profits on early voyages; (c) soldiers and sailors, deploying force in garrisons, police actions and not infrequent wars (against other Europeans as well as indigenous peoples), often with small numbers and more advanced technology than indigenous groups; (d) administrators, following the traders and establishing bureaucracies that expanded slowly as trading turned into colonialism with its authoritarian paternalism, along with families and transplanted aspects of home-life as expatriates in settlements having various quarters for the different races; and (e) the adventurers who worked along a line parallel to the traders and bureaucrats.

All these agents both read and ordered their activities in the light of particular sets of expectations and ideas. The sets of ideas brought to bear on a given situation would of course be very particular. In the period of expansion the activities of the various agents provided a rich stock of new

3 The long process of the global expansion of capitalism has been a particular concern of neo-marxist theorists; see I. Wallerstein 1974 *The Modern World System*, New York, Academic.
4 G. Woodcock 1969 *The British in the Far East*, London, Weidenfeld.

ideas: (a) the traders provided stocks of travellers' tales of exotic places; (b) the mariners provided the same plus adventures with natural hazards; (c) the soldiers provided stories in respect of military campaigns waged against successive indigenous groups which were popular amongst domestic audiences and which provided a rich stock of images of savages;[5] (d) administrators[6] discovered incompetence and laziness[7] and set about correcting it; and (e) the adventurers provided copy in respect of more exotic adventures.[8] The practical expression of these ideas shaped the nature of expansion (the use of violence, the assumption of superiority, the strong predilection for trade, and the self-justifying ideologies of superiority and responsibility) and the eventual colonial systems (where sets of ideas and prejudices found routinized and institutionalized expression). These sets of ideas also shaped both the nature of the decolonization process, where colonial state-regimes acquiesced with widely varying degrees of good grace to the inevitable, and subsequent links with newly independent countries.[9]

The long phase of the expansion of the European capitalist system is one in which the patterns of understanding of indigenous peoples were slowly overborne by the more powerful incomers. As the pattern of exchanges between the incomers and the indigenous peoples developed over time the versions of events promulgated by the incomers came to have priority.

However, we can pull back from the detail of particular sets of ideas and suggest that over time broad sets of cultural expectations, stereotypes and prejudices were put in place. It was in the light of these regular patterns of understanding that relationships between the members of the various groups would have come to be ordered over the longer run. It is these sets of ideas that can be taken to inform the residual common sense of people in the First World, including development theorists.[10]

Changing general sets of ideas

The significance of the ways in which one culture construes another can be seen in the pattern of characterizations made by Europeans of non-Europeans in the process of the slow European subjugation of the peoples of the world. The process can be treated in terms of the power of myths,

5   V. G. Kiernan 1982 *European Empires from Conquest to Collapse*, London, Fontana.
6   A rich source of material on the early period of expansion. A classic example of a colonial administrator/scholar was Stamford Raffles who 'founded' Singapore. The administrators kept private journals, began official records, sponsored research, and so on.
7   S. H. Alatas 1977 *The Myth of the Lazy Native*, London, Frank Cass.
8   A detailed review of the more equal exchange between Europe and Japan in the late nineteenth century is given by E. Wilkinson 1990 *Japan versus the West: Image and Reality*, Harmondsworth, Penguin.
9   H. Grimal 1965 *Decolonization: The British, French, Dutch and Belgian Empires 1919–1963*, London, Routledge.
10   P. W. Preston 1983 'A Critique of Some Elements of the Residual Common Sense of Development Studies', *Cultures et Developpement*, 15.

including those promulgated at the time and those which have been presented subsequently.[11] The ways in which myth acts to constitute and structure power relationships as one group moves through the process of absorbing or subjugating another is made clear by the two prototypical 'voyages of discovery' of early medieval Europe: the one to the west by Christopher Columbus (1492) which led to the exploitative commercialization of the empires in Latin America; the voyage to India by Vasco da Gama (1497–8) which began a more enduring commercial relationship with the countries of Asia.[12] It can be argued that the whole problem of the Third World is concerned at base with power relationships of dominance and dependence. It is here that we find the practical centre of gravity of all theorizing about development.

The earliest European contacts of the emerging capitalist period were construed in terms not of an exchange of equals but in terms of opportunities for the exercise of power over other groupings. Hernán Cortés in Mexico was regarded as a crusader, not an invader.[13] It is also the case that the native populations of both northern and southern America were swept aside and came to occupy marginal positions within the subsequent societies. However, a little later in Europe at the time of the Enlightenment *philosophes* and the early voyages of discovery in the South Pacific we have the presentation of the image of the noble savage. The reports of the mariners James Cook, Louis Antoine de Bougainville and others into the island peoples of the South Pacific presented them as communities free of the distortions of civilized life. In these island communities it was supposed by the mariners that they had found empirical evidence of the perfectibility of humankind. The reports of the mariners fed into the political-philosophical work of the *philosophes* and thereafter to the European Enlightenment generally. The early voyages of discovery were widely influential within educated circles in regard to matters of trade, art and ideas.[14]

As Europe's interests in the non-European world become more extensive, as the capitalist system in the metropoles develops, so the imagery alters and the notion of the uncivilized savage comes to be used. An example is the change in the reading of the Australian aboriginals, from figures taken as exotic to becoming figures of fun, and a little later, as they were exterminated in Tasmania, rather less than this.[15] In the non-European territories as the colonial system advanced the imagery of the local people shifts – they

---

11 P. Worsley 1967 *The Third World*, London, Weidenfeld, pp. 1–20.
12 H. Brookfield 1975 *Interdependent Development*, London, Methuen, ch. 1.
13 Worsley 1967 op. cit.
14 It would seem to be the case that variants of these images were reworked in the inter-war period by the anthropologist Margaret Mead, and they certainly find routine current expression in the realms of the consumptionist ideologies of tourism. Margaret Mead carried out extensive fieldwork in the South Pacific in the inter-war period and wrote on sexual mores: see her *Coming of Age in Samoa* 1928, New York, Morrow.
15 See R. Hughes 1988 *The Fatal Shore*, London, Pan; see also H. Reynolds 1982 *The Other Side of the Frontier*, Penguin Books Australia, Ringwood.

become uncivilized or backwards and thus justifiably subject to the control of the incoming Europeans. The key agency comes to be the colonial state with its machineries of administrators and their transplanted metropolitian cultures. In this sphere a rich stock of work is assembled as colonial officials produce private journals, official records and reports, and as missionaries, businessmen and scholars also produce this style of material.

One aspect of the European expansion reflected the actual demographic balance of populations with very few colonizers and a mass of those colonized. In respect of Asia, for example, we have a nineteenth-century idea of the 'yellow peril'. The exchange of European and non-European could find expression in racist terms.

Recent critics working in the area of cultural studies have looked at this long period, most especially as it feeds into ideas of modernity with its implicit contrast with the pre-modern rather than with the non-modern, which subsequently find further expression in the ideologies of the colonial period, and which subsequently feed into ideas of development, and have argued that European culture remains extensively suffused with these ideas and that they act today to misdirect European thinking in respect of non-European peoples.[16] In recent years these culture critics have looked at this imagery and have attempted both to deconstruct the ideologies, which are often understood in their popular expression in terms of racism, and to reach back to pre-contact days which are taken to offer an undistorted sphere where the matter of identity can be addressed to some extent outside the European frame.

Colonization and Decolonization

The expansion of European capitalism can be understood in terms of the dynamics of structural change and agent response. The patterns of structural change driving the expansion of the capitalist system were fundamentally political-economic and the key agent groups would thus be the merchants, traders, manufacturers and financiers. However, the key institutional vehicle of the colonial period which effectively integrated global system and local agents was the machinery of the colonial state based in a territory's capital city with its characteristic patterns of activity: (a) law and administration; (b) trade and development (oriented to the needs of the metropole); and (c) social regulation of European and indigenous or immigrant non-European populations.[17] At the same time, over this period, elaborate ideologies detailing the character of natives and the responsibility of the more civilized to attend to their long-term needs found expression in administrative, popular and scholarly forms.

16   Said 1993 op. cit.; Kabbani 1986 op. cit.
17   Worsley 1967 op. cit., ch. 1; see also A. D. King 1990 *Urbanism, Colonialism and the World Economy*, London, Routledge.

System, agent and theory

In the eighteenth century the European powers began to establish extensive trading networks in Latin America and Asia. In the nineteenth century Africa was drawn into the system. The trading networks were slowly extended geographically and their regulation made more detailed. A slow process took place whereby European trading factories became trading ports which became small territorial holdings which became colonial holdings. Over this long period the economies of the various territories slowly became integrated and it became possible to speak of a global system. The system slowly expanded to cover most of the world until it reached an apogee in the years before the Great War. The colonial system regulated trade and drew the global system into a series of blocs. There was routine conflict between the European powers. Within each bloc the metropolitan power established a distinctive pattern of rule. It is possible to speak of British, French, Dutch, Belgian, Portuguese, Spanish, Italian, German, American and Japanese colonial systems. We can pursue the nature of the overall process in terms of the logic of the capitalist system which was driving the expansion, the role of the various agents involved, and the ways in which they understood and ordered their activities. In terms of this process of system expansion and peripheral absorption, the key location was the colonial capital city and the key institution was the state machine.

The colonial city was often a primate city and the base for the colonial state machine. It was therefore the key location of the linkage of peripheral territory to the metropolitan core of the wider global system. The importance of the colonial state was interleaved with the importance of the colonial city.

The shift to the towns had been taking place down through history with the rise and decline of civilizations.[18] It is with the rise of capitalism that the growth of urbanism accelerates significantly. In nineteenth-century Europe there is a massive shift from the land to the cities. The shifts now taking place in the Third World are even greater in terms of numbers and they began with the colonial period as the global system reached into these areas and made them elements in the wider system. As the colonial system took root there were migrations to serve the needs of mines and plantations and the cities that acted to link system and locality. In the First World the historical record involves urbanization coupled to industrialization and whilst the conditions of cities were bad they improved from the late nineteenth century. At the present time in the Third World there seems to be urbanization with only partial industrialization and the conditions of cities are poor. What we find in Third World cities today is a very mixed pattern with areas of prosperity linked to the state-machine, branch offices of MNCs or the established production and service activities of the city, and areas of relative insecurity which are found in the extensive marginal patterns of

18 P. Worsley 1984 *The Three Worlds: Culture and World Development*, London, Weidenfeld, pp. 168–78.

life (some speak of urban petty subsistence on the analogy of rural peasant subsistence).

Third World cities should be regarded as being integral parts of the global system.[19] In the colonial period colonial cities were the mechanism whereby the European-centred global system drew in its new territories. The ideal-type of this relationship takes colonial cities as exchange points with manufactured goods coming in and primary products flowing out. The colonial city can be characterized in the following terms: (a) the focus of city is outwards to the global system; (b) power is in the hands of a non-indigenous minority; (c) the colonized majority are culturally distinct; (d) the city is segregated residentially, ethnically and by wealth/power; and (e) the focus of the colony is on the city as the centre of administration, economy, society and culture.

The colonial state was an administrative state.[20] It was the source of legitimate violence which was the base line of the control of the territory. In places a distinction was drawn between direct and indirect rule with the later system leaving in place local rulers who acted as a buffer between colonizers and colonized. The colonial state raised taxes and provided the basic infrastructure of metropolitan life and this included: (a) a legal system (whereby the law of the incomers was integrated as the superior system with the law of the locals and provided a formal structure for all the population); (b) a communications system (ports, roads, railways, telegraphs and so on); (c) an economic system (in the sense of supporting traders, merchants, manufacturers and financiers); (d) a social system (housing, health, police, recreation); and (e) a cultural system (both formal in terms of the practices necessary to the functioning of the colony and informal in terms of supporting the expatriates and absorbing the locals). It is a very particular social situation which generated its own scholarship, policy analysis, politics and culture (both peripheral and metropolitan).

The contribution of policy-related social science to the work of the colonial administrative state should be noted.[21] In particular it is to this quite particular location that the development of contemporary anthropology can be traced. The pursuit of anthropological knowledge could be dated from the late nineteenth century and it was pursued through the colonial period. It is now of course an integral part of the spread of contemporary social science disciplines and may be taken to have a particular contribution in respect of the matter of elucidating patterns of culture.[22] However, it can be argued that anthropology is uniquely marked by the colonial episode to the extent that one line of reflection amongst anthropologists at the present time suggests that the discipline needs must turn away from an exclusive concern with the Third World and return to the Enlightenment

19 King 1990 op. cit.
20 Worsley 1967 op. cit.
21 Ibid.
22 Worsley 1984 op. cit.

tradition in order to reconstitute itself as an integral part of the social scientific concern to elucidate the dynamics of the modern world.

The general sets of ideas

The nineteenth-century expansion of formal colonial holdings involved ideas of the civilizing mission of the advanced countries. The late nineteenth- and twentieth-century period of high colonialism saw ideas of the superiority of the colonists and their responsibility for their charges. However after the debacle of the Great War, and in the light of the model of the USSR, ideas of independence began to be advanced by metropolitan critics and colonial nationalists. It is the case that very slowly within the metropoles responsibility for colonies came to be taken to entail their eventual independence.

However, it is the case that the crucial inter-war phenomenon was the reaction against colonization which took place amongst the colonized peoples. Amongst the elite of the colonial holdings there was a process of learning and dissent and eventually colonial nationalisms of one sort or another formed. And whilst the metropolitan powers did belatedly acknowledge a responsibility towards those territories which they had come to occupy, Hobsbawm makes clear that it was the long period of catastrophe stretching from 1914 through to 1945 which destroyed the colonial holdings.

It was in the early years of the twentieth century that the populations of the colonial territories of Asia and Africa came to resist the established domination of the European colonists and the process can be understood in terms of the transfer and use of the metropolitan ideas of nationalism to the territories of the colonies.[23] The two events which precipitated the rise of nationalism amongst the peoples of the colonized peripheries were the Japanese defeat of Russia in the war of 1904–5, and the Russian revolution of 1905, which produced hardly any response in Europe but which influenced the revolutions in Persia (1906), Turkey (1908) and China (1911), and gave renewed impetus to the Congress Party in India. After the outbreak of the Great War in Europe the various belligerents encouraged nationalist groups in each other's colonies and by the end of the war the entire edifice was seriously cracked. In this vein the crucial encouragement and example of the Russian revolution of 1917 should also be noted.[24]

It is clear that two other factors were important in the long run: (a) the assimilation by the colonized peoples of European ideas which came to be turned against the incomers; and (b) the vitality and capacity for self-renewal of societies which Europeans had far too easily dismissed as uncivilized.[25] In Asia and Africa the Europeans provoked the nationalist reaction

23 G. Barraclough 1964 *An Introduction to Contemporary History*, Harmondsworth, Penguin, chs. 6, 7.
24 E. Hobsbawm 1994 *Age of Extremes: The Short Twentieth Century, 1914–1991*, London, Michael Joseph, chs. 2, 7.
25 Barraclough 1964 op. cit.

which was to sweep them away and subsequently remake the territories which they had temporarily absorbed. The European powers responded initially with a variety of stratagems to delay the inevitable, and the overall process saw repression, accommodation, war and finally withdrawal.

The learning experience of the elites of the colonial holdings can be characterized in terms of the notion of colonial pilgrimages within the school and administrative systems.[26] In each case the local recruit was introduced to metropolitan ideas and offered the experience of membership of a broad trans-ethnic community whilst simultaneously being denied the opportunity to achieve full membership simply by virtue of a background amongst the colonized peoples. The experience of learning, membership and rejection was easily read into early programmes of nationalism which saw the reinvention of community, or its invention where it had never really existed, as the basis both for demands for independence, an equality of political status with the colonizers who provided the models, and promises to the masses of the territories of growth and welfare. The nationalists of the colonial territories deployed European ideas to invent modern nations from the residues of pre-contact forms-of-life and the confused patterns of the colonial system.

Colonial nationalisms took various forms. An elite could look to a series of sources of legitimacy: (a) pre-contact forms; (b) traditional authority and practices; (c) revolutionary ideas; or (d) the demand that colonizers put into practice the ideas they preached. The responses of the colonial powers took a variety of forms through the sequence of repression, accommodation, wars and acquiescence. It is also the case that these complex exchanges were shaped both by economic circumstances, including local ones in terms of the patterns of development and global ones in terms of the levels of prosperity (or not) of the territories, and by the pattern of social life which had grown up over time and which could differ from colony to colony in terms of the possibilities for change seen by the colonized and acknowledged by the colonizers.

The notion of eventual decolonization did come to be accepted by colonial powers in the wake of the upheavals of the Great War but very little was done to prepare for independence until the greater upheavals of the Second World War made the whole business inevitable.[27] The period from 1919 to 1939 was a phase of preparation. The impact of the Great War is the key matter and it operates in four related areas. First, the stability of the empires was undermined as colonial resources and personnel were used in the war. This left a residue in the form of the idea that the centre owed the periphery some sort of moral debt – here is an early source of the idea that development should be acknowledged as the legitimate goal of the colonial territories. Second, there were reactions in the colonies to the

26   B. Anderson 1983 *Imagined Communities*, London, Verso.
27   Grimal 1965 op. cit., introduction.

problems which resulted from the war, and in particular the ways in which the victors carved up the spoils, including colonial territorial holdings, was seen to cut against the claims about freedom that had been used to justify the war. Third, some of these territories were placed under League of Nations mandates which meant little in practice but did grant the moral force of the claims to freedom. And fourth, in the mandated territories of the Middle East in the inter-war period there was a measure of nationbuilding.

There were a trio of factors at back of this slow movement away from colonial ideologies towards ideas of independence.[28] First, the conservative reaction amongst colonizers in the metropoles and peripheries which saw the continued affirmation of the view that the colonized were not able to deal with their own affairs and should rely on the good intentions and judgements of the colonial authorities who would set down their administrative burdens as soon as their civilizing mission had been completed. Against this was, second, the challenge to the concept of colonialism which was made in Europe, in particular amongst the political left. However, it was, third, the rising tide of action within the colonies that provided the major impetus to change with the model of Japan cited, the resurgence of Islam advocated and ideas of Africanism advanced (including negritude, pan-Africanism and the celebration of Africa directly).[29]

The presence of the Europeans generated nationalist sentiment and this occasioned rather different responses in the various colonial systems. In the British sphere policy entailed the eventual independence of colonies. In the case of the white dependencies of Canada, Australia and New Zealand this was quickly achieved. However, for the other holdings the prospect of independence was a distant and vague goal for the colonial power except where, as in India, civil strife was pushing it up the agenda. In contrast, in the French sphere there was a debate between proponents of association and assimilation and the central government vacillated and followed the British line by default. And in the Dutch sphere the grip of the colonial power was relaxed only very slowly as the territories were regarded as an important source of mercantile surplus. In the years prior to the Second World War an ethical policy was followed which looked to synthesize the best of the metropolitan and peripheral ways of life in a variety of capitalist controlled development. On all this, we can cut through the debate about slowly changing views on the part of the colonial powers by citing the episode of the Second World War because what 'fatally damaged the old colonialists was the proof that the white men and their states could be defeated, shamefully and dishonourably, and that the old colonial powers were patently too weak, even after a victorious war, to restore their old positions'.[30]

---

28 Ibid.
29 Worsley 1967 op. cit. ch. 4.
30 Hobsbawm 1994 op. cit. p. 216.

War and decolonization

The European colonial system in Asia was fatally disturbed by the episode of the Second World War. The Japanese conquest gave a great boost to Asian nationalism and it shattered colonial structures of power. In the confusion of war a series of nationalist groups attained a measure of influence in the area and when the colonial powers looked to return they were resisted with, it should be noted, the tacit support of the USA which wanted the system of empire-centred trading blocs broken. The countries of Asia rapidly attained independence albeit with a measure of violence amongst the indigenous groups of the area and between the departing colonists and the nationalist groups. It was only in Indo-China that the withdrawal was significantly delayed and this was a matter of the rapidity of the onset of the Cold War and the US determination to oppose what it took to be communist advance in the region.

In the wake of the Second World War the withdrawal from the Arab lands was fairly quickly accomplished with the exception of the small statelets of the Persian Gulf whose strategic importance to the West ensured their extended colonial status and thereafter an independence that seemed to entail a measure of patron–client dependence.

In the case of Africa the experience of the Second World War was indirect. However, the colonies did experience the upheavals of economic change as the demands of the allies fell upon their resources. In the post-war period the symbolic date is 1955 when the Bandung Conference of Asian and African nations condemned colonialism. The withdrawal was spread over the next decade or so and was accomplished with varying levels of difficulty and violence. In all cases the key problem was the settler communities in the British, French, Portuguese and Belgian territories. A measure of violence was necessary to expel the colonialists and their pattern of withdrawal, coupled with the radical rhetoric of independence and the US-sponsored reaction of the 1980s led to extensive warfare with consequent political-economic and social breakdown.

In brief, overall, the colonial territories each had a different internal character and the disruption of war led to slightly different patterns of withdrawal and this in turn generated slightly different patterns of post-colonial linkages.[31] In the post-war period the overarching idea which shaped relationships after the episode of decolonization was formally completed was the idea of development.

The Pursuit of Development

As the global system was reconfigured in the wake of the Second World War the system requirement for access to territories of the Third World coupled to the developmentalist rhetoric of the independence movement

---

31   Grimal 1965 op. cit., and C. Thorne 1986 *The Far Eastern War: States and Societies 1941–45*, London, Unwin.

coupled to the available interventionist Keynesian theories of growth and welfare issued in the imputation to the replacement elites of the goal of the pursuit of effective nationstatehood. In respect of the spread of exchanges between First and Third World states a particular sphere of activity came to be picked out: that is, the concern with development.

If we consider an ideal-typical exchange in respect of development between two states then we can note the following features: (a) it establishes some sort of exchange between states in respect of securing planned change in one state with the assistance of another; (b) it identifies a complex spread of changes; (c) it typically demands the involvement of a variety of groups, and is sustained through a variety of institutional channels; (d) it is also clear that it is an asymmetrical exchange in terms of the powers of the states involved. The familiar sphere of talk about development is thus institutionally extensive as there are many groups, agencies and organizations involved in theorizing, commentating and acting in regard to development. The talk is also intellectually-ideologically extensive as the discourse of development comprises a stock of ideas that informs the praxis of many groups. The talk is also popular as it is clear that technical ideas have become part and parcel of the routine experience of many people in both Third and First Worlds.

The goal of the pursuit of effective nationstatehood has been affirmed by the participants in the development game and has shaped post-Second World War development theorizing. It has also nominally shaped the practical actions of the key players: (a) the international agencies such as the IMF, World Bank and UN; (b) the state-regimes in the Third World with their particular linkages and agendas; and (c) the state-regimes in the First World with their ODA programmes. It might be taken to have shaped rather more directly (that is, honestly) the thinking of charities and NGOs. However, it is from this last-noted group coupled to analogous groupings within recipient countries that doubts have been raised as to the plausibility and appropriateness of the generally taken-for-granted goal.

In recent years various criticisms have been advanced ranging from culture-critical suggestions of subtle error in the generally accepted goal of development, often expressed in terms of Eurocentrism, through to policy analytical criticism of state/institutional preferences for projects reflecting the needs of the donors, often expressed in debates about aid being wrongly focused on infrastructure or otherwise tied to the donors, and finally through to political agent suggestions of collusion and corruption in the whole development game such that the interests of the rich in the metropoles and the corrupt elites in the periphery are served at the expense of the poor. The debates generated within these lines of reflection have been extensive.[32] It is also the case that they tend to be somewhat separate. However, in recent years it is safe to say that the more critical material has grown in influence.

32 See B. Hettne 1990 *Development Theory and the Three Worlds*, London, Longman, ch. 3.

Chapter Summary

The European capitalist system expanded from the fifteenth century and slowly reconstructed the non-European societies it contacted. The colonial episode can be taken to have structural, institutional and cultural legacies which continue to shape the thought and action of the present. The ways in which the non-European world was understood by European traders, missionaries, settlers and so on varied. In the period of the Enlightenment non-Europeans are taken to represent innocence and we have ideas of the noble savage. However, as the European empires expand the imagery shifts and we have ideas of uncivilized savages. In the period of formal colonialism the European ruling elites adopt a posture of taking responsibility for civilizing the less advanced peoples and this modulates into an early acknowledgement of a responsibility to organize development for eventual independence. The colonial powers adopted different schemes and most advanced slowly until the Second World War undermined the European empires and ushered in the phase of decolonization.

9

Decolonization, Cold War and the Construction of Modernization Theory

Overview of Early Post-war Theories of Development

In the years following the Second World War a series of factors occasioned the production of a theory of economic growth which was applicable to the Third World. The crucial factors included political pressure flowing from the desire of the USA to order the post-war world, the interests of capitalist business in maintaining access to the territories of the Third World, nationalist developmentalism amongst replacement elites and the example of the Marshall Plan in Europe. However, in time, as the role of the USA within the post-war global system increased, the early material of growth theory was superseded by the more robust formulations of modernization theory.

Background to Growth Theory

It is possible to identify four elements in the background to growth theory: (a) the intellectual influence of the work of the economist John Maynard Keynes; (b) the political agenda of the USA as it moves to a position of dominance in the short twentieth century;[1] (c) the Marshall Aid programme and the reconstruction of Western Europe; and (d) the demands of nationalist developmentalism which was the ideology of the emergent new nations (see figure 10).

The Keynesian revolution

There are three general elements in the overall Keynesian revolution in economic theorizing which came to underpin intellectually the prosperity of the post-Second World War period.[2] The first was the inter-war experience of the Great Depression which was an event which could not happen according to orthodox neo-classical economics which insisted that if the marketplace was left to its own devices then all would be well in the long run. The second element was the impact upon intellectual and political opinion of the apparent success of the planned economy of the USSR. In the inter-war period the USSR embarked upon a series of large-scale economic development projects whose success was in marked contrast to the failures of economic liberalism in the West. And the third element was the radical overhaul of technical economic argument effected by Keynes.

In the 1930s the economic orthodoxy rested upon the work of the equilibrium theorists, men such as W. S. Jevons, Alfred Marshall, Léon Walras and Vilfredo Pareto who argued that the free market left to its own devices would spontaneously order society in such a fashion as to maximize human well-being.[3] Against the sanguine view of the orthodoxy, Keynes showed that it was possible for economies to go into depression equilibrium where the various factors of production were not used to achieve optimum economic configurations. And the question of theory and policy thereafter concern the precise conditions which will ensure full employment. The answers made to the question by Keynes opened the way for a new idea of the role of the government in managing the economy.

In general, the *laissez-faire* scheme had been attacked on three points: (a) the persistence of unemployment; (b) the misuse of available resources; and (c) the trend towards monopoly firms within the economy. The alternative Keynesian view suggested that if the level of total expenditure falls below that which is necessary to sustain full employment, then the shortfall should

1   E. Hobsbawm 1994 *Age of Extremes: The Short Twentieth Century, 1914–1991*, London, Michael Joseph.
2   See ibid. chs. 3, 9.
3   C. Napoleoni 1972 *Economic Thought of the Twentieth Century*, London, Martin Robertson.

Figure 10   Growth theory

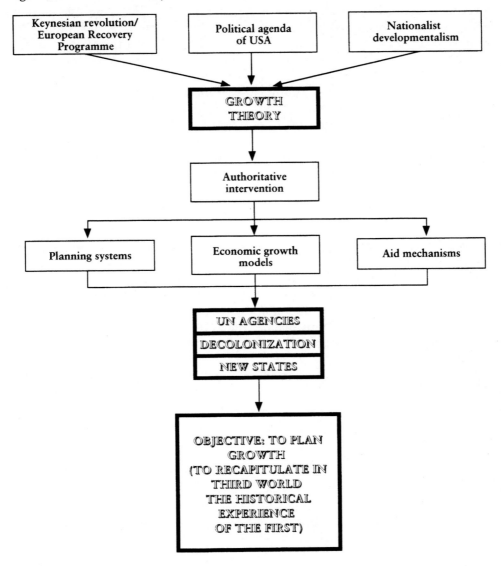

be made up by government spending. The proposal rests in turn on the notions of deficit financing and the multiplier. Keynes argued that government borrowing to finance expenditures was justified as each unit of expenditure would have its beneficial effect multiplied as economic activity in general was encouraged and eventually the higher levels of economic activity would generate higher tax returns and the government's deficit could be removed and debts repaid. Overall, the role for the government is sharply altered in line with revisions to the established conception of the market.

It is clear that the establishment of the first centrally planned economy in the USSR and the Great Depression of the 1930s had a profound impact upon the work of Keynes who thereafter managed to plot a middle course through the alternatives of anarchic *laissez-faire* market capitalism and the authoritarian state intervention of the Second World of official socialism.[4] Keynes establishes three key policy-analytic points in the light of the experience of economic depression and the state planning of the USSR and these are the notions of depression equilibrium, deficit finance and the multiplier. Overall, the Keynesian analysis makes clear that state planning to secure full employment is compatible with the political concerns of liberalism for the freedom of the individual. With Keynes the economic orthodoxy was very sharply overhauled,[5] resulting in a style of government regulation that was taken to have tamed the system's periodic crises.[6]

The political agenda of the USA

The initial set of political factors which gave shape to the subsequent efforts to make use of Keynesian work in guiding policy with regard to development revolve around the determination of the USA to order the post-war world in a fashion acceptable to the demands of international business, in particular its US-based components. A crucial concern was for access to those territories which had been protected behind colonial preference systems within trading blocs in order to construct a liberal global trading system.

It has been argued that three issues dominated US thinking in the period 1943–5: 'First was the . . . disintegration of the pre-war social systems and the growth of revolutionary movements and political upheaval everywhere in the world. Next was the problem of the Soviet Union . . . Finally there was the issue of Great Britain, invariably set in the context of the future of the world economy and its present and future relationship to the US'.[7] Once the Americans became involved in the war they began to establish a series of economic war aims. This task fell to the Department of State under Cordell Hull, a disciple of President Woodrow Wilson's *laissez-faire* liberalism and a man marked (as was Keynes) by the experience of the Great Depression. Hull's conclusions in respect of ordering the global system centred on the pursuit of an open international trading system centred on the USA.

The two major elements in US thinking were finance and trade. The discussion of finance was initiated in 1942 with a British submission prepared

4   See R. V. Eagly ed. 1968 *Events, Ideology and Economic Theory*, Detroit, Wayne State University Press.
5   See J. Robinson 1962 *Economic Philosophy*, Harmondsworth, Penguin; P. Ormerod 1994 *The Death of Economics*, London, Faber.
6   Hobsbawm 1994 op. cit. ch. 9.
7   G. Kolko 1968 *The Politics of War: US Foreign Policy 1943–45*, New York, Vintage, p. 4.

by Keynes which envisaged the growth of world trade with an international fund to smooth over budget deficits and channel investment money into development projects. The USA replied to the proposal with the White Plan (named after Harry White, a senior member of the US Treasury) and debate thereafter revolved around the control of the proposed institutions and the ground-rules of their operation. The debate continued until the Bretton Woods conference of July 1944 and the final compromise established the US view of the post-war world economy as one run by business on business principles. The Bretton Woods conference led to the establishment of the International Monetary Fund (IMF) and the International Bank for Reconstruction and Development (IBRD, or World Bank). A little later a body to regulate trading was proposed which was to have been known as the International Trade Organization (ITO) but this was not successful and eventually the GATT (General Agreement on Tariffs and Trade) was established.[8] These institutions were thereafter the key vehicles in ordering the economic, social and political development of the First World in the post-war period, and they were the starting point for work in respect of Third World development. The general way in which the USA was later to approach matters of development is also clear and critics have argued that America's 'foreign policy at the end of World War Two necessitated the ability and desire to employ loans, credits and investments everywhere to create a world economic order to its own desires'.[9]

The European Recovery Plan

The interventionist nature of US policy at this time means that the European Recovery Programme encapsulates a wealth of tensions. At the outset it is quite clear that 'the most dramatic . . . contribution to recovery was the announcement in the summer of 1947 . . . of the so called Marshall Plan'.[10] The aid programme provided a source of credit to war-damaged Europe which allowed the reconstruction to begin. Yet the justification of the programme in the USA focused on the fear of communism. A contemporary commentator remarked that self-interest 'rather than charity inspired the ERP'[11] and went on to record that 'frightened by the onward movement of communism . . . the American people rallied to the support of the Marshall Plan . . . Americans realised also that economic recovery in Western Europe

---

8   See A. Harrison 1967 *The Framework of Economic Activity*, London, Macmillan, ch. 3, pp. 82–6, for a discussion of these Keynesian-inspired institutions. See also, for more detailed discussions, W. M. Scammel 1980 *The International Economy Since 1945*, London, Macmillan, ch. 2. On this matter, the recent 1994 completion of the GATT Uruguay Round marks a further advance towards the original goals.

9   Kolko 1968 op. cit. p. 624.

10   M. M. Postan 1967 *An Economic History of Western Europe 1945–1964*, London, Methuen, p. 14.

11   S. Harris 1948 *The European Recovery Programme*, London, Harper and Row, p. 3.

would rebound favourably on the American economy'.[12] The mixture of political and economic concerns is quite clear and they informed the overall approach of the USA to the recovery of Europe.

The major formal political event of the period was the promulgation of the Truman Doctrine in March 1947. The essence of the doctrine was that political change not agreed by the USA was to be blocked and in this 'Truman spoke for the bulk of American conservatives and allied himself with reaction around the globe'.[13] The implementation of the Marshall Plan within Europe was informed by this political stance and the powers were used to discourage social reform. An American critic noted that 'the effect of our economic intervention in Europe has been not only to oust communists from the governments but to put the socialists out or decrease their influence'.[14]

In terms of the economics, and apart from the business of self-interest, what is novel is that 'the Truman Doctrine contained a concept of international aid based on the need to promote a suitable rate of growth in the receiving countries, a prototype thus of modern development aid'.[15] That growth could be described theoretically and actually promoted as a matter of policy were intellectual and policy analytic novelties. Paul Streeten suggests that it was the dramatic recovery of Europe's economy that lent credence to the notion that deliberate intervention in an economic system to raise its level of activity was possible.[16]

Nationalist developmentalism

The intellectual mainstream of development theory derives from the historical episode of the dissolution of the mainly European system of formal colonial territories. At this particular time a series of factors came together, including the logic of the capitalist system, available theory and nationalist rhetoric. Any review of the historical expansion of the capitalist system reveals a system-requirement of access to various territories for resources, trade and markets. In the colonial period this access was secured via the machineries of the colonial regime. With the collapse of the colonial system a replacement political form was needed. The available idea was that of the nationstate, which was part and parcel of the nationalists' ideology of independence and taken for granted within contemporary social theory. It is clear that other political forms were available in principle and one could cite UN trusteeship, continued linkages with the relevant colonial power and

12   Ibid.
13   D. F. Flemming 1961 *The Cold War and Its Origins*, New York, Doubleday, p. 447. On the Cold War see also M. Walker 1993 *The Cold War and the Making of the Modern World*, London, Fourth Estate.
14   Ibid. p. 501.
15   G. Zeylstra 1977 *Aid or Development*, Leiden, A. W. Sijthoff, p. 31.
16   P. Streeten 1972 *The Frontiers of Development Studies*, London, Macmillan, ch. 16.

various returns to the pre-colonial situation. However, none of these were acceptable to the aspirant power-holders within the countries which were forming within the territories of the dissolving colonial territories. The rhetoric of nationalist developmentalism which had been used by local leaders in pursuit of independence affirmed the model of independent nationstatehood which was to be the vehicle of the achievement not merely of political freedom for the elite but also growth and welfare for the masses.

It is clear that for the new replacement elites in the Third World a set of demands coincide: the demands of the global capitalist system, the demands of their own people which flow from the rhetoric deployed by nationalists in their pursuit of independence, and the intellectual demands of available theory. The goal of the pursuit of effective nationstatehood is embraced by the new elite. On this view, ruling elites will face the complex task of building new nationstates. They must rapidly engender sentiments of political and cultural coherence because citizens must live the experience of membership of a single nation, a single community. The elite must secure political and social stability and in place of colonial arrangements there must be new patterns of authority and new political mechanisms to absorb and resolve inter-group conflicts. Finally, the new elite must pursue economic development as this is the base line of claims to legitimacy.

The Logic of Authoritative Intervention

Out of the melange of theoretical possibility, political and economic necessity, successful European examples and the demands of nationalist developmentalism the theorists of development created an intellectually coherent and politically relevant scheme. An approach to analysing complex change was produced which was both prospective in orientation and practical in intention. It was essentially an ideology of authoritative intervention oriented to national development. The theory involved claims in respect of the fundamental nature of economic growth, the effective role of state planning and the rationale of aid transfers.

Authoritative intervention

Intervention in a social system might be understood as deliberate action whose objective is to bring about a particular change in some set of circumstances and thereby achieve a preferred state of affairs. There are three basic aspects of this approach: (a) the supposition that there is something to be acted upon, an object; (b) the expectation that it will respond and do so in a predictable fashion; and (c) the idea that the intervention is accomplished by an actor in a precise manner according to a clear set of expectations; that is, authoritatively and not randomly or accidentally.

It is clear that for the intervention to be successful it must be a knowing intervention that is in the right place, at the right time and of the right kind. It is clear that authoritative intervention demands a descriptive general theory of the social world. This intellectual strategy can be called policy science and the term designates the assumed product of mainstream social science such that in response to the question 'why have a social science' the answer is given that 'it will enable humankind to control their social environment'.[17] An analytical strategy centred on authoritative intervention requires a legitimating intellectual core, and thereafter it needs organizing and implementing.

Growth theory, development planning and aid

In the early work on Third World development, intervention was legitimated by being based upon economic growth theory, and these were in turn extensions made to the work of Keynes. Roy Harrod[18] 'established growth economics as a going concern on the foundations of Keynes' saving investment theory'.[19] Harrod's famous essay[20] focuses on 'the necessary conditions for equilibrium between aggregate saving and investment in a dynamic economy'.[21] The basic proposition is that Ga=s/v, where 'Ga' is the actual rate of growth of national income, 's' is the marginal propensity to save, and 'v' is the marginal capital–output ratio. This fundamental relation can define a growth path if it is linked to a statement of the entrepreneur's estimations of future trends. The notion of warranted growth ('Gw') is introduced to fulfill the Keynesian role of the entrepreneur. The entrepreneur invests and investment today depends upon estimation of tomorrow's possibilities. If the investor is to be reassured that the reading of the economy is correct, then Ga will have to be equal to Gw. In addition to Ga and Gw, Harrod has 'Gn' which is the natural rate of growth flowing from given rises in population where more people imply more production.

If all these are put together we have the first major conclusion to issue from Harrod's work: 'If, by coincidence the actual rate of growth equalled the warranted rate, which itself equalled the rate of growth of the labour force, then steady growth at full employment would occur'.[22] The second conclusion Harrod makes is that such a state of affairs is unlikely to come about and even if it did it would be unstable. In the notation of the economists what has to happen for there to be steady growth of the system is that Ga=Gw=Gn. If the equation has the determinants of the various elements inserted then the problem becomes clear. The elements that determine

17   B. Fay 1975 *Social Theory and Political Practice*, London, Allen and Unwin, p. 19.
18   The American economist E. D. Domar independently offered similar ideas.
19   K. Kurihara 1968 'The Dynamic Impact of History on Keynesian Theory' in Eagly op. cit. p. 137.
20   R. Harrod 1939 'An Essay in Dynamic Theory', *Economic Journal*, 49.
21   H. Jones 1975 *An Introduction to Modern Theories of Economic Growth*, London, Nelson, p. 44.
22   Ibid. p. 53.

the three growth rates are independently set and only an accident will bring them into the relation demanded by steady growth at full employment. This is the 'First Harrod Problem' and is a step towards his aim of showing that the system tends to stagnate. Apart from the inherent pessimism, this view clearly places a huge burden upon planning agencies for when they intervene they do so in a system that is not disposed to assist them. The 'Second Harrod Problem' is the problem of stability. If Ga diverges from Gw then within limits it is likely to carry on doing so. Once the growth path is lost the rational corrective behaviour of the entrepreneur is such that things get worse not better. Overall, three things are clear: 'the possibility of steady growth at full employment . . . the improbability of steady growth at full employment . . . the instability of the warranted rate of growth'.[23]

Harrod's work does identify a long-term stable growth path but suggests that it would be difficult to find and difficult to follow. In an economic theory underpinning an approach to development predicated upon the notion of authoritative intervention, the pessimism came to be seen as rather awkward. However, Harrod's work was widely used and remained serviceable in its legitimating role. As an approach within development studies the theory of growth was elaborated from the 1940s to the mid-1950s when it was absorbed into modernization theory.

Having looked at the legitimation of intervention it is appropriate to turn to its organization; that is, to ideas of planning. The conceptual relation is in outline straightforward but the notion of planned intervention has been contentious throughout the short twentieth century. The familiar debate about economic planning begins with the Austrian economist Ludwig von Mises who reacted against the rise of arguments for socialism and the example of the USSR and argued in the 1920s that a planned economy could not work rationally. The gist of his argument was that if the job of an economic system was to allocate scarce resources between competing ends then this required indices of scarcity which had to be established by allowing the free market to determine prices. An economy with no free market could not provide any index of scarcity and therefore could not rationally allocate scarce resources. Unfortunately for von Mises it was possible to answer his argument by manipulating the formal machineries of neo-classical economics so as to abolish the need for a market to determine indices of scarcity. And throughout the 1920s and 1930s debate centred on whether, and if so how, the theoretical possibility of planning could actually be translated into practice. It is not necessary to pursue the detail of these debates as for our purposes; it is enough to note that when in the post-Second World War period a demand arose for a planning system the notion was already well known.[24]

It was real-world changes that called planning machineries into being. A

23 Ibid. p. 59.
24 See Napoleoni 1972 op. cit.

contributory factor in the rise of the preoccupation with growth was the reconstruction of capitalism that was evident in the 1920s and 1930s, specifically the emergence of monopoly forms of enterprises and a recasting of the relationship of state and industry. It can be said that there was nothing new about the partnership between capital and state but what was novel was its respectability.[25] The changes were evident in the 1930s and were extensively developed in the wartime period. When it came to dismantling war economies the legislative, institutional and psychological requirements of a Keynesian-managed economy were already in place. In brief, the work of Keynes legitimated a reworking of the public view of the relationship of state and industry.[26]

The implementation of intervention takes a series of forms and they have typically revolved around aid programmes. We can understand aid generically to be piecemeal interventions in the system having the aim of contriving a preferred state of affairs. Aid can take the form of single projects, sets of related projects, programmes, emergency one-off exercises, and so on.[27] Two early sources of interest in aid-giving can be identified. In the first, aid is given to allies, as exemplified by the Marshall Plan, and subsequently given to other allies, particularly in Asia, as political need dictates. In the shift to the Asian sphere the perceived task for aid is broadened and the notion of development comes to the fore. There are various reasons for this and chief amongst them are the changed nature of the recipients (economies and societies unlike those of Europe) and Cold War-fuelled competition between the USA and the USSR as aid-donors for influence amongst the newly emerged non-aligned group. The second source of interest in aid-giving flows from the process of withdrawal from empire. In the case of Asia withdrawal was understood as marking the end of any responsibilities on the part of the ex-colonial power for its ex-colony. In the case of withdrawal from Africa there was an assumption of continuing assistance in the form of aid. In this process aid-giving is increasingly understood in non-context-specific terms and the idea that the rich have a responsibility to aid the poor comes to be taken for granted.

On this last noted point it should be added that over the post-Second World War period the general concern of the international community for the business of development grew. As the issue moved up the agenda of newly created international bodies such as the UN the flow of aid from various donors to the multilateral agencies grew along with bilateral aid programmes. In this context a series of unforeseen developments came to pass. The flow of military aid became quite large. The practice of tying aid

---

25   H. Brookfield 1975 *Interdependent Development*, London, Methuen, p. 25.

26   None of this, let us note, went unchallenged. In the USA and in the UK especially (and also in mainland Europe) there was strong opposition to the notions of planning. In 1944 Friedrich von Hayek published a critical text entitled *The Road to Serfdom*: Hayek and his views came back into fashion in the Anglo-Saxon world in the 1980s epoch of the 'New Right'.

27   Zeylstra 1977 op. cit. discusses an ideal-type of aid; see pp. 15–19.

to purchases in the donor country grew. The administrative apparatus of development grew. The whole business became very contentious with critics on the metropolitan political right arguing that the whole endeavour was unnecessary as economic growth would happen when the conditions in the global marketplace were suitable, whilst critics on the metropolitan left suggested that far from the monies being wasted they were both hugely important and clearly insufficient to the task at hand. In more recent years critics have tended to add two further lines of commentary, first in respect of the lack of any very obviously positive results from all these efforts and secondly the suggestion that as the business of aid giving becomes lodged within the ambit of established institutional networks the whole business loses any very obvious connection with its original concerns and becomes a self-perpetuating activity which primarily serves the needs of those involved.[28]

The Work of Arthur Lewis

The historical context and intellectual milieu within which growth theory was constructed fed into to the actual use of the theory. The work was deployed to provide practical advice to planning agencies in respect of the pursuit of economic growth. Arthur Lewis made a series of early and influential contributions: (a) contributions to the 1951 UN report *Measures for the Economic Development of Underdeveloped Countries*; (b) the essay *Economic Development with Unlimited Supplies of Labour*; and (c) the monograph *The Theory of Economic Growth*.[29]

Measures for economic development

The United Nations report was written by a group of experts who were invited to prepare 'a report on unemployment and underemployment . . . [in underdeveloped countries], and the national and international measures required to reduce such unemployment and underemployment'.[30] The authors began by redefining their task as concerned with 'economic development rather than . . . unemployment',[31] and their treatment involves six major elements.

First, they consider the preconditions for progress. The authors see the establishment of 'proper cultural orientations' as a necessary condition of growth. Then, secondly, the central role of the state is acknowledged. The

28 See G. Hancock 1989, *Lords of Poverty*, London, Macmillan.
29 On Lewis, see G. Meier and D. Seers eds. 1984 *Pioneers in Development*, Oxford University Press.
30 United Nations 1951 *Measures for the Economic Development of Underdeveloped Countries*, p. 9.
31 Ibid.

argument here rests upon the analogy of the government of the UDCs facing development and the governments of the DCs facing depression.

Thirdly, they treat technical matters. In this case domestic saving is discussed and a tacit definition of their assumed goal is offered. In DCs they observe a ten per cent of national income rate of capital formation, whereas in the UDCs this rate is only five per cent. A key problem is thus how to raise the rate of capital formation.

In their fourth point, where they treat the notion of planning, it is made clear that the role of the expert is crucial. They consider neo-classical economics adequate at the micro level when precise data are available, but inadequate at the macro structural level when precise data are not readily available. The authors suggest that it is not possible to offer any general rules governing economic planning: 'those who are responsible must soak themselves in the facts of each particular case and must then use their best judgement as to what will be the most desirable directions of movement'.[32] This is one of the most optimistic sections of the report and the world of *laissez-faire* is left far behind – indeed the authors call for *carte blanche* for the economic planners.

In the fifth point, the authors turn to look at terms of trade. On this they affirm a loose internationalism that is in accord with the style expected of a UN study and, more relevantly, it fits in with the views of the USA on the proper development of post-war trade.

Finally, in point six, they tackle the matter of external sources of capital. Here we see two points of interest. First, they answer the question of the extent to which capital is needed from abroad by seeking to indicate a quantity. This, they grant, is difficult, but important. Then, secondly, with regard to the government's role as provider of infrastructure, they say 'we do not suggest that aid should be given unconditionally . . . This would not be wise. Each grant should be linked to a specific function, and there should be international verification that the funds are used only for the purposes for which they have been granted'.[33] Thus aid is targeted and monitored according to wise prescriptions. This is what we would expect to find. It is the practical expression of a policy science, and it is also entirely typical of the mode of argument of UN specialist commissions with their concern to establish what J. K. Galbraith will later generically tag as 'institutional truths' which are the sets of semi-formal ideas to which organizations give assent and which express political-bureaucratic compromises amongst competing groups.

Unlimited supplies of labour

The essay *Economic Development with Unlimited Supplies of Labour*, published in 1954, marked an explicit recovery of the legacy of the classical

32   Ibid. p. 50.
33   Ibid. p. 85.

political-economists of the nineteenth century with its central concern for the conditions of long-run growth. Lewis looked at the nature of the typical underdeveloped country and identified two sectors: the one was capitalistic and the other traditional. The business of economic development could be theoretically described in terms of the relationship of the two sectors over time. In this dualistic model the capitalist sector is dynamic and reinvests the profits it generates and thereby acts to move the social system forward whereas the traditional system of subsistence agriculture does not generate investable profits but acts only to sustain its current condition. The expansion of the capitalist sector can proceed on the basis of drawing in labour from the subsistence sector and this will allow long-run growth. The process of long-run growth will continue in this fashion until the surplus labour of the traditional sector has all been absorbed. At this point the modern sector will both dominate the economy and be self-sustaining.[34]

It should be pointed out that the work of Lewis acted to reintroduce many of the concerns for long-term growth and its sectoral or class impact which were typical of classical political-economics.[35] It is also clear that Lewis had correctly seen that the business of analysing the economies of the underdeveloped countries demanded analytical machineries which were quite different from the machineries available within the framework of the neo-classical economics of self-regulating markets.[36]

Economic growth

Lewis worked on the 1951 UN report which was one of the earliest attempts to make sense of the matter of Third World development. However, we can pursue the matter of the export of Keynes a little further in a more academic context by looking at Lewis's *The Theory of Economic Growth* which was published in 1955 and which offers a more theoretical statement of his position.

Lewis declares in the book's preface that he is not presenting original ideas but offering a framework for studying economic development. The level of enquiry is general. Lewis identifies three proximate causes of growth and development. These are, first, the 'effort to economise', which Lewis uses to characterize the DCs. Included within it or as illustrations of it we find listed: experimentation; risk-taking; mobility; and specialization. We can take this as fairly straightforwardly descriptive of the industrial capitalist world and it is liable to criticisms of oversimplification, aggregation and value-bias. The second proximate cause is the increase of knowledge and its application. It would seem that this point can be taken as a simple

34 See M. P. Todarao 1982 *Economics for the Developing World*, London, Longman, pp. 209–11.
35 W. J. Barber 1967 *A History of Economic Thought*, Harmondsworth, Penguin, pp. 107–15.
36 The subsequent more descriptive notions of dualism came to be heavily criticized; see H. Brookfield 1975 *Interdependent Development*, London, Methuen, ch. 3.

corollary of the first: thus Ernest Gellner remarks that 'science is the mode of cognition of industrial society'.[37] Finally, we are reminded that growth depends upon increasing the amount of capital, which is a fairly obvious reflection of contemporary Keynesian economic ideas.

From these three elements Lewis follows a procedure of unpacking: thus he shifts ever closer to history and to the real world by asking why these proximate causes operate in some societies more strongly than in others. This is a search for those configurations of institutional and cultural factors which are compatible with the logic of economic development. All the non-economic factors must be consistent with the demands of economic logic. In general we can ask what an environment conducive to growth looks like. At this point the questions are reformulated to focus on the evolutionary aspects of the process. It can be asked how it is that environments change so as to become more or less conducive to economic growth. In this way Lewis links themes within classical political-economy, material drawn from Keynesian-influenced economic growth theory and descriptive historical and social scientific material related to the condition of the underdeveloped countries. In all this he both recalls the concerns of the classical tradition with its focus on the analysis of complex change and anticipates the particular schedule of interests of the approach which came to dominate much of First World development theorizing; that is, modernization theory.

The Construction of Modernization Theory

The background to the construction of modernization theory is suffused with the political concerns of the USA in the late 1950s and early 1960s. The general ethos of the period finds intellectual expression in the social scientific concern with the structural-functionalist analysis of industrial society. The social scientific material can be taken to comprise a package deal which specifies the nature of industrial society, indicates how non-industrial societies might be expected to modernize, argues that capitalism and socialism will converge as the logic of industrialism drives the global system forward, and suggests that the system will produce widespread prosperity with a consequent diminution of conflict-occasioned ideological debates. The background to the production of the theory of modernization can be said to have three elements: bipolarity; containment; and aid-donor competition (see figure 11).

International bipolarity, containment and aid-donor competition

Hobsbawm analyses the short twentieth century in terms of the eclipse of the optimistic project of the European Enlightenment.[38] There are two

37   E. Gellner 1964 *Thought and Change*, p. 179.
38   E. Hobsbawm 1994 *Age of Extremes: The Short Twentieth Century, 1914–1991*, London, Michael Joseph.

Figure 11   Modernization theory

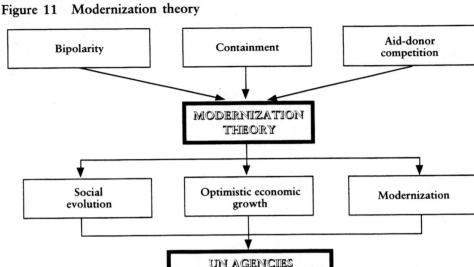

elements to the analysis. The major theme deals with a series of disasters which overtook the Europeans and these included war, revolution, depression and, after a brief economic and social golden age, a return to drift and unclarity. The minor theme deals with the shift in power within the global system of industrial capitalism away from Europe and towards the USA.

The changing nature of power relationships within the capitalist global system is a familiar issue for economic and political historians. The standard story involves an opening phase centred on the rise to global prominence of the UK in the nineteenth century followed by the rise of competitors in the USA, Germany and Japan. The Great War sees the Europeans locked in conflict while the Americans (and the Japanese) advance. In the period following the Great War the centre of the capitalist world economy is the USA.

In the post-Second World War period the European powers are finally eclipsed. The effective removal of the major colonial economic blocks with their centres in Paris, Amsterdam and London leaves the USA as the un-challenged leader of what comes to be called the Free World, or the West. However, as the post-Second World War period sees the decline of Euro-pean power and the rise to pre-eminence of the USA it also sees the parallel rise of the USSR. The dominance of the USA and the USSR within the international system was understood in terms of the notion of bipolarity.

The USA prepared for its global role as the core power of the liberal capitalist system and the machineries of the Bretton Woods system of inter-national economics were predicated upon the notion of open liberal trade.[39] The Bretton Woods system along with the dominant role of the USA was successful. Hobsbawm notes that the period from 1945 to 1970 was in ret-rospect an economic golden age,[40] notwithstanding that no one can quite explain why it all happened.[41] However, for present purposes we can set these debates aside. It is enough to record the division of Europe into an eastern bloc and a western bloc. It was this Cold War situation which coloured the thinking of American policy-makers, political agents and scholars.[42]

The notion of containment expressed the resolution of the USA to halt the spread of communism. The concern of the USA was initially focused on Europe in the wake of wartime upheaval. In particular the occupation of eastern Europe by the USSR and the activities of the left in western Europe. Subsequently, the attention of the USA extended to the Third World.

In the period of the 1950s when the first work that was to issue in modernization theory was undertaken, the model of the modern was not merely the image of the USA writ large, but an image suffused with the demands of the 'patriotic imperative'.[43] It was widely supposed that it was the business of the USA to reconstruct the world in its own image. The ideological position typical of American thinking equated: (a) the interests of the USA; (b) functioning liberal market economies; (c) resistance to communism; and (d) the future prosperity of the world. This doctrinal package was labelled the 'Free World'. The mere existence of the USSR was a challenge and it seemed within the logic of this ideology that peace and stability required that the USA adopt the role of protector of the Free World. It was President Harry S. Truman's March 1947 address to the Congress that officially launched the doctrine of containment. The US government was attempting to proscribe any change – political, social, or economic – to which it had not given its assent.

---

39   G. Kolko 1968 *The Politics of War: US Foreign Policy 1943–45*, New York, Vintage.
40   Hobsbawm 1994 op. cit.
41   P. Krugman 1994 *Peddling Prosperity: Economic Sense and Nonsense in an Age of Diminished Expectations*, New York, Norton, speaks of the post-war 'magic economy' which arrived unexpectedly and then went away equally unexpectedly.•
42   In substantive vein, see T. Spybey 1992 *Social Change, Development and Dependency*, Cambridge, Polity, ch. 7.
43   D. Caute 1978 *The Great Fear: The Anti-Communist Purges Under Truman and Eisenhower*, London, Secker and Warburg, p. 21.

The third element in the background to modernization theory involves aid-donor competition. In the history of aid-giving it is possible to distinguish between two broad phases.[44] At first aid was internally oriented and concerned with the reconstruction of Europe. In the second phase however the attention of First World theorists was outwardly oriented and concerned with development in the Third World. The key events which marked the change of focus were the Bandung Conference of 1955 when a group of newly independent countries founded the influential non-aligned movement, and a few years later the entry onto the aid-giving scene of the USSR. Overall, this is the period during which modernization theory was constructed.

In the early post-war years the USSR regarded the world as split into hostile camps and any suggestion of non-alignment was viewed with suspicion. However with Stalin's death in 1953 there was a relaxation in that stance which coincided with a thaw in the Cold War. The first sign of this was the pledge by the USSR of one million dollars to a UN aid programme. In 1956 Nikita Khrushchev announced that the USSR was now willing to offer the underdeveloped countries development aid. This offer saw practical expression when in the wake of the USA's withdrawal of financial support for President Nasser's Aswan High Dam (in Egypt) the USSR stepped in with aid.

As a consequence of these events there opened up an area of competition between the super-powers. The competitive aid-giving took the form of offers of socialism on the one hand and membership of the Free World on the other. In the USA the latter scheme was presented within the ambit of development studies as modernization theory. A recent discussion of the impact of the competition of the USA and the USSR in the Third World indicates that extensive disruption has been caused. In respect of the activities of the Americans it is possible to identify a series of overt and covert interventions within the Third World which have had a catastrophic impact.[45] In general, where we looked earlier at the crystallization of Keynesian-derived growth theory within the context of decolonization, here we look at the construction of modernization theory within the context of bipolar competition between super-powers.

The Logic of Modernization Theory

In the process of the construction of modernization theory there were two major areas of intellectual resources available to the theorists and these were the work of the economists who confront the problems attendant upon the scale and complexity of the macro-economics of growth and the work of the broad spread of social scientists who concerned themselves in one way or another with the problem of analysing industrial society.

44   J. White 1973 *The Politics of Foreign Aid*, London, Bodley Head.
45   F. Halliday 1989 *Cold War, Third World*, London, Radius.

The economics of modernization

The debate in respect of the possibilities of stable growth can be seen as an element in the wider debate around the implications of the work of Keynes for economics in general. In this debate two tendencies can be identified. First, the 'new Cambridge school' in the UK which seems to have taken Keynes to have reinvented political-economy. Second, the continued neo-classical line promoted by scholars at Cambridge, Massachusetts, which takes Keynes to be assimilable to the neo-classical line where economics is taken to be a matter of the construction of formal economic-analytic calculi. Overall, the hesitant rediscovery of political-economy made by the new Cambridge school is echoed and elaborated by later theorists of development whilst the work of Keynes is simultaneously absorbed into a revivified neo-classical orthodoxy.[46] Indeed in the 1980s the anti-Keynesian economic liberalism of the New Right attained a measure of fashionable acceptance in parts of the First World.

The history of technical growth economics can be characterized as a sustained attempt to weaken the unpalatable implications of Roy Harrod's work,[47] and in this restricted sphere 'growth theory quickly became highly elaborated and often esoteric'.[48] In 1956 Solow presents a revised model of economic growth in which the uncomfortable elements of Harrod's work are simply removed and no longer is the growth path difficult to find and hard to keep to but on the contrary it is easy to find and thereafter self-sustaining.[49] In the practical political context of aid-donor competition this is a much more attractive position. A related series of revisions are made and models of the growth process are made more sophisticated by using material from 'theories dealing with the processes of social and institutional change'.[50] Overall the models became more complex and less narrowly economic and the distinction between economic growth theories and theories of social change grew increasingly blurred.

The problem of social change and modernization

Theories of social change constitute the second area of substantive interest that carries over from the earlier discussions of growth theory and here we can trace the emancipation of the broad range of the social sciences from their status as under-labourers to economics. With regard to the origins of modernization theory commentators are clear that 'the idea of modernisation

46   P. Ormerod 1994 *The Death of Economics*, London, Faber, ch. 3.
47   H. Jones 1975 *An Introduction to Modern Theories of Economic Growth*, London, Nelson, p. 53.
48   H. Brookfield 1975 *Interdependent Development*, London, Methuen, p. 30.
49   R. Solow 1956 'A Contribution to the Theory of Economic Growth', *Quarterly Journal of Economics*, 70.
50   R. F. Mikesell 1968 *The Economics of Foreign Aid*, London, Weidenfeld, p. 32.

is primarily an American idea, developed by American social scientists in the period after the Second World War and reaching the height of its popularity in the middle years of the 1960s'.[51] The period saw an attitude of complacency towards American society which had its counterpart in social theory when a mixture of structural-functionalism, social psychology and empirical survey analysis was deployed to elucidate the nature of industrial society and it was claimed that all societies were 'converging towards a common destination dictated by the technical and organisational imperatives of advanced industrialisation'.[52] The fate of the Third World was one of disintegration and reformation in line with this trend. All this can be read in the light of American intellectual traditions and 'in such a way contemporary history was assimilated to the foreshortened historical understanding in American social thought so that the diverse peculiarities of other societies and the worrying features of America itself could always be explained away'.[53] The general ethos of the period finds intellectual expression in the social scientific concern with the structural-functionalist analysis of industrial society. The material gathered under this general approach was very influential within the West and it may be said to have attained for a brief period in the 1950s and early 1960s the status of an unquestioned consensus position.

In producing this approach the work of Talcott Parsons was a key resource. Parsons offered a very complex general theory of social action which comprised four aspects: the analysis of the fundamental logic of social action; the scheme of the pattern variables which govern the orientation of action; the identification of the functional requisites of systems of action which allow the system to be maintained; then finally the idea of equilibrium is introduced as the endpoint to which all systems tend when disturbed. The business of disturbance and restoration of equilibrium generates system learning. The system as a whole can be said to experience differentiation, reintegration and evolution. Parsons then used this general theory of action to analyse existing society. It was argued that the general social system comprised a set of sub-systems which could be dealt with by the various social sciences (economics, sociology, politics and psychology).

It is on the basis of the work on general action theory that the familiar structural-functionalist analysis of industrial society is constructed. What we have is a model of the social world as a self-regulating harmonious whole held together by common values. The approach developed through the post-Second World War period into the modernization, industrialism,

---

51 D. C. Tipps 1976 'Modernisation Theory and the Comparative Study of Societies: A Critical Perspective' in C. E. Black ed. 1976 *Comparative Modernization*, London, Collier, p. 71.
52 G. Hawthorn 1976 *Enlightenment and Despair*, Cambridge University Press, p. 242.
53 Ibid.

convergence and end-of-ideology package. In this essentially ideological celebration of the model of the Free West: (a) modernization was the process whereby the less developed countries would shift from traditional patterns of life to become developed; (b) industrial society was the goal, where society was driven by the demanding logic of industrialism; (c) the logic of industrialism would lead to the convergence of political economic systems (in particular those of East and West); and (d) the achievement of prosperity as in the USA of the 1960s would mean that ideological debate occasioned by conflict in respect of scarce resources would wither away.[54]

Criticisms of Modernization Theory

The whole episode of modernization is characterized by its adherence to dichotomous characterizations of the issue of development.[55] Having conceptualized the whole business in terms of the dichotomy between traditional and modern, the theorists of this school then proceed to attempt to elucidate matters by deploying a further set of dichotomous constructs such as agricultural and industrial, rural and urban, religious and secular, literate and pre-literate, and so on.[56] Yet the terms traditional and modern are merely 'the latest manifestation of a Great Dichotomy between more primitive and more advanced societies which has been a common feature of Western social thought for the past one hundred years'.[57] The following influential typifications have all been offered: Maine's status/contract; Durkheim's mechanical/organic; Tonnies' Gemeinschaft/Gesellschaft; and Weber's traditional/rational.[58] The strategy of argument entails that 'the bridge across the Great Dichotomy between modern and traditional societies is the Grand Process of Modernisation'.[59] Overall, it seems clear that what we have in these schemes of modernization is an attempt to construct a descriptive general policy science which characterizes the process and goal of modernization and identifies specific points of intervention. However, the theory of modernization has been extensively criticized.

54   A fine example of the package is offered by C. Kerr et al. 1973 *Industrialism and Industrial Man*, Harmondsworth, Penguin. For a general rebuttal see A. MacIntyre 1971 *Against the Self-Images of the Age*, London, Duckworth.
55   Brookfield 1975 op. cit. p. 53.
56   See B. Hettne 1990 *Development Theory and the Three Worlds*, London, Longman, ch. 2. See also H. Bernstein 1971 'Modernization Theory and the Sociological Study of Development', *Journal of Development Studies*, 7; H. Bernstein 1979 'Sociology of Underdevelopment Versus Sociology of Development' in D. Lehman ed. *Development Theory*, London, Frank Cass.
57   S. P. Huntington 1976 'The Change to Change: Modernisation, Development and Politics' in C. E. Black ed. op. cit. p. 30.
58   See R. A. Nisbet 1966 *The Sociological Tradition*, New York, Basic Books, ch. 3 which deals with community.
59   Huntington 1976 op. cit.

Criticisms of the models of traditional and modern

We can begin with the attacks that have been made on the two central notions of traditional and modern. The characterizations offered have typically been based on the scheme of pattern variables advanced by Talcott Parsons. In Parsons' work the pattern variables were designed to characterize the ways in which social agents approached social action. However, in the theories of modernization the pattern variables are reworked to offer characterization of the general nature of societies. The five pattern variables offer a way of characterizing the shift from traditional to modern which is taken to be necessary in the process of development. However, the characterizations of both traditional and modern society have been criticized as highly dubious descriptions.

The modern world is thus only restrictedly universalistic as society is fissured by class, ethnic and religious affiliations. The extent of achievement-orientation may also be questioned, as the attitude of the middle-class careerist is not that of either the landed aristocrat or the working-class labourer. The extent of self-orientation may also be questioned because modern society continues to evidence a concern for the community. In a similar fashion, when we turn to the model of the traditional we find that the criticisms have been sharper. The image of traditional society contains flaws which are similar to those indicated for the model of the modern. It is clear that traditional societies do evidence self-orientation, universalism, and concerns for achievement. It is also the case that in addition to the type of descriptive imprecision noted there is an ethnocentric bias insofar as the model of traditional society is presented merely as a collection of ways in which these societies diverge from the model of the modern.[60] If it is now retorted that these are 'ideal-typical' characterizations (and thus inevitably problematical in concrete application), then we can say that as heuristic devices they are low grade because of their imprecision, and that their manner of construction is not satisfactory.

The theoretical objection in respect of the strategy of concept construction used by the theorists of modernization is to the way in which the category of traditional is simply defined negatively in relation to the modern. The procedure of the modernization theorists has been to define first the modern; the non-modern or traditional is what is left over. The category of 'traditional' is a residual category. It is clear that residual categories are beset with problems. If we begin by taking note that the modernization theorists aspire to produce a policy science – which understands knowledge of the social as being the same as knowledge of the natural – then it is clear that the fundamental concepts they use must (on their own arguments) stand in some clear relationship to the facts, to the concept's empirical

60 See A. G. Frank 1969 'Sociology of Underdevelopment and Underdevelopment of Sociology' in idem *Latin America: Underdevelopment or Revolution*, New York, Monthly Review Press.

referents. We can agree that the category of the modern, even if the characterizations produced are faulty, does at least stand in some sort of clear and direct relationship to the material circumstances it would grasp; and even, to go one step further, if we note that abstracting and generalizing are faulty procedures we can nonetheless grant that with the modern the procedure is at least minimally plausible. This is not so with the category of the traditional. This concept is not made by abstraction and generalization, but by detailing the way in which non-modern societies fail to measure up to the model of the modern. The notion of traditional is thus a residual category and dichotomies 'which combine positive concepts and residual ones . . . are highly dangerous analytically'.[61] It is from this fundamental incoherence that the intellectual problems of modernization theory flow. It is little wonder that their characterizations of traditional society were attacked as unconvincing and ethnocentrically biased.

Criticisms of inbuilt bias

If we move on to the issue of bias we can see that it is inherent in the use of residual categories. A dichotomous typification which affirms one category and then identifies the other as a concatenation of non-prime category elements is immediately biased. The notion of the modern within modernization theory is taken as self-evidently given, and the non-modern constitutes just so many deviations from it. In this way a schedule of judgements gets built into the very machineries of analysis.

With modernization theory the bias works in several interesting ways. I will note one: the abolition of the history of Third World countries. Thus A. G. Frank notes of Rostow's stage theory, that the scheme presupposes a primitive starting-point from which the presently developed are taken to have emerged.[62] Frank thinks this reasoning is flawed: 'This entire approach to economic development and cultural change attributes a history to the developed countries but denies all history to the under-developed ones'.[63] The presently developed countries have the history of their emergence whilst the presently underdeveloped have yet to move and consequently have no history. Now clearly this is ludicrous, but what is happening is that classifying the Third World as comprising traditional societies neatly begs the issues in respect of their character. Frank argues that far from the Third World countries having no history, it is precisely the histories they do have that explain their present circumstances. And the history of many involves, crucially, the episode of colonialism and the manner of their insertion into the expanding world economy of First World capitalism. The modernization

---

61   Huntington 1976 op. cit.
62   Frank's work is discussed in ch. 13.
63   Frank 1969 op. cit. p. 40; see also R. I. Rhodes 1968 'The Disguised Conservatism of Evolutionary Development Theory', *Science and Society*, 32.

approach is condemned as theoretically incapable of what on any plausible account would be part of the commonness of enquiry. The formulation traditional/modern is thus skewed or biased in that it rules out consideration of the part played by the developed in creating the circumstances of the underdeveloped.

Walt Rostow's Stages of Economic Growth

The discussion of modernization theory can be concluded by looking at Rostow's *The Stages of Economic Growth* which represents the apogee of modernization theory. Rostow identifies five stages of economic growth and then observes: 'They constitute, in the end, both a theory about economic growth and a more general, if still highly partial, theory about modern history as a whole'.[64] To this he adds that 'the dynamic theory of production ... is their bone structure'.[65] The stages and mechanism combined thus address the issues tackled by Marx; hence the book's subtitle – *A Non-Communist Manifesto* – and Rostow's claim to have replaced Marx. The stages comprise the following five-element sequence.

The initial situation is that of traditional society which Rostow characterizes as 'one whose structure is developed within limited production functions, based on pre-Newtonian science and technology, and on pre-Newtonian attitudes towards the physical world'.[66] It does not mean that the traditional society was wholly static and indeed improvements in agriculture could enhance levels of living. However, the absence of modern science and technology imposed inevitable limits upon such a society. Rostow goes on to characterize this traditional society in terms of its agricultural base, clan-based polity, and fatalistic mentality.

The second stage of the process has to establish the pre-conditions for take-off into self-sustained growth. The second stage is exemplified by western Europe in the late seventeenth and early eighteenth centuries as medieval society disintegrates, modern science grows and trade develops. In this period the possibilities for production opened up by modern science find acceptance within society and as a consequence the whole slow business of remaking traditional society begins. In contrast to the traditional societies of the Third World, which are dislodged by incursions of external powers, in seventeenth-century Britain reactive nationalism was generated by the wars against the Spanish, Dutch and French. Once the economic and social dynamic had been initiated it was quickly extended to other European states.

In the third stage of take-off economic growth becomes normal. Rostow

---

64   W. W. Rostow 1960 *The Stages of Economic Growth: A Non-Communist Manifesto,* Cambridge University Press, p. 1.
65   Ibid. p. 3.
66   Ibid. p. 4.

argues that the take-off 'is the interval when the old blocks and resistances to steady growth are finally overcome'.[67] Rostow continues by arguing that the 'forces making for economic progress, which yielded limited bursts and enclaves of modern activity, expand and come to dominate the society'.[68] A particular group has to seize the opportunities provided by their resources within the expanding economy. The typical rate of capital investment rises from five to ten per cent of national income and a series of sectors of industry are quickly established. Rostow comments that in 'a decade or two both the basic structure of the economy and the social and political structure of the society are transformed in such a way that a steady rate of growth can be . . . regularly sustained'.[69]

In the fourth stage of the drive to maturity there is a long period of progress with ten to twenty per cent of national income invested in new production capacity. As a consequence industries now forge ahead, mature and level-off. At the same time new industries arrive on the scene. There is a period of fine adjustment to social and institutional arrangements such that eventually a mature economy and society is established which rests on the absorption of home-generated new technologies.

In stage five, which is the period of high mass consumption, the leading sectors shift away from heavy industries towards the provision of consumer durables and services in the consumer marketplace, and at the same time social welfare provisions are made. At this point the society in question has accomplished fully the shift from traditional to modern society.

Rostow links this stage theory to a mechanism, which he has to in order to block the criticism that all he has produced is an arbitrary periodization of history. Rostow insists that his stages 'are not merely descriptive . . . They have an analytic bone-structure, rooted in a dynamic theory of production'.[70] Rostow's dynamic theory of production is a derivation it seems of Keynesian work and he looks at savings, investment and sectoral performance, and postulates for an economy a set of optimum paths of sectoral development. The course of history will inevitably see divergences from this optimum path but essentially development is 'the effort of societies to approximate to the optimum sector paths'.[71] In terms of a mechanism then, what we have in addition to the above noted element of reactive nationalism is a mixture of growth economics after the style of Harrod–Domar and sectoral analysis after the style of the economist Colin Clark.[72]

67   Ibid. p. 7.
68   Ibid.
69   Ibid. pp. 8–9.
70   Ibid. pp. 12–13.
71   Ibid. p. 14.
72   Clark analysed societies in terms of sectoral maturation: primary sector, secondary sector, tertiary sector and quaternary sector. The shift is from raw-material producing through manufacturing to knowledge-based industries. On Clark, see Brookfield 1975 op. cit. ch. 2.

Rostow criticized

If we look to the general response to Rostow's book it is clear that whilst it was well received by lay readers, in particular amongst the various policy communities associated with the business of development, it was badly received by specialists. Baran[73] and Hobsbawm remarked that the closest the author came to offering a mechanism of growth comprised 'little more than verbiage . . . based on . . . coffee-house sociology and political speculation'.[74] The popularity of Rostow's book amongst policy-makers was based on the timing and origin of his message, and the optimistic generality of the content.

The work was first presented in a 1956 essay[75] and re-presented in its now familiar form in 1960. It was the pre-eminent theory of modernization in the early 1960s. The initial publication of the material coincided with the challenge to the USA in respect of aid donation made by the USSR. In the context of aid-donor competition between super-powers and the subsequent search by the Americans for an elaborated theory of modernization the work of Rostow was ideologically serviceable. In the 1960 publication the policy-scientific core of the scheme plus its anti-communist theme fitted Rostow neatly into the New Frontier.[76] It is here that we find the highest expression of the notions of interventionism. Rostow was a part of this establishment.

The counterpart is the acceptability of the message. In the 1960s a confluence of factors had effectively shifted international discussion of aid and development on to a very general level. The debate came to focus on the rules of the game, and questions about the real purpose of aid, concern with how it was supposed to work and what existing analytical conceptions supposed and entailed, dropped away. In their place there was a presumption of self-evidence. Here the descriptive, unreflective generality of the Rostowian scheme was wholly appropriate. It can also be suggested that the scheme had detailed stylistic advantages for any policy-maker: thus take-off was scheduled to run over a 20-year period – both short enough to be conceivable and long enough not to be oppressive. The scheme's persuasiveness can be summarized as follows: 'It seemed to give every country an equal chance; it "explained" the advantages of the developed countries; it offered a clear path to progress – without spelling this out in detail; it identified the requirements for advance with the virtues of the West; it suggested comfortingly that the communist countries were in fact following Western recipes, with a difference; it debunked the historical theories of Marx'.[77]

73   Baran's work is considered in ch. 13.
74   P. Baran and E. Hobsbawm 1961 'The Stages of Economic Growth', *Kyklos*, 14.
75   W. W. Rostow 1956 'The Take-Off into Self-Sustained Growth', *Economic Journal*, 66.
76   The phrase 'New Frontier' was President Kennedy's and marked the intention of his administration to tackle social reform.
77   Brookfield 1975 op. cit. p. 38. For further material see W. W. Rostow 1990 *Theorists of Economic Growth from David Hume to the Present*, Oxford University Press.

Chapter Summary

I have now discussed the historical milieu of growth theory, its logic of explanation, and have looked at two influential early applications of the position. It is clear that these theorists were sensitive to the difficulties of shifting established intellectual tools to the Third World and they appreciated that complexity of the issues themselves. Given the demand that they produce something by way of a theory of development, their procedure was what we would expect, which is to say that they began with the intellectual tools at their disposal and fashioned a plausible scheme around the economics of Keynesian growth theories. Second, we can note that their work subsequently fell out of fashion as it became clear that the basic metaphor was false, because tackling development was not like tackling unemployment. Streeten remarks that they miscast their starting point and confused complex problems of social, political and economic change with the range of technically detailed aspects of managing sophisticated economies.[78] It is also clear, thirdly, that we should not dismiss their work because their work saw both an initial restatement of some of the core concerns of the classical tradition of political-economy and relatedly the initial presentation of a series of ideas revolving around the ideology of authoritative interventionism which in the guise of modernization theory subsequently became part of the common coin of development studies.

The theory of modernization follows on from growth theory but is heavily influenced by the desire of the USA to combat the influence of the USSR in the Third World. The theory of modernization offers the new nationstates of the Third World an easy route to the status of developed economies and societies. The theory of modernization typically makes use of the work of all the social sciences to offer a general description of the shift to the modern world. The theory of modernization rests an optimistic version of economic growth models and on theories of stable change. A simple dichotomy is proposed between traditional and modern societies with modernization as the process of moving from one situation to the other. The theory of modernization was very influential in the 1950s and 1960s. However, modernization theory has subsequently been criticized for illegitimately generalizing the model of the West and more particularly the model of the USA.

78   Streeten 1972 op. cit.

10

The Development Experience of Latin America: Structuralism and Dependency Theory

Overview of Structuralist and Dependency Theories

In the years prior to the depression of the 1930s the economies of the countries of Latin America had been oriented to exporting primary products to the European and American markets. However, the response of governments to the economic dislocation of the depression and subsequent war years had the effect of encouraging import-substituting industrialization. After the end of the Second World War this situation was theorized by Raul Prebisch and the social scientists of the UN Economic Commission for Latin America, ECLA. The standard theories of international specialization and trade which argued for a complementary international division of labour were rejected. A structuralist economics was formulated to model realistically local economies so that governments could effectively plan for national development. The influence of structuralist economics declined as the drive to industrialize faltered in the early 1960s and theorists came to stress the more radical political implications of the structuralist centre–periphery motif. As the material of structuralism was reworked the approach known as dependency theory emerged. On the dependency view the upshot of the historical experience of the countries of Latin America is that the region has come to occupy a position of subordinate incorporation in the global economy.

Latin America between the Wars

After the disintegration of the Spanish colonial empire in Latin America around the turn of the nineteenth century A. G. Frank[1] identifies the emergence of two factions amongst the newly independent peoples who came into conflict in respect of the future pattern of development: the 'Europeans', who were advocates of free trade and thus a continuing role as primary product exporters; and the 'Americans', who were nationalistic and advocates of industrialization behind protective tariff barriers.[2] In the event the views of the Europeans prevailed and the countries of Latin America embarked on a long period of economic development centred on primary-product exporting. In the years before the Great Depression of the 1930s Latin American countries pursued policies of primary-product exporting, an outward-directed pattern of development which looked primarily to Europe. Alongside this outward direction there was an available theory in the form of Ricardian ideas in respect of the nature of international trade. David Ricardo was a nineteenth-century English political-economist who was the key theorist of the rising industrial bourgeoisie in England.[3] The particular element of Ricardo's work which was invoked in the context of Latin American debates in respect of economic policy was the idea of international specialization. Ricardo suggested that each country would have a specific set of local resources, a natural endowment of material, cultural and geographical opportunities, and that a country's economic development would benefit from specialization on these particular strengths coupled to widespread international trade. As each country maximized its own economic strengths and thereafter traded, the system as a whole would achieve a maximum level of operation. In a system of specialization and trade all would benefit.

This view of the benefits of international specialization was essentially an ideological reading and justification of the position of the UK within the world economy during most of the nineteenth century, when the industrial world economy was more or less equivalent to the UK economy. The theory guaranteed the industrial pre-eminence of the UK and relegated the rest of the world to the status of raw material suppliers and consumers of finished products.

In the depression years the economies of Latin America were very badly hit as demand for their products fell, in line with falls in production within the industrialized economies of the First World. As exports of primary products fell, so too did the income which Latin America derived from them. The automatic defensive reaction of Latin American governments seeking to adapt to these adverse circumstances had the effect of initiating a programme of import-substituting industrialization as goods which had

1   A. G. Frank 1972 *Lumpenbourgeoisie-Lumpendevelopment*, New York, Monthly Review Press, ch. 4. A. G. Frank's work is discussed in ch. 13.
2   On the politics of identity in colonial and post-colonial Latin America see B. Anderson 1983 *Imagined Communities*, London, Verso, ch. 4.
3   W. J. Barber 1967 *A History of Economic Thought*, ch. 3.

been bought abroad were now produced locally. The Second World War continued and reinforced this pattern as the markets in Europe to which Latin America had historically looked were cut off by military activity. Once again the pressure to produce at home that which had usually been imported was reinforced. After the end of the wartime period there was a general revival in world trade and in the long period of remarkable post-war prosperity[4] the economies of Latin America were successful and grew rapidly. The entire episode became the theoretical concern of a group of economists lead by Prebisch at the UN Economic Commission for Latin America, ECLA. A theory offering an explanation of the mechanisms of import-substituting industrialization was constructed and the governments of the region were urged to continue with their established development plans[5] (see figure 12).

The Structuralist Work of Raul Prebisch

Raul Prebisch is widely taken to have been instrumental both in establishing the intellectual machineries of structuralist economics and in establishing an appropriate international institutional vehicle for the deployment of these lines of argument and policy.[6] The crucial intellectual insight which came to be known as the 'Prebisch thesis'[7] was that the global system was not a uniform marketplace with producers and suppliers freely making mutually beneficial contracts but was in fact divided into powerful central economies and relatively weak peripheral economies. The economics of structuralism rejected the formal model-making of orthodox economics and addressed the situation of peripheral economies directly and pragmatically. It was on the basis of these analyses that Prebisch was active in the newly established institutional mechanism which served to order the global system in the post-Second World War period. Prebisch was a key figure in the UN Economic Commission for Latin America (ECLA) which was founded in 1948, and made an important contribution to the early development work of the UN through helping to set up the first UNCTAD in 1964. It has been argued that the 'creation of UNCTAD was . . . the result of Prebisch's personal efforts',[8] and was concerned, they point out, 'to discuss the international economic relations linking industrialised and less-developed countries'.[9]

4   See E. Hobsbawm 1994 *Age of Extremes: The Short Twentieth Century, 1914–1991*, London, Michael Joseph, ch. 9.
5   An excellent overview is offered by M. Blomstrom and B. Hettne 1984 *Development Theory in Transition*, London, Zed, chs. 2, 3.
6   For an overview see L. E. DiMarco ed. 1972 *International Economics and Development: Essays in Honour of Raul Prebisch*, London, Academic Press.
7   L. E. DiMarco notes (ibid. p. 5) that there were two crucial early essays: R. Prebisch 1959 'Commercial Policy in Underdeveloped Countries', *American Economic Review*, 49; and R. Prebisch 1949 'The Economic Development of Latin America and its Principal Problems', *Economic Review of Latin America*, 7.
8   A. A. Dadone and L. E. DiMarco 1972 'The Impact of Prebisch's Ideas on Modern Economic Analysis' in L. E. DiMarco ed. 1972 op. cit. p. 23.
9   Ibid. p. 24.

182

Figure 12 Structuralist economics and dependency theory

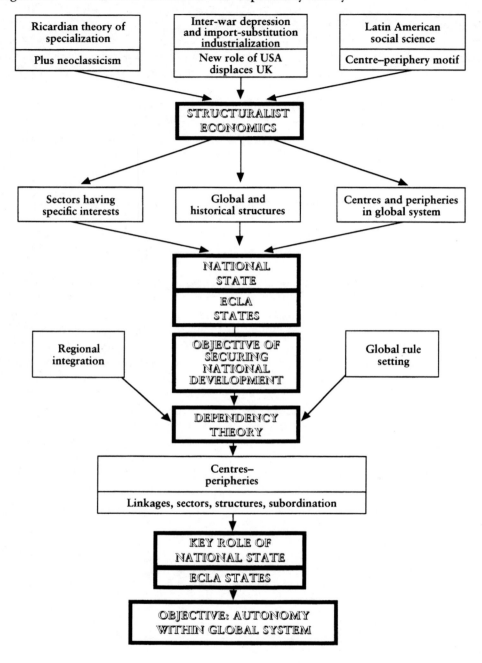

Background concerns

The principal position against which Prebisch developed his views[10] was the claim of orthodox Ricardian-inspired economic theories that international specialization conferred benefits upon all those involved.[11] Against this argument Prebisch used a version of the centre–periphery idea which was available not only in marxian but also in indigenous Latin American anti-imperialist writings which had been produced over the 1930s and 1940s. The lines of criticism of the orthodox view of the benefits of international specialization and exchange run back to the late nineteenth century when the USA, Russia, Germany and Japan all confronted the problems of being 'late industrializers' within a global system dominated by the British. In all these cases a preference for industrialization behind protective tariff barriers was favoured. In the light of these considerations, Prebisch argued that the orthodox theory condemned Latin American economies to a secondary and relatively declining position as primary product exporters. It was in fact the position which had been occupied in the years prior to the depression and which was inherited from the colonial period. Prebisch rejected the argument in favour of international specialization and in addition to challenging the orthodox conception of the appropriate position of Latin American economies within the world economy makes a concurrent reworking of the explanations of the nature of peripheral economies. The market equilibrium model of neo-classicism is rejected in favour of an empiricist-style, pragmatic and problem-oriented approach known as structuralism which insisted that the economies of the countries of Latin America should be analysed as a loosely integrated set of separate sectors, each of which had a particular role within the global system bequeathed by the dominance of the metropolitan economies. The new policy solution was to pursue a national programme of industrialization behind protective tariff barriers: precisely the pattern which had grown up in the wake of the crises of depression and war.

Structuralist economics

The structuralist approach starts with the attempt to model the local situation realistically rather than formally. In place of the orthodox neo-classical economics of the self-regulating market system with its predilection to formal models, the structuralists look to the actual historically generated pattern of real economic activity. As soon as this procedural change in strategies of social scientific explanation is made a very different story in respect of the economies of Latin America emerges. The putative single national economy is seen as split into a loosely integrated set of quasi-autonomous sectors. In place of the smooth interaction of the various elements of the single economy there is a diverse spread of conflicts of interest between the

10 R. Prebisch 1950 *The Economic Development of Latin America and its Principal Problems*, New York, United Nations Publications.
11 See M. Blomstrom and B. Hettne op. cit. chs. 2, 3.

various sectors. In the actual historically generated economies of the countries of Latin America each of the various sectors of the economy of the present day represents either a residue of the historical process of the expansion of Western European capitalism or a present requirement of contemporary capitalism. The distinctively national and integrated economy does not exist and instead there is a collection of residues, enclaves and various parasitic forms. In the light of these analyses it can be argued that an 'underdeveloped country is underdeveloped precisely because it consists of different structures each with a specific type of behaviour'.[12]

The origins of structuralism lie in the concern which Prebisch had in respect of the relations between Latin America and the industrialized economies.[13] The notion of the key relationship being between centre and periphery 'was derived from the preoccupation with economic cycles during the immediate postwar period'.[14] It is clear that from this perspective 'the distinction . . . was principally inspired by the unequal role played by the two segments of the world's economy in the system's periodic fluctuations: the first playing an active role; the second a passive or reflexive role'.[15] The distinction also pointed to the different roles assigned to 'primary exporters and industrial exporters by the international division of labour, whose end result was an unequal distribution of technical progress'.[16] The upshot is that the powerful core economies both drive the system generally and tend to accumulate an ever greater technological lead in industry which in turn secures their dominance. Overall it became clear to Prebisch that the relative lack of advance of the economies of Latin America could not be explained in terms of deficiencies within the local economy but should be explained with reference to the debilitating structural circumstances of the economies of Latin America within the global system.

The major claims of the structuralist position were constructed on the basis of these analyses. There was a more particular occasion for the presentation of structuralist economics insofar as they 'dealt with the implications of the substitution of the US for the UK as the system's principal centre'.[17] As the disruptions of the inter-war depression gave way to the greater systemic upheaval of the Second World War the metropolitan centre to which the economies of Latin America had looked over the long period of their independence, which had been secured from Spain and Portugal in the early nineteenth century, namely the UK, became enfeebled and was eclipsed by the USA. It was the USA which became the dominant centre to which the economies of Latin America looked in the post-Second World War period.

12   P. J. O'Brien 1975 'A Critique of Latin American Theories of Dependency' in I. Oxaal et al. *Beyond the Sociology of Development*, London, Routledge, p. 9.
13   J. Knakal 1972 'The Centre-Periphery System Twenty Years Later' in DiMarco ed. op. cit.
14   Ibid. p. 97.
15   Ibid.
16   Ibid.
17   Ibid.

In general terms the ECLA line of analysis involved a series of interrelated claims. The first claim was that the economy of the USA was relatively self-contained and therefore its responsiveness to the periphery was less in comparison to that of the previously more open economy of the UK. The shift in focus from the UK to the USA found a more advanced liberal market economy whose centres of power were not particularly disposed to continue the styles of interaction established by the British over their long period of association with the countries of Latin America. In brief, a new metropolitan centre entailed a new schedule of demands upon the peripheral countries of Latin America. The second area of concern was with the terms of trade between centres and peripheries which were seen to have moved against the peripheries as primary product prices fell relative to the prices of manufactures. In this situation the general position of the periphery is weakened significantly as the capacity to finance imports is reduced. The third related concern points to the capacity of the centre to import independently of its exchanges with the periphery. In other words the centre could source its imports from any number of locations within the global periphery. In the case of Latin America the freedom of the centre weakens the position of the periphery in vital trade relations. Again, fourth, the imports of the centre are of raw materials and their prices fluctuate sharply which is to the detriment of the periphery which cannot rely upon a steady stream of income. And finally, the theorists of ECLA took the view that the post-Second World War 'dollar shortage'[18] revealed that the USA is unused to a world role, in contrast to the UK, and that this impacted negatively on the peripheral economies. Overall, the ECLA analysis of the situation of the peripheries in relation to the new metropolitan centre of the USA was pessimistic in that the new centre was seen to be both powerful and unsympathetic.

It is with the addition of one further set of reflections that the full ECLA argument emerges. In this early formulation the role of global financial mechanisms was omitted but this was quickly remedied and it was pointed out that the major global sources of finance were controlled and regulated by the metropolitan capitalist countries, and indeed that the major new institutions of the Bretton Woods system were located within the American capital. It is at this point that the ECLA structuralist diagnosis of a global economy divided into a powerful autonomous centre surrounded by dependent peripheral economies was finally stated.[19] The policy conclusions flowed from the analysis and revolved around the affirmation of a strategy of industrialization in the peripheries such that they could over time become non-dependent economic agents within an interdependent global system.

18   In the immediate post-war period the US economy was dominant and all other economies were war damaged. In this situation they could not export goods to the USA in order to earn dollars to pay for their imports – hence a shortage of dollars. In Europe the aid programme known as the Marshall Plan solved the problem.
19   Knakal 1972 op. cit. p. 100.

The broad sweep of structuralist analysis can be summarized in terms of the three key implications of the rejection of the Ricardian-inspired theories of international specialization and exchange: (a) the analysis of relationships in terms of centres and peripheries, rather than equal market players; (b) a focus on industrialization as a means to catch up and join in with the core economies, in preference to continued dependence; and (c) a concern for the social and cultural implications of dependency.[20] The crucial element of the overall position was the view that technical progress was concentrated at the core and in character was slowly diminishing the importance of primary product inputs – hence, over time, the declining terms of trade. The expectation was that industrialization would address directly the issue of the technical advantage of the core and would help mop-up unemployment by providing new industrial jobs. Government finances would be improved by broadening the economy and thus the tax base, and the balance-of-payments position would be improved by making at home what had previously been imported. These policies met with early success and there was extensive industrialization and urbanization. However, there were unanticipated problems in that industrialization depended on foreign supplies of sophisticated manufactures and thereafter served relatively small local markets. The benefits were thus less than expected and the financial costs were higher than expected. The strategy of import-substituting industrialization turned out to have only limited effect and in the case of Latin America a mix of overenthusiasm, incompetent and corrupt First World bankers and a subsequent flood of petro-dollars led to economic, political and social problems which culminated in the debt crisis of the late 1970s and 1980s.[21]

The practical record

The practical record of structuralist-inspired policy advice has been mixed. In Latin America the move towards industrialization, which was begun in the difficult period of the depression and which continued over the wartime episode, has continued as a central concern of the policies of governments in the post-Second World War period. In all cases the drive towards an industrial developed economy continues. It is also clear that the record is uneven and shows a mixture of partial success and clear failure. The approach has seen as series of phases.

The reformist structuralism of ECLA belongs to the first of what the noted dependency theorist Celso Furtado has called 'three easily identifiable periods' in the economic history of post-war Latin America.[22] The first

20   H. Brookfield 1975 *Interdependent Development*, London, Methuen, pp. 139–42.
21   See S. George 1988 *A Fate Worse than Debt*, Harmondsworth, Penguin; P. Korner et al. 1986 *The IMF and the Debt Crisis*, London, Zed.
22   C. Furtado 1976 *Economic Development in Latin America*, Cambridge University Press, p. 298.

is characterized as one of rapid growth based on favourable terms of trade, accumulated reserves from the war years, and currencies strong enough to be able to withstand gradual devaluation in the face of already active inflationary pressures. However, by the mid-1960s the position had changed and the strategy of import-substituting industrialization was apparently failing. In this second period there was a sharp deterioration in the terms of trade and a slackening of the rate of growth. On top of this the Cuban revolution provoked widespread questioning of the nature of Latin America's recent development history. A third period is also identified in the early 1970s which saw something of an economic boom on the back of vast imports of capital as petro-dollars were recycled and a little latter the debt crisis of the 1980s emerged.

The deteriorating situation of phases one and two was interpreted by ECLA in terms of problems with small local markets, and the associated difficulties of securing overseas markets, and the disadvantageous nature for Latin American economies of established patterns of international exchange. In response to these problems ECLA 'pursued a two pronged strategy of pressure and persuasion in the 1960s: the first, on Latin American governments in favour of regional integration; the second, on governments of the developed countries for more liberal trade and financial policies'.[23] However, by the late 1960s the ECLA model of development was in severe crisis.[24]

A variety of problems were noted. There was, firstly, the continuation of economic dependency despite import substitution (as the drive to upgrade local industry progressed a strong demand for the import of First World sophisticated technology was created). Once the drive to industrialize was initiated the demand for further imports of technology and supplies continued to grow. The paradox of import-substituting industrialization was that it demanded a significant supply of foreign imports all of which had to be paid for by export earnings or by the accumulation of debt. In the wider economy, secondly, as the drive for industrialization continued the urban employment structure began to become sharply divided as those with employment in industries sponsored by governments, or overseas companies became relatively prosperous, whilst those in the unprivileged local sectors found their incomes falling behind. This situation was to become more problematical as inflation took hold and various groups moved to protect themselves from any loss of earning power. In the rural areas the established primary product operations continued but with diminished political support. As poverty increased there was pressure for rural–urban migration. It was clear that the impact of the economic developments of the period was that income inequality was becoming worse. So, thirdly, large sections of the population were marginalized as they shifted out of any formal

23 N. Girvan 1973 'The Development of Dependency Economics in the Caribbean and Latin America: Review and Comparison', Social and Economic Studies, 22.
24 O'Brien 1975 op. cit. p. 11.

employment and into the myriad activities which are summed as the 'informal sector'.[25] Then, fourthly, the role of foreign capital was increasingly in evidence as the state, the industrial sector and the rural primary producers sought to support their activities by drawing in foreign capital. In general, fifthly, a consequence of the economic, social and political problems of the period was that the military came to seize political power in many places.[26] Overall, it could be argued that the approach favoured low-quality high-cost manufactures, neglected agriculture and entrenched the role of foreign capital.[27] In the light of these developments it soon came to be argued that the structuralist remedy was better seen as 'the cause of the economic illness'.[28]

It was at this point that the argument moved out of the structuralist frame used by Prebisch to embrace work from wider traditions within the social sciences. A significant area of concern was the critique of the model of modernization which had been assiduously developed by US theorists in the late 1950s and throughout the 1960s. The exchange with modernization theory can be taken to have issued in the representation within Latin American social science of the concerns of the classical nineteenth-century tradition of social science with its concern to elucidate the dynamics of complex change.[29]

A series of objections were made to the modernization theory analysis of the countries of Latin America. The idea that they were dual societies with a traditional and a modern sector was rejected (as the whole of the territories were influenced by the demands of the global system). The idea that modernizing impulses would spread to the backward areas was rejected (as the impact of global system on poor areas was at best unpredictable). The idea that the poor traditional areas represented a handicap to progressive national bourgeoisies was rejected (as such an elite did not exist).[30] The general strategy of looking to a series of stages of economic development was rejected in favour of a more richly elaborated historical analysis which would deal with the normality of the pattern of underdevelopment within Latin America given its particular position within the global system.[31]

It is out of this complex pattern of debate which revolved around the

25   On urban poverty and the vitality of the informal sector, see P. Worsley 1984 *The Three Worlds: Culture and World Development*, London, Weidenfeld.
26   On the collapse into military rule, see J. Linz and A. Stepan eds. 1978 *The Breakdown of Democratic Regimes*; see also for a discussion of the return of democracy, D. Reuschemeyer et al. 1992 *Capitalist Development and Democracy*, Cambridge, Polity.
27   R. Peet 1991 *Global Capitalism: Theories of Societal Development*, London, Routledge, pp. 43–5.
28   Ibid. p. 45.
29   See for example, F. H. Cardoso and E. H. Faletto 1979 *Dependency and Development in Latin America*, University of California Press. See also J. A. Kahl 1976 *Modernisation, Exploitation and Dependency in Latin America*, New Brunswick, Transaction.
30   See R. Stavehhagen 1968 'Seven Erroneous Theses on Latin America' in J. Petras and M. Zeitlin eds. *Latin America: Reform of Revolution*, Greenwich, Fawcett.
31   See O. Sunkel 1969 'National Development Policy and External Dependency in Latin America', *Journal of Development Studies*, 6.

exchange of metropolitan centres and Latin American economies that the notion of dependency crystallizes. The theory of dependence is a response to the problems of structuralist analyses.[32] In the dependency analysis the familiar structuralist themes in respect of the fragmented nature of the local economy are firmly lodged within an explanatory frame which details the historical development of the asymmetrical relationships of economic power between the metropoles and the peripheries and thereby locates crucial elements of local problems beyond the control of the local state. At this point the familiar themes of external dependency and the related internal debilitating stability of social and economic structures are presented.

The Dependency Work of Celso Furtado

The work of Celso Furtado encompasses a number of themes: (a) the slow revision of an early adherence to structuralist economics such that in the later work a dependency theory is produced; (b) the related slow shift in orientation of Furtado's work away from technical solutions cast in terms of economic policy towards analyses which are concerned with the sphere of the political; and finally, drawing on both these movements, (c) a shift away from narrowly discipline-bound work towards a routinely multi-disciplinary style of analysis redolent of the material of the classical nineteenth-century European tradition of social science oriented to the elucidation of the dynamics of complex change in the industrial capitalist system.

The revision of structuralism and the presentation of dependency theory

Furtado's *Development and Underdevelopment*[33] begins with a discussion of existing treatments of economic growth and from this he derives the idea that:

> The theory of development endeavours to explain, from a macro-economic point of view, the causes and mechanisms of the persistent growth in productivity of the labour factor and the repercussions of this growth on the organisation of production and on the distribution and utilisation of the social product.[34]

On the basis of this understanding Furtado goes on to identify two further related styles of enquiry: the abstract and the historical. Of the first,

32   O'Brien 1975 op. cit. p. 11.
33   C. Furtado 1964 *Development and Underdevelopment*, Berkeley and Los Angeles, University of California Press. In the preface the author explains that having begun as a neo-classical theorist he derived further inspiration from marxism and Keynesianism and came to move towards a structural analysis of development and underdevelopment. The intellectual movement from structuralism towards dependency theory is evident in the trio of works considered here.
34   Ibid. p. 1.

'in which abstract formulations prevail',[35] Furtado argues that it 'comprises analysis of actual mechanisms of the process of growth'[36] and the strategy of enquiry involves 'building models or simplified schemes of existing economic systems'.[37] What we have here is an acknowledgement of the post-Second World War neo-classical informed language of the precise identification of mechanisms via model-building. Furtado continues by introducing his second, related, style of enquiry. It is the 'historical plane, [and] comprises critical study in the light of a given reality and on the basis of the categories defined by the abstract analysis'.[38] In this way the theorist can refine formal models and better grasp the real world processes of growth.

Furtado's early approach may be characterized as structuralist, and he is concerned to fashion a set of models of Latin American economies which will reveal how they have changed through time and how they are presently constituted. What is most intriguing in this early work is the way in which Furtado runs together attention to the historical detail of the Latin American case with a deference to orthodox economic ideas of scientific explanation which expresses itself in the pursuit of models.

As Furtado deploys the structural approach in the case of the economies of Latin America, the substance of the analyses which he presents already contains in outline the dependency position. Furtado considers the historical expansion of industrial capitalism and observes:

> The advent of an industrial nucleus in eighteenth century Europe disrupted the world economy of the time and eventually conditioned the later economic development in almost every region in the world.[39]

The nucleus expanded in three directions: internally, in Europe itself; into the 'empty lands' of North America and Australasia; and, third, into already inhabited lands in Latin America. It is the matter of the types of economies and societies produced – especially in the last noted case – that is of interest to Furtado, and he argues that the 'effect of the impact of capitalist expansion on the archaic structures varied from region to region; the result, however, was almost always to create hybrid structures'.[40] At this point we have a first statement of the core of the dependency analysis which is that underdevelopment is not an original condition but is historically generated in the process of the expansion of capitalism. The impact of the expansion of industrial capitalism upon the various colonized territories has the effect of producing economies comprised of distinct sectors. Furtado identifies three typical sectors:

> one was the 'remnant' economy with a predominance of subsistence activities and a minor money flow; the second comprised activities

35   Ibid.
36   Ibid.
37   Ibid.
38   Ibid.
39   Ibid. p. 127.
40   Ibid. p. 129.

directly connected with foreign trade; the third consisted of activities directly connected with the domestic market.[41]

Using this scheme, Furtado takes note of the situation of the Brazilian economy, and he concludes his remarks by remarking that 'Again we see that underdevelopment, specific phenomenon that it is, calls for an effort of autonomous theorising'.[42]

Furtado's ideas of an appropriate theory of underdevelopment are pursued in *Diagnosis of the Brazilian Crisis*.[43] Thus far we have met the ideas of sectors and structures, and the importance of historical analysis has also been stressed. Furtado has emphasized that enquiry into the circumstances of underdevelopment in Latin America, which is his particular area of concern, must focus upon the actual local situation and hence his calls for autonomous theorizing. In *Diagnosis of the Brazilian Crisis*, which was written at a time of political crisis in Brazil, we find three crucial revisions to the analysis thus far made. Furtado, first, invokes the Hegelian and marxian idea of dialectical change. This, argues Furtado, is the best available general orienting frame for enquiry. However, Furtado immediately goes on to say that at a practical level it is not much use and other modelling exercises are needed. The second revision made involves acknowledging the idea of class and class struggle. Furtado has discovered the diversity of political class interests in Brazil. However, again he quickly softens his argument by treating class in the style of orthodox sociology. Finally, the third revision entails speaking of institutional flexibility, and here Furtado extends his argument into the political realm. The Brazilian economy and society lacks a ruling class committed to industrialization and the emergence of such a group will depend upon the flexibility of present institutional arrangements. Unfortunately for Furtado's analysis, and Brazil, the actual result of the crisis was a military coup.

In the text *Economic Development in Latin America*,[44] the dependency line is fully presented. The economic and social structures of present-day Latin American countries are presented as being the result of the manner of that continent's incorporation into the world capitalist economy. The production of the dependency position over the period can be characterized as follows:

> the developments in thought, generally, took the forms of (i) adding a historical perspective and analysis to the structural and institutional method, (ii) giving the historical/structural/institutional method the kind of theoretical and empirical content needed to construct a general theory of dependence and underdevelopment.[45]

41   Ibid. p. 136.
42   Ibid. p. 139.
43   C. Furtado 1965 *Diagnosis of the Brazilian Crisis*, Berkeley and Los Angeles, University of California Press.
44   C. Furtado 1969 (2nd edn 1976) *Economic Development in Latin America*, 2nd edn Cambridge University Press.
45   Girvan 1973 op. cit. p. 12.

The nature of this historical, structural and institutional method is exemplified in the analyses presented. Thus, given circumstances which admit of a description (or disaggregated modelling informed by generally true economic propositions) in terms of economic structure also admit of a complementary description in terms of a functionally necessary institutional framework. Historical analysis provides data for examples and the construction of a sequence of models; and, further, borrowing from classical economics and the marxian traditions, an overarching framework which firmly locates the Latin American economies in the dependent peripheral areas of the world capitalist economy. Problems of development are then treated in terms of the lack of fit between, on the one hand, the possibilities for development provided by technological levels and, on the other, the restrictions and possibilities attendant upon given structural and institutional circumstances.

The presentation of new policy work

In the text *Economic Development in Latin America* Furtado presents a detailed analysis and treats the historical genesis of the contemporary situation. The work ends with a chapter summarizing his argument and identifying the necessary conditions of any future advance. Furtado observes that:

> There can be no doubt that development based on exports of raw materials and import substitution industrialisation has reached the limits of its possibilities . . . Similarly the institutional framework inherited from the colonial period . . . seems to have exhausted its possibilities of adaptation to development needs.[46]

And he adds that discussion has increasingly turned, not surprisingly, to the business of structural and institutional reform. When we look at the broad areas of specific policy proposals he makes, dealing with reforms to internal and external structural linkages, what is abundantly clear is that the dependency approach is both politically explosive in its implications and that the reform tasks he identifies are dauntingly difficult. The key problems lie in the present make-up of the political-economy and its associated structures of political power. The dilemma for the theorist in respect of identifying possible routes to the future is that subordinate peripheral capitalism generates a particular pattern of class-based groups, some of whom have a direct interest in established patterns of outward-directed growth. Furtado confronts this dilemma with a reform package. Externally, there are three problems: (a) the re-entry of regional economies into the expanding mainstream; (b) the reshaping of economic relations with the USA; and (c) the reshaping of economic relations with the multinational corporations.[47] And, internally, five problems are noted: (a) the reconstruction of economic structures to permit the use of modern technology; (b) the avoidance of social

46   Furtado 1976 op. cit. p. 300.
47   Ibid.

marginalization of large sections of the population; (c) the reorganization of the state sector so as to enable the state to assume its proper role as the agent of development; (d) the pursuit of technological autonomy; and (e) the establishment of regional cooperation.[48]

It is clear that these represent an essentially political programme cast in terms of policy proposals. I have followed Furtado in noting the broad headings and it is clear that they admit of detailed elaboration. However, what is. interesting is the political reform strategy they embody. Furtado's dilemma is that of reform-minded theorists generally in that whilst his own work disposes him to reliance upon persuasion his circumstances are not obviously conducive to the efficacy of reasoned debate. Furtado's solution revolves around the key role of the state in the pursuit of development, but the present state represents the interests of specific groups whose interests are not general. In other words the vehicle of the solution to the problem of development is actually a part of the problem. Furtado offers a reformist politics. For the moment we can note that in Furtado's work the dependency approach emerges in all its subtlety and intellectual power. In a subsequent 1978 text entitled *Accumulation and Development*,[49] Furtado tackles a broad-scale discussion of dependency, seeing it as a structural condition bequeathed by history. The themes of the earlier work are here pursued in a broad cultural, historical and theoretical text which the author calls an 'academic anti-book'[50] as the issues will not fit into available social science categories.

The Legacy of Dependency Theory

In recent years one might suggest that the broad tradition of work known as dependency theory has been out of fashion in the First World. The initial English-language presentation of the material of this tradition took the form of polemical interventions within intra-First World theoretical debates and this had the unfortunate effect of confusing the reception of the lessons of dependency theory as those ill-disposed on political grounds were able to dismiss the entire approach as left-wing propaganda.[51] Nonetheless it seems to me that we can take from this material a useful concern for linking structural and agent-centred explanations. It is clear that dependency theory has been presented in diverse guises and that it has generated extensive critical debates. In its initial formulations it was shaped by the particular historical experience of Latin America in the 1940s and 1950s when long-established trading and economic patterns were disturbed by the episode of the Second World War and occasioned a measure of import-substituting industrialization. These circumstances were theorized by the group of economists at ECLA led by Prebisch[52] and their work issued in a novel structuralist economics oriented to informing the policy positions of

48 Ibid.
49 C. Furtado 1978 *Accumulation and Development*, Oxford, Martin Robertson.
50 Ibid. p. i.
51 See P. W. Preston 1987 *Rethinking Development*, London, Routledge, chs. 6, 7.
52 See P. W. Preston 1982 *Theories of Development*, London, Routledge, ch. 6.

governments concerned specifically with national development. This work provided the intellectual base upon which the broader schemes of dependency theory were articulated.

Against the schemes of analysis and policy advice derived from the work of orthodox First World economics and development theorists the proponents of dependency stressed: (a) the importance of considering both the historical experience of peripheral countries and the phases of their involvement within wider encompassing systems; (b) the necessity of identifying the specific economic, political and cultural linkages of centres and peripheries; and (c) the requirement for active state involvement in the pursuit of development.

The work of the modernization theorists was essentially ahistorical. The diverse experience of the countries of the Third World was aggregated in terms of a notion of traditional society which in turn was merely a residual category which summarized the ways in which these countries failed to exhibit the traits of modern societies. The model of the modern was the model of the USA. In this way the historical experience of the countries of the Third World was both denied and assimilated to the historical experience of the developed West. As A. G. Frank was to point out, the theorists of modernization managed both to deny any history to the countries of the Third World by simply calling them traditional and moreover managed to ignore the fact that it was precisely the history that they did have that explained their present dependent underdeveloped situation. A related further revision to the familiar modernization theory story is generated by looking at the experience of history not as a smooth evolutionary progress from traditional to modern, or uncivilized to civilized, but in terms of a series of relatively discrete phases within which patterns of development are developed over time. In the case of the countries of the Third World the dependency theory position offers a story of the incorporation of these territories within the expanding sphere of the metropolitan industrial capitalist system and the subsequent reworking of this relationship according to the schedules of demands of the developing core. The present phase of peripheral capitalism is but the latest in a series of asymmetrical relationships of periphery and core.

The theory of modernization worked with an evolutionary model of change which was unpacked in terms of the structural-functionalist analysis of the logic of industrialism. The approach was focused on dynamics of change which were internal to the countries in question. However, the dependency theory approach recalled attention to the whole issue of the broader political-economic contexts within which particular nationstates operated. The dependency theorists argued that the relevant context within which the historical development of the countries of Latin America could appropriately be analysed was the global industrial capitalist system. In place of the modernization theory's focus on economic, social and cultural patterns internal to the countries of Latin America the dependency theorists insisted that a crucial aspect of the entire experience of these countries was to be found in the pattern of linkages which they had with the wider global system. A new schedule of questions was developed which dealt with the economic, social and cultural linkages which the peripheral countries had with the powerful metropolitan core countries.

The conclusions which the theorists of dependency drew in respect of the appropriate spread of policy for local national governments committed to the pursuit of national development goals was sharply different from the proposals of modernization theory. Against the modernization theory informed proposals to rely upon the marketplace, which entailed simply reaffirming an upgraded version of the historically generated and debilitating role of primary product exporter, the theorist of dependency looked to foster an independent pattern of development. The strategic differences with modernization theory came to revolve around the role of the state, which was to become the key vehicle of the new political-cultural project of autonomous development. This was to be the overriding objective in the attempt to remove the damaging handicaps of dependency.

It is clear that many development theorists would regard these three broad ideas as the positive legacy of dependency theory. In the work of Cardoso and Faletto the material of dependency theory offered a restatement of the core concerns with analysing complex change in the industrial capitalist system which had been addressed by the classical theorists of the nineteenth century.[53] The work of dependency theory recalls a very rich intellectual tradition.[54]

Chapter Summary

The central claim of dependency theory was that the circumstances of the underdeveloped were to a significant extent shaped by the global structures within which they found themselves, in particular the dominance of the West. An analysis was presented which spoke of the historical development of powerful centres and weak peripheries. The peripheries supplied primary products and low-tech manufactures to the First World in exchange for high-tech goods. This economic dependency was further expressed in political and cultural dependency. The overall result was the condition known as underdevelopment which would continue for as long as the structural conditions. The solution was therefore to weaken the grip of the global system with trade barriers, controls on multi-nationals, and the formation of regional trading areas so as to permit nationalist governments to pursue goals of national development. It was an influential approach in the 1960s and 1970s, although in its radical political forms it subsequently became unfashionable.

---

53   Cardoso and Faletto 1979 op. cit.
54   An influential reconsideration of the approach is D. Seers ed. 1981 *Dependency Theory: A Critical Reassesment*, London, Pinter. See also M. Bienefeld and M. Godfrey eds. 1982 *The Struggle for Development: National Strategies in an International Context*, London, Wiley.

11

The Pursuit of Effective Nationstatehood: The Work of the Institutionalist Development Theorists

Overview of Institutionalist Theory

The work of institutional economics offers a distinctive way of grasping the issues of development. Against those who would accept that markets are the outcome of many individual decisions the institutionalists insist that markets are lodged within societies. It is a sociologized economics oriented to the elite pursuit of state planning for development. Institutional economics has its roots in the USA but found an influential voice within development theory in the work of the Swede Gunnar Myrdal who argued that Third World countries must struggle to solve economic, social, political and cultural problems all at the same time. A notion of circular cumulative causation is presented which implies that once a direction of change is set it will continue. The Third World needs to be shifted by planning onto an upward development track.

The Occasion of Institutionalism in Development Theory

The particular historical occasion for the work of the institutionalists is to be found in the late 1950s and early 1960s as the European colonial powers withdraw from Africa south of the Sahara. The institutionalists are not immediately concerned with confronting a supposedly expansionist communism, as was the case with modernization theory. Nor are they attempting to interpret a rather general commitment to development, as was the case with growth theory. What they are concerned with is the project of reworking long-established colonial relationships such that over a period of time a replacement ruling elite, which would affirm ideas of nationalist developmentalism, could safely be installed. The project of reworking an established relationship is understood as involving: (a) the First World's experts deploying a reflexive social science; (b) the indigenous replacement rulers oriented to an agreed goal; (c) a significant measure of continuing aid from the departing colonial power; and (d) an expectation of a long period during which the exchanges between the various actors will be for mutually agreed goals; that is, the co-operative pursuit of development[1] (see figure 13).

Resources used in Institutionalist Development Theory

The resources invoked by the institutionalists include the following: (a) the actual experience of the colonial episode; (b) a history of close relationships between social scientists and governments which generally has had a social reformist character; and (c) a distinct European tradition of social thought which we can, for our purposes, trace back to Thorstein Veblen[2] and which is concerned with controlling the free market.

The colonial episode

The resources available to the institutionalists from the colonial episode were of great significance. This is clear if we compare the idea of intervention as it appears in US modernization work with how it appears in institutionalism. The European colonial powers had long years of experience with their colonial territories, and even if such knowledge was partial, it was nonetheless available. The social scientists of the USA never had an

1   See E. Hobsbawm 1994 *Age of Extremes: The Short Twentieth Century, 1914–1991*, London, Michael Joseph, ch. 7. The exchange of metropole and periphery was for a long time asymmetrical with the models of the modern being derived from the example of the metropole. The episodes of industrialization outside the core countries of the West have been limited: the USSR in the 1930s and Pacific Asia in recent years.
2   To locate Veblen, see P. Ormerod 1994 *The Death of Economics*, London, Faber, ch. 3; K. Cole et al. 1991 *Why Economists Disagree*, London, Longman, ch. 6. Also J. P. Diggins 1978 *The Bard of Savagery: Thorstein Veblen and Modern Social Theory*, Hassocks, Harvester.

Figure 13 Institutional development theory

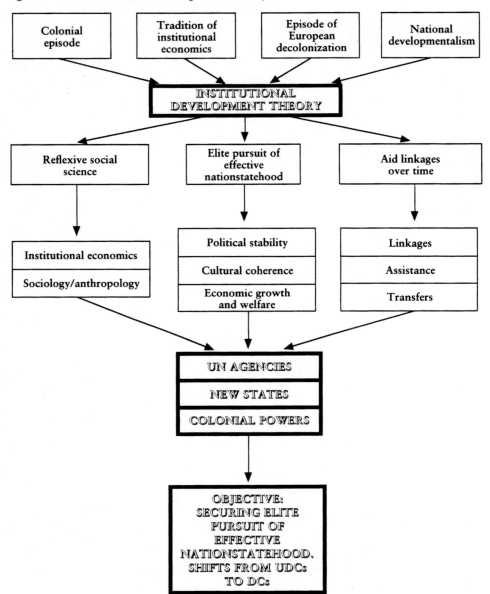

equivalent stock of knowledge. When the demand came to theorize 'development', the institutionalists could draw on the body of knowledge and local contacts established over the years (merely by being there) and within this body of knowledge there was the idea of 'stewardship' because, however grudgingly, it had been acknowledged that the ethical end of colonialism was the abolition of the system. It can be argued that stewardship is a richer idea (and presents a subtler view of the relationships of First and Third Worlders) than that of containment which was the notion central to modernization theory. It can be said that institutionalism evolves out of an ongoing European colonial situation whereas modernization theory is cobbled together in the USA in response to a developing competitive situation with the USSR.

Practical theorizing

It is appropriate to add to the lessons available within the experience of the colonial situation a second element within the resources of institutionalism and again it points up differences in the European and American situations. It has been argued that national sociologies can be identified and characterized, and that the peculiar characters of such national sociologies owe much to the relationship of the community of sociologists to the state.[3] The same can be taken to be true of the community of social scientists generally. In Europe there has been a tendency for social theory and political practice to be distinctly liberal-reformist in character. In contrast, in the case of the USA such liberal reformism has not been the general rule and social scientific knowledge has tended to be construed as discipline-bound technical expertise which was available to be deployed in the knowledge marketplace. In the case of institutionalism the general European intellectual and social milieu permits the expression of a characteristic political ethic and the work of these theorists centres upon the ideal of rule by people of enlightened goodwill.

The tradition of institutional economics

The orthodox tradition within development theory is an internally diverse one and the more narrowly economic traditions that it draws upon are themselves diverse.[4] In considering the work of mainstream economists it is possible to identify a position which dissents from the central idea of the regulative discipline of the marketplace. The first statement of institutional economics is usually associated with Veblen who was a stern critic of the unregulated market. It is characteristic of institutionalism that it argues for governmental control of business activity. In the 1930s in the USA institutionalism was the intellectual counterpart to President F. D. Roosevelt's New Deal policy which involved an extensive programme of government public works designed to ameliorate the effects of the Great Depression. In place of the notion of the market the proponents of institutionalism substitute a scheme of rational and reasonable control of the marketplace via mechanisms of regulation and planning. In the wake of the marginalist revolution of the 1870s we find a steady stream of institutionalist theorists, including

3 G. Hawthorn 1976 *Enlightenment and Despair*, Cambridge University Press.
4 See K. Cole et al. 1991 op. cit.

Thorstein Veblen, J. K. Galbraith, Gunnar Myrdal and Paul Streeten. It is common to all these various schemes of institutional analysis that economics is understood to be social-economics. In the work of these theorists economic analyses are routinely and self-consciously couched in terms which acknowledge that economies are simultaneously social systems and have their own distinct socio-cultural patterns and histories.

The typical core claims of institutionalist economics have been restated by Hodgson[5] who argues that the manifest deficiencies of the neo-classical orthodoxy place the approach beyond repair and necessitate a rigorous development of the comparatively neglected tradition of institutionalism. At the outset it is argued that the neo-classical approach survives only because of the ideological serviceability of its intrinsic commitment to market liberalism within the metropolitan capitalist countries of the global system. It is clear that the approach offers little by way of plausible analysis or policy advice in respect of the contemporary problems of First World countries. The attack on neo-classicism centres on the intellectually impoverished nature of its core commitments – to economic rationality, to the availability of knowledge throughout the system, and to the tendency of the system to equilibrium – which are taken to be sustainable only at the cost of shutting economics off from the wider social sciences. In place of this essentially ideological discourse it is proposed that economics must turn to the resources of the wider social sciences in order to study economies as social phenomena.

The institutionalist view of economies takes them to be complex social phenomena which have to be analysed in appropriate terms – using the materials of sociology, politics, anthropology, history and so on. Once economies are viewed as lodged within social systems which are themselves lodged within history then analyses automatically turn away from the sterile formalistic and mechanistic model-building of the orthodoxy and towards a richly detailed exposition of the actual dynamics of actual economies/societies. It can be argued that this approach is not a variant on the orthodoxy but is in fact quite distinct, and this is a point we can pursue in the company of Gunnar Myrdal.

The Work of Gunnar Myrdal

In the areas of development theory Myrdal has presented institutionalist analyses of the causes of persistent poverty in Third World economies and societies. Myrdal's writings are very extensive and commentators have called him a 'generalist'.[6] The work involved a reaction against mechanico-formal neo-classical equilibrium theory and in its place Myrdal offered a substantive institutionalist analysis which had at its centre the idea of circular

---

5   G. M. Hodgson 1988 *Economics and Institutions: A Manifesto for a Modern Institutional Economics*, Cambridge, Polity.
6   H. Brookfield 1975 *Interdependent Development*, London, Methuen, p. 99.

cumulative causation. It was claimed that the general direction in which a socio-economic system was developing would be self-reinforcing so that the countries of the Third World, with their weak position within the world system and weak internal institutional structures, tended to fall into a position of low-level equilibrium whereas the countries of the First World were firmly lodged on an upward development path.

In Myrdal's work the economic system is no longer seen as a self-regulating and instead has to be seen as an element of a complex social system. A social system has to be analysed realistically and this requires detailed studies of the economic, social, political and cultural aspects of the system as a whole. It is only on the basis of a detailed knowledge of all the aspects of the social system that any grasp of the system as a whole can be secured and subsequent policy-making attempted. In respect of the business of ordering change in the system, Myrdal has a particular view of social system change and argues that once a direction of change is set then the social system adjusts to reinforce that direction of change. What we have is an idea of social inertia. Myrdal speaks of this in terms of the notion of circular cumulative causation. In the case of the Third World the original condition of underdevelopment, a low-level equilibrium, was altered in the colonial period but only to the pattern of a dual economy with a traditional and a modern sector. The dual economy of the colonial period was only a slight advance on pre-colonial forms. However, in the period of independence as the institutional development of the typical Third World country is low, with institutional arrangements only working with limited efficiency, and as the position of these economies within the global system is weak, then the countries tend to stay in a position of low-level equilibrium. The solution so far as Myrdal was concerned was for the state in the Third World to struggle on a broad front of social, economic, political and cultural reforms so as to redirect the socio-economic system onto an upward path of development.

Myrdal applies his notion of circular cumulative causation both to the Third World position *vis-à-vis* the world economy and to its internal social and institutional structures and his conclusions are pessimistic. As the Third World nations are understood to be locked into a debilitating low-level equilibrium position, the remedy is to use national planning to shift individual economies into an upward dynamic. Myrdal argues that 'what in fact we all mean by development is the movement upward of the whole social system'.[7] Myrdal's analyses translate into practice via the machineries of the state and his work is an example of the ideology of the First World planner in its most obvious form. It is the machineries of state planning which are the vehicles for contriving an upward dynamic of development within the countries of the Third World. In the work of Gunnar Myrdal the business of social scientific analysis, the pursuit of development and the realm of political action all coincide in state ordered planning. It is a

7   G. Myrdal 1970 *The Challenge of World Poverty*, London, Allen Lane, p. 268.

distinctive position and one which owes, as he reports, much to the experience of the Great Depression.[8] It is clear that Myrdal's work has had a widespread influence within contemporary development theory and it is to the particular intellectual logic of his work that we can now turn.

The Logic of Myrdalian Institutionalism

Myrdal locates his earliest work within the traditions of the early-twentieth-century Swedish School of economists[9] and reports that the established members of the group evidenced a 'rather uncompromising laissez faire attitude'.[10] The general flavour of the period is recorded by Myrdal as optimistic. The Great War was regarded as an aberration and 'the twenties were an era of gradually increasing confidence in restored stability and progress'.[11] The older members of the school regarded this positively – in particular it meant an end to irritating wartime economic controls. However, the younger members of the school had become quite used to crisis and the business of government controls over economic activity seemed quite familiar and unproblematical. On the basis of these differences in experience and outlook, Myrdal records that the younger theorists were more disposed to confront problems directly with the intention of finding solutions. Nonetheless, in his own case Myrdal reports that by the late 1920s his own scholarly economic work was making little progress. Myrdal comments:

> Meanwhile the happy 'twenties had ended. The gathering Great Depression and the practical economic problems raised in its wake rescued me from my critical philosophy and restored my scientific productivity. My outer life had already placed forcefully before me that important phenomena: Social Crisis; and I have remained, with the rest of the world, under that sign ever since.[12]

It was in the severe social crisis of the 1930s that Myrdal rediscovered not only his scientific productivity but also the way in which social crises could act to simplify ideological debate in society and scholarship such that agreed lines of action could be undertaken. Myrdal also notes the influence of the American institutional economists with whom he was in contact around this time. In the 1930s the collective desire to address the problem of mass unemployment and collapsing industrial production was enough to overcome doubts about value-engaged social scientific work and turn the attention of social theorists to the solution of practical problems.

Myrdal's later approach to development expresses a similar view of the

8   G. Myrdal 1958 *Value in Social Theory*, London, Routledge, pp. 242–58.
9   See ibid.
10   Ibid. p. 243.
11   Ibid. p. 247.
12   Ibid. p. 255.

nature of social science and it has been reflected in a diverse group of social reformers, all of whom attempt to use a sceptical and reflexive approach to the construction of realistic[13] models upon which piecemeal planning can be based. There are three issues which flow from the approach adopted by the institutionalists: (a) the use of the resources of the social sciences; (b) the solution to the problem of values; and (c) the business of agency. We can pursue these matters in the company of Paul Streeten whose work interprets Myrdal and is itself a sophisticated version of the institutionalist tradition.

The use of the resources of social science

The use made by the institutionalists of the resources of the social sciences is typically piecemeal, sceptical and empiricist. It pursues realism in modelling as a means to order planned social change and the key idea in respect of the construction of such models is that concepts are seen as working only in particular circumstances. So, for example, the familiar economists' term 'unemployment' can be considered and it is clear that far from this notion being an abstract generally applicable notion, as the orthodox economists would claim, it is only usable in a particular context.[14] When the economist uses the term, the analyst thereby supposes all the social and institutional arrangements of mature capitalist society.[15] In the case of any Third World economy a detailed knowledge of the society is a prerequisite of concept-formation.

In contrast to the procedures of orthodox economists Streeten presents no abstract general models of growth and instead works in a piecemeal, sceptical and empiricist fashion in pursuit of realistic models. Streeten argues that 'the bias in our view of economic and social reality enters before the model building begins, at the level where concepts are formed'.[16] Streeten notes that 'All thought presupposes implicit or explicit model building and model using. Rigorous abstraction, simplification and quantification are necessary conditions of analysis and policy'.[17] In Streeten's view the business

13   By 'realistic', Myrdal and others seem to mean a model which is adequate to the fine grain of the 'real world'. It is to be contrasted to the abstract formal models of growth theory and the somewhat schematic models of modernization theory. The neo-institutionalists made much of this pursuit of realistic models as vehicles for understanding and ordering development. The earlier concern for economics, narrowly understood – that is, as one orthodox discipline of social science amongst others – drops out of sight.
14   D. Seers 1963 'The Limitations of the Special Case', *Oxford Bulletin of Statistics*, 25. The essay is reprinted in K. Martin and J. Knapp eds. 1967 *The Teaching of Development Economics*, London, Frank Cass.
15   R. A. Gordon 1963 'Institutional Elements in Contemporary Economics' in J. Dorfman ed. *Institutional Economics: Veblen, Commons and Mitchell Reconsidered*, Berkeley and Los Angeles, University of California Press.
16   P. Streeten 1970 'An Institutional Critique of Development Concepts', *Journal of European Sociology*, 11, p. 69.
17   P. Streeten 1972 *The Frontiers of Development Studies*, London, Macmillan, p. 52.

of model-building is not only inevitable but must be pursued in a sceptical fashion. As Streeten puts it: 'it is of the essence of what is sometimes called the institutional approach to probe into the psychological, social, political and cultural justification for the formation of certain concepts'.[18] In respect of the matter of the formation of concepts Streeten argues that model-building typically reveals four systematic biases.

The first of these concerns the decision as to what counts as a variable and what counts as a parameter. Streeten notes that 'the separation of parameters from variables in Western orthodox models is partly determined by what is appropriate for advanced industrial nations, partly by ideology and vested interest, and partly by convenience of analysis'.[19] Against the style of argument of the free market economists, with their *a priori* argument, Streeten suggests that we focus on the problems which confront us in practice. The problem will reveal what is to count as a parameter and what as a variable. Streeten insists on the specificity of analysis, and urges that 'to be useful models will have to be, at least initially, much more specific to individual cases and much less general and "theoretical"'.[20]

Using the distinction between parameters and variables, Streeten defines his position in relation to both the economic orthodoxy and marxist theorists. The orthodox treat economic variables and eschew engagement with social parameters (setting them aside under *ceteris paribus* clauses), and the marxists in essence do the same (looking to economic change causing social change *mutatis mutandis*). So far as Streeten is concerned, these two very different analyses manifest a convergence-in-neglect of the institutional, political and cultural circumstances of economic development.

The second systematic bias is introduced, by Streeten, with the aid of the notion of fashion, and this enables the juxtaposition of the pursuit of various putative 'strategic factors of development' (for example, capital, or education, or health, or marketization and so on) with the broad, problem-relevant and catholic analysis offered by institutionalism. It is certainly the case that development theory has seen a series of fashions, and Streeten ridicules this habit, observing that 'numerous . . . conditions both account for past growth in advanced countries and are required for development in underdeveloped countries'.[21]

The third source of bias is the habit of shifting from regarding some features of the situation of a developing country as being an explanatory necessary condition for the given overall circumstances, to seeing the features in question as an explanatorily sufficient condition for the given overall circumstances. In other words, certain features are picked out and made to explain the whole situation. Streeten calls this tendency illegitimate isolation. So, consistent with an analysis of the system-as-a-whole, Streeten is

18   Streeten 1970 op. cit. p. 69.
19   Streeten 1972 op. cit. p. 52.
20   Ibid. p. 52.
21   Ibid. p. 54.

able to indicate the foolishness of aid missions to developing countries recommending assistance in this or that sector of the society in the expectation that the rest of the system will thereafter respond favourably.

The final source of bias identified in modelling by Streeten refers to the data of social science and to their context-dependence. Streeten observes: 'Almost all concepts formed by aggregation suitable for analysing Western economies must be carefully considered before they can be applied to underdeveloped economies'.[22] Streeten does not object to aggregative concepts in themselves, but to the use of such concepts where their cultural prerequisites are absent, or in brief where they do not make sense. The unconsidered and uncritical use of familiar Western social scientific concepts in the novel circumstances of other cultures is likely to lead to category errors. Here Streeten is taking an idea from the philosopher Gilbert Ryle[23] who used the notion of a category mistake to indicate that our ordinary language worked correctly only in restricted and given spheres of thought and action. If a concept adequate to one situation was transferred to another then the possibility arose of making a category error – of systematically misunderstanding the new situation. In a similar way Streeten would argue that to use the familiar notion of 'unemployment' in the situation of a Third World country – with peasant communities and urban informal workers – would be to commit a category error simply because these economies and societies work differently.[24]

The conceptual repertoire developed by Streeten owes much to the work of the broad spread of the social sciences. These intellectual resources are used in order to get clear the overall outlines of the character of the economy with which he is concerned. Overall, we can see that Streeten like the other institutionalists is making extensive use of the resources of the social sciences: epistemological, methodological and procedural.

Streeten takes empirical concepts to be simplifying abstractions from raw data; that is, aggregative isolations from experience. Thus, a subtle grasp of the data of an economy is a necessary condition for concept formation and subsequent model-building. A poor grasp of data will result in a greater likelihood of the construction of inadequate concepts. In general it is facts that determine concepts. Epistemologically, fine-grain social science data are thus necessary to Streeten so as to be able to construct and check concepts, the bases of realistic models. And at this point Streeten's notion of biases indicates errors of analysis which serve to misdirect enquiry (perhaps in a direction which serves the interests of the status quo).

Methodologically speaking, since Streeten regards empirical concepts as

---

22 Ibid. p. 55.
23 G. Ryle 1949 *The Concept of Mind*, London, Hutchinson; see also J. Passmore 1968 *A Hundred Years of Philosophy*, Harmondsworth, Penguin, pp. 442–50.
24 Streeten is clearly correct in his general point. However, there must be some doubt that it is necessary to invoke Ryle at this point – these errors of misplaced concept transfer seem gross compared with the subtle errors pursued by Ryle. A simpler notion of ideologically driven misreading might secure Streeten's point more easily.

abstractions from particular concrete situations, he is able to ask of any concept: what is the empirical situation from which it abstracts? Thus he may check the argument machineries of other theorists. Yet, rephrased, we see that as his economics are lodged within an institutional frame, then his concepts (insofar as they are social and not just economic) are borrowings from the conceptual store of social science. Social science data establish the possibility of realistic concepts, whilst social science concepts provide the governing frame for concept-formation. All this follows the institutional-ists' problem-centred empiricism, in contrast to the abstract-formal style of the neo-classical-dominated orthodoxy. Coupled up to their ideology of plan-ning, this reveals the source and impetus in their work to the construction of realistic models.

There is a related procedural point here. Since social science (concepts and data) provides a technique for testing the adequacy of data, and as Streeten takes economies to be intimately lodged within institutional frame-works, the habit of thought of social science is used to generate criticisms. Social science both orders the data brought to bear on concepts suspected of being unrealistic, and is the point of departure of critical speculations, a source of questions to put to otherwise innocent data. In this way the thoroughly sceptical character of social science is used. Rather than accept-ing that which is taken for granted or obvious, and so on, the familiar critical habits of social science are invoked. And this critical element is reflexively deployed as Streeten, and those in the institutionalist tradition, routinely critically inspect their own work.

The problem of values

As regards the role of the theorist Streeten takes Myrdal to have posed the tripartite question 'can one be at the same time objective, practical and ideal-istic?'[25] Streeten notes that Myrdal's career 'looks almost like a series of attempts to extort from concrete problems . . . the replies to these and sim-ilar fundamental questions'.[26] Myrdal's solution to the problem of values in social science involves invoking the notion of crisis politics. In periods of crisis it becomes generally obvious what ought to be done.

Myrdal reports that the issue of values arose in the context of academic work in Sweden. The orthodox argued for an ideal of value-neutrality whilst clearly having an impact in the realm of practical politics. Myrdal comes to the view that any principled striving after value-neutrality is futile as social scientific work is always, one way or another, engaged in practical problems. The key experience seems to have been his exchanges with the US institutional theorists in the 1930s, whom he regarded, in this matter, as intellectually naive, and thus the issue of how to integrate values within

---

25   P. Streeten 1958 'Introduction' in G. Myrdal *Value in Social Theory*, London, Routledge, p. ix.
26   Ibid.

social scientific research was directly raised. However, Myrdal reports that he found no solution until the Great Depression. Myrdal reports that the depression itself presented a solution because the demanding urgency of the social crisis put academic questions in respect of values into perspective at the same time as generating a crisis-driven consensus in respect of what must be done. Myrdal writes:

> The crux of the matter is, of course, that when the old liberal postulate of harmony of interests is renounced, political conclusions – and ultimately theoretical research – must be founded on explicit value premises which must be concrete and take into account the actual conflict of interests between different social groups. However in a situation experienced as crisis, it is a matter of empirical fact that interests converge and conflicts of valuation disappear. Political conclusions can then be drawn from value premises which are homogeneous and defined in concrete terms.[27]

Myrdal's dilemma was resolved by practical activity within the context of social crisis, and this solution was affirmed in subsequent work. Streeten reports that in *An American Dilemma*, begun in 1938, Myrdal distinguishes between the concepts of 'programme' and 'prognosis', and adds that these two key concepts 'open the door to his approach to the whole problem of values'.[28]

Streeten defines a programme as a 'plan of intended action . . . it consists of certain objectives or ends, and rules about the manner in which these objectives are to be pursued'.[29] The complementary concept of prognosis is 'a forecast of the probable or possible course of events'.[30] Here we can see how the Myrdalian solution to the fact/value problem flows out of the position of centrality given to a certain type of practical activity. Streeten notes that the distinction is 'related to the more familiar one between analysis and policy'.[31] It also resembles the distinction between means and ends, although it is not the same. Where the means/end split lets the practitioners of the conventional wisdom assimilate matters of value to given ends, and thereafter treat the means as an entirely technical issue, Streeten sees the programme/prognosis distinction as preventing such a manoeuvre.

Streeten observes that a programme is a 'complex of desired ends, means and procedures . . . all of which is conditioned by valuations'.[32] The core of this Myrdal/Streeten solution is a denial of the orthodox means/ends split in the context of a certain sort of practical theorizing-and-activity. The programme, by definition, includes both means and ends. It is thus a counterstance that rules out the position followed by the conventional wisdom. The

27 Myrdal 1958 op. cit. p. 256.
28 Streeten 1958 op. cit. p. xiv.
29 Ibid.
30 Ibid.
31 Ibid.
32 Ibid.

style of validation that it would have applied to itself are the tests of realism and relevance: realism because it claims to produce a better model of what in fact is the case, and relevance because the whole effort takes as its point of departure a reading of some problem inherent in social crisis. The relationship of programmes and prognoses is dialectical, and Streeten notes that:

> A programme without a prognosis is an impotent utopian dream. On the other hand, a prognosis without a programme is necessarily incomplete. Prognosis depends upon programme in two distinct ways. First and obviously, the programmes of others are data for the social observer and theorist . . . Second, and perhaps less obviously, the observer and theorist himself has something like a programme which determines his analysis and prognosis.[33]

The first point calls attention to the complexity of the environment of theorizing which must be acknowledged. The social world is not a static environment but one containing a multiplicity of actors. The second point calls attention to the engagement of the theorists in this complex and dynamic environment.

In Streeten's view social theorizing is an active business pursued in dynamic circumstances by engaged actors, and in all these areas the claims of the orthodoxy to value-freedom simply break down. However, Streeten's movement away from the orthodoxy is restricted and the place of values in social research is simultaneously granted and taken to be problematical. If social crisis gives us a consensus about matters of value, thereafter, it would seem we have to guard against any value-seepage disturbing the pursuit of practical analyses. Streeten is clear that social scientists should not 'plunge at once into valuation and ideologies'[34] and that the pursuit of realistic and relevant models to inform practical courses of action should govern their work. In both Streeten and Myrdal the final value commitment is to a style of social scientific work which is dominated by the image of rational and reasonable social reform.

As regards the institutionalist treatment of the issues of value and the role of the theorist, we can summarize as follows: (a) Myrdal raises the issue of valuation in the context of debates with colleagues in the 1930s but fails to secure a plausible solution; (b) Myrdal instead offers a parallel solution in terms of the crisis-engendered obviousness of certain schedules of values, which can thereafter govern practical research; (c) Myrdal argues that crisis politics lets basic values be assumed, and thereafter the problem is simply one of the removal of idiosyncratic valuations; and (d) Myrdal adopts the stance of the reasonable man addressing reasonable people about obviously urgent issues and takes the coherence and plausibility of his work to flow from this stance.

33 Ibid. p. xvii.
34 Streeten 1958 op. cit. p. xxxiv.

The mechanisms of change

Myrdal argues that the state planning machine run by reasonable people can order and implement programmes of social change. What Myrdal does is to reduce politics to planning. Like the other institutionalists, Myrdal argues in reaction to the conventional wisdom of neo-classicism and the experience of the Great Depression to the rational necessity of planning. Myrdal reveals this as the core of his theory's practical engagement when he observes that:

> what a state needs, and what politics is about, is precisely a macro-plan for inducing changes, simultaneously, in a great number of conditions, not only in the economic, and doing it in a way so as to coordinate all these changes in order to reach a maximum development effect of efforts and sacrifices. This may, in popular terms, be a definition of what we should mean by planning.[35]

In observing that the situation in many Third World countries simply does not measure up to the requirements of his theory, Myrdal introduces the notion of the 'soft state', which is effectively one that covers the extent to which reality diverges from the requirements of theory. Myrdal writes that the soft state is characterized by 'a general lack of social discipline',[36] and adds that his discussion 'should rightly lead up to an investigation of the policy issue of by what means the "soft state" can be changed into more of a "strong state" . . . This is, in my view, the most important task to be fulfilled in order to make possible rapid development'.[37]

Myrdal is rather pessimistic about the chances of the countries of the Third World putting their own houses in order; with good reason, since his policy proposals take the form of the vague injunction that: 'the underdeveloped countries have to struggle on a broad front to make their states less soft'.[38] But the agents of this activity are never clearly identified, much less openly discussed. The role of the more developed countries is ambiguous. Myrdal advocates the use of 'leverage' but this strategy in turn rests on the assumption of the power of liberal progressives in the governments of the developed countries. In respect of the states of the Third World, Myrdal observes that little can be done before the 'power structure has been changed by evolution or revolution'.[39] The reform of the political and social structures of the underdeveloped countries, plus changes in orientation on the part of the more developed, are made the pre-requisites of planning the development of the Third World. It seems that it is the planners, the reasonable men, who must press for these reforms.

35 G. Myrdal 1970 *The Challenge of World Poverty*, London, Allen Lane, p. 21.
36 G. Myrdal 1970 'The Soft State in Underdeveloped Countries' in P. Streeten ed. *Unfashionable Economics: Essays in Honour of Lord Balogh*, London, Weidenfeld, p. 229.
37 Ibid. p. 241.
38 Ibid. p. 242.
39 Ibid. p. 248.

There are a number of objections to these suggestions. Perhaps the most familiar objection is a tactical one: those who have made this point ask why a part of the problem (the present nature of the state) should be made into a vehicle for the solution of social and economic problems as a whole? It is suggested that this contradiction within the analysis cannot be glossed over by arguing for the internal renewal of the state whereby the reasonable men gradually extend their hold over the machineries of the state.

Moreover, we can go further than this with a related technical version of this criticism which can be generated from the argument that prospective social theorizing is incoherent without an identified agent for the execution of the theory.[40] It can be argued that a complete analysis entails prescription because the analysis itself necessarily involves some suppositions as to mechanisms for the realization of the solution presented. In other words, theories are not simply constructed for somebody to use or not; rather they involve as necessary assumptions agents acting in line with the proposals of the theory. The corollary is that any theory which has no agent whereby the theory can be translated into practice is an incomplete analysis and is consequently disengaged from the world. If we ask about the status of Myrdal's agent, the state, it is clear that Myrdal's treatment is dominated by how the state ought to be rather than how Third World states typically are at the present time. In considering Myrdal's treatment of the state, it seems that having just established by moral and practical reflection how the world is and how it ought to be, he then proceeds to search for an agent to change it. Myrdal does not begin his analysis of the state in the Third World from how it is, which would be consistent with his methodological insistence on realism; rather he begins with how it has to be if Myrdalian theory is to be executed. It is clear that the Myrdalian reforming state is the minimum necessary acknowledgement of the logical requirement to identify an agent for the execution of the theory. It is not any extant state in the Third World.

A third related line of criticism can be generated by considering the version of progress which is tacitly affirmed by Myrdal. The notion of the perfectibility of humankind comes down to us from the ancient Greeks.[41] Prior to the Renaissance such discussions of perfectibility were couched in metaphysical or religious terms, and concerned the pursuit of the goal of perfection. The philosopher John Locke transforms the idea by arguing that men are capable of being improved by moral education; that is, social action. This is the key idea which was influential in the eighteenth and nineteenth centuries: the focus is on the role of education, and the process of improvement. However, a damaging criticism of this line is to point out that the educator is a member of a corrupt society and presumably corrupt also. Marx will accuse Locke and his followers of forgetting the matter of

40   See M. Dobb 1973 *Theories of Value and Distribution Since Adam Smith*, Cambridge University Press.
41   J. Passmore 1971 *The Perfectibility of Man*, London, Duckworth.

the education of the educator. This opens up a search for a guarantor – if Locke established the possibility of the moral advancement of the citizens and their society, the question becomes one of securing the fact. And two lines of argument flow from this point. The first, presented by the French *philosophes*, who were very much aware of their own novel social status, argued for the rule of the best – a version of the Platonic 'philosopher-king' idea – and advanced an early version of governmentalism, with its stress on the role of the state. This line moves via Jeremy Bentham and J. S. Mill down to the Fabians and contemporary ideas of the role of the state. On the other hand, the second line of development has recourse to the model of the natural sciences and here the need for a guarantor focused on a method. The extension of the method of natural science into the realm of the social was entailed, as was the dissemination and use of the result-ant knowledge. The notion of progress is presented, and is taken to be normal insofar as it is not blocked by sinister partial interests. However, both these lines of response to the need for a guarantor fail as neither states nor methods can guarantee that social learning and progress will proceed. The further refinement of the debate takes the issue of progress and lodges it in tendential historical mechanisms – from Charles Darwin ideas of social evolution, and from Marx ideas of historical dialectics.

Myrdal refers to himself as 'a student in the great liberal tradition of the Enlightenment'.[42] Myrdal is clearly drawing on both the government- and method-focused lines of analysis of progress. In the analysis of the situation of the Third World the two elements come together in that the state is both the agent of change and the locus of the deployment of reason; hence Myrdal's claim that: 'what the state needs, and what politics is about, is precisely a macro-plan for inducing changes . . . This may in popular terms, be a definition of what we should mean by planning'.[43] However, neither of the two lines of argument used by Myrdal carries conviction; nor does the practical stance advanced.

In summary, the Myrdalian state is an epistemic device to secure a grounded theory and it represents a minimum response to the demands of the logic of theorizing. The Myrdalian treatment of the state is in conflict with the avowed method of the pursuit of realism in modelling and is too weak to carry the general argument. Furthermore, combining the role of the state with the method of science is insufficient to secure development if this is regarded as synonymous with progress.

The best of the orthodox?

In the end, the institutional approach is one of the most plausible of the post-Second World War theories of development. The work of the institu-tionalists is a significant advance over modernization theory. The general

42   Myrdal 1970 op. cit. p. 435.
43   Ibid. p. 21.

procedural dictum of institutionalism is the pursuit of problem-specific formulations rather than general theories and its analytical machineries are subtle in contrast to those of growth theory and modernization theory. It is also true that the claim to the crisis-engendered obviousness of their reformist stance may well be taken as a part of the common sense of development studies. The approach has found widespread support amongst the state machines of the new nationstates and within the various agencies of the United Nations.[44]

Chapter Summary

The institutionalist school can be taken despite its internal diversity to represent a coherent and distinct position within development theorizing. These theorists – with the figure of Myrdal made central – tended to the view that development studies was a novel and distinct social science. These theorists denied the simple transferability of social scientific concepts that had been produced in the First World to the circumstances of the Third World. The emphasis on situating analysis is taken up by Paul Streeten,[45] who is the most theoretically subtle member of this group. But it is Myrdal who is the pre-eminent figure amongst the institutionalist theorists of development. A notion of circular cumulative causation is presented which implies that once a direction of change is set, it will continue. The Third World needs to be shifted by planning onto an upward development track.

---

44   The approach has inspired for example the UNDP *Human Development Report* – a kind of institutionalist reply to the World Bank's *World Development Report*.
45   P. Streeten 1972 *The Frontiers of Development Studies*, London, Macmillan.

12

The Critical Work of Marxist Development Theory

Overview of Marxist Development Theory

Within the broad marxist tradition it can be argued that there have been three major attempts to grasp the situation of the underdeveloped countries.[1] The first was the work of Marx and Engels who saw capitalism as destructive of non-capitalist social forms and thereafter as progressive. The second was the work of the theorists of imperialism who initially expected capitalism to act progressively once the colonial system had been dismantled but who later became more pessimistic. The third and most recent grouping began with the optimistic work of the neo-marxists in the immediate post-Second World War period. The neo-marxist line revolved around the work of Paul Baran who analysed the situation of the Third World in terms of how local economic surplus was realized and used. As with the dependency theorists, he diagnosed subordinate and deforming incorporation within a world capitalist economy. The key to development was disengagement from the deforming impact of the world economy and the prerequisite was socialist revolution. However, the early optimism waned and subsequent marxist work has looked to consolidate intellectually the contribution of the tradition.

---

1   G. Palma 1978 'Dependency: A Formal Theory of Underdevelopment or a Methodology for the Analysis of Concrete Situations of Underdevelopment', *World Development*, 6.

The Rediscovery of Marx

In the years prior to the 1960s Western social scientists did not pay much attention to the marxian tradition of social theorizing. The intellectual and political rediscovery of Marx in the late 1960s was brought about by a combination of the collapse of consensus politics, the failure of the Americans to win a decisive victory in Vietnam, and the moribund nature of academic social science. In the USA the collapse of consensus was bound up with the issues of civil rights, university reform and the episode of the war in Vietnam. In Europe the key issues were university reform and the war in Vietnam which for Europeans was redolent of other colonial wars. A new political movement emerged which acquired the label New Left. It developed in the 1960s as a broad activist progressive movement and it also came to adopt as its own the struggles of the Third World anti-colonial movements.

In the USA the civil rights movement began to gather influence with the 1954 Supreme Court decision which desegregated the public school system. Many students came to the South in order to assist civil rights workers. The political intention of these activities overlapped with the movement for reform of the universities. In Europe the student movement began in Germany, in particular at the Free University of Berlin.[2] The scope of the protest was ever widening and Vietnam became the crucial issue. The universities came to be seen as exemplifying in microcosm the paternalistic, authoritarian, hierarchical and non-democratic character of the society of which they were a part. The New Left became to a significant extent transformed into a 'youth movement'[3] focused on the general issue of democracy.

A series of features of the colonial and post-colonial situation were taken as the basis for an identification with the local people on the part of radicals in the developed world. In the period of decolonization there had been a widespread optimism for the future. However, it soon became clear that replacement elites were often less than innovative in their economic, social and political programmes and confidence in the imported political model collapsed. The spectacle of corrupted elite groups and successions of military coups led to the recognition that any affirmation of the notion of democracy would entail a sharp revision in political theory and practice. A new politics slowly began to emerge which proposed ditching elite-ordered capitalist nationbuilding in favour of an identification with the problems of the masses and this 'new politics . . . became known as the politics of liberation'.[4] The experiences of Vietnam, Algeria[5] and Cuba are central to the manner of cooption by the New Left of the experience of groups in the Third

2   G. Statera 1975 *Death of a Utopia*, Oxford University Press.
3   N. Birnbaum 1969 'The Staggering Colossus' in J. Nagel ed. *Student Power*, London, Merlin Press, p. 149.
4   B. Davidson 1978 *Africa in Modern History*, London, Allen Lane, p. 328.
5   A brutal war traumatised Algeria and France. It produced the great influential work of F. Fanon 1967 *The Wretched of the Earth*, Harmondsworth, Penguin.

World. It can be read as a way of learning the lessons of a series of brutal colonial wars. It issued in the creation of a myth of Third World struggle which pointed to extensive poverty and the likelihood of rapid change once the grip of the metropolitan centre had been weakened.[6]

The rediscovery of Marx and the marxist tradition took place in the period of the disintegration of the post-Second World War mood of consensus within the First World. The experience of the civil rights movement, the reform of the universities and the lessons of the Vietnam war all contributed to a revival of radical thought. The upshot of these events was that once again social theorists paid serious attention to Marx and when radicals in the First World turned their thoughts to a general theory of development and underdevelopment there was an available explanation in the form of the work of Paul Baran (see figure 14).

The Work of Paul Baran

Paul Baran was one of a small number of scholars based in the West who kept the intellectual tradition of marxism alive at a time when it had effectively died out in the form of its enshrinement within official Marxism–Leninism, the official ideology of the USSR. Baran along with his co-worker Paul Sweezy presented a novel marxist analysis of the condition of capitalism in the mid-twentieth century in terms of an idea of monopoly.[7] The capitalist system can no longer be regarded as having a competitive market; nor can it be regarded as a progressive social form. In a monopoly capitalist situation the economy is dominated by a handful of giant firms and they operate to control competition. They use their monopoly power to defend the status quo in which they have a crucial interest and dominant position.

Baran extends the argument to the sphere of the underdeveloped in *The Political Economy of Growth*.[8] The crucial idea is that of surplus. Baran remarks: 'I consider [economic surplus] to be the key to the understanding of the general working principles of capitalism'.[9] The idea of surplus used by Baran is not that of Marx, where the idea is rooted in the labour theory of value; rather it is the total material output of an economy. What Baran is going to do is to argue that monopoly capitalism both fails to realize the economic surplus that could be generated with presently available factors of production and that it diverts much of the economic surplus that is realized into wasteful and immoral consumption. Baran identifies three related notions of surplus: (a) actual surplus, which is just that which an economy actually produces; (b) potential surplus, which the economy could produce given available factors of production; and (c) planned surplus, which

6 G. Challiand 1977 *Revolution in the Third World*, Hassocks, Harvester.
7 See P. Sweezy 1942 *The Theory of Capitalist Development*, Oxford University Press; P. Baran and P. Sweezy 1968 *Monopoly Capital*, Harmondsworth, Penguin.
8 P. Baran 1973 *The Political Economy of Growth*, Harmondsworth, Penguin, with an introduction by R. Sutcliffe.
9 Ibid. p. 29.

216

Figure 14   Marxist development theory

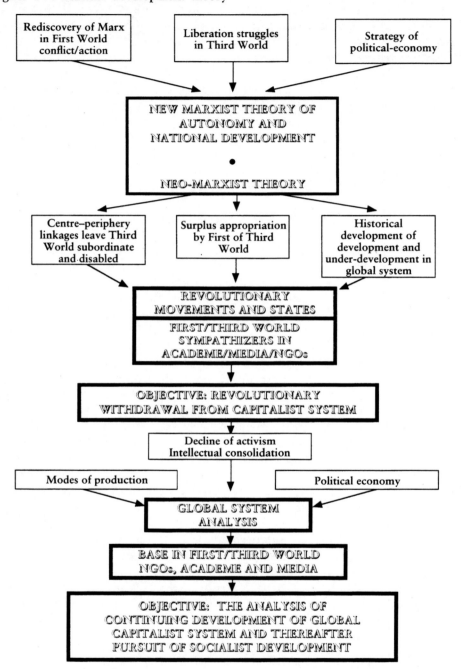

is what could be produced in a rational and humane system. It is the relationship of these three that lets Baran make his analysis of monopoly capitalism and by extension the situation of the Third World.

In a monopoly capitalist economy there is an inbuilt tendency towards stagnation which flows from insufficient consumer demand. The monopoly capitalist system continually faces the problem of avoiding a slump. The remedy identified by Baran was the role of the state as consumer. State spending underpins the monopoly capitalist system. In particular Baran points to military spending as this is the one kind of spending that does not obviously raise general questions about social arrangements in society. Baran's view of monopoly capitalism was that it was irrational and wasteful.

Baran argues that the global capitalist economy is divided into the two historically generated sectors of the advanced and the underdeveloped countries. The key to unravelling the logic of this historical development lies in the issue of the generation and subsequent use of economic surplus. The history may be traced back to the mercantile capitalist appropriation of economic surplus from those territories which now comprise the underdeveloped countries of the world. As regards the present-day circumstances of the Third World two issues emerge: first, how is the economic surplus of these countries realized, and second how is it then used? Baran's answer to this double question entails the identification of a series of sectors within the Third World economy. We have, firstly, the agricultural sector of either peasant farming or commercial plantation. It is the case that neither part of this sector is historically progressive as surplus is realized and either consumed immediately or removed as profits. Then, secondly, there is the merchant sector, with money lenders, traders, middlemen and so on, and this essentially parasitic grouping is not progressive as the economic surplus which does accrue to it is merely diverted into consumption. The third sector comprises the local industrial groups. However, because these industrial groups face daunting problems of internal handicaps and external competition, their contribution to total economic surplus is depressed and they are not progressive. Baran goes on to identify a fourth sector, which is the state, and argues that the state should use the economic surplus at its disposal to foster development. However, this does not happen. The state, even if uncorrupted, has the unenviable task of trying to balance the conflicting demands of internal agricultural, mercantile and industrial capital. Additionally the state employees come to have a powerful interest. And externally, there is the power of overseas capital (the multinationals and the agencies of the capitalist system such as the IMF and World Bank). Baran thinks that the state is either probably incapable or already corrupted and thus the available economic surplus is either drained away to the metropolitan centres or misused in the peripheral states. The economic surplus that the Third World economy does produce is not effectively utilized and nor, within the context of the world capitalist system, can it be. The solution to which Baran points is that of the withdrawal from the world capitalist system and the state-socialist pursuit of development.

The Work of A. G. Frank

A. G. Frank is probably the best-known theorist working within the general marxist line. Frank's background is that of an economist turned political activist.[10] The decisive events in Frank's career centre upon his experience of Latin America. Out of a recognition of the long-term foreign dominance of the area, in particular by the USA, and the experience of the Cuban revolution, and within the intellectual context of a rejection of orthodox economic approaches, Frank conceives the task of contributing to a revolutionary critique of orthodox theorizing and expectations. The available resources are threefold: (a) the neo-classical economics informed theories of modernization provide an object against which the new departure may be defined; (b) the analytical machineries are largely provided by the structuralist line associated with ECLA whilst the political reformism of that organization provides another negative defining element; and (c) a simple strategic metaphor which involves the crucial idea of surplus is borrowed from the marxism of Baran and we have the notion of the debilitating metropolitan extraction of economic surplus from the peripheral areas.

The position of A. G. Frank

A simple statement of Frank's overall position in presented in the text *On Capitalist Underdevelopment*[11] Frank states:

> All serious study of the problems of development of underdeveloped areas and all serious intent to formulate policy for the elimination of underdevelopment and for the promotion of development must take into account, nay must begin with, the fundamental historical and structural cause of underdevelopment in capitalism.[12]

Frank identifies three contradictions which characterize capitalist development and the development of underdevelopment. They are:

> the expropriation of economic surplus from the many and its appropriation by the few, the polarisation of the capitalist system into metropolitan centre and peripheral satellites, and the continuity of the fundamental structures of the capitalist system throughout the history of its expansion and transformation.[13]

The first noted contradiction (expropriation/appropriation) deals with the way in which the economic surplus generated within an economy is removed from the hands of those who actually produce it. Frank argues that

---

10   An autobiographical sketch is offered in A. G. Frank 1976 *Economic Genocide in Chile*, Nottingham, Spokesman.
11   A. G. Frank 1975 *On Capitalist Underdevelopment*, Oxford University Press.
12   Ibid. p. 96.
13   A. G. Frank 1967 *Capitalism and Underdevelopment in Latin America*, New York, Monthly Review Press, p. 3.

this results in the economy functioning poorly and the division of society into 'haves' and 'have nots'. The image he uses is of a chainlike expropriation/appropriation of economic surplus. This chain stretches from the poorest landless labourer, up through landlords, regional elite groups, national elites, and finally joins the metropolitan capitalist centres. An economic model is conjoined with a geographical pattern as surplus shifts up the chain and moves from peripheries to centres. This is pursued in the second contradiction (polarization), where Frank argues that the immanent tendency towards centralization within capitalism has manifested itself on a world scale in the form of a split between metropolitan centres and peripheral satellites. Thus he argues: 'Economic development and underdevelopment are the opposite faces of the same coin'.[14] Then, the third contradiction (continuity in change) allows Frank to urge that capitalism does not and has not changed its character and that to understand the circumstances of Latin America one has to think not in terms of underdevelopment but in terms of capitalist underdevelopment. All other economic, social and cultural phenomena revolve around this basic point. Latin America, argues Frank, has been capitalist ever since the Conquistadors arrived.

With this basic position sketched, Frank then goes on to review the history of Latin America. In general, a series of phases can be identified, beginning in the sixteenth century and culminating in the twentieth-century situation, which is characterized in terms of the incapacity of national bourgeois groups to fulfil their historical role of securing development. Only socialist revolution can now advance matters.[15] And at this point we can take note that we now have two of the characteristic elements of the Frankian mode of analysis: (a) the analytical framework which is a mixture of Latin American social science run together in a distinctly activist fashion with the material of Baran; and (b) the detailed attention to history. It all amounts to a quite distinctive way of making and deploying social scientific arguments which may be characterized as 'political writing'.[16]

The World Systems Approach

Wallerstein argues that analysis must begin with social systems regarded as totalities, and not with nationstates seen thereafter as interacting.[17] A social system is characterized by an internal division of labour: there is specialization and exchange. In history there are only three identifiable sorts of social systems: closed local economies, world empires (where a core extracts tribute from its peripheries) and world economies (where the world economy is a single economic division of labour, and thus pattern of specialization and exchange, with multiple cultures within it and no central

14   Ibid. p. 9.
15   A. G. Frank 1972 *Lumpenbourgeoisie–Lumpendevelopment*, New York, Monthly Review Press.
16   See P. W. Preston 1987 *Rethinking Development*, London, Routledge.
17   I. Wallerstein 1974 *The Modern World System*, New York, Academic.

authority). Substantively, the modern world system is capitalist. Wallerstein takes the notions to be equivalent: thus capitalism is a world market system.

The capitalist world system is divided into tiers of states: core, semi-periphery, and periphery. There is a transfer of wealth through asymmetries of state power from periphery to core. The state is a key actor in manipulating the world market to the advantage of local traders. The core–periphery division is historically given through technology developments in Europe requiring free labour, and which made strong states. Peripheral economic areas had weak states that were overborne by the core states. Once in place the core–periphery system is reproduced over time.

So now we can ask, recalling the classical marxian tradition, just what happened to productive relations and classes? The answer seems to be that Wallerstein abandons marxian notions of class and the dynamic of capitalist production-driven accumulation, in favour of a world market system with groups manoeuvring for advantage. The dynamic of the world capitalist system shifts from production and class conflict within the capitalist heartland to trade flows between the various polities within the one world market capitalist system. To characterize very briefly the world system procedure in contrast to the political-economic, the style of social theorizing which I take both to encompass Marx and represent the core of our distinctively European tradition, we find, in place of the intellectual reconstruction of the real orientated to uncovering dynamics of change in pursuit of democracy, the deployment of economic history to establish what looks like a descriptive general model.

Wallerstein has been criticized by Brenner[18] and Palma,[19] amongst many others, who argue that he has mistakenly identified capitalism with a trade-based division of labour where the system dynamic flows from market pressure. Thus we have a neo-Smithian inversion that repeats that theorists err in placing the market at the core of human social life, and thus orthodox economics at the centre of analysis with society following on. The reverse is the case: economics must be reduced to society as Marx argued. What then becomes the focus in respect of the origins of capitalism is the precise concatenation of class circumstances that gave rise to and then fixed in place the technologically innovative and capital accumulative dynamic of the capitalist system. Thereafter we study the reproductive mechanisms of the inherently dynamic social system of capitalism.

The place of the notion of the market in world systems theorizing is thus suffused with ambiguity: at base there is a strong argument to the effect that a neo-classical conception of the market is deployed. However there is clearly a lot more to it than this, and what world systems theory does do, against the liberalism-writ-large of orthodox economics with their focus on nation-states as separate and competing in an essentially time-less market milieu,

18 R. Brenner 1977 'The Origins of Capitalist Development: A Critique of Neo-Smithian Marxism', *New Left Review*, 104.
19 Palma 1978 op. cit.

is to reintroduce both an element of history into the analysis and to de-centre theorizing so that the familiar nationstate drops away in favour of a world market system having points of power within it (and here extant states would be such points). This is very much the credit side of the equation.[20]

Criticisms of Neo-marxism in General

The work of Paul Baran, A. G. Frank and Wallerstein has been subject to a series of general lines of attack. These lines of criticism are often directed both at a particular figure and at the approach as a whole. The criticisms can be considered under three headings: (a) objections to the notion of surplus; (b) objections to the characterization of capitalism; and (c) objections to the ethics affirmed.

The notion of surplus

The notion of surplus has figured centrally in the work of the neo-marxists. We can pursue the notion in the company of Baran with whom the concept originates. The idea of surplus is crucial to Baran's analysis of underdevelopment and there have been two main lines of criticism. First, the orthodox have lodged charges of ambiguity and difficulty of measurement; but these attacks need not be pursed as they are besides the point because Baran is offering a political-economy of underdevelopment not an orthodox empirical model. Second, radical marxists have lodged similar criticisms claiming that Baran's work owes more to Keynesian aggregate analysis than it does to Marx. It has been argued that:

> The conceptual difference is that Marx's 'surplus value' is defined in relation to the ownership of property while Baran's 'surplus' is defined more in relation to consumption needs. It is therefore to Baran something which exists in all societies.[21]

What we have here is a fairly complex distinction: what is most obviously relevant in the present context is that, on the one hand, we have, with Marx, an essentially economic notion defined with reference to the historically specific circumstances of capitalism, whereas, on the other hand, we have an abstract and idealist notion.

In a similar way it has been suggested that the idea of surplus labour and the related idea of surplus value are specific to capitalist social relations. Yet Baran's idea of 'economic surplus' relates to the excess of production over consumption and could be called a pre-marxist notion which understands surplus as material quantity of goods produced.[22] It is in this context

20   T. Schiel 1987 'Wallerstein's Concept of a Modern World System: Another Marxist Critique' in *University of Bielefeld Sociology of Development Research Centre Working Papers*, 89. See also D. Smith 1991 *The Rise of Historical Sociology*, Cambridge, Polity.
21   R. Sutcliffe 1973 'Introduction' in Baran op. cit. pp. 90–1.
22   A. Brewer 1980 *Marxist Theories of Imperialism*, London, Routledge, pp. 138–41.

that Baran introduces an idea of human need so as to characterize different production schedules as either wasteful or rational in respect of their usage of realized economic surplus.

The matter of the ethics lodged in Baran's analytical machineries can be pursued in a little while. For the moment, however, we can grant that it is true that Baran's notion of economic surplus is different from that used by Marx. Yet one wonders if this is really all that interesting because the real question cannot be simply whether or not Baran alters the analytic machineries of Marx but whether or not the theory which he does present makes good or bad sense, and this is clearly an issue that extends far beyond mere comparative textual exegesis.

The notion of capitalism

Brenner says that neo-marxist theorists argue in a circular fashion. They assume the existence of capitalistic social relations in their attempts to explain the rise of capitalism. Brenner analyses Paul Sweezy's work by unpacking the model offered and asking after the plausibility of its assumptions about the behaviour of the historical actors mentioned. The conclusion presented is that 'the entire account of the transition from feudalism to capitalism is based on the implicit assumption that capitalism already exists'.[23] Sweezy's work is taken to reduce to the view that the transition from feudalism to capitalism is a matter of the appropriate adjustment in society to the demands of the market. But the relationship of economics to society is not one of simple determination of social relations by economic forces and nor can capitalism be defined just by the existence of a market. Brenner is suggesting that Sweezy and the rest offer an economistic reading of Marx which contains amongst its assumptions precisely those individualistic ideas in respect of the pursuit of individual satisfactions in the market that underlie orthodox economics.

Brenner also claims that the entire neo-marxian line in this area of debate reduces to a polemical inversion of Adam Smith. Most broadly, where Smith argued that the free market would maximize progress the neo-marxists argue that it actually has generated a moribund monopoly. In more detail, it is argued that the neo-marxists follow Smith in equating capitalism with a trade-based division of labour where innovation is determined by market pressure and class relations adjust thereafter. It is argued that it is misconceived. Instead analysis should reduce economics to social relations after the style of Marx. The core of the matter is the particular set of class circumstances that trigger and sustain the innovative dynamic of capitalism.

The neo-marxists displace the dynamic of the system from the social relations of production into the business of market exchanges in pursuit of profit. The conditions of development and underdevelopment are seen as aspects of this same world market. It is noted that Wallerstein 'straightforwardly defines capitalism as a trade-based division of labour, and it is

23 Brenner 1977 op. cit. p. 48.

here that he locates the dynamic of capitalist development'.[24] Against this, Brenner argues that capitalism is a specific social form which requires that productive forces are continuously upgraded:

> In short the uniquely successful development of capitalism in Western Europe was determined by a class system, a property system, a system of surplus extraction, in which the methods the extractors were obliged to use to increase their surplus corresponded to an unprecedented, though imperfect, degree to the needs of development of the productive forces.[25]

It is in this historical conjunction that the search for an explanation of the genesis of capitalism is to be conducted, not in any behaviour of an abstractly regarded world market.

Frank repeats this neo-marxist line when he argues that development and underdevelopment are explained by reference to international trade-based extraction of surplus, and not the particular conjunctions of class circumstances and technological possibility. It is argued that 'the method of an entire line of writers in the [neo] marxist tradition has led them to displace class relations from the centre of their analyses of economic development and underdevelopment'.[26] And the upshot of these errors is a wholly implausible analysis of the present circumstances of the underdeveloped. An analysis which is both economistic and heavily skewed to the single issue of the deleterious effects of external dependency.

So, picking up the question raised at the end of the first objection – do the neo-marxists make good or bad sense – can we now say anything more? Evidently there are good reasons for doubting that Baran and others had their analyses rigorously worked out. Both Baran and his early co-worker Sweezy were writing in a period of Keynesian reformism and it would be easy to derive material from that tradition. Frank's work is often strongly politically engaged, and the early work of Wallerstein was analytically schematic. However, at the time Baran and others produced their material it was both novel and progressive. It certainly anticipated many areas of subsequent work and this must be evidence of its intellectual vitality.

The ethics affirmed

There have been a variety of objections to the ethics embodied in the work of the neo-marxists. It has been argued that the work of the key figure Paul Baran is fundamentally a moral critique. This line of criticism focuses on the idea of economic surplus. The notion of potential surplus represents some sort of a theoretical maximum of production in an economy, and the planned surplus is that which could or should be produced in a rational and humane socialist society. It is suggested that the position is essentially

24   Ibid. p. 61.
25   Ibid. p. 68.
26   Ibid. p. 27.

utopian and that the whole of the work undertaken by Baran and his neo-marxist co-workers is an elaborate expression of disapproval. With the work of Baran and others it is certainly the case that we have what looks like idealist argument. The notion of surplus is distinctly redolent of Keynesian aggregative macro-economic analysis and of the liberal reformist ethic affirmed in the work of Keynes. However, all social theorizing is value-based and what is at issue is not whether or not the work of Baran and his colleagues is tainted by ethical valuation but the precise nature of the moral core of the work and the manner of its insertion into analysis.

In the case of Marx the moral core of his work was a philosophical anthropology which issued in the critical notion of alienated labour.[27] The ethic of human emancipation was central to his substantive political-economic analyses. A series of explicit arguments about the nature of persons in general are linked to the basic strategies of analysis in order to argue that the dynamic of capitalism has ushered in a system which denies the fundamental nature of humankind as creative labour is degraded into mere work. If we compare the evaluative stance of Baran, the key figure in neo-marxist work, then it may be that there is some cause for concern. Baran's evaluative stance, which condemns the system's present irrationality of use of economic surplus and points to a rationally ordered future, is pitched at such a general level as to tend to be indistinguishable from any other socially liberal critique. Related to this is the manner of the insertion of the ethic into analysis. It is suggested by critics that Baran's economics are not linked to his ethics, and indeed that the economics are merely a vehicle for the application of otherwise established moral views. There is something to be said for these points but we can disarm these criticisms for the time being by concluding that Baran offers a simple political-economic analysis affirming an easily recognizable ethic.

The idea of development is best seen as an ethico-political term which has to be cashed in specific circumstances. In respect of the way in which Baran cashes the term in substantive analysis, two points might be made. First, that Baran is talking in rather general terms; that is, he is not saying what will count as development in a specific country or region. He is, rather, discussing the plight of the Third World in general. In addition to this, we can see that his ethic is relatively unconsidered. A defence can easily be mounted in terms of the context-boundedness of all theorizing. In this case Baran's work was both novel and innovative. However, there is a second line of criticism which does have more force. It has been suggested that the idea of development affirmed by Baran is pessimistic and static: thus the capitalist system has become a monopoly system and no longer progressive, and what chances there are for change have been displaced into the periphery. It has been argued that the politics of the neo-marxists are naive and Third Worldist. A mixture of wrong conceptions of the dynamic of capitalism coupled with an enthusiasm for activism have issued

27   K. Marx 1957 *The Economic and Philosophical Manuscripts*, London, Lawrence and Wishart.

in an apocalyptic politics of disengagement in the peripheries, the location that is seen as the next step in world history given that the First World proletariat has been bought off by consumerism. The critics suggest that this is simply not plausible. However, overall, the neo-marxist line has opened up a host of novel questions and it is fair to say that is has thrown much light on the historical dynamic of capitalist exchanges with peripheral areas. It is as well to recall the remark of Colin Leys to the effect that whilst the neo-marxists may have got much of the story wrong they did rescue enquiry into matters of development from the veritable 'intellectual deserts' of modernization theory.[28]

Contemporary Marxist Debates

The rediscovery of the marxist tradition in the 1960s and its widespread promulgation amongst practitioners, theorists and commentators led to a surge of optimism in respect of the classical political agenda of the marxist tradition. It was supposed that the global capitalist system was in crisis and that a progressive shift towards a socialist world system was in process. However, as the decade of the seventies turned into the eighties this optimism at first waned and then disappeared. A number of factors can be cited: (a) a series of failures of development in Asia, Latin America and Africa; (b) the rise of a powerful political reaction[29] in the USA which sponsored low intensity conflict (LIC) to undermine regimes which were not to its political taste;[30] (c) the evident moribund nature of the USSR and a similar fading of confidence in the example of the People's Republic of China (and other officially socialist states);[31] and (d) the rapid process of the maturation of recently represented marxist scholarship which led to a precipitate fall in earlier simplistic overconfidence.

A period of critical work followed. A core preoccupation which was addressed in different ways was with the nature of a plausible, grounded and intellectually defensible marxism.[32] A series of First World debates were pursued and these included the philosophically structuralist marxism of Louis Althusser, the critical work of the Frankfurt School, the culture-criticism inspired by Antonio Gramsci and the concern for the history of the common people pursued by the British marxist historians.[33] In a similar fashion, the discussions of development have been extensive and three major

28 C. Leys 1977 'Underdevelopment and Dependency: Critical Notes', *Journal of Contemporary Asia*, 7, p. 93.
29 J. Toye 1987 *Dilemmas of Development*, Oxford, Blackwell.
30 F. Halliday 1989 *Cold War, Third World*, London, Radius; V. Brittan 1988 *Hidden Lives, Hidden Deaths*, London, Faber; N. Chomsky 1991 *Deterring Democracy*, London, Vintage.
31 E. Hobsbawm 1994 *Age of Extremes: The Short Twentieth Century, 1914–1991*, London, Michael Joseph.
32 On this see the survey of R. Peet 1991 *Global Capitalism: Theories of Societal Development*, London, Routledge.
33 On all this, see, P. Anderson 1976 *Considerations on Western Marxism*, London, Verso; P. Anderson 1983 *In the Tracks of Historical Materialism*, London, Verso.

themes can be picked out: (a) a rather deterministic and distinctly scientistic approach concerned to uncover the dynamics of particular modes of production and their complex articulations with the developing global system; (b) an approach which eschews the pursuit of substantive theory in favour of the political-economic elucidation of the dynamics of specific situations of underdevelopment; and (c) a recent concern to uncover the mechanisms of the global capitalist system.

Modes of production

The idea of mode of production has been represented in Louis Althusser's structuralist reading of Marx and it is used to designate a particular sort of social production.[34] Marx had understood capitalism as a particular sort of social production and had most famously in the Preface of 1859 deployed the notions of forces of production plus relations of production and summarized their complex patterns of interaction under the heading of 'mode of production'.[35] A capitalist mode of production is characterized as involving the private control of social production. The system was understood as historically dynamic and unstable. Marx also identified other modes of production: primitive communism, ancient slave-based production, feudalism, capitalism, communism, and the Asiatic. The list varies somewhat[36] and there is a large amount of then contemporary ethnographic material discussed but, except for some work published by Engels, little of this material was ever set out in an ordered form. It was this complex of ideas that was picked up by French theorists and used in the context of discussions of development.[37]

The gist of the French approach, inspired as noted by the work of Althusser, is as follows. The Third World is no longer seen as being an underdeveloped social form but as comprising very many modes of production. Each of these modes of production represents a particular historically generated pattern of life, an arrangement of social relations around a particular sort of production. These modes of production have their own internal dynamics as any mode of production must be able to reproduce itself. Further, it is pointed out that these modes of production interact in specific and complex fashions: pre-capitalist modes with each other, and all these with capitalism. So, to analyse any particular part of the world, we have two problems: first, to specify the character of the local modes of

34   Althusser was trained as a philosopher and deployed a structuralist epistemology which insisted on the rationalist theory-driven nature of enquiry. The theories of Marx were considered to be formal theories. These could be deployed to read the confused empirical situation obtaining in reality. See J. Sturrock 1986 *Structuralism*, London, Palladin. See also J. G. Taylor 1979 *From Modernization to Modes of Production*, London, Macmillan.
35   K. Marx 1859 Preface to *A Contribution to the Critique of Political Economy*, reprinted in Marx 1957 op. cit.
36   See P. Worsley 1982 *Marx and Marxism*, Milton Keynes, Open University Press, ch. 3.
37   See J. Clammer 1978 *The New Economic Anthropology*, London, Macmillan; M. Bloch 1983 *Marxism and Anthropology*, Oxford University Press.

production, indicating how they reproduce themselves and how they interact with one another; and second, to detail the way in which these local modes of production interact with the incoming capitalist mode of production. This complex set of circumstances will have its own dynamic and this will condition the chances of development.

The idea of modes of production is taken to permit the pursuit of enquiry which is faithful to the work of Marx, sensitive to empirical detail and scientifically rigorous. All this is taken to be in marked contrast to the overgenerality of Paul Baran and the neo-marxists. The neo-marxists were criticized for oversimplifying the issues of development and underdevelopment by taking capitalism as essentially a market-centred exchange relationship; that is, for equating the existence of individual pursuit of profit within a market for capitalism. The Third World is taken to comprise many modes of production, and these can coexist with each other for long periods of time, and the business of the transition from one pre-capitalist mode of production to the capitalist mode is typically a long drawn out and thoroughly complex business. The idea of a sequence of modes of production, which can be discerned in the work of Marx, is thus revised and the crucial question – given an interest in development – becomes the way in which different modes of production interact, either facilitating or retarding the emergence of capitalism. This is referred to as the articulation of modes of production. The most important articulation is that between capitalism and various precapitalist modes of production. The value of this approach is much debated. The rather scientistic notion of marxism affirmed, plus the influence of Althusser as a philosopher, issue in a tendency to produce elaborate, rather general and formal schemes. Nonetheless, the insistence upon paying attention in a detailed and rigorous way to the differences, and differing patterns of change, between modes of production within the Third World is a useful corrective to the arguably overschematic work of the neo-marxists.

P. P. Rey makes use of the notion of modes of production.[38] The way in which the term was used by Marx and Engels was, as noted, largely unformalized. However, subsequent orthodox marxists presented the idea of modes of production as a series of stages, or a sequence punctuated with periods of transformation, where one mode of production turned into the next. Rey reworks this image so that transition is seen as typical: the two (or more) modes of production will coexist and the process of replacement is slow. Rey calls this the articulation of modes of production.

The expanding mode of production is capitalism, and here Rey returns to the old marxist idea of capitalism as progressive, in contrast to the views of the neo-marxists. Why, then, have some areas advanced and others not? Rey's answer is that it depends on the interaction or articulation between the incoming capitalist mode of production and the existing mode of production.

---

38   In this discussion I draw on A. Brewer 1980 *Marxist Theories of Imperialism*, London, Routledge, ch. 8.

In the heartlands of capitalism, in Europe, the historical articulation of the feudal mode of production with the nascent capital mode issued in the relatively straightforward succession of the latter. Elsewhere in the world pre-capitalist modes of production did not generate their own internal progressive dynamic and have subsequently been drawn into the general world system via exchange with the established and external capitalist mode of production.

Rey analyses in detail the case of the Congo in West Africa. He identifies firstly the local mode of production which he calls a 'lineage mode'. This lineage mode is analysed as comprising two classes: chiefs (or elders) and dependants (or juniors). Allocation of tasks is by kinship relations and the whole is a subsistence type production. A crucial aspect of this lineage mode is the exchange of slaves between related groups. Slavery within the lineage mode was not slavery as we would now understand it. Rather it was a small-scale circulation of population and not the 'chattel slavery' of plantations in the New World.

The lineage mode interacted with the capitalist mode via the slave trade. The slave trade was supportable for the lineage mode for a long time: slaves were drawn from the interior and shipped out by coastal lineage modes and European goods moved inwards from coastal trading stations. Thus were the two modes of production articulated.

As the slave trade declined, European traders looked for other goods, such as ivory, rubber and so on; the typical products of the subsistence pattern of the area. The colonial power, having taken a formal responsibility, attempted to rationalize production by allocating areas to trading companies. However, this did not succeed, and Rey points to this as evidence that purely economic exchanges could not effect any radical change in the lineage mode because when the chiefs had enough prestige European goods, they simply stopped supplying the ivory and so on. At this point we have the imposition of colonial authority and the creation of what Rey calls the 'colonial mode of production'.

The imposition of the colonial mode involves the forced destruction of the lineage mode simultaneously with the implantation of modern production forms. Subsistence farming is replaced and the key is the setting up of a money economy. In this period we have the usual range of colonial developments – railways, ports, plantations, mines and towns – plus all the social changes that go alongside these obvious economic changes. The upshot is that the traditional lineage mode is effectively destroyed. A final shift, for this area, was from the colonial mode to the 'neo-colonial mode' of production: patterns of economic and political dependence on the metropolis assume their present and familiar form and within the peripheral territory we find the familiar disintegrated sectoral pattern. Rey argues that development within the peripheral territory is held up by the alliance of the 'neo-colonial mode' with the 'capitalist mode' and the majority of the people continue in their now degenerate lineage mode. Politically, and here Rey's analysis comes to resemble that of the neo-marxists, a socialist revolution is the prerequisite of change. The present alliance of peripheral and metropolitan capitalism will only advance development for the mass of the people at a very slow pace.

Thus does Rey offer his version of an analysis of the Third World that is sensitive to the detail of actual Third World societies and rigorously marxist. There are three points which we can make at this stage: first, the insistence upon conceptual rigour and sensitivity to empirical detail are unobjectionable, although whether it is fair for the proponents of this approach to contrast their work favourably with that of the neo-marxists is much less clear; second, the opening made to the work of anthropology is surely wholly correct; and third, the Althusserian syntax of scientificity is deeply unpersuasive.[39]

Political-economic analysis

A similar insistence upon attention to detail and patterns of change is found in the differently premised and oriented work of those theorists who have had recourse to the strategy of enquiry of political-economy.[40] The theorists typically characterize political-economy as a holistic approach to analysing society which contrasts sharply with the discipline-bound fragmentation of the orthodox social sciences. The work of Marx is taken to exemplify the strategy of political-economic analysis, which was the premier social science of the nineteenth century, the period of the first phase of theoretical attempts to read the shift into the modern industrial capitalist world, and which is characterized by its reflexive and engaged attempts to grasp the dynamics of complex political-economic, social-institutional and cultural change. The Latin American social theorists F. H. Cardoso and E. H. Faletto have used this approach to grasp the circumstances of Latin American societies in terms of the particular balances of class forces in various countries as they have successively presented themselves through history.[41] The contemporary conjunction of classes is analysed and political alternatives to dependent development are thereby identified.

If we consider political-economy as a general style of analysis then we can see that 'much of the effort of political economists went into what appears today to be a very general enquiry, with statements and defences of their views on definitional questions, and some of the moral and political issues entailed'.[42] In addition to the catholicity of intellectual interest involved in the construction of their efforts, we must also note their practical

39   Engaging with the Althussarian tradition is not easy: see, A. Foster-Carter 1978 'The Modes of Production Controversy', *New Left Review*, 107; A. Hoogvelt 1982 *The Third World in Global Development*, London, Macmillan, pp. 174–84; Brewer 1980 op. cit. and J. C. Taylor 1979 *From Modernization to Modes of Production*, London, Macmillan.
40   Some material bridged this gap, see J. Clammer ed. 1978 *The New Economic Anthropology*; J. Clammer 1985 *Anthropology and Political Economy*, London, Macmillan.
41   F. H. Cardoso and E. H. Faletto 1979 *Dependency and Development in Latin America*, Berkeley and Los Angeles, University of California Press.
42   T. Carver 1975 *Karl Marx Texts on Method*, Oxford, Blackwell, p. 7.

intent as theorists seek to advance their own understandings of the circumstances they confront.

This characteristic breadth of scope is picked up by those who would affirm the utility of this approach. An explicit contrast is often drawn with the restricted, partial, institutionalized discourses of the various orthodox social sciences. This rejection of intellectual fragmentation is the most general starting point for Cardoso and Faletto who in recording general terms their intellectual history take note of the impact of US academic social science and detail their response to it. They state: 'We attempt to re-establish the intellectual tradition based on a comprehensive social science. We seek a global and dynamic understanding of social structures'.[43] Beyond this they lodge themselves specifically within a tradition; hence, 'we stress the sociopolitical nature of the economic relations of production, thus following the nineteenth century tradition of treating economy as political-economy ... which found its highest expression in Marx'.[44]

The strategy of political-economy is not only distinguished from orthodox social science by the catholicity of its intellectual interest and practicality of intent but also in the overall shape of its method. It can be argued that Marx draws a distinction between logical analysis 'in which something complex is resolved or broken up into simple elements'[45] on the one hand, and on the other, logical synthesis which 'proceeds in the opposite direction in order to reproduce the concrete in conception'.[46] It is the second procedure which is taken by Marx to represent the proper direction of enquiry for political-economy. The effort is one of the intellectual reconstruction of the real. Thus it is noted that:

> Marx develops the view that this concrete result, achieved by a process of synthesis, is also the 'actual starting point', the starting point which actually exists; in other words to perform the synthesis properly he must, at the beginning, presuppose actuality in order to arrive at the summarised conceptualised concrete.[47]

As a scheme of enquiry and explanation, political-economy is clearly sharply distinct from the orthodoxy. Enquiry does not proceed by abstraction from the given, generalization and model-building; nor is explanation linked with or made in some fashion analogous to causal predictiveness. Instead, enquiry proceeds by the technically explicit categorial reconstruction of the real. To explain is to make sense. Of Marx's notion of science, we can note that the

> searching process for Marx was essentially active, investigative, critical and practical; a scientific presentation, in his view, seems to have

43 Cardoso and Faletto 1979 op. cit. p. ix.
44 Ibid.
45 Carver 1975 op. cit. p. 129.
46 Ibid. p. 130.
47 Ibid. p. 132.

been one which solved conceptual mysteries and presented the human world accurately, intelligibly and politically.[48]

The differences just noted have been represented in recent critical-theory inspired work in the guise of a distinction between validation and authentication.[49] Cardoso and Faletto seemingly anticipate this distinction when they treat the issue of measurement. They reject the model of social scientific explanation presented in orthodox US work, and assert that the 'accuracy of a historical-structural interpretation has to be checked by confronting its delineation of structural conditions and trends of change with actual socio-political processes'.[50] They speak of two elements, 'construction and interpretation and . . . its practical validation',[51] and note that 'the demonstration of an interpretation follows real historical processes very closely and depends to some extent on its own ability to show socio-political actors the precise solution to contradictory situations'.[52]

Cardoso and Faletto offer an example of the strategy of analysis at work.[53] In the preface to the second edition of their book *Dependency and Development in Latin America* the authors remark that:

> If the analytical effort succeeds, general platitudes and reaffirmations about the role of capitalist modes of production can turn into a lively knowledge of real processes . . . It is necessary to elaborate concepts and explanations able to show how general trends of capitalist expansion turn into concrete relations amongst men, classes and states in the periphery . . . This is the methodological movement constituting what is called the passage from an 'abstract' style of analysis into a 'concrete' form of historical knowledge.[54]

The analytic strategy at work in respect of Latin America will point to those historically generated class groupings, each with their own immediate concerns, which presently make up a country, and then to a state unable to reconcile incompatible demands and consequently drifting into effective immobility. In this fashion Cardoso and Faletto can trace the patterns of class relationships over time. A concern to deploy analytical strategies to quite specific situations in the pursuit of practical lines of advance is the key to their approach. It has been characterized as being centred on the 'specificity

---

48 Ibid. pp. 40–1.
49 Critical theory is the particular style of work of the humanist marxist tradition known as the Frankfurt School. On the distinction noted, see Z. Bauman 1976 *Towards a Critical Sociology*, London, Routledge.
50 Cardoso and Faletto 1979 op. cit. p. xiv.
51 Ibid.
52 Ibid.
53 A further introductory review can be found in M. Staniland 1985 *What is Political Economy?* New Haven, Conn., Yale University Press. See also M. Barret-Brown 1984 *Models in Political-Economy*, Harmondsworth, Penguin.
54 Cardoso and Faletto 1979 op. cit. p. xiv.

of enquiry'.[55] The political-economies of the countries of Latin America are presented in terms of a shifting scene of competing, cooperating, cohabiting and mutually unconnected groups. The whole configuration is subject to the impact of the world capitalist economy which is beyond the control of any one group. It is the business of the logic of the global system that has become a new concern for many social theorists.

The logic of the global system

It has been noted that the structuralist style of analysis associated with ECLA, which was absorbed into the more familiar dependency approach, has continued to be explored and developed.[56] It is possible to speak of an approach in which 'the world economy constitutes a structured whole, and its constituent parts display various forms and degrees of dependency.[57] With this general orientation it is possible to add three sorts of related analyses: (a) first, to plot in some detail the ways in which an individual country actually fits into the wider global system; (b) second, to detail the overarching global institutional structures which regulate and order the system as a whole (multi-lateral organizations and treaties, and the dense network of bi-lateral treaties); and (c) third, to detail the radical asymmetries of power lodged within this densely ordered global system.

In the first place, any country will be dependent on flows of economic power (patterns of trade), financial power (flows of money and credit), military power (networks of force), and cultural power (flows of intellectual resources).[58] It is the precise context within networks of global power that will shape the situation of the people of a particular country.[59] It is clear, secondly, that the global system is clearly an ordered and integrated system. There is a dense network of institutions which together can be taken to constitute the system at a global level. Theorists have spoken of the transnational capitalist system.[60] The idea can be unpacked along two axes.[61] The first is the development of a global culture carried by international institutions, including TNCs, which is generating a global community. At the present time the membership, so to say, of this community is heavily restricted and limited; thus few participate directly and many participate only via mass media images (archetypically, a mix of Coca Cola and CNN). The second axis, by way of a logical corollary, is the partial

55   G. Palma 1978 'Dependency: A Formal Theory of Underdevelopment or a Methodology for the Analysis of Concrete Situations of Underdevelopment?', World Development, 6.
56   B. Hettne 1990 Development Theory and the Three Worlds, London, Longman.
57   Ibid. p. 133.
58   The work is pointed to by Hettne ibid. See D. Seers 1979 'Patterns of Dependence' in J. J. Villamil ed. Transnational Capitalism and National Development: New Perspectives on Dependence, Hassocks, Harvester.
59   This insight is picked up and put to effective use by the school of 'international political-economy'; see S. Strange 1988 States and Markets, London, Pinter.
60   O. Sunkel and E. Fuenzalida 1979 'Transnationalization and Its National Consequences' in Villamil op. cit.
61   See Hettne 1990 op. cit.

disintegration of national communities, as powerful groups pull away from a local commitment towards the new and burgeoning global community. The local area, the erstwhile national community, becomes less important and subject to more authoritarian control. In this way the development of the global system can run alongside the continuation or even deepening of distress amongst the disadvantaged.[62] It is at this point, thirdly, that the asymmetries of power within the global system can be addressed. It is not the case that all players within this integrated system are equal. The metropolitan centres continue to dominate. However, as capital migrates to find new sources of opportunity the overall pattern of the global system shifts as areas experience relative decline and relative advance. Overall, these themes have formed a new area of concern for social theorists dealing with development and it is to these debates that we must now turn.

Chapter Summary

Marxist work on the Third World can be divided into three phases: (a) the efforts of Marx and Engels who seem to have expected the capitalist system to expand and draw in other cultures to their eventual benefit; (b) the efforts of Lenin and the theorists of imperialism who expected capitalism to be progressive but who came to adopt a more cautious position seeing the outline of a possible stable and enduring exploitative relationship; and (c) in the early post-Second World War period the neo-marxism inspired by Paul Baran who argued that local Third World economies were condemned to a distorting subordinate position within the global system which could only be remedied via revolution and disengagement. The neo-marxist work was influential in the 1960s and 1970s, in particular as it was disseminated by A. G. Frank, but it has subsequently been much criticized. Marxist-inspired work has continued in a number of ways and three strategies have been particularly influential in the 1970s and 1980s: (a) the concern to elucidate the formal logic of discrete modes of production, often via anthropological ethnographic fieldwork, where each mode of production is a coherent mix of economic and cultural patterns, and which interact in complex ways as the powerful capitalist mode of production expands to remake and absorb the less powerful; (b) the reassertion of the methodological value of political-economy, which deals with the overall logic of the system and which can be used to elucidate the detail of social processes within the ongoing dynamic of the development of the global capitalist system; and (c) a concern to elucidate the broad pattern of the historical development of the world capitalist system. Overall, marxist-inspired theorizing has amounted to a contentious but influential and important area of work.

---

62   See A. Sklair 1991 *The Sociology of the Global System*, Hemel Hempstead, Harvester, Wheatsheaf.

13

The Assertion of Third World Solidarity: Global Development Approaches

Overview of Global Development Approaches

The notion of global development covers a series of related approaches which stress the interdependent nature of the global system, the special concerns of the Third World and the interests which the First World has in seeing the situation of the Third World improved. In this case we can note: (a) the general development arguments stressing the unity of mankind made by the United Nations and other international organizations with declarations of Development Decades, the programme for a New International Economic Order, and the programme of basic needs; (b) a concern for environmental pressures first expressed in the Club of Rome's reports on the limits of the earth and recently restated at the Rio Earth Summit; and (c) a concern for the poverty of the Third World when measured against the need for markets of the hugely productive First World which generates after the fashion of Keynesian pump-priming the thought that the rich should underpin the growth of the poor to everyone's benefit.

Patterns of Reconsideration in Development Theory

It is probably true to say that growth theory was an early and quickly superseded approach to the problem of development. On the other hand modernization theory did for a time attain the status of an unchallenged orthodoxy within Western discussions of development. However, it is with institutional development theory that we find the most intellectually sophisticated version of the orthodox line of analysis. The work of the institutionalists offered a sharp criticism of the economistic bias of the orthodoxy and attained a wide and continuing influence amongst specialists in various agencies dealing with development. Overall, we have considered the process of the construction of a series of delimited-formal ideological positions which although different in detail have it in common that they evidence a predilection for expert intervention in social systems to secure development goals established by First and Third World elites.

The period of the construction of the orthodox position in development theory was one of general optimism. The various agents involved in development work were all confident that the goal of effective nationstatehood lodged in the orthodox approach could be realized. The goal of development was taken to be clear in principle and attainable in practice. However, the early optimism slowly faded as old problems unexpectedly persisted. As old problems persisted and new problems emerged those involved in working for development began to look for new approaches. The conventional wisdom entered a long slow period of drift and decline during which old ideas were reconsidered and reworked, or discarded, and new ideas were presented, considered and sometimes pursued. The business of the decline and dissolution of the orthodox interventionist position is important because it is via this process of dissolution and reconsideration that a new approach to development emerged to secure a brief period of influence.

I will begin the discussion of the decline and dissolution of the orthodoxy around the substitution of the core idea of global interdependence for recapitulation and the affirmation of the policy programme of international Keynesianism. The treatment will be divided into three parts: (a) an overview of the shift in debate and proposed action in respect of development; (b) a review of the debates surrounding the rules of the game, in particular the programme for the new international economic order (NIEO); and (c) a review of the debate surrounding the business of resource transfers, in particular the notions of basic needs. In the light of this review we can add a note on the subsequent continuing influence of the work produced[1] (see figure 15).

The Shifts in Debate in the 1970s

It can be argued that modernization theory represented for a period something like a consensus within orthodox development theory. However, that

---

1 A. Hoogvelt 1982 *The Third World in Global Development*, London, Macmillan, offers a useful review of these matters which I draw on in this chapter.

Figure 15 Global development approaches

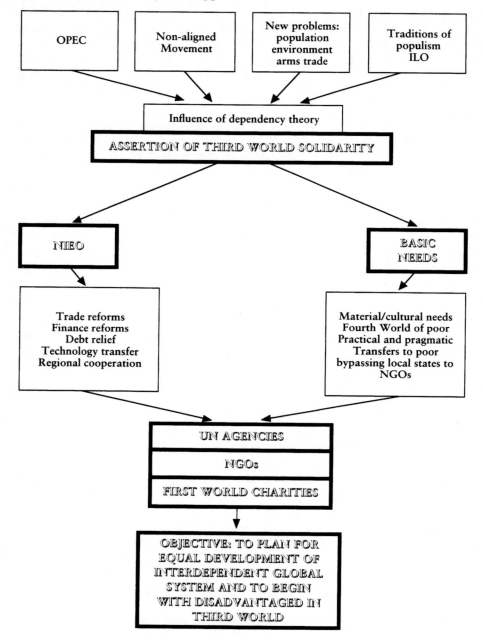

consensus broke down in the 1970s and although the work of the institutionalists attained great professional influence no new consensus emerged. In its place a diffuse body of work was presented which we can grasp with the notion of global development approaches. In its earliest phase in the 1970s there was a pronounced concern for the mutual interests of all those working within the global system, and the interlinked set of concerns presented have been called international Keynesianism. The particular institutional location of these approaches has been the United Nations, NGOs, charities and pressure groups. The governments of the countries of the First World and the key institutions of the post-Second World War liberal-capitalist system, the World Bank and the IMF, have had to accommodate to the pressures for reform. Overall, the key idea presented in the 1970s is that of global interdependence and there are two major areas of concern: first, with the calls for a new international economic order (NIEO); and second a concern for the transfer of resources to the poor to meet basic needs in development.

The NIEO was presented to the United Nations in the early 1970s as a series of proposals for the reform of the world economic system. Around the idea of global interdependence the NIEO programme looked to shift the balance of economic power towards the countries of the Third World. A series of issues which concerned the proponents of the programme, the countries of the Third World, were advanced and included the following: trade reforms; monetary reforms; resource transfers; debt relief; and technology transfer. It was an ambitious programme to upgrade the economies of the poor countries and to integrate them as equal partners within the global system. In this way the 'rules of the game' could be made more equitable in principle and operation to the benefit of all.

An aspect of the NIEO programme was the transfer of resources from the First to Third World and in the mid-1970s the matter came to be addressed in a quite particular fashion. The idea of basic needs derives from a utopian Latin American group concerned with arguing that a little more equality in the world would mean rather less poverty and a much easier development task. The basic needs approach found favour with international agencies. It was argued that basic needs were obvious targets for urgent help and amenable to authoritative expert treatment. At the same time it was argued that a basic needs approach entailed targeting aid on the poorest, those most in need. Overall, it is clear that the fundamental strategy of orthodox interventionism is here conjoined with a grassroots activism, as NGO groups became involved in running local level development projects, to the detriment of the autonomy of the states and governments of the countries of the Third World.

A significant element of international political manoeuvring can be identified. As the NIEO programme implied a shift of power to the states of the Third World, so the basic needs programme implied a shift of power away from states towards development projects closely overseen by experts from the First World. The debates can be traced over the immediate post-Second

World War decades within the non-aligned group and other groupings organized in the context of the United Nations. Overall there was a long-drawn-out assertion of Third World solidarity. On the basis of general arguments in favour of solidarity and the dramatic example of the economic power of OPEC in the early 1970s, the drive to bring the plight of the poor countries of the world to the centre of the international political stage reached a peak in the proposals for the NIEO. Thereafter, it would be fair to say that whilst both areas of debate, the NIEO and basic needs, have continued and have seen action, it is the notion of basic needs which has received by far the greatest attention from development theorists in the First World.

The background considered

There was a series of circumstances which together conspired to redirect the attention of development theorists and which undermined their hitherto remarkable optimism in respect of the future of development work: (a) the end of the post-Second World War economic boom; (b) the rise of OPEC; (c) shifts in the terms of trade which disadvantaged the Third World; and (d) new problems of population growth, environmental degradation and the generally detrimental impact upon development work of the burgeoning global arms trade. It should also be noted that there was a new alternative theoretical approach to development available in the form of Latin American dependency theory which called attention to the role of the First World in creating and sustaining the relative poverty of the Third World.

The optimism in respect of the future of the countries of the Third World had been strongly assisted by the long experience of economic prosperity which unexpectedly characterized the early years of the post-Second World War period. However, the Bretton Woods institutional structures which underpinned the successful US-centred global economy came under severe pressure in the early 1970s. A combination of factors meant that the post-Second World War economic boom faltered throughout the late 1960s and then in the early 1970s drifted to a halt with the collapse of the Bretton Woods system of fixed currency exchange rates. The shift to floating currency rates was initiated by the USA in response to the demands upon its economy of the costs of the war in Vietnam. The new financial system of unregulated financial markets introduced great instability into the global economy and generally reduced economic growth rates. Overall, the global economy experienced a general downturn in economic activity.[2] The new situation of downturn and instability cut against the economic optimism which underpinned modernization theory.

2   E. Hobsbawm 1994 *Age of Extremes: The Short Twentieth Century, 1914–1991*, London, Michael Joseph, ch. 9; See also E. A. Brett 1985 *The World Economy Since the War: The Politics of Uneven Development*, London, Macmillan, chs. 3, 5, 7.

A related problem at this time was generated by the decisions of the oil producers' cartel the Organization of Petroleum Exporting Countries (OPEC) to raise the price of oil. In the early 1970s OPEC was dominated by the countries of the Arabian Gulf region and together they produced a major part of the oil used by the Europeans and the Japanese. A general concern to increase their revenues and thereby finance the development of their own countries coincided with a further episode of conflict between the state of Israel and its Arab neighbours. The rise in the price of oil was used as a political and diplomatic weapon against the countries which had generally been sympathetic to Israel. The rise in the price of oil contributed directly to a sharp reduction in economic activity in the developed countries and to a rise in inflation. The OPEC action was expressive not only of short-term concerns in respect of finance and politics but also of a new assertiveness on the part of those whom the global community had regarded as under-developed and relatively powerless. The notion of recapitulation which lay at the back of modernization theory and which looked to the slow evolutionary process of the Third World catching up with the First World was directly challenged. The determination of the members of OPEC to use oil money to build industrial economies offered a general example to the countries of the Third World of a development strategy which did not depend upon First World models or aid money.[3]

A third issue relates to the terms of international trade, that is to the relative position of Third World exporters/importers compared with the exporters/importers in the First World. In brief, the terms of trade moved against the essentially primary product exporters of the Third World who saw the prices their crops realized fall at the same time as the prices realized by First World manufactures rose. As the situation of the countries of the Third World deteriorated the optimism of modernization theory in respect of the process of economic and social development was further undermined.

A series of new problems also made their first appearance within development debate: overpopulation; environmental degradation; and the proliferation of armaments throughout the Third World. And all three problem areas coincided in their impact upon development work in that they drew resources away from the task of raising levels of living for the peoples of the Third World. The rapid growth of population placed severe demands upon governments and resources. The degradation of the environment compounded these problems (and they were often seen as interlinked). And the rapid growth of the global trade in armaments had the dual effect of drawing resources away from development projects whilst at the same time promoting the interests within the countries of the Third World of the

---

3   Which is not to say that these countries were politically, economically or socially progressive as many were feudal countries. See F. Halliday 1979 *Arabia Without Sultans*, Harmondsworth, Penguin; F. Halliday 1979 *Iran: Dictatorship and Development*, Harmondsworth, Penguin.

military machines. The major exporters of weapons at this time were the USA, the USSR, France and Britain.

If all these represent real world problems, it is also the case that there was an influential general counter-view to modernization theory available. The mixture of changing circumstances and new ideas combined to push debates about development in new directions. The influential new theories came to be known as the dependency approach. The theory originated in Latin America and its softer versions have been widely used by development theorists, policy-making agencies and political commentators. In brief, dependency theory contains the key idea that development can only be understood as an historical and global process. In other words, the object of enquiry of development theorists shifts from the recapitulation by the poor countries of the historical experience of the rich towards the question of how the global system developed over time to produce a system having both rich and poor. An idea of the historical creation of present global interdependence is advanced.

In the light of this new overarching conception the circumstances of the Third World countries cannot now be discussed in terms of how they can modernize and thereby catch-up with the countries of the First World, but in terms of their continuing role within the global system. The role of the countries of the Third World has to be characterized in detail so as to display the responsibilities of the powerful for creating and sustaining the subordinate role. In an interdependent world the onus for achieving development no longer rests exclusively with the ruling groups of individual countries because the possibilities for the development of any Third World country are conditioned by the global contexts within which they operate. Accordingly, the rich and powerful are now directly implicated in the business of securing development as the centres of power within the global system lie within the countries of the First World.

The early theories

The earliest theorists of the global system evidenced a 'kaleidoscopic diversity'[4] of approaches to the future development of the system and first and second generations can be identified. The former are the futurologists who tried to plot the macro development of the system such that governments at an international level could order the future, and the latter are the theorists of international interdependence who looked rather more plausibly to presently identifiable areas of possible practical cooperation between governments in respect of common problems.

The 'world futures theorists' tried to sketch likely future lines of development for the whole global system.[5] The methods used include the production

---

4   Hoogvelt 1982 op. cit. p. 128.
5   Ibid. p. 123.

of large-scale models, the attempt to make long-range extrapolation of macro trends, and the speculative and formal simulation of alternative scenarios of long-term change. All this rests on general systems theory which is an intellectual relative of modernization theory and it is similarly interventionist. It attempts to reduce the intervenor to the status of extra-systemic cause. As this position is unavailable the theorists fall back on appeals to reasonable people acting on behalf of humankind. The members of the 'first generation' include people like the 'futurologist' Herman Kahn who offered broad predictions/scenarios of future global trends, and the various eco-doomsday theorists of the Club of Rome.[6] I shall ignore these people as they are peripheral to the main trend of development thinking at this time although their concerns do continue and in the case of environmental concerns do attain significance in the late 1980s.

The second generation are the proponents of international Keynesianism who argue that where Keynes urged national governments to stimulate demand within their economies during times of depression so as to preserve the system, the international community must grant the necessity of international agreement on a new economic order lest the Third World countries collapse back into a miserable poverty and in so doing damage the interdependent economies of the countries of the First World. It is possible to identify two areas of concern for international Keynesianism: first, the business of the rules of the game which can be discussed in the context of the NIEO programme; and second the business of reforms in resource transfers and utilization, all of which can be pursued under the heading of the programmes of basic needs provisions. In the first noted area development theorists looked to the business of stimulating economic growth in the Third World and its better integration within the global economic system (thereby providing reliable economic partners for First World countries). In the second noted area development theorists looked to the provision of better fundamental conditions for the majority of the people of the Third World, who comprised in fact the majority of humankind, in the long-term expectation of lifting their levels of living which was seen as a matter of mutual benefit to Third and First World.

Overall, it should be noted that the period of the 1970s when these debates were underway saw considerable economic upheaval as inflationary pressures moved through the global system. The post-Second World War Bretton Woods system had produced a long period of growth and stability but the 1970s and 1980s were to prove to be much more unstable. In the 1970s there was a long period of recession plus inflation in the developed countries and recession coupled to the accumulation of debt in the under-developed countries. The optimism for a new international economic order rapidly faded as countries came to face problems of debt and economic

---

6 The Club produced a series of reports, beginning in 1972, which argued that there were limits to the economic growth which the planet could sustain.

regression. In due course the problems of debt spill over into the 1980s and become a matter of central concern for the New Right.

The Debate on the Rules of the Game

The UN was originally established with a relatively small membership in the period following the Second World War and the expectation of the First World was that the organization would naturally be dominated by their interests. However, as the period of decolonization ran its course a series of new nationstates took their seats in the UN organization. The UN has subsequently become both a major platform for the expression of the concerns of the Third World and a key centre of formal political conflict within the global system between First and Third Worlds. The UN has become an important arena of debate and political activity as the organization is not restricted in membership unlike the major economic and financial institutions of the post-Second World War global system.

The presentation of the NIEO programme in the United Nations is a complex story in itself. The matter can be summarized as follows: 'the *Declaration on the Establishment of a New International Economic Order . . .* and the accompanying Programme of Action, were adopted without a vote at the Sixth Special Session of the UN General Assembly in May 1974, and were confirmed in November 1974 in the *Charter of Economic Rights and Duties of States*'.[7] These texts contain declarations of principles and programmes of action in respect of development and they were further elaborated in a series of subsequent and related conferences. The detail of the institutional politics of the UN can be set aside and we can look simply at the NIEO and its concern to adjust the rules of the game in favour of the countries of the Third World.[8] The NIEO can be taken to have had two main elements: a general declaration in respect of the economic development of the countries of the Third World enshrined in the Charter and a more specific and concrete agenda of reforms presented in the Programme. The latter identified five principal areas of concern: trade reforms; monetary reforms; debt relief; technology transfer; and regional cooperation.[9]

In respect of international trade the concerns of the proponents of the NIEO centre on the problem of the declining value of the primary products which are the principal export of the countries of the Third World. The proposals advanced included both the establishment of buffer stocks which can be used to smooth out price fluctuations and the global redistribution of industrial production in favour of the countries of the Third World which could be aided by the setting of targets for such a redistribution and the provision of liberalized trade preferences for Third World economies.

7 Hoogvelt 1982 op. cit. p. 79.
8 On the record of the UN see United Nations 1995 *Yearbook of the United Nations: Special Edition UN Fiftieth Anniversary*, The Hague, Kluwer Law International.
9 Hoogvelt 1982 op. cit. p. 81.

In respect of international monetary arrangements the proposals for reform advanced by the proponents of the NIEO began with the observation that the Bretton Woods system with its key institutions of the World Bank and the IMF had been designed by the developed countries with the interests of the First World economies in view. Moreover the current location and functioning of these institutions reflected the overwhelming influence of the developed countries. The Bank and the Fund are located in Washington. It was proposed that the rules of association of the institutions be adjusted to raise the power of the countries of the Third World and that the rules of procedure of the institutions be similarly altered to reflect the needs and aspirations of the countries of the Third World.

In respect of the issue of debt relief and the related matter of resource transfers the proponents of the NIEO called attention to the heavy burdens of debt payments carried by many Third World countries and to the related restricted and limited nature of resource transfers from rich to poor countries. In the matter of resource transfers a series of proposals to increase both bi-lateral transfers and multi-lateral transfers were made with mixed overall success. On the other hand a series of proposals were made in respect of debt relief including debt forgiveness, moratoriums on repayment, the transfer of debt into equity and various strategies of debt refinancing. All these issues came to be very important in the 1980s when the levels of Third World debt became not merely a problem for the poor countries but a threat to the banking system of the developed countries.

In respect of the issue of the transfer of technology the proponents of the NIEO pointed out that the countries of the Third World were not merely technology-deficient but were having to pay large sums in royalties and licences for the First World technology which they had managed to acquire. It was noted that much of the technology transfer was accomplished in the context of the operations of commercial multi-national corporations whose key interest was to establish enterprises which were profitable. This concern could conflict with the development needs of the host country. The proposals which were made included revisions to international patent law to permit the easier and cheaper import of technology and suggestions for regulating the activities of MNCs so as to encourage technology transfer. Overall, the policy concern was with maximizing the benefits to host countries of the operations of the MNCs and minimizing the costs of bought-in technology.

In respect of the matter of inter-regional cooperation the proponents of the NIEO pointed out that patterns of trade tended to follow a centre–periphery pattern which favoured the already rich and powerful centres. It was proposed that the countries of the periphery in the Third World could strengthen their local economies and their bargaining power with the centres if they encouraged and built up intra-peripheral economic linkages.

After the presentation of the NIEO programme the First and Third Worlds manoeuvred for position within the various institutional forums of the United Nations. The reaction of the developed countries to all these proposals was initially strongly negative but the reaction was modified shortly thereafter when it was realized that suitably reworked the proposals could be made to fit with the interests of the rich countries. Over the decade of the 1970s the debate continued in the United Nations and other international organizations. The upshot was the slow winding down of the radicalism of the NIEO programme at the same time as the dialogue between what were now referred to as North and South continued. However, as the debate continued it came to be thought, in particular by the development experts within the various organizations,[10] that a related area could usefully be explored, that is the business of the receipt and use of resource transfers. The shift of attention to basic needs also undermined a key aspect of the NIEO programme, namely the concern to strengthen the countries of the Third World in relation to the First World, because the new strategy of focusing the attention of development agencies on the needs of the poorest entailed the submission of the countries of the Third World to greater external direction of their development efforts.

The lessons of the debate

The drive for the NIEO represented a particular expression of Third World solidarity in regard to their dealings with the developed countries.[11] The assertion of solidarity was a product of events which were particular in time and place. The institutional vehicles of this expression of solidarity were found within the various organizational structures of the United Nations. The debate about the NIEO proposals generated considerable interest amongst development theorists. The debate also generated conflict amongst governments but little by way of direct practical results. The countries of the First World were not prepared to countenance the scale of the reordering of the global balance of economic power which was implied in the programme. It is also true that the countries of the Third World began to discover quite sharp divergences in interest amongst themselves. Overall, the episode offers a number of lessons: (a) that the Third World is not and cannot be regarded as a unitary phenomenon as the interests of those countries thus labelled are divergent; (b) that the role of the United Nations is severely limited and cannot be treated as some sort of world government-in-waiting which might properly attend to the matter of the development of the presently disadvantaged countries within its remit as the interests of its members are widely divergent; (c) that the particular interests of the First World will not be overborne by abstract general arguments presented in international institutional gatherings; and finally (d) that there is indeed a global system which is extensively interdependent and in the 1990s this last noted lesson was once again presented in broad debate when the issues of how to characterize, explain and order the global system became important.

10   Ibid. p. 96.
11   Ibid. ch. 2.

The Debate on Basic Needs

The idea of basic needs originated with a group of Latin American theor-ists[12] and 'was officially launched at the ILO World Employment Confer-ence in 1976'.[13] The basic needs approach was constructed so as to deny the pessimistic position of the first Club of Rome report which spoke of the limits to growth and asserted that in a radically changed world economic system all people could have an acceptable standard of life. Rather more specifically they argued that a more egalitarian national and international system would allow basic needs to be achieved with much lower economic growth rates than were needed in the present inegalitarian world system.

The basic needs debate drew an important distinction between economic growth and the provision of the basic necessities of life. The debate about development was pulled away from narrowly economic discussions which were inevitably biased in favour of the schedule of assumptions which governed debate within the First World. The drive to attend directly to the needs of the poor of the Third World opened up the range of relevant debate. In the work of the ILO this was expressed directly in the preference for employment creation over economic growth and in practical terms this focused attention on employment in agriculture and the informal sector as these were where the majority of the populations of the countries of the Third World made their livelihoods.[14] It can be argued that the approach adopted by the ILO was heir to a long tradition of thought which in vari-ous ways preferred to stress the value of the small-scale and local in the face of the demands of the encroaching industrial capitalist system.[15] It is also clear that the idea of basic needs has been easily associated with a spread of other critical ideas which have it in common that they stress the value of established patterns of life and deny the assumption of the self-evidently beneficial nature of economic growth which is made by orthodox development theory.[16]

The debate on the idea of basic needs quickly became extensive with many groups contributing. A key distinction in reflection on the issue was between universal and objective needs on the one hand and culturally shaped needs on the other. The former definition implied a concentration on the minimum physiological needs of humanbeings whereas the latter implied a broader set of concerns which embraced both material minima and the minima of particular cultural forms-of-life. In other words, basic needs were seen to involve not merely survival but also participating in the life

12 In a report prepared by the Barlioche Foundation, Canada, and presented by A. O. Herrera et al. eds. 1975 *Catastrophe or a New Society*, Ottawa, Barlioche Foundation.
13 Hoogvelt 1982 op. cit. p. 100.
14 See B. Hettne 1990 *Development Theory and the Three Worlds*, London, Longman, ch. 5.
15 See G. Kitching 1982 *Development and Underdevelopment in Historical Perspective*, London, Methuen, ch. 4. The author takes the view that the approach is essentially 'popu-list' and unrealistic.
16 See Hettne 1990 op. cit. ch. 5.

of the particular community. The former approach came to be associated with World Bank versions of the basic needs approach which tended also to stress the efficiency of delivery of these basic needs, which in turn implied directing or bypassing the governments and state machines of the recipient countries. It is clear that the idea of basic needs was picked up by theorists in the orthodox tradition and by international institutions – the World Bank in particular – and used to justify a reworked interventionist stance. The general notion of basic needs implied that aid and development work had to be targeted at the poorest and that success had to be carefully monitored. It was made more or less clear that both elements of the approach would have to be pursued in such a way as to protect the work from the interference of the local state and local politics. The governments of the countries in receipt of basic needs funding were required to acquiesce in their own downgrading. It quickly became clear that the autonomy which the governments of the countries of the Third World had been pursuing in the context of the NIEO proposals was being subtly undermined and the governments of the countries of the Third World quickly came to see the basic needs approach as thoroughly ambiguous.

If we simplify matters, we can see that the basic needs approach involves the following elements: (a) it calls attention to the needs of the poorest of the poor, those who have been called the inhabitants of the Fourth World; (b) it attempts to define basic needs in operational terms with food, water, health and thereafter education, work and political participation; (c) it seeks the establishment of targets for countries and the specification of criteria of performance so that progress can be measured; and (d) it makes an acknowledgement of the necessity for internal structural transformations in the economic and socio-political patterns of the countries of the Third World.[17] In general the basic needs approach has three obvious characteristics and they recall the orthodoxy in development theory: (a) an appeal to the obviousness of certain problems, as (b) the basis for the intervention of the planners, (c) in pursuit of a series of crucial internal reforms.

The covert appeal to obviousness lies in the focus on the poorest of the poor. The distress of the people of the Fourth World is such as to constitute a presently extant crisis. In the circumstance of crisis what ought to be done is not in general in doubt. The crisis must be confronted in terms of immediate attempts to alleviate the distress of the people concerned. Thereafter the way to deal with the crisis is via expert guided intervention. It is perfectly clear with basic needs approaches that we have not left the realm of aid targets, aid flows, aid projects and performance criteria and monitoring. It is clear that the basic needs approach is far from being a radically new departure in theorizing and action. However, there is some novelty in the way in which the approach urges the necessity for internal social, political and economic reform. It is here, with the concern for schedules of internal reforms to be secured by outside expert assistance which may

17 See P. Streeten 1981 *Development Perspectives*, London, Macmillan, ch. 19.

well bypass the host country government, that we come across the reasons why Third World governments have viewed the approach as ambiguous. Perhaps more interestingly it is also clear that we now confront the apparent limitations of the theorists of basic needs in respect of the role of the global system in creating the problems of corruption, inefficiency, and wastefulness which they are at such pains to address, and the impossibility of reducing the political realities and development problems of the present global system to a size that can be encompassed by authoritative planning interventions.

Basic needs and global systems

In the arguments of the advocates of the basic needs approach the politics of the real world, involving patterns of power and economic advantage,[18] tend to be presented as a problem for the planners. It is assumed that the problems of the poor are of such demanding urgency that a simple measure of attention on the part of the established structures of power would be enough to ensure that action could be taken. However, it seems clear that matters of internal social, political and economic change cannot be treated in this oversimplified fashion. The substantive realities of the societies of the Third World cannot be thus elided because making social reforms the precondition of effective planning begs the question of how such changes might be brought about in the first place. Paul Streeten, who has been an eloquent proponent of a basic needs approach, illustrates this point quite clearly.[19] Streeten argues that the schedule of basic needs lists concrete goals which are obvious and specific. Streeten goes on to say that the basic needs approach: (a) reminds us that development studies are about making better lives for people; (b) spell out in detail the human requirements of food, water, health, housing and so on; (c) remind us that economic and social models are abstract and that theorists should be specific; (d) appeal to the international community because the idea is clear; and (e) have great intellectual organizing power as all other development problems fall into place around them. Streeten adds:

> In one sense, this is a home-coming. For when we embarked on development 30 years ago, it was surely the needs of the poor of the world that we had in mind. In the process we got sidetracked, but we also discovered many important things about development . . . We are now back where we started in the 1950s . . . But we are back with a deeper understanding . . . [and] with a clearer vision of the path.[20]

Streeten thinks that the work of thirty years has been useful in learning what development studies are about even if the successes have been less than had

18   See S. Strange 1988 *States and Markets*, London, Pinter.
19   Streeten 1981 op. cit. ch. 18.
20   Ibid. pp. 332–3.

been hoped. It is true that there is something in this claim although it would be remarkable if no learning had taken place. However the basic needs are still presented as crisis-engendered obvious goals for technical expert intervention in the context of world community approval. The substantive judgements that Streeten makes in favour of a helping hand to the poor are unexceptionable and the recent work of the United Nations Development Programme (UNDP) in presenting a human development report which addresses these concerns[21] is wholly to the good, but the idea that the global system might be structured in a fashion that effectively reduces the plight of the poor to a marginal issue amongst power holders escapes the compass of the basic needs approach.

The lessons of the debate

The basic needs approach has continued to exercise considerable influence amongst those who concern themselves with development. The approach has gained over the years further refinements and would now encompass not merely the basics of human life, but also the need for a clean and viable environment and an appreciation of the value of diverse cultural traditions. A series of key lessons can be derived from this debate. Firstly, the role of NGOs and charities in encouraging basic needs approaches to development has secured widespread support amongst the populations of the countries of the First World and has revealed a preference amongst these populations for effective action to assist the poor in preference to aid linked to trade. Secondly, in many countries of the First World pressure groups targeted at their own governments are increasing in strength as it becomes more widely realized that governments running ODA programmes can be indifferent to interests outside those of their own industries. Thirdly, the pursuit of basic needs, with its concern for the detail of the lives of ordinary people in the Third World, has fostered amongst First World populations an appreciation of the diversity of the cultures of the world and an appreciation of the ambiguous nature of the notion of development. Finally, amongst Third World countries the preference for basic needs has directed attention to the needs of the poorest and has drawn local-level support and action.

Global Development Approaches in Retrospect and Prospect

In order to summarize this review of the period of the decline of the orthodoxy we must note that the relationship of the NIEO and basic needs

---

21   See United Nations Development Programme 1990 *Human Development Report 1990*, Oxford University Press. The first report contains a wealth of statistical information on levels of living in the Third World. It is the broad social scientific counterpart to the narrowly laissez-faire economic material presented each year by the World Bank as the *World Development Report*.

approaches was complex, and the relationship of both to the interventionist ethic of the orthodoxy in development theory is also complex. The key idea to have come to the fore in this general line is that of global interdependence. It is suggested that the present world system is an integrated and interdependent system and can only be saved from decline and failure if this is acknowledged. However, the governments of the First World have acted cautiously and defensively in the area of the overall setting of the rules of the game (NIEO) but have acted rather more aggressively with respect to basic needs analyses which focus attention upon the recipients' use of resource transfers. It is clear that the overall strategy of interventionism both in rule-setting and resource-using continues to lie at the core of this orthodox position.

It might also be noted that the global development line has subsequently generated a series of concerns related to the notion of basic needs. The core ideas of basic needs have been pursued in a wide range of contexts. Hettne summarizes the range of debates under the heading of alternative approaches and traces the spread of new ideas back to a UN-sponsored symposium on development in Mexico in 1974 which announced its findings by issuing the Cocoyoc Declaration.[22] It is reported that the declaration affirmed the importance of basic needs and then added that a richer set of goals centred on human freedom was required, as was a critique of overconsumptionist patterns of life in the West. It is possible to identify four variants of the alternative approach: (a) egalitarian development or basic needs which looks to attend to the basic requirements of human life; (b) self-reliant development which implied a criticism of the existing global system's demands on the poor and suggested a strategy of withdrawal in order to pursue development free of existing distorting demands and which also implied a preference for democratic and small-scale activity; (c) eco-development which acknowledges the concern for the environment which emerged in the First World in the 1970s and which implies small-scale industry which is sustainable over the long run; and (d) ethno-development which notes that development processes have often fostered ethnic conflict and insists that this be addressed and the diversity of cultures in the world be respected.[23]

However, in the metropolitan heartlands of the global system a new intellectual and political project emerged at the start of the 1980s and, notwithstanding the intrinsic interest of many of these alternative development ideas, as the balance of political power within the First World changed so too did approaches to development theory. The analysis of the global economic, social and political situation offered by the New Right begins from a diagnosis of far too much government and agency intervention and a return to the sovereign joys of the free market is urged. As the agenda of the New Right gained in influence within the First World in the early years of the 1980s the arguments of the proponents of both the NIEO,

22 Hettne 1990 op. cit. pp. 152–67.
23 Ibid. pp. 167–94.

basic needs and other alternatives were swept away. When the nature of the interdependence of the global system reemerged it did so in the very different context of talk about free-market-driven globalization.

Chapter Summary

The notion of global development covers a series of related approaches which have it in common that they stress both the interdependent nature of the world system and the interests which the First World has in seeing the situation of the Third World improved. In this case we can note: (a) general development arguments stressing the unity of mankind made by the United Nations and other international organizations; (b) a concern for environmental pressures first expressed in the Club of Rome's reports on the limits of the earth and later restated at the Rio Earth Summit; and (c) a concern for the poverty of the Third World when measured against the need of the hugely productive First World for markets – hence, after the fashion of Keynesian pump-priming the thought that the rich should underpin the growth of the poor to everyone's benefit. It is an important area of work which has continuing intellectual and organizational influence.

14

The Affirmation of the Role of the Market: Metropolitan Neo-liberalism in the 1980s

Overview of the Position of the New Right

The work of the New Right neoliberal theorists on development has been characterized as a counter-revolution whose aim has been to undermine and replace orthodox notions of how development in the Third World might be achieved.[1] When we examine the claims of the New Right we find a complex group of claims in respect of the scientific status of their work and its centrality within social science coupled to an unrestricted celebration of the power of the unregulated free market. Against these claims, theorists have offered replies which effectively dispose of the arguments of the New Right,[2] but there are wider debates beyond the narrow confines of recent polemics dealing with the relationship of state, economy and political action. The debates about states and markets evolve out of the slow collapse of the post-Second World War political settlement which in turn can be seen as an element in the wider shift towards an integrated tripolar global system.

1   J. Toye 1987 *Dilemmas of Development*, Oxford, Blackwell.
2   See, for example, D. Seers ed. 1981 *Dependency Theory: A Critical Reassessment*, London, Pinter; M. Bienefeld 1980 'Dependency in the Eighties', *Institute of Development Studies Bulletin*, 12; M. Bienefeld and M. Godfrey eds. 1982 *The Struggle for Development: National Strategies in an International Context*, London, Wiley.

The Eclipse of the Liberal-democratic Orthodoxy

In the early 1970s the post-Second World War welfare state settlement between capital and labour in the metropolitan heartlands of capitalism drifted into crisis. The steps on the road to political and intellectual collapse were many but commentators cite as a key moment the US decision in 1973 to end the Bretton Woods system by allowing the dollar to float. Over the period of the 1970s there were severe upheavals within the First World economies and there was rising concern with the apparent inability of established national and international mechanisms to deal with the new economic problems.[3] In the wider international system there were political problems as the bipolar system of the USA and USSR came under pressure. In particular the USA become embroiled in a futile war in Vietnam designed to 'contain communism'. It has been suggested that this involvement was an instance of imperial overstretch[4] but more mundanely one can point to the burden of the war on the US economy and the collapse of its moral claims to leadership of the Free World. Relatedly we may note the rise of new economic and political powers in Japan and the European Union.

The relative eclipse of the post-Second World War liberal-democratic welfare state compromise has seen both a regressive and a progressive response. The progressive reply within the First World countries of the capitalist system has been presented by theorists of democracy[5] but the immediate advantage was seized by the political right. After some thirty-odd years of opposition[6] it was with the elections of Ronald Reagan and Margaret Thatcher that the New Right finally took power.[7] The extent to which the theorists of the right can be taken to have provided new ideas and strategies as opposed to ideological public-relations fig-leaves vehicled through sympathetic media commentators is a matter of debate. However,

---

3   E. A. Brett 1985 *The World Economy Since the War: The Politics of Uneven Development*, London, Macmillan.
4   P. Kennedy 1988 *The Rise and Fall of the Great Powers*, London, Fontana.
5   I have in mind the work of J. Habermas, A. MacIntyre and C. B. Macpherson in particular.
6   It was European democratic reformism plus the active promulgation of emerging US hegemony that acted to structure the post-Second World War compromise in Europe. Yet, in the construction of this compromise there were irreconcilable opponents who saw post-war liberal-democratic polities as socialistic Amongst the early intellectual critics were Friedrich von Hayek, Karl Popper and Milton Friedman. In the early post-war period the re-writing of history proceeded apace and soon the European fascists were linked up to Soviet communism under the umbrella label of totalitarianism. The culpability of the Western powers in regard to the pre-war rise of European fascism, and the aggressive US drive against the left and the USSR after the war, were rapidly and actively forgotten. An extensive vocabulary of legitimation was developed, and free enterprise was equated with free economies, which were equated with the Free West, which in turn was equated with freedom.
7   See J. Krieger 1986 *Reagan, Thatcher and the Politics of Decline*, Cambridge, Polity; on Thatcher see B. Jessop et al. 1988 *Thacherism: A Tale of Two Nations*, Cambridge, Polity, and S. Hall and M. Jacques eds. 1983 *The Politics of Thatcherism*, London, Lawrence and Wishart.

to take them at face value initially, what the New Right theorists claim is that the modern free-market capitalist system is maximally effective in producing and equitably distributing the economic, social, political, and intellectual necessaries of civilized life (see figure 16).

The Logic of the New Right Position

The theorists of the New Right offer a stark restatement of economic liberalism with its central role for the free market. An overarching claim is made that free markets maximize human welfare and in turn this unpacks as a series of interlinked claims: (a) economically, the claim is that as free markets act efficiently to distribute knowledge and resources around the economic system, then material welfare will be maximized; (b) socially, the claim is that as action and responsibility for action reside with the person of the individual, then liberal individualistic social systems will ensure that moral worth is maximized; (c) politically, the claim is that as liberalism offers a balanced solution to problems of deploying, distributing and controlling power, then liberal polities ensure that political freedom is maximized; and (d) epistemologically, the claim is that as the whole package is grounded in genuine positive scientific knowledge then in such systems the effective deployment of positive knowledge is maximized.

The substantive core of the package is made up of the claims in respect of the functioning of the free market. The free market comprises atomistic individuals who know their own autonomously arising needs and wants and who make contracts with other individuals through the mechanism of the marketplace to satisfy those needs and wants. The market is a neutral mechanism for transmitting information about needs and wants, and goods which might satisfy them, around the system. A minimum state machine provides a basic legal and security system to underpin the individual contractual pursuit of private goals.

A key figure in all this has been Milton Friedman who has presented his views in both technical and popular form. Some of the technical material will be dealt with later but for the moment the popular material will allow us to grasp the conservative political ideology. Friedman argues that *laissez-faire* capitalism is a necessary condition of political freedom.[8] In a competitive capitalist society individuals freely enter into exchanges in the marketplace and in society. The role of the state is minimal: economic power is dispersed in a competitive capitalist economy and political power must also be dispersed. The separation of economic power from political power lets the former act as a check on the concentration tendencies in the latter: the proper role of the latter, the state, is in setting the rules of the social game and arbitrating disputes. This position is taken to rule out not only the historical objective of socialism but also the social-democratic welfare

8   M. Friedman 1962 *Capitalism and Freedom*, University of Chicago Press.

Figure 16   Neoliberalism in the 1980s

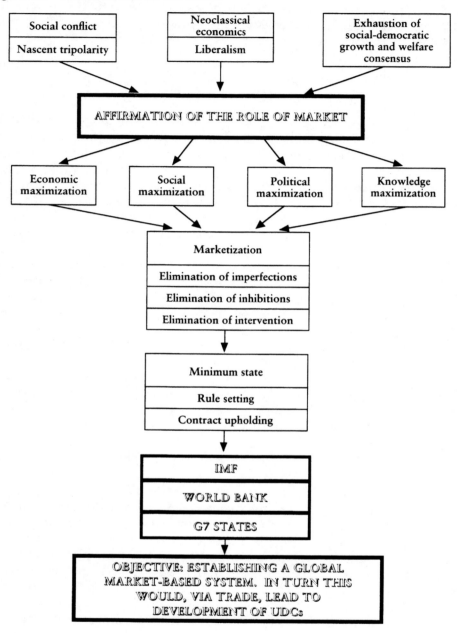

states of the post-Second World War First World.[9] In the light of the evident ideological commitments of the New Right the attempt to reduce the scope of economics and of political and policy analysis to the sphere of the proper functioning of a putatively self-regulating equilibrium system is deeply unpersuasive.

The general pro-market position of the New Right has informed the policy of the World Bank, the IMF and the US government over the 1980s. The position of the New Right translates into policy advice for Third World countries around the core commitment to free markets. The argument has been unpacked in terms of a series of principles which guide policy advice for Third World countries:[10] (a) any regulation of the market is to be avoided, save for crises and the removal of malfunctions or inhibitions to full functioning; (b) any intervention in the market is to be avoided, save to remove causes of price distortions, so subsidies should be abolished, tax rates adjusted to encourage enterprise, tariff barriers removed along with other non-tariff barriers or disguised restrictions; (c) any government role in the economy should be avoided, as private enterprise can usually do the job better, and when governments do become involved it should be both market-conforming, short-term and involve a minimum of regulations; (d) any collective intervention in the market should be avoided, so labour unions must be curbed; and (e) international trade should be free trade with goods and currency freely traded.

The work of the New Right in respect of the development of the Third World has been much discussed and it is suggested that they are guilty of oversimplification and sloganeering.[11] It has been noted that both the political left and the right came to agree in the 1970s that the Third World did not exist separately from the global system. The former assimilated it into the world capitalist system as a degraded dependent sector and the latter assimilated it into a mythic functioning world market system. Against this orthodox critics insist that the Third World does indeed exist as an internally complex sphere which is integrated within the global system which must be studied in a pragmatic fashion.

The New Right came to prominence in the wake of the slow collapse of Keynesianism which was the intellectual counterpart to the post-Second World War liberal-democratic welfare state compromise. The collapse was a mixture of the impact of real world events, in particular the surge in inflation coupled to a lack of very obvious success in securing development, plus the intellectual impact of structuralist economics (a progenitor of dependency theory which we will consider later). The New Right seized the opportunity to advance their long prepared restatements of economic liberalism.

9   On Friedman's ideas of freedom see C. B. Macpherson 1973 *Democratic Theory: Essays in Retrieval*, Oxford University Press.
10 K. P. Clements 1980 *From Right to Left in Development Theory*, Singapore, Institute of Southeast Asian Studies, p. 16.
11 Toye 1987 op. cit.

Critics have suggested that this was often accomplished with scant regard
to the truth of particular cases, as when for example New Right theorists
pointed to the example of the growth of East Asia as supporting their position where in fact East Asian development has been state-centred and routinely regulated-market in character. The entire New Right approach was
always strongly ideological in character and the approach captured the World
Bank, IMF and development agencies of those First World governments
wedded to the ideals of free markets. In the space of a few years the New
Right celebration of the market became a new orthodoxy.

In general all this economics work, by both the orthodox professional neo-
classical theorists and the overt ideological celebrants of the unregulated
market, revolves around the model of the pure market economic system.[12] We can summarize the core elements of this model of a satisfaction-
maximizing automatic asocial mechanism as follows: (a) in respect of goods
and services there is a fundamental underlying naturally given situation of
scarcity; (b) there is legally guaranteed private ownership of the means of
production; (c) there is pervasive perfect competition amongst suppliers
who operate in a complex division of labour and who are aiming to meet
the demands of sovereign consumers, all ordered via the market; and (d)
there is a definite politics attached to this model – thus the free market is
taken to underpin human freedom in general. So far as the New Right are
concerned this model represents the essential character of all human economic activity in society. However, this pure market model is a sophisticated intellectual construct and when it is examined it rapidly disintegrates.[13]

The 1980s have seen the New Right experiments in the First World fail
as the experiment has produced unemployment, reductions in general welfare, social dislocation, declining manufacturing production, and extensive
debt burdens. In the Second World the post-1989 rush to celebrate the 'end
of history', understood as the triumph of the ideas of liberal-democracy,[14]
via the rapid marketization of the old Eastern Bloc countries has proved ill
judged as the reform processes in these countries have drifted to a halt as
the intractable problems of these areas have continued and deepened. It is
now clear that any social change will be slow. In the Third World the work
of the New Right as it has been vehicled through the IMF and World Bank
has been regarded as less than helpful. In general, against these ideological
schemes, in regard to the First and Second Worlds European commentators
look to the model of Germany where the social market system is a variety
of consensus-centred corporatism. And against the claims of the proponents
of the sovereign joys of the marketplace, development theorists cite the
models of Japan and East Asia as examples of state-assisted development.[15]

12   M. P. Todaro 1982 *Economics for a Developing World*, London, Longman.
13   See P. Ormerod 1994 *The Death of Economics*, London, Faber, ch. 3.
14   F. Fukuyama 1992 *The End of History and the Last Man*, London, Hamish Hamilton.
15   Indeed the World Bank and IMF are even now presenting their ideological counter-
offensives on behalf of their fantasy model of the market. See, for example, World Bank
1993 *The East Asian Miracle*, Oxford University Press.

Overall, in place of celebrations of the ordering capacity and benefit-maximizing properties of the free market, an analysis informed by the classical social scientific tradition with its concern to elucidate the dynamics of complex change would look to offer characterizations of the global system and the actions of powerful agents within this system. The relevant intellectual resources would comprise the strategies of political-economic analysis, institutional analysis and the critical interpretation of culture. In substantive terms, we have the issue of the emergent blocs of Japan/Asia, the Americas, and Europe. And relatedly, in regard to development, the issue is one of the continuing extension of the capitalist mode of production with the consequent remaking of the economies and societies of the countries of the Third World.

The Overall Record of the New Right

The theorists of the marketplace offer strong claims in respect of both the coherence of their views and the success of policy positions informed by these views. In recent years the track records of various countries and regions within the global system have been subject to competing claims from the New Right and their opponents in respect of the appropriate explanation for recorded success.

In the First World

In discussions of the monetarist aspect of the New Right experiment (the scheme of reducing government intervention in the economy to a narrow technical sphere of monetary control in the expectation that after a period of adjustment as the Keynesian poison worked itself out of the system market forces would thereafter maximize benefits), commentators have argued that it has been a failure both in the USA and in the UK.[16] These two countries have seen clear tests of the theories of the New Right.[17] The free marketeers would offer a reply to this in terms of the test having been not quite correct or otherwise defective by virtue of a lack of policy clarity or rigour but this is not persuasive.

However, there are further questions and disaggregating the UK record we can say that there has been no state withdrawal from the economy, merely a different pattern instituted. A similar argument could be made for the experience of the USA under Reagan.[18] In general what seems to have been done is that the post-Second World War liberal-democratic settlement has been rewritten such that the economic direction of society is no longer a tripartite matter for government, industry, and unions, but is increasingly

16   D. Smith 1987 *The Rise and Fall of Monetarism*, Harmondsworth, Penguin.
17   On the UK see J. Mitchie ed. 1992 *The Economic Legacy 1979–1992*, London, Academic Press; on the USA see Krieger 1986 op. cit.
18   Krieger 1986 op. cit.

a matter of government and large corporations.[19] There has been a marked shift of economic power away from formal democratic institutions, which at the very least paid some deference to the ideal of the responsibility of the economic sphere to consider and consult wider constituencies representing society in general, into the modern monopoly marketplace. Economic power, and relatedly social, cultural and political power have been removed from the public and state spheres and lodged in the private market. However, when power is shifted from the state and the institutions of the public sphere into the market it is not shifted into the ambit of a neutral efficiency-maximizing mechanism; rather it is shifted into the hands of the monopoly firms, the multi-nationals, the big banks and their allies in the higher echelons of government and para-statal organizations. The slogans used to legitimate this shift of material and ideological power have been drawn from the lexicon of the free marketeers and ideologues and have spoken warmly of the processes of privatization, liberalization, enterprise, competition, free trade and the related rise in individual responsibility. The machineries of social control of the marketplace which were intermediate between citizen and market, the realm of the public sphere ordered by the state, have been dismantled. Individuals, taken atomistically as mere consumers and no longer citizens even in aspiration, now face an enormously more powerful and unconstrained array of giant firms. Any perception of enhanced economic, political or social freedom is on any routine social scientific description an illusion for all but a tiny elite minority.[20]

In the Second World

In the period following the 1989–91 upheavals in the old East European Bloc there have been a series of distinct phases in the commentaries offered by New Right theorists based in the West: (a) celebrations of victory; (b) the deployment of recipes for rapid marketization; (c) a muted and puzzled recognition of evident failure; and (d) the slow growth of a realistic social scientific approach to these issues.

The initial reaction of Western New Right commentators to the upheavals in eastern Europe was an attempt to assimilate the changes to the positions of the New Right. It was suggested that here was the inevitable drive to market freedom reasserting itself against tyranny and socialism. The end of history in the final victory of the notions of liberal-democracy was confidently announced.[21] In fact the changes in eastern Europe had nothing to do with the New Right and everything to do with the final revolt of ordinary people, organized by citizen groups, churches and artists, against

19   See E. Hobsbawm 1994 *Age of Extremes: The Short Twentieth Century, 1914–1991*, London, Michael Joseph, ch. 14.
20   The postmodernist view that celebrates the 1980s as a new sphere of consumption centred freedom I dismiss as fantasy. See D. Harvey 1989 *The Condition of Postmodernity*, Oxford, Blackwell.
21   F. Fukuyama 1992 *The End of History and the Last Man*, London, Hamish Hamilton.

a moribund and discredited state-capitalist system that had been in terminal decline ever since its aged rulers declined the opportunity to effect reforms in the 1960s.[22]

In the wake of the collapse of the old USSR and its satellites there was a rush of Western advisors offering bizarre blueprints for a rapid transfer to market systems. The argument was made by these policy advisors that a rapid shift to the market was both possible and desirable. However, the exercises in social reconstruction which were advocated were not available in reality. The proposals owed more to dogma that any defensible social science. In the swathe of countries bordering the European Union the model which has been pursued has been that of a German-style social market and not the free market advocated by the ideologues of the New Right. It is also clear that social and economic change will be slow because in most of the areas of the former Soviet bloc there is neither a pristine capitalism nor an historical memory of such an order ready to spring into life at the moment governmental regulation is removed.[23] As the institutionalists argue, all economic systems are lodged in social systems and change is slow. Indeed, most recently, this seems to have been accepted. The return of socialist governments in several of the old Eastern Bloc countries in protest against the upheavals and failed promises of the marketeers came as a surprise to Western right-wing commentators. Of late, their celebrations of victory and statements of confidence in the marketplace have been considerably less emphatic. It might be suggested that a pragmatic and rational approach to the analysis of complex change in these territories is slowly gaining ground.[24]

In the Third World

In respect of the Third World the ideology of the free marketeers has governed the major institutions of capitalist development efforts since the early 1980s. The IMF and World Bank have pressed for economic liberalization and proposals have involved: (a) the elimination of market imperfections, thus the removal of controls on the private sector, the privatization of state assets, the liberalization of foreign investment regulations and so on; (b) the elimination of market-inhibitory social institutions and practices, thus curbing trades unions and professions, abolishing various subsidies, liberalizing employment regulation and so on; (c) the elimination of surplus government intervention, thus the imposition of restrictions on government spending, the reduction in government regulative activity, the reduction of government planning activity, the abolition of tariff regimes and

22   See Hobsbawm 1994 op. cit. chs. 13, 16. See also A. Callinicos 1989b *The Revenge of History*, Cambridge, Polity; B. Denitch 1990 *The End of the Cold War*, London, Verso; T. Garton-Ash 1989 *We The People*, London, Granta.
23   The one exception is the Czech Republic which was both an advanced economy before disaster overtook it in 1938 and which now shares a common border with Germany. In similar terms one might also point to Hungary – again, having close links with Austria.
24   The problems are severe: see M. Glenny 1990 *The Rebirth of History*, Harmondsworth, Penguin; M. Ignatieff 1994 *Blood and Belonging*, London, Vintage.

so on; and (d) it might be noted that such programmes of liberalization have usually required parallel programmes of political repression.

The New Right has argued that the 'Third World' only exists as a figment of the guilty imagination of First World scholars and politicians. They argue that the idea should be set aside in a return to analysis conducted in the light of market principles. The celebration of the marketplace was effectively advanced within professional and public debate towards the end of the 1970s when the existing technocratic Keynesian consensus was wrestling unpersuasively with problems of stagflation. The ideological position was given a superficial plausibility in the contrast of (state-directed) misdevelopment in India and (market-ordered) successful development in the Asian NICs. As these arguments were advanced and gained widespread influence within the key institutional centres of the global system, many other social science analyses were pushed to one side. However, the schedule of reforms inaugurated by the New Right have not generally proved to be successful.[25] It is also true to say that the rhetorically important attempt to annex the development experience of Pacific Asia to the position of the New Right has been widely ridiculed by development specialists.[26]

In all, the affirmation of the role of the marketplace has led to untold damage to the fragile economies and societies of the Third World.[27] It has been cogently argued that the machineries of the IMF and World Bank can be taken to be primarily concerned with the task of making the world safe for business.[28] Such strong claims in regard to the role of the IMF and World Bank are quite familiar.[29]

New Right Ideas on State, Market and Economy

It is possible to move beyond the specific debate on the ideology and policy positions of the New Right to consider some of the more detailed debates pursued in recent years on the relationship of state, economy and political action. We can consider four points: firstly the emergence of the broad agenda of the New Right from the confines of the 1970s issue of inflation; second the way in which these thinkers actually argued their case; thirdly how the case which they did argue functioned to read out all those structural-historical circumstances which militated against acceptance of their views and solutions; and fourthly the progressive reply to the collapse of

25   Toye 1987 op. cit.
26   G. White ed. 1988 *Developmental States in East Asia*, London, Macmillan; R. P. Appelbaum and J. Henderson eds. 1992 *States and Development in the Asia Pacific Rim*, London, Sage.
27   Susan George for example, has traced the links between US agricultural problems, the World Bank's preference for market-oriented agricultural development programmes and the consequent inability of African nations to feed their populations. See S. George 1984 *Ill Fares The Land*, Washington, Institute for Policy Science.
28   S. George 1988 *A Fate Worse then Debt*, Harmondsworth, Penguin, and in this vein see also W. Sachs ed. 1992 *The Development Dictionary*, London, Zed.
29   P. Korner et al. 1984 *The IMF and the Debt Crisis*, London, Zed.

the post-Second World War liberal-democratic compromise advanced by the theorists of democracy.

The debate about inflation

The problem of inflation came to dominate economic thinking in the late 1970s and it was within this particular setting that New Right work attained its fashionable status. The theorists of the New Right argued that inflation was a phenomenon generated in the money economy (the sphere of the circulation of money as opposed to the real economy which was the sphere of the circulation of manufactured goods) and that it was caused by government over-spending; that is, putting too large a quantity of money into the system. The remedy was quite simple. All governments should stop their oversupply of money. Thereafter, it was argued that governments should look to the reinstitution of the free market as this would maximize human welfare.

The debate in respect of inflation may be seen to turn on the matter of the cause of inflation. Keynesians do not distinguish between the money and real economies and have spoken of two varieties of inflationary pressure: cost-push inflation, so called because costs push up prices; and demand-pull inflation, which occurs when many consumers compete for scarce goods. The Keynesian concern with inflation, which was secondary to the focus on maintaining high levels of employment, centres on the efforts of governments to curb rises in prices and incomes. The right mix of policies was always a matter of debate. However as the post-Second World War economic boom faded away a new situation combining economic slump and inflation came into being and was dubbed 'stagflation'.[30] The circumstances of the political-economies of the First World in the early 1970s were very difficult for social theorists to understand.

The early theorists of the New Right offered a simple cure to the disease of inflation. Milton Friedman adopted the strategy of the American economist Irving Fisher and distinguished between the real economy and the money economy and then announced that 'inflation is always and everywhere a monetary phenomenon' which is caused by governments taking the easy way out of economic problems by printing money.[31] The solution was to curb government spending and thereby reduce the quantity of money in the system. The message has the great merit of simplicity: analogies can be drawn between profligate householders who spend all the money they have and responsible householders who budget carefully and live within their means. The monetarists suggested that the key problem was the profligacy of governments.

The New Right did not believe that governments have much influence on rates of economic growth or rates of unemployment. However, they did think that governments had a major impact on rates of inflation and that

30 P. Donaldson 1973 *Economics of the Real World*, Harmondsworth, Penguin, ch. 6.
31 M. Freidman and R. Friedman 1980 *Free To Choose*, London, Secker, p. 224.

this should be addressed by spending cuts. As the government cuts its spending so the inflation rate will drop and the self-regulating system attain its equilibrium position, and thereafter it will function smoothly. In the short term there will be unpleasant side-effects such as a dramatic fall in the output of the economy and an equally dramatic rise in the rate of unemployment. And all this, say the Keynesians, is little more than a recipe for a slump and there are no reasons to suppose that this slump will cure itself.

In contrast, Celso Furtado presents a structuralist analysis of inflation which begins with a denial of the relevance of either Keynesian or neo-classical economics to the circumstances of Latin America.[32] Furtado insists that the economies of Latin America must be modelled directly and not in terms of the *a priori* schemes imported from the First World. In this case the typical Latin American economy presents itself as comprising a loosely related set of quasi-autonomous sectors each of which represents either a residue of the historical processes of the expansion of European capitalism or a present requirement of the newly dominant capitalist centre of the USA. The distinctively autonomous national economy of orthodox economics simply does not exist in Latin America where there is rather a concatenation of historical residues, introjected enclaves and various parasitic forms. The structuralist analysis of inflation[33] begins by noting the inflation proneness of traditional primary-product exporting economies and then goes on to note that the pursuit of industrialization 'based on import substitution started a new inflationary cycle'.[34] Any weaknesses in the capacity to import were met by generating local credits (or in monetarist terms printing money) and this 'sparked off a number of structural tensions which were translated into an inflationary process'.[35]

The debate around the matter of inflation lets Furtado counterpose a structuralist approach to those orthodox discussions which regard inflation as a matter of the poor functioning of money flows. Furtado insists that even if familiar patterns of inflation did occur then they were more often than not the outcome of 'more complex processes, whose main ingredients were structural inflexibility and the determination to press ahead with a development policy'.[36] This argument is unpacked in terms of the various responses contrived by the different sectors of the economy in endeavouring to avoid the burden of financing (through increased taxes or reduced subsidies and so on) the government's deficit. Thus Furtado deploys notions such as basic inflationary pressure, circumstantial pressures, propagation mechanisms and decision centres. The decision centres include the financial authorities of the state, the treasury and the state-bank, and it is here that

---

32 C. Furtado 1976 *Economic Development in Latin America*, 2nd edn, Cambridge University Press.
33 See 1981 edition dealing with monetarism, *Institute of Development Studies Bulletin*, 13.
34 Furtado 1976 op. cit. p. 118.
35 Ibid.
36 Ibid. p. 126.

the arguments of the monetarists start. In sum, Furtado attempts to provide an analysis of inflation which acknowledges the particular circumstances of Latin American economies in contrast to the analyses presented by the orthodoxy which rest in his view on models of self-regulating equilibrium systems and which elide the complexity of real-world politics in favour of the presentation of spuriously technical solutions.

Joan Robinson, reviewing the attraction of Irving Fisher's quantity theory of money which is the starting point for Friedman's approach comments that its 'enormous ideological attraction . . . [which] kept it going for nearly forty years after its logical content was exploded [by Keynes], is due to the fact that it conceals the problem of political choice under an apparently impersonal mechanism'.[37] And more broadly, in a discussion of the fierce resistance put up against Keynes by the orthodoxy in the 1930s and subsequently, it is precisely the matter of having to make explicit argument. Robinson comments that there

> is also a psychological element in the survival of equilibrium theory. There is an irresistible attraction about the concept of equilibrium – the almost silent hum of a perfectly running machine; the apparent stillness of the exact balance of counteracting pressures; the automatic smooth recovery from chance disturbance. Is there perhaps something Freudian about it? Does it connect with a longing to return to the womb? We have to look for a psychological explanation to account for the powerful influence of an idea that is intellectually unsatisfactory.[38]

Arguing the New Right case

Celso Furtado's view of economic analysis requires that it is adequate to specific situations, and thus he addresses the sociology, the politics and the history of the given situation. The orthodox theorists of economics tend not to do this and the neo-classical theorists, and the New Right, deliberately omit these concerns. There is an issue here in respect of the nature of economics, and thereafter of social science generally.

In terms of my distinction between empiricists and rationalists, the New Right conception of the status of economics is firmly empiricist. The science of economics is construed as a narrowly technical discipline which deals with matters of fact and eschews discussion of values. In a noted essay Friedman argues that:

> Positive economics is in principle independent of any particular ethical position . . . Its task is to provide a system of generalisations that can be used to make correct predictions about the consequences of any change in circumstances. Its performance is to be judged by the precision, scope, and conformity with experience of the predictions it

---

37 J. Robinson 1962 *Economic Philosophy*, Harmondsworth, Penguin, p. 93.
38 Ibid. pp. 77–8.

yields. In short, positive economics is, or can be, an 'objective' science, in precisely the same sense as any of the physical sciences.[39]

A little later we are told that the role of theory is simply the systematization and abstraction of the essentials of reality. In other words, social theory is a complex summary description. In economics scientific prediction is difficult and testing awkward but these problems are not insuperable. Against those who would say that the assumptions of economics are unrealistic, it is stated that assumptions are in practice relatively unimportant as it is accurate predictions which are the key. In sum, positive economics can be seen to be 'a body of tentatively accepted generalizations about economic phenomena that can be used to predict the consequences of changes in circumstances'.[40]

Against this, Keynesianism in its original form was an economics and politics of social reform. Joan Robinson offers a series of points on this matter and contrasts Keynesian economics with the neo-classical orthodoxy which it had been taken to have replaced. Robinson argues that Keynes brought back into economics the 'hard headedness of the Classics';[41] that is, he speaks directly to the dynamics of the historically existing capitalist system. Keynes reintroduces a series of aspects of analysis which the neo-classical theorists had been happy to ignore: history (and thus no more ahistorical enquiry); ethics (and thus no more easy value-freedom as economists needs must make and defend choices); and time (and thus no more timeless perfect equilibrium worlds). Robinson summarizes the impact of the work of Keynes by saying that these revisions made

> it impossible to believe any longer in an automatic reconciliation of conflicting interests into a harmonious whole, [Keynes] brought out into the open the problem of choice and judgement that the neo-classicals had managed to smother. The ideology to end ideologies broke down. Economics once more became Political Economy . . . The Keynesian revolution has destroyed the old soporific doctrines . . . We are left in the uncomfortable situation of having to think for ourselves.[42]

Against this backdrop it is clear that the theorists of neo-liberalism were concerned to overthrow Keynesianism which was taken to be the main intellectual vehicle of liberal-democratic interventionism. This objective was accomplished in its narrowly intellectual aspect by launching a revised version of an old element of neo-classical equilibrium economics, quantity theory, supported by a study of historical econometric statistical data.[43] The proponents of monetarism focused on the matter of inflation and laid the blame at the door of government, arguing that if too much money is fed into the system then inflation will be the inevitable result. This claim cut at the heart of the Keynesian role for the state. In place of the interventionist

39   M. Friedman 1953 *Essays in Positive Economics*, University of Chicago Press, p. 4.
40   Ibid. p. 39.
41   Robinson 1962 op. cit. p. 71.
42   Ibid. p. 73.
43   See ibid.; D. Smith 1987 *The Rise and Fall of Monetarism*, Harmondsworth, Penguin.

role of the state securing stable growth at full employment through judicious deficit-financed spending, we have not merely inflation but also a higher rate of natural unemployment than would otherwise have been the case. If this central claim, in respect of the occasion of inflation could be secured then the Keynesian project was effectively dead. This was the strategy adopted by Friedman.[44]

The intellectual aspect of Friedman's work centres on econometric analysis and the claim to positive scientificity. The procedure involves modelling on the basis of large sets of economic data. In regard to econometrics, however, critics report increasing doubt amongst economists as to the value of the procedure as little has been achieved by way of defensible results.[45] Relatedly, a critique of positivist models in social science is available which points out that all that can be claimed for these efforts is an arbitrary plausibility in respect of their relation to their object-spheres.[46] If there are doubts about econometrics and modelling, then there are also doubts about the way in which Friedman has handled these strategies. One commentator reported that 'Friedman's most notable research work was *A Monetary History of the United States* published in 1963 . . . [and there] is a sense, running through Friedman's research work, of reading a "whodunit" having already glanced at the final page'.[47] Others have noted the commitment of the New Right and have argued that, whilst social theory properly addresses real world problems, the robust intellectual pragmatism of Keynes has 'become, in the hands of the counter-revolution, a much more manipulative approach to the intellectual standards of economics'.[48]

In my terms what we have from the New Right is the promulgation of a delimited-formal ideology in the form of a restatement of the model of free-market capitalism. The original ideas of monetarism were sold in the UK by a comparatively small group of people who assiduously fed policy ideas to those likely to be sympathetic within the media-city-parliament arena: a few professors, a few journalists, and a couple of right-wing think tanks were particularly important.[49] The issue of the relationship of scholarship to political spokesmanship and the role of both styles of enquiry/action in the public sphere are difficult matters. The work of the New Right has the intention of eliminating from debate the historical and structural

44   Smith Ibid.
45   J. Pheby 1988 *Methodology and Economics: A Critical Introduction*, London, Macmillan.
46   See B. Hindess 1977 *Philosophy and Methodology in the Social Sciences*, Hassocks, Harvester.
47   Smith 1987 op. cit. p. 20.
48   Toye 1987 op. cit. pp. 23–4.
49   Smith 1987 op. cit. This is also an issue much debated in Australia, another site of New Right experimentation, where commentators diagnose a similar capture of influential points in policy and state system. See D. Horne ed. 1992 *The Trouble with Economic Rationalism*, Newham, Scribe, and M. Pusey 1991 *Economic Rationalism in Canberra: A Nation-Building State Changes its Mind*, Cambridge University Press. For the USA, J. Krieger 1986 *Reagan, Thatcher and the Politics of Decline*, Cambridge, Polity, speaks of the construction of an arithmetical coalition based on particular interests articulated around the celebration of the market.

circumstances of particular economies. The problem is not the New Right's attempt to persuade a wide audience amongst politicians, policy-makers and public but the flawed nature of their argument which by misrepresenting delimited-formal ideology as positive science does indeed look manipulative.[50]

State, economy and action in the global system

I remarked above that there was a progressive reply to the collapse of the post-war contested compromise of liberal-democracy. In respect of the First World this reply, to cast the matter in general terms, is carried by the critical-theoretic attack on the technocratic invasion of the life world and the decline of partially realized democracy.[51] Thus the civil sphere of private economic action is increasingly subject to regulation and control via giantism of monopoly capitalist firms, and the public sphere of citizen discourse is shrinking as power becomes concentrated in an opaque state machine clearly concerned more with its linkages to the business world than with ordering the public sphere. Thus the spheres of civil society – the public sphere and the arena of state activity – are increasingly subject to the complex of economic, social and political demands which flow from the particular interests of the monopoly capitalist sector of the economy. Habermas speaks of the political project of reconstructing the public sphere, such that decisions in respect of core industrial and scientific activities are taken by the community. There are many strands to the present theoretical and practical drive in Europe for a more effective formal and substantive democracy. Where the New Right would affirm albeit spuriously the relative separateness of state and economy, and the liberal-democratic orthodoxy would affirm the general subordination of economy to enlightened state, the question to be addressed for the democratic line is the precise nature of the exchange between state, economy and political action. What might be known and how might such knowledge be deployed to secure agreed social goals?

Offering at this stage a schematic treatment of a key issue in social theory we can distinguish between three spheres of relevant debate: (a) the narrowly polemical where the issue is whether or not the state can influence or direct the economy; (b) the political-theoretical where the issue is the nature of the exchange between state and economy; and (c) the abstract-theoretical where the matter of structure and agency in the spheres of economy, society and polity might be raised.

Against the New Right claim that the state can do no more than play the role of underlabourer to market forces which are to be seen as a reality *sui generis*, we can begin by insisting that political power shapes economics both directly and indirectly. The occasion and intention of the original

---

50 On the issue of political writing see P. W. Preston 1987 *Rethinking Development*, London, Routledge; and on the political writing of the monetarists, with their substitution of purportedly technical argument for explicit political judgement see C. Furtado 1976 *Economic Development in Latin America*, 2nd edn, Cambridge University Press.
51 These terms are used by the German social theorist Jürgen Habermas, who draws on the Frankfurt School tradition to characterize the increasing *rationalization* of human life. See J. Habermas 1989 *The Structural Transformation of the Public Sphere*, Cambridge, Polity.

marginalist theorists have been noted earlier, and their inheritors, the New Right, offer claims in respect of the relationship of state and economy that are, if taken seriously, simply incredible. The real questions centre on the nature, extent, occasion and character of state involvements in markets.

Looking at the matter generally, in the case of direct state influence upon matters economic we can recall episodes ranging in social scale from securing strategic class interests (for example Weber's work on the role of political action as against economic forces which was addressed to the sleepy German bourgeoisie[52]) through to the establishment of formal institutional mechanisms of economic control (as with Bretton Woods), down to simple pork-barrel politics in respect of the distribution of government largesse. The point here, broadly, is that economic structures are to be seen as social structures which are created and recreated in routine social practice, and not as absolute and given as the free marketeers would have us believe.

Turning now to the political-theoretical issue of how to conceptualize the relationship of state and economy it is clear that this matter has been extensively discussed within social science. Thus for the free marketeers the relationship of state to economy is one of subordination and rule protection. The self-regulating maximizing market may be minimally assisted by the state to better realize its potential: a framework of law to protect that self-generating and regulating market. The extent of available economic knowledge, upon which a state would act were it necessary to restore system self-regulation, is minimal: this is one of the paradoxes of naturalistic economics: they commit themselves to strong models of knowledge and then report that only a very little of this knowledge can be provided. Enough to correct but, emphatically, not enough to direct.

For the liberal-democratic orthodoxy the state is the overseer of the economic activities of society. This line of theorizing can be traced back into the late nineteenth century and the beginnings of a reaction on the part of the reform-minded bourgeoisie to the evident problems of emergent industrial society. In social science this reform line is developed at the same time as classical political-economy fades away and the marginalist anti-socialist theories take hold in economics. State direction of the economy, both directly, as in state industries, and indirectly as in fine-tuning or, later, development projects, is necessary as the free market left to its own devices is productive of extensive mal-development. Optimistically these theorists take the view that the knowledge necessary to order this active interventionist role is also in principle available; usually it is a product of the range of social sciences, not just the economists.

For the democratic line the state is one major locus of citizen activity in regard to ordering society and economy. The state is an institutionally elaborate membrane ordering internal and trans-national flows of economic and political power, such trans-national flows of economic and political power being taken as the out-turn of the structured activities of other groups,

52 A. Giddens 1972 *Politics and Sociology in the Thought of Max Weber*, London, Macmillan.

other communities. The neo-liberal realm of markets *sui generis* is not accepted, but the notion of a trans-national global system is affirmed.[53] The political-economic system is taken as both complex and extensively knowable, and in regard to the metropolitan capitalist heartlands the requirements by way of knowledge to order the system are available but as political-dialogic rather than technical knowledge. It has been argued in recent years that social theorizing must grant that agents are widely knowledgeable about the social worlds they inhabit. There seems to be little reason to suppose that this could not hold true for abstract knowledge of political-economy.[54] It is of course true that presently the state is a closed-off sphere with access and activity being restricted by the special interests of capital but the project of de-mystifying and democratizing these opaque state-machines is now a strong theme in European politics.

In this democratic line recent work has looked to unpack the dynamics of the exchanges between state, global system and relevant population groups. It is a relatively straightforward matter to analyse the political projects of extant state-regimes in terms of accumulation strategies (how the state attempts to position the economic sphere under its influence within the encompassing regional and global networks) and related regulation strategies (how the state orders the population within its control – both via the force inherent in any state machinery and, importantly, with ideological hegemonic projects).

Finally, moving one step beyond these obvious remarks, there remains the wider issue of how we are to handle the business of structure and agency in the spheres of economy, society and polity, plus, evidently, their manifold interweavings. Such general issues have been a major part of the work of Giddens whose theory of structuration draws on both classical and contemporary social theory to offer an answer, in brief that structures are the ground of action which in turn is the occasion of structure. Clearly it would be beyond my scope here to attempt to deal with these problems. However, one might say that the patterns of human interaction centring upon material/social needs are the given that has to be accepted, all of which follows classical nineteenth-century social scientific thinking, and of course Marx. We need to reduce the economic to the social so as to make it clear that economic structures, like social, political and cultural structures, are generated within the routine practices of ordinary social life.[55]

The New Right Episode in Retrospect

The comparative eclipse of the post-Second World War liberal-democratic compromise consensus in the American sphere of metropolitan capitalism[56]

53   See L. Sklair 1991 *Sociology of the Global System*, Hemel Hempstead, Harvester Wheatsheaf; S. Strange 1988 *States and Markets*, London, Pinter.
54   A. Giddens 1979 *Central Problems in Social Theory*, London, Macmillan.
55   R. Dilley ed. 1992 *Contesting Markets: Analyses of Ideology, Discourse and Practice*, Edinburgh University Press.
56   See J. Krieger 1986 *Reagan, Thatcher and the Politics of Decline*, Cambridge, Polity;

has seen a dual reply on the part of social theorists and political comment-ators/activists. The regressive reply to this real-world-occasioned eclipse is that of the New Right ideologues who claim that the free market provides the sovereign remedy to all our ills, but who are in reality merely servants of metropolitan capitalism. In the USA and the other Anglo-Saxon econom-ies the track records of right-wing governments over the last decade have been poor. The New Right have of course typically backed reaction in the Third World.[57] The progressive reply may be said to encompass all those who would analytically reduce the sphere of the market to the sphere of the social in order to fashion programmes of democratization.[58] Against the New Right's celebration of the sovereign role of the market and the inevit-able incapacity and incompetence of the state, it can be safely asserted that the state can be mobilized for democracy and development. In recent years it is quite evident that states have been mobilized for authoritarian non-democracy and thoroughly dubious patterns of development.[59]

Chapter Summary

The 1980s saw a resurgence of theories of society which stressed the role of the market. These theories came to prominence in the West in the wake of the seeming failure of post-Second World War Keynesian growth and welfare schemes. These celebrations of the market have been influential in development theory and practice, especially via the activities of the World Bank and the IMF. The intellectual core of the New Right approach is the neo-classical model of the market as a self-regulating system which maximizes the benefits of all participants. In development work it led to a stress on outward-directed development strategies and the encouragement of unregulated markets. As the 1980s progressed two lines of criticism were made: (a) that the market model at the centre of the programme was radically unsatisfactory intellec-tually; and (b) the policy flowing from the model did not seem to be working in either the First or Third World where, if anything, poverty seemed to be increasing. New Right theory was a contentious area of work which was very influential in the 1980s.

A. Woodiwiss 1993 *Postmodernity USA: The Crisis of Social Modernism in Postwar America*, London, Sage.

57 N. Chomsky 1991 *Deterring Democracy*, London, Verso.

58 Habermas 1989 op. cit.; D. Reuschemeyer et al. 1992 *Capitalist Development and Democracy*, Cambridge, Polity.

59 We might also note that the intellectual imperialism of neo-classical economics has been recently expressed in the guise of 'rational choice theory' whereby a methodological individualism coupled to an ethical preference for liberalism is presented as a procedural requirement of positive social scientific enquiry. A brief discussion is offered by H. Ward 1995 'Rational Choice Theory' in D. Marsh and G. Stoker eds. *Theory and Methods in Political Science*, London, Macmillan.

PART IV
New Analyses of Complex Change

15

Global System Interdependence: The New Structural Analyses of the Dynamics of Industrial-capitalism

Overview of New Structural Analyses

In the 1980s a new concern for analysing the global industrial-capitalist system has been expressed. A newly intensified interdependence has been identified. There are a number of ways in which this emerging global system has been theorized: (a) from the market-oriented postmodernist theorists we have had ideas of the transformation of capitalism such that the knowledge-based system was now global in reach and geared to consumption in the marketplace; (b) from the dependency and marxist theorists we have had ideas of the global reconstruction of the capitalist system as patterns and styles of production change with the rise of East Asia, the collapse of the Second World bloc, and the further partial dependent integration of areas of the Third World; and (c) from those identifying mutual interdependence and interest and who are concerned with global development there has been an increasingly vigorous concern both to detail the ways in which various groups live within the global system in order to identify common problems, and to reinforce global-level rule-setting in place of simple power relations (see figure 17).

Figure 17   New structural analysis of the global system

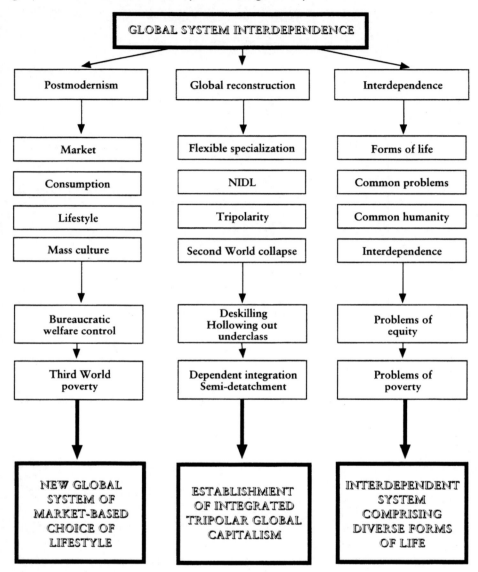

The Postmodernist Theory of the Global Cultural Marketplace

An influential new analysis has been presented by the market-oriented post-modernist theorists. The theory of globalization details the transformation of industrial-capitalism such that the system is now knowledge-based, geared to consumption in the marketplace and global in its reach. The power of the marketplace in the First World is taken to be self-evident whilst the Second and Third Worlds are assimilated to the overall perspective via the notion of emerging markets.[1]

The general theory reviewed

The decade of the 1980s has seen the extensive presentation of a fashionable theory to the effect that we now live in a knowledge-based post-industrial world with a postmodern culture. It has been suggested that three cultural trends came together to fashion the postmodernist package. The first involved a shift from the aesthetics of modernism to those of post-modernism in the arts, in particular a 'reaction against . . . functionalism and austerity . . . in favour of a heterogeneity of styles drawing especially on the past and on mass culture'.[2] Then, second, the epistemological shift from structuralism to post-structuralism 'stressed the fragmentary, heterogeneous and plural character of reality'.[3] And third, a 'version of the transformations supposedly undergone by Western societies in the past quarter of a century was provided by the theory of post-industrial society'.[4] Critics have argued that much of the general package of postmodernism has expressed the unhappy consciousness of the radical intelligentsia as the 'running has been made . . . primarily by North American philosophers, critics, and social theorists'.[5] The roots of postmodernism 'are to be found in the combination of the disillusioned aftermath of 1968 throughout the Western world and the opportunities for an overconsumptionist lifestyle offered upper white-collar strata by capitalism in the Reagan/Thatcher era'.[6]

These three themes were run together by the French theorist Lyotard[7] who argues that the two great nineteenth-century European metanarratives of progress which were constructed alongside the rise of science-based modernity, the French-inspired ideas of the Enlightenment and the German-inspired systems of speculative idealism, have undergone a dual process of decline. Intellectually they have undermined themselves in shifts towards either statelinked bureaucratic control, or abstract, formalized, and finally empty disciplines of learning (especially philosophy). In practical terms the political-economic systems in which they operate have become dominated by the pragmatics of the power of technical means, and the ends of action. The points of orientation of the metanarratives are no longer of any great concern.

This dual process of decline has allowed the expression of a new political-economy and culture. The global political-economy of the present

1 R. Robertson 1992 *Globalization: Social Theory and Global Order*, London, Sage.
2 A. Callinicos 1989a *Against Postmodernism*, Cambridge, Polity, p. 2.
3 Ibid.
4 Ibid. pp. 2–3.
5 Ibid. p. 5.
6 Ibid. p. 7.
7 F. Lyotard 1979 *The Postmodern Condition*, Manchester University Press. See G. Bennington 1989 *Lyotard Writing the Event*, Manchester University Press.

is dominated by flows of knowledge or information, produced via a natural science oriented to discontinuities and novelties rather than the task of uncovering a single coherent truth, and within these flows groups and individuals compete for the means to fashion discrete life-styles. It may all be viewed in an optimistic libertarian fashion, a system offering freedom to choose and construct life-styles from open flows of knowledge, but the pessimistic reading sees a renewed centrality for capitalist market relations, and these are unequal.

Lyotard argued that the contemporary world is best seen as a field of language-games through which individuals move. It is a relativistic, provisional and fragmented social world where received metadiscourses of progress are abandoned as patterns-of-life structured by the practices and cultures of capitalist-industrialism give way to life-style creation within the knowledge-based global system of post-industrial society.

One important aspect of the postmodernist material is its insistence that received patterns of social theoretical argument are now in need of radical renewal. In place of the experience of continuous intelligible progress, the experienced world of postmodernity has become one of partial truths and relativistic subjective perspectives. In our ordinary lives we are invited to select from proffered consumer alternatives in order to construct a life-style, and in the realm of social theorizing we are similarly enjoined to reject received traditions aspiring to universal knowledge in favour of the local, the partial and the contingent.[8]

The political-economy of postmodernity

The political-economic changes within the global system which are taken to underpin this shift to a postmodernist culture can be elucidated around the marxist regulationist school[9] distinction between fordist and post-fordist modes of production: the former characterized in terms of mass production, extensive state regulation, corporatist industrial relations and mass consumption of essentially common products; whilst the latter is characterized in terms of flexible production, restricted state-regulation, market-based industrial relations and personalized schedules of consumption from a varied menu of consumer goods.[10]

This broad characterization can be unpacked by reference to the detail of the political-economy of both Western and non-Western countries over the period since the First World War. The 1930s can be read as the confused episode of the construction of the fordist system, from New Deal politics in the USA, and Keynesianism in the UK, through to National Socialism in Germany. The essence of the productive system was the mass production of standardized products for a mass consumer market. The technologies, patterns of

8 A general survey is offered by B. Smart 1993 *Postmodernity*, London, Routledge.
9 D. Harvey 1989 *The Condition of Postmodernity*, Oxford, Blackwell, ch. 10.
10 Ibid. chs. 7–11.

industrial organization, patterns of political ordering and expectations in regard to consumption of the output all took time to fix in place. Indeed, the shift to a widespread use of fordist modes of accumulation and regulation belongs to be post-Second World War period of Keynesian demand management and the economic long boom. The goals of the early phases of optimistic decolonization and nationbuilding were similarly fordist.

The shift to post-fordist accumulation and regulation strategies can be dated with reference to familiar political-economic and political events. The episode of inflationary pressures compounded by the oil-price hike of the early 1970s tipped the fordist system into crisis. The post-fordist mode of production is thereafter taken to be in process of construction. The theorists point to a new rapidity in technological innovation, and to patterns of production which are decentralized, multi-plant, multi-national and which adopt the flexible specialization strategy such that a wide range of products can be made with designs quickly changed. The new pattern of production requires an educated, adaptable and complaisant workforce, coupled with government deregulation of the market. The restructuring of production takes place on a global scale, and the countries of the Third World are automatically drawn in as new locations for both production and consumption of global products.

However, against the theorists of postmodernity, critics have argued that it is not clear that the system has changed fundamentally. The 1980s might simply have seen reactionary political regimes in power in the countries of the First World who took advantage of improved transport and communications network to engineer a further round of dependent development by relocating a limited spread of production units in low-cost Third World countries.

The social-institutional order of postmodernity

The theorists of postmodernity analyse the shift from the modern to the postmodern world in terms of a series of characterizations. In the sphere of social institutions the complex changes can be grasped in terms of the shift from a core of institutions surrounding the state and embracing the community to a set of institutions surrounding the individual and extending through the marketplace.

The modern state ordered a series of key social institutions (family, welfare, employment and security) and fostered a wide spread of informal associations which were oriented towards the community (citizen groups, sports groups, community groups, churches, charities and the like). In all, a dense network of association bound each individual into the wider community where membership was construed as a matter of both rights and duties.

In the post-war period this is the form of social institutional life which was typical of European welfare capitalist systems. It is also the form of life which commentators now discern in the countries of Pacific Asia.

In the postmodern period social institutional order revolves around the individual who freely chooses patterns of association and consumption in order to construct a life-style. The private companies of the marketplace offer those family supports, welfare provisions and security forces which had been the concern of the state in the modern period. A key difference is the reliance on the unregulated market as a source of employment. All these relationships are mediated by the marketplace and are essentially voluntaristic and contractual.

In the post-war period this is the form of social institutional life which has been typical of the American free-market capitalist system.

The culture of postmodernity

Notwithstanding the available doubts in respect of the precise nature of recent political-economic and social-institutional changes, it has been argued that postmodernist culture has to be taken seriously as it could be the cultural form of a new stage in the development of the world capitalist system.[11] The culture of postmodernism centres upon the pre-eminent position in contemporary life of the commercial consumer marketplace. The ideas of progress which we take from the classical social scientific traditions of the nineteenth century are rejected. All that is available to humankind are the consumption opportunities offered by global capitalism. The individual exercise of choice within the marketplace is the basis of arbitrarily constructed life-styles. In this vein, those earlier cultural schedules which distinguished high culture from low culture are dismissed. In postmodernist culture any product offered on the cultural marketplace is as good as any other. In a similar way, by extension, those earlier schedules of the socially acceptable and unacceptable are dismissed because any product may be taken up into a life-style package. Indeed in the context of the marketplace-centred non-aesthetic and non-ethic of postmodernism, the production and consumption of novelties become prized simply because they are novelties. Overall, commentators identify certain key characteristics of postmodern culture: (a) depthlessness, as in place of structural analyses and understandings the surface image is stressed; (b) ahistoricism, as in place of analyses and understandings that place events and processes in history, the present is stressed; (c) intensities, as in place of considered ethics and aesthetics, subjectivist emotionality is stressed; (d) technologies, as in place of a view of technology-as-servant the power of technology is stressed; (e) pastiche, as in place of realism the play of invention is stressed; and (f) episodicity, as in place of the coherence of sequential discourses, the broken nature of discourse fragments is stressed.

It is clear that there is a link between liberal-individualism and postmodernist consumerism[12] because the idea of positive liberty,[13] the freedom of

11   F. Jameson 1991 *Postmodernism, Or the Cultural Logic of Late Capitalism*, London, Verso.
12   Z. Bauman 1988 *Freedom*, Milton Keynes, Open University Press.
13   I. Berlin 1989 *Four Essays on Liberty*, Oxford University Press.

agents in charge of their own lives, has been rejected in favour of an idea of negative liberty, the freedom from imposed restriction that lies at the core of the liberal-individualist political philosophy. It can be argued that the modernist project of democracy, the pursuit of positive liberty,[14] was forgotten long ago. Hannah Arendt has argued that the rise of the social question of poverty in the late nineteenth century turned attention away from fully realizing the public sphere of positive liberty, and the pursuit of democracy declined into the amelioration of poverty and the pursuit of material consumption, and the consumption sphere became self-perpetuating.[15] In this way it is argued that consumer-capitalism has both offered freedom-as-consumption (the negative liberty of freedom from the constraint of want and uncertainty) to all, or most, and has effectively blocked the modernist project. The consumer-capitalist system is now stable and successful. The individual and the system are linked via consumption of goods. Once inside the ideological circle it all makes perfect sense.

The power of the language of postmodernist politics centres on the notion of the market.[16] The notion of the market is a political resource which serves the interest of ruling groups. The pure market never did exist so debate about it is not debate about real social processes; rather the idea is a crucial area of ideological struggle. It can be granted that the language of the market superficially describes present patterns quite well – after all, ideology and reality intermingle as we (mis)organize our lives in the light of (mis)descriptions, but as an intellectual analysis it is vacuous[17] and as a prescriptive programme it is reactionary. The peculiar sexiness of the idea of the market can be traced to the 1980s' linkages of market and media. The realm of media-carried consumerism became the illusory exemplar of market freedom, and the notion of the market was taken into common thought as both a natural system-given and a realm of freedom.

The postmodern Third World

Notwithstanding the generally much lower levels of material living experienced by the peoples of the Third World, postmodern theory has been used to make sense of their changing circumstances. A series of changes are adduced as evidence of the rapid integration of these poor countries within the global consumer capitalist system. Postmodernists argue that the extent of penetration of industrial capitalist forms of life into Third World countries has increased very rapidly in recent years. A series of particular areas of activity are cited: (a) global production systems which ensure that schedules of material goods which were restricted in their availability to the rich West are now widely available (brand names like Sony or Ford or IBM are

---

14 C. B. Macpherson 1973 *Democratic Theory: Essays in Retrieval*, Oxford University Press.
15 Arendt is cited by Bauman 1988 op. cit. pp. 96–8.
16 Jameson 1991 op. cit.
17 Recall the arguments of P. Ormerod 1994 *The Death of Economics*, London, Faber.

now recognized globally); (b) global cultural forms which revolve around expressive consumption which used to be restricted to the West are now widely available (Hollywood movies, Coca-Cola, satellite TV are now consumed globally); and (c) global travel in the forms of migration (of poor people to richer areas) and mass tourism (often of rich people to poorer areas) ensures both a mixing of people and a standardization of activities (as the international style of airports, hotels, shops and leisure activities becomes more widespread).

The theorists of postmodernity have argued strongly that a process of globalization of culture is slowly taking place as patterns of consumption across the global system grow ever more similar. The theorists of the emergent markets of the Second and Third Worlds point to the growth of consumerism amongst those groups able to take advantage of the new opportunities within the marketplace. In this way the theorists of postmodernity draw the poor of the Second and Third Worlds into a global-market-based expressive consumerism which has recently been celebrated as the political-philosophical end of history.[18] However, critics have suggested that these patterns of consumption are available only to a narrow group and that the poor who lie outside the consumer sphere are subject to severe control. In First World consumer capitalism the poor are subject to the control of the bureaucratic-welfare system. Similarly the citizens of the Second World state-socialist systems prior to the revolutions of 1989 inhabited a culture which resembled the bureaucratic welfare control system. At the present time the poor who make up the majority of the populations of the countries of the Third World are excluded. In the context of the patterns of power within the global system these groups are not sources of alternative thinking, they are merely failed or aspirant consumers.[19]

The Reconstruction of Global Industrial-capitalism

A series of tendencies within the global system can be identified as patterns and styles of production change. First, the intermingled upgrading and hollowing out of the metropolitan core economies (flexible-specialization and the new international division of labour). Second, the rise of East Asian developmental capitalism as a discrete and novel variant of the industrial-capitalist form-of-life (tripolarity and the eclipse of the liberal market model). Third, the collapse of the Second World state socialist bloc and its confused shift towards market-based political-economies (a mixture of political collapse and thereafter general reconstruction in the USSR and Eastern Europe, and authoritarian market reforms in China and Indo-China). Fourth, the further partial dependent integration of areas of the Third World (in Asia, Latin America and the oil-rich Middle East). And fifth, the slow shift

---

18   F. Fukuyama 1992 *The End of History and the Last Man*, London, Hamish Hamilton.
19   On the globalization of culture see M. Featherstone 1991 *Consumer Culture and Postmodernism*, London, Sage.

of areas of the Third World into a situation of apparent semi-detachment from the global system (much of Africa south of the Sahara).

Flexible specialization and the new international division of labour

The notion of flexible specialization is associated with the institutional economic analyses of Piore and Sabel.[20] They focus on the industrial sociology of contemporary society and consider the nature of technology, the organization of the workplace, the demands of the labour force and the interaction of the place of work with the wider society. The authors argue that the familiar pattern of geographically concentrated large-plant fordist mass production of standard products has given way in the 1980s to the geographically dispersed small-plant post-fordist innovative production of individualized products. The mass production of similar products has given way to the large-scale production of a diversity of products.

It is suggested that there are two alternate reasons for the problems of fordist mass production: (a) a series of external shocks to the fordist system including labour problems and the oil crises of the 1970s which issued in the problems of inflation and slump and provoked an attempt by firms to ameliorate these difficult circumstances; (b) the internal needs for reform of a mass production system which could no longer respond to the increasingly sophisticated demands from consumers. On the basis of this analysis, there are two ways in which the problems of the breakdown of fordist mass production can be addressed: (a) an increase in global demand such that the system is reinvigorated (this could be achieved after the suggestion of the Brandt Commission of 1980 which looked to an international Keynesianism which identified the Third World as a potential marketplace for the First World in a mutual interdependence); (b) a shift to new patterns of production which are knowledge-based, small scale, and oriented to an individualized product spread, or the flexible specialization of a post-fordist system of production.

A related analytical concern has been with the changing geographical pattern of production within the global industrial capitalist system. In the 1980s some industrial production was relocated from First World to Third World and some newly established industrial production was set up in the Third World in preference to the First World. The change has been noted by the theorists of the new international division of labour.

Frobel and Heinrichs referred to the theoretical machineries of world system analysis, which are a variant of Latin American dependency analysis, and pointed out that in the 1970s a new phase of the development of world capitalism could be identified.[21] It took the form of the relocation

20   M. Piore and C. Sabel 1984 *The Second Industrial Divide*, New York, Basic Books.
21   F. Frobel and J. Heinrichs 1980 *The New International Division of Labour*, Cambridge University Press.

of certain industries in the Third World and the establishment of some new industries in that region rather than in the First World. A complementary development took place with First World industries relocating to the Third World as these countries pursued export-oriented development strategies. It is certainly the case that over the late 1970s and 1980s some areas of the Third World saw rapid export-oriented industrial growth. The export goods produced have in significant measure served the demands of the First World consumer markets. The new global market for goods and the rise of the MNCs favour the new international division of labour. The other factors which helped this new pattern to develop included the labour reserves of the Third World, the advance of technology such that tasks could be simplified and easily relocated to traditionally low-skill areas, and the development of transport and communications such that multi-national production and distribution could be achieved by the MNCs.

In the First World two concerns about the nature of the global system have been voiced: (a) the social implications of the upgrading of the core economies where the demand for semi-skilled or unskilled labour falls away rapidly which in the absence of state corrected action leads to structural unemployment of a large scale and long duration; and (b) the hollowing out of core economies as industrial production is relocated to low-cost off-shore production platforms leaving head-office functions in the production sphere and an ever larger service sector. In the Third World the concerns about the changing nature of the global system revolve around the character of the industrialization that has recently occurred and the stability of the commitment of the First World to the relatively open trading economy which has in part underpinned this development. However, the long-term implications of these observed patterns of change in production patterns are far from entirely clear.[22]

Tripolarity and the eclipse of the liberal market model

One aspect of the recent debates about patterns of global change has been a rise of concern for the tripolar nature of the system. The global system has been taken both to be in the process of becoming more integrated and to be forming into three distinct blocs: the Americas, Europe and Pacific Asia. The characteristic form-of-life of the peoples within these blocs and their interactions within the global system have become important issues. It has been suggested that within each of the three spheres a distinctive form of life is developing where each presents a particular version of industrial-capitalism. At the global level it is suggested that the system is increasingly shaped by the flows of material goods, finance and cultural resources between

22 A review of these debates is available in J. Allen and D. Massey eds. 1988 *The Economy in Question*, London, Sage.

these three spheres as the post-war period of Cold War division and US hegemony over the market sphere comes to a close. The emerging sphere of Pacific Asia has occasioned considerable interest.

In the case of Pacific Asia it has been argued that a novel form of industrial-capitalism has been developed. Pacific Asia has been a significant base for export-oriented production destined for the First World countries of America and Europe. It is also the case that since the 1985 Plaza Accord[23] that a new round of export-oriented development has taken place as Japanese firms have relocated within Pacific Asia so as to escape the problems of the high yen. The result of these changes in production within the global system has been that over the period of the 1980s the economies of Japan, Southeast and East Asia have grown very rapidly. It is possible to analyse the Pacific Asian model in terms which gesture to the idea of a typical political-economic configuration with related social-institutional structures and associated cultural forms.

In the post-Second World War period the political-economies of the countries of Pacific Asia have undergone extensive change and there are a series of versions of the political-economic aspect of the story. The development orthodoxy would speak of the evolutionary and planned achievement of effective nationstatehood. In the case of Pacific Asia this would seem to find familiar expression in terms derived from modernization theory. The Pacific Asian countries have successfully achieved take-off and as their economies mature so their societies are being remade in a fashion similar to that in other industrial countries. In time their polities might be expected to shift away from their presently authoritarian style towards the liberal-democracy familiar in the West. On the other hand, in contrast, the recently influential economic liberals would offer a different tale. In place of the stress on planning they would bring to the fore the dynamism of the free market. Economic liberals would point to the dynamic nature of the Pacific Asian economies and would read this as evidence of the spontaneous order which minimally regulated capitalistic business enterprise might be expected to produce. Expectations in regard to the future seem to be cast in terms of more of the same. The notion of a 'borderless world'[24] has been advanced.[25]

There is also available a thoroughly sophisticated political-economy reading of the Pacific Asian model in its Japanese form. In this perspective the development experience of Japan which is the core country of Pacific Asia is read in terms of the exchange between an oligarchic ruling group (involving the bureaucracy, business, politicians, and in earlier versions the military),

23 An agreement made in New York which revalued the yen upwards.
24 K. Ohmae 1990 *A Borderless World*, Tokyo, Kodansha.
25 There are also conservative American commentators who look at East Asia with unease. See P. W. Preston 1995 'The Debate on the Pacific Asian Miracle Considered' in idem *Aspects of Complex Change in Asia*, Occasional Paper 7, Department of Anthropology and Sociology, Universiti Kebangsaan, Malaysia.

determined to secure the position of a late-developer within the expanding global system, and the structures of that system, which flowed from the activities of the other major participants/players.[26] In the post-Second World War period this drive to achieve position and security has evidenced itself in strategic concern for economic expansion. It can be said that Japan is a capitalist developmental state.[27]

If the political-economy of the Pacific Asian model has been a success it is often argued that this is in no small measure due to the particular character of Pacific Asian society. In particular, society is held to be familial and communitarian, and not individualistic on the model of the West (a model dominated by the experience of the USA). Relatedly society is held to be disciplined and ordered (unlike the West, again with the image of the USA to the fore, which is taken to be riven by the unfortunate consequences of excessive individualism).[28]

In a similar way the political life of these countries has routinely diverged from the model of the West. In terms of overall political-economic, social institutional and cultural packages it is possible to speak of models of democracy: the Northwest European; the North American; and now the Pacific Asian.[29] It has been argued that the Pacific Asian model centres on an Asian communitarian politics stressing community, hierarchy, consensus and a strong dominant party state.[30] It can be noted that democracy is a real world historical achievement which is neither spontaneously generated by systemic evolution nor to be considered a recipe to be authoritatively applied by an enlightened elite. It is rather a laboriously achieved set of ideas, institutions and routine social practices. Overall, the Pacific Asian model is distinct from the received models of American liberal market and European social-democratic polities. The pattern is undoubtedly coherent and effective and in general offers an interesting example to other countries in the Third World peripheries.

Partial collapse and partial renewal in the socialist bloc

In the People's Republic of China in the late 1970s Deng Xiaoping inaugurated an economic policy turn towards the marketplace. Over the period of the 1980s China has taken its place within the burgeoning Pacific Asian region. The patterns of political-economic and social institutional change

26   B. Moore 1966 *The Social Origins of Dictatorship and Democracy*, Boston, Mass., Beacon. R. Dore 1986 *Flexible Rigidities*, Stanford University Press; K. van Wolferen 1993 *The Enigma of Japanese Power*, Tokyo, Tuttle.
27   C. Johnson 1982 *MITI and the Japanese Miracle*, Stanford University Press.
28   E. Vogel 1980 *Japan as Number One*, Tokyo, Tuttle.
29   C. B. Macpherson 1966 *The Real World of Democracy*, Oxford University Press.
30   H. C. Chan 1993 'Democracy: Evolution and Implementation – An Asian Perspective' in R. L. Bartley ed. *Democracy and Capitalism: Asian and American Perspectives*, Singapore, Institute of Southeast Asian Studies.

within China have been extensive and suffused with conflict.[31] However, the overall success of the Pacific Asian region and the lack of any political reform has meant that the changes have not been widely remarked. The changes in China have been read in the First World as one further episode in the very slow renewal of the state socialist sphere. However, in contrast the events of 1989–91 in eastern Europe have begun a series of complex changes where the final equilibrium point of the emergent system is most unclear. Overall, a transition is in process from the command economies of state socialism towards a market-based system with a pluralist polity.[32]

The dramatic reform movements in the old Eastern Bloc had a series of elements. The process started with the democratization and liberalization moves within the USSR initiated by Mikhail Gorbachev's government in the late 1980s. The most dramatic upheavals took place in 1989–91, and reform continues within Russia. The depth of the problems facing the new leadership are clearer – as are the apparent difficulties of securing desired change. In the old Eastern Bloc territories of Europe the situation is at once clearer in some respects whilst in others earlier clarity has given way to deeper confusion. In the case of political reforms the generally peaceful shifts from bloc-given Stalinist style command political-economies to a mix of variants on the Western model was completed with elections throughout 1990. However, it has become clear that many tensions within these countries will have to be resolved. The reappearance of nationalism is one problem. In regard to economic matters the situation is more obscure and an initial enthusiasm for models of *laissez-faire* capitalism is giving way to a dawning appreciation of the difficulties of securing economic reform and of the problematical nature of the pure market schemes advocated both by intellectual groups within eastern Europe and by western experts in the guise of the IMF/World Bank.

Credit for these changes has been claimed by the American market liberals and commentators have spoken of the West having won the Cold War with the consequence that further development within the global system would necessarily follow the Western model. One commentator offers a celebration of westernization as the ethico-political end of history.[33] However, it was the people of eastern Europe who made their revolution. It was a revolution led by intellectuals, trades unionists, Church groups and artists. The final resting point of these upheavals is yet to be established and their politics are in flux. It has been suggested that the crucial distinction in respect of eastern European politics will be between backward-looking nationalists and European modernists.

It is clear that laying claim to the events of eastern Europe is a New

31 See J. Howell 1993 *China Opens its Doors: The Politics of Economic Transition*, Hemel Hempstead, Harvester; D. Goodman and G. Segal eds. 1994 *China Deconstructs: Politics, Trade and Regionalism*, London, Routledge.
32 See E. Hobsbawm 1994 *Age of Extremes: The Short Twentieth Century, 1914–1991*, London, Michael Joseph, ch. 16.
33 F. Fukuyama 1992 *The End of History and the Last Man*, London, Hamish Hamilton.

Right tactic. It continues their hitherto domestic ideology of the Free West by imputing this idea-system to eastern Europe. It has been argued that it was a mistake for the New Right to lay claim to the revolutions in the eastern Europe.[34] It has been suggested that the Right's aim is to present the 'East Europeans as a living, historical proof of the common sense (and clichéd) truths of free-market Western capitalism'.[35] Against this strategy of analysis, what 'is actually happening there is the collapse of the state, around which the old system was based'.[36] It seems clear that the natural resting point for an eastern European politics was social-democratic. Nonetheless if social-democracy did not succeed in eastern Europe then the alternative was the extremes of racist and nationalist movements.

If anything, subsequent events have tended in the direction of a new Third World. The early optimism in eastern Europe for the liberal market faded as IMF and World Bank austerity-adjustment went ahead. With the December 1991 dissolution of the USSR in favour of the seemingly politically inchoate and economically damaged Confederation of Independent States (CIS) all the conditions for 'third worldization' were in place. Overall it seems that the real battle is not about which model of development eastern Europe should adopt but is about the shape of an emergent Europe as political and economic reforms continue in Russia, and as the European Union moves towards some sort of unification. The attempt of the New Right to annex the events in eastern Europe to its liberal market position is essentially a defensive manoeuvre within a broader game about the shape and nature of the tripolar system.

The situation of the Eastern Bloc countries as they move to reassert local political-economic and cultural models in the wake of the abrupt ending of bloc-imposed conformity is difficult. Problems are legion, of which two may be cited: the resurgence of nationalism; and the severe problems of economic adjustment in the face of a legacy of problems, debts and Western market-nonsense coupled to practical indifference.[37] A series of conclusions about the situation of eastern Europe can be presented:[38] (a) the political-cultural framework of the Cold War era, with ideas of socialism and talk of 'middle Europe', is now disregarded or of no help; (b) relatedly there are ambiguous new cultural idea-sets being drawn down upon, in particular varieties of nationalism; and (c) the most often cited new political-cultural notion is that of a return to Europe, where this is neither left nor right and counts as some sort of coming home. By way of response, commentators offer two thoughts: the first is that the resurgence of nationalism is a danger; and the second is that it is precisely the indifference of the West, illustrated in their thoughtless market recipe-ism, that is most likely to trigger

34   O. Figes in *The Guardian*, London, 17 February 1990.
35   Ibid.
36   Ibid.
37   M. Glenny 1990 *The Rebirth of History*, Harmondsworth, Penguin.
38   Ibid.

political and social upheavals in the Eastern Bloc as they flounder under their received economic problems.[39]

Dependent integration and semi-detachment in the Third World

The initial post-Second World War enthusiasm for the pursuit of development slowly waned as the early efforts at industrialization ran their course in a mix of success and failure as import-substituting industrialization strategies reached their low maximum potential. The global system context within which early development work had been pursued changed as the long post-Second World War economic expansion came to an end in the early 1970s. In addition the oil-shock damaged Third World economies as markets for their products contracted and at the same time recycled petro-dollars fuelled ill-advised attempts to carry on with established development work. In Africa the result was stagnation and in Latin America inflation and the debt crisis of the early 1980s. The experience of the countries of the Third World in the post-colonial period has evidenced a diverse mix of advance, drift and stagnation.

If we consider the very broad sweep of the countries of Pacific Asia, Latin America and the oil-rich Middle East it is clear that there has been a sharp process of differentiation within the Third World. In the case of Pacific Asia the basis for economic success is elusive. In the 1980s the New Right claimed that the success of the area proved the correctness of market-oriented development policies. However, the countries of the area have all pursued state-directed development. The core regional economy has been Japan which industrialized in the late nineteenth century and which has subsequently played a key role in the development of Pacific Asia. The pace of development in the region as a whole over the 1980s has been so rapid that Pacific Asia is now spoken of as one of the three major economic blocs within the global economy. In the case of the Middle East it is clear that the basis for its economic success is primary product exporting, in particular oil, but these countries have also invested heavily in industrial development. It is also clear that many of the countries of the Middle East have experienced considerable political dislocation in the shape of war and revolution. At the same time the progress of what has been called westernization, the introduction of modern social patterns, has been deeply problematical. In the case of Latin America the extent of success is more problematical as social inequalities, environmental problems and political instability work against economic successes.

In Africa the initial legacies of the colonial period included state and administrative machineries, legal systems, educated and mobilized populations,

---

39 Ibid. See also B. Denitch 1990 *The End of the Cold War*, London, Verso. On the model of eastern Europe within development theory, see B. Hettne 1990 *Development Theory and the Three Worlds*, London, Longman, pp. 18–21, 220–31.

and so on. All these slowly ran down. As the economic changes of the post-colonial period progressed the residual pre-contact and colonial patterns of life began to be reworked. This could include the decay of traditional patterns of family and kin. It could also involve problems with tribalism. In Africa there were problems of political corruption, incompetence and instability. The role of the military increased. A series of internal conflicts occurred. These problems were internal to the new countries of the Third World and were acutely felt in Africa.[40] At the same time African countries experienced interference from the two great powers as they pursued a series of overt and covert proxy wars.

If we try to summarize the period as a whole then we can say that by the mid-1970s the orthodox optimism of the immediate post-Second World War period had dissipated and was beginning to be replaced by fears about debt, instability and failure which were to come to the fore in the 1980s. At the same time the counter-optimism of the critics of the orthodoxy was similarly beginning to decline as unease grew about the further unequal development of the global system. It is also true to say that the unease about the post-Second World War settlement which underpinned the discussion about development also became acute as First World economies suffered economic slowdowns and societies saw rising problems. In the First World the intellectual and political confusion of the period saw the emergence of the Anglo-Saxon New Right. In the Third World the New Right sponsored a counter-revolution which aimed to sweep away the developmental role of the state in favour of the marketplace.[41] The period of the 1980s was thus one of reduced expectations for both the orthodoxy and their radical critics. However, the position of the radical democrats was further undermined by the ferocious political reaction of the 1980s. The overall impact upon the Third World has been to reinforce the diversity of the area's patterns of integration within the global system; a mixture of dependent development and semi-detachment.

In the case of Pacific Asia it is clear that large areas of what might a few years ago have been called countries in the Third World have experienced relatively rapid development. In the case of Pacific Asia they have been drawn into the Japanese orbit within the tripolar global system. It is similarly the case for other areas of what would have been called the Third World a few years ago that they have experienced a further round of dependent capitalist development. It is possible to point to the oil-rich states of the Middle East and to parts of Latin America and the Caribbean. These last two fall within the ambit of the USA-centred sphere of the global capitalist system. In 1993 the NAFTA agreement was inaugurated which looks to a free trade zone within the Americas. In sharp contrast to the countries of Pacific Asia, the Middle East and Latin America, the countries of Africa have experienced

40 See B. Davidson 1968 *Africa in History*, London, Weidenfeld; idem 1994 *The Search for Africa*, London, James Currey.
41 J. Toye 1987 *Dilemmas of Development*, Oxford, Blackwell.

little progress in the period of the 1980s. In the case of Africa development specialists tend to speak of a lost decade. The African countries' share of world production and world trade is shrinking and is now slight. In the case of Africa it seems to be possible to speak of a slow detachment from the mainstream of the global industrial capitalist system.

Strategies for analysing complex change in the global system

In recent years a body of work has grown up which is called international political-economy. It offers a schematic way of framing analyses of patterns of complex change in the global system. The track records of particular state-regimes can be read as exemplifying a series of projects, where such projects represent creative responses to the enfolding dynamics of the global capitalist system. A context-sensitive analytic strategy dissolves the actions of the state-regime into a much more complex trans-state system. Analysing state-regimes as if they were autonomous units is misleading, and the familiar talk about nationstates, taken as somehow essentially self-contained, is an error which reifies a contingent set of relationships thereby obscuring the very processes under consideration.

Over the post-Second World War period, by way of example, this is precisely how orthodox development theory analysed problems of Third World development. The early expectations of the First World theorists, shaped in a period of optimistic decolonization and bipolarity, the high-tide of fordism, were that the Third World would recapitulate the historical experience of the West. The discourse of development saw the elaboration of a complex package oriented to the goal of the pursuit of effective nation-statehood which the experts imputed to the replacement elites of the new nationstates of the Third World. This ideal goal can be unpacked to reveal a triple task involving the engendering of political and cultural coherence, the securing of political and social stability, and the achievement of economic growth and welfare. However the assumptions built into this model are extensive, and when examined untenable. There is a triple claim to knowledge (of claimed development sequences), to expertise (in regard to ordering the process), and ethic (in regard to the obligation of First World to Third, and the nature of the overall goal of liberal-democracy). The model slowly collapsed because the experts did not have the knowledge or the expertise, and their Western ethic was only dubiously relevant.

As the model collapsed First World development work divided into three broad channels: state aid programmes continued for various reasons (which may or may not have included 'development'); practitioner groups looked to small-scale 'empowerment', a much more plausible engagement; and relatedly theorists looked to revise the whole panoply of received expectations.[42]

42 See Hettne 1990 op. cit.

Here we find a shift away from exporting recipes to analysing the detail of actual political-economic, social-institutional, and cultural processes using the established repertoire of concepts carried in the central tradition of European social science. The upshot has been a return to core concerns with the interpretive and critical analysis of complex change within the context of the on-going development of the global capitalist system.[43]

Once the analysis of the new nationstates has been contextualized in terms of their position within the global system, a plausible way of handling the development experiences of these new nations is generated. In place of evaluations of track records according to the model of the pursuit of effective nationstatehood, which often generates tales of breakdown or falling away from liberal democratic grace,[44] or in terms of the pursuit of free markets, which generates an analogous literature of market-inhibitory failure, we can look at track records as exemplifying the political projects of state-regimes. Such political projects represent the agency of state-regimes within the structural circumstances they inhabit. In practice, of course, all this is fraught with the usual problems of coalition building and conflict control internally, plus reading global structures and thereafter formulating practical programmes. The general point that countries operate within wider systems was very well illustrated by the four little tigers of Asia where internal class-groupings came to power and then seized the opportunities provided by the expanding global economic system to carve out distinctive economic spaces.[45] In sum, the material of development theory considered in the light of the remarks on international relations theory reveals that to grasp the nature of a particular state-regime it is necessary to consider the projects pursued by these agents within the context of global system structures.

There is a variety of approaches to the analysis of the projects of state-regimes, and all revolve around the political-economic, social-institutional and culture-critical analysis of the dynamics of the exchange of internal and external systems, where these structural dynamics constrain the possibilities open to agent-groups. An interesting approach looks to construct an international political-economy (IPE).[46] It is argued that orthodox international relations work is deficient because it focuses exclusively on the relations of governments. Similarly, orthodox economics and political-science are also rejected as both inhabit closed intellectual spaces and take their spheres of enquiry to be similarly closed – where economics is blind to issues of power, political-science typically ignores economics in its focus on governmental

43   See P. W. Preston 1994 *Discourses of Development: State, Market and Polity in the Analysis of Complex Change*, Aldershot, Avebury.

44   B. N. Pandy 1980 *South and Southeast Asia 1945–1979*, London, Macmillan; see also R. H. Jackson 1990 *Quasi-States: Sovereignty, International Relations and the Third World*, Cambridge University Press.

45   C. Hamilton 1983 'Capitalist Industrialisation in East Asia's Four Little Tigers', *Journal of Contemporary Asia*, 13; see also W. Bello and S. Rosenfeld 1990 *Dragons in Distress: Asia's Miracle Economies in Crisis*, San Francisco, IFDP.

46   S. Strange 1988 *States and Markets*, London, Pinter.

machineries. Work from outside these usual areas is invoked and includes development economics, historical sociology and economic history. The key is an idea of the basic needs of any polity in respect of wealth, security, freedom, and justice. Any polity will evidence some mix of these four. An international political-economy approach can lodge agents (states or polities) within global structures of power and thus uncover the trans-state mechanisms which underpin given empirical configurations of wealth, security, freedom and justice. It is possible to distinguish structural and relational power where the former sets the broadest of agendas, the frames within which people and groups have to act, and the later focuses on specific episodes of agent exchanges.

On the IPE analysis structural power is found in the four spheres of security, production, financial credit, and knowledge; where the first is the familiar realm of state–state relations, the following pair note the crucial role of economic power. Finally, the importance of the subtler sphere of culture is acknowledged. The first noted, the security structure, comprises the networks of relationships between states which revolve around, and order, the use of force. These structures are extensive, and cover diplomatic, military, and security linkages. In regard to the second pair, the production structure, the sphere of the military overlaps in the history of the development of the modern First World-dominated global system with the rise of industrial production and global trade. Relatedly, the financial structure comprises an integrated global network, with major centres in Europe, the USA and Japan. This network is the source of credit, and the ability to generate credit confers significant power. Finally the knowledge structure is one of the underpinnings of the entire system, the production not merely of scientific and technical knowledge but also social technologies of management involved in the business of putting knowledge to work.

These networks of power constitute the underlying structure of the global system. Whilst resources of power, production, finance and knowledge are unevenly distributed they provide the start-point for the activities of any extant state-regime. Overall, the idea is that of a world system comprised of a variety of power structures within which states (and other actors) are agents: lines of power are relatively fixed and the polity itself given shape. We have a strategy of analysing the axes of structural power which necessarily constrain/enable the actions of state-regimes (as agents). In place of state–state relations we have a picture of many states-within-the-global-system enmeshed in a network of power relations. Most broadly, the IPE approach offers the model of a world system comprising a variety of power structures within which agent-groups, primarily states, move, and where the specific exchanges of agent-groups and global structures generate the familiar pattern of extant polities.

One particular problem with the IPE approach is that it reduces the business of the internal make-up of any state-regime to a reflection of trans-state flows of power. A corrective to this can be found within the regulationist school which has offered not dissimilar analyses which do pay attention to the internal dynamics of state-regimes within the shifting patterns of power of the global system. The literature flows from the work of Aglietta[47] and centres on the identification of patterns of accumulation and regulation within state-regimes and across wider sweeps of the global capitalist economy. This school gives us the recently familiar analysis of the post-oil shock shift from fordist to post-fordist political-economic modes of accumulation and regulation.[48]

The Claims to a Logic of Ever Greater Global Interdependence

A further series of arguments have been advanced by theorists working with global development. In these new structural analyses of interdependence there has been an increasingly vigorous concern to detail the ways in which various groups live within the global system (characterizing diverse patterns-of-life), to identify common problems (e.g., environment), and to reinforce global-level rule-setting in place of simple power relations (affirming a common humanity).

The concern for global cultural diversity can be taken to be a counterpart to an increasing appreciation of interdependence. As the global system becomes more integrated there is a corresponding concern to affirm the value of local cultures. We can speak of a kind of global multiculturalism. A key vehicle of such a celebration of diversity would be the UN and its various agencies. A related concern with the interdependence of the peoples of the global system is evidenced in the concerns of the environmentalist movement. It is proposed that there are a series of 'global commons' which are the common concern of humankind and should be dealt with accordingly. In this context the problems of population control, resource depletion, and pollution are cited. Again the UN is a key institutional vehicle for the dissemination of information. On the basis of an appreciation of interdependence there is a related concern to advance a global-level process of rule-setting which can supplement the inherited patterns of nationstate relations. A preference for multi-lateral rather than bi-lateral treaty making. And a preference for multi-lateral agency initiatives in place of bi-lateral work. Again, a key agency is the UN.

In the work of the theorists of global development there is a strong concern to attend to the detail of the lives of ordinary people. In practical terms this is evidenced in a preference for local small-scale development work organized via NGOs. The intellectual counterpart involves asserting the value of agent-centred analyses in contrast to the more familiar structural style of development theory, and it is to these matters that we can now turn.

47 M. Aglietta 1979 *A Theory of Capitalist Regulation*, London, Verso.
48 See J. Allen and D. Massey eds. 1989 *The Economy in Question*, London, Sage.

Chapter Summary

In the 1980s a new concern for analysing the global industrial capitalist system has been expressed. A newly intensified interdependence has been identified. There are a number of ways in which this emerging global system has been theorized. The market-oriented postmodernist theorists have presented ideas of the transformation of capitalism such that the system was now global in reach, knowledge-based and geared to consumption in the marketplace. The dependency and marxist theorists have spoken of the global reconstruction of the capitalist system as patterns and styles of production change with the rise of East Asia, the collapse of the Second World bloc and the further partial dependent integration of areas of the Third World. The theorists who identify mutual interdependence and who are concerned with global development have shown an increasingly vigorous concern to detail the ways in which various groups live within the global system, and to identify common problems in order to reinforce global-level rule-setting in place of simple power relations.

16

Agent-centred Analyses of the Diversity of Forms-of-life

Overview of Agent-centred Analysis

In the post-Second World War period development theorizing has tended to focus on structural change with a view to informing intervention. In recent years critics have suggested that this approach misses the detail of forms-of-life. The matter of agent-centred analysis of development problems may be approached both formally and substantively. In the first place it is possible to review a series of sophisticated critiques of structural styles of argument within development theorizing. In the second place it is possible to review the practical efforts of various social movements which have centred on the efforts of particular social groups. The key social movements which have had a major impact on development theorizing comprise three broad groups/concerns: (a) environmentalism; (b) the situation of women; and (c) the area of work by Non-Governmental Organizations or NGOs (see figure 18).

Figure 18   Agent-centred analysis

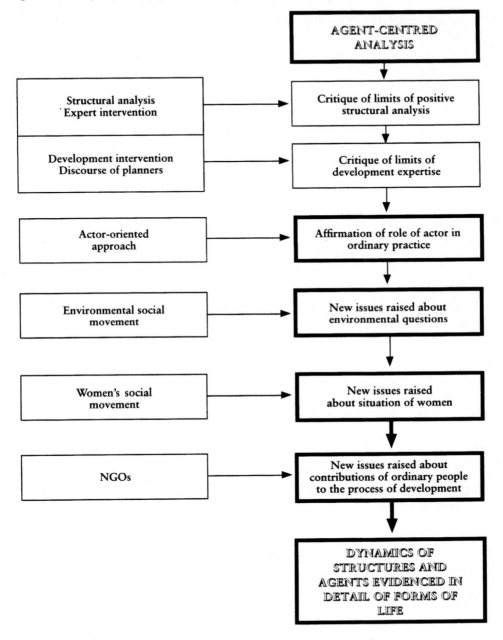

Agent-centred Analysis

The critics of structural analyses within development theory have made three broad points: (a) that development theory must pay attention to the micro-scale detail of the social processes of the construction of patterns of life; (b) that development theory must deconstruct notions of intervention and shift away from untenable rational models of plan-making followed by plan-execution, and grant that intervention itself is a drawn-out and complex social process involving many agents; and (c) that the further theoretical elucidation of these matters requires the supersession of the distinction between structure and agency. In this way both social scientific enquiry and development interventions are recast and the expectation is of dialogic exchanges in pursuit of piecemeal change.

Global structures and agent responses

In the area of debate about development the post-Second World War period has seen a variety of responses to the dominant discourse of technical planning which has relied heavily on structural argument. A general criticism has been made that structural explanations miss the detail of ordinary people's lives and that in doing so they vitiate their own analyses and inhibit the practice they would foster. In simple terms, it is suggested that as development plans are always translated into practice at the local level then a knowledge of local-level cultural patterns is seen as a logical precondition of the success of planning. In a related fashion the specific argument is also made that if social movements based on grassroots activism have been influential in the areas of food, health, environment and women then development theory should acknowledge this by attending to the business of agency.

The business of expert intervention

The first presentation of development theory in the period of rapid decolonization saw the imputation to replacement elites of the goal of attaining effective nationstatehood. Such a goal was to be achieved most centrally by expert intervention. This celebration of the role of the expert has figured not only within development theory but also within the wider traditions of Western social science.[1] It would now be argued that such a view of the role of social scientific work, and the implied claims in respect of general nature and distribution of knowledge of the social world, stands in need of correction. It is also clear in the wake of the failure of the 1980s enthusiasms for market solutions to human social problems, announced recently in Moscow in terms of the end of 'market romanticism',[2] that the multifarious ways in which the social world is ordered, the traditional

---

1   See Z. Bauman 1987 *Legislators and Interpreters*, Oxford, Polity.
2   The UK press reported that this was a phrase from Russian Prime Minister Viktor Chernomyrdin in the wake of the January 1994 government changes in Russia following the election of a new parliament.

concern of the core traditions of social science, cannot be set aside in the expectation of spontaneous social order. In this way the core concern of social science, like development theory, can be seen to be with the interpretive-critical elucidation of the dynamics of complex change within the global system.[3]

It has been argued that knowledge of how the social world works is widely distributed within society and that all social actors should be regarded as knowledgeable.[4] In this way we could speak broadly of a hierarchy of familiar ways of knowing: the personal knowledge of the local and domestic sphere; the common sense of the community within which people live; the folk knowledge of the culture within which people move; and the official knowledges of great traditions, which typically have been religious but now are more familiarly secular ideologies of one sort or another. It is within the frameworks of these subtle cultural patterns of understanding that agents pursue their particular projects. In the light of these claims, the business of knowing is not passive; rather, it is an active achievement of social beings who are extensively knowledgeable about their societies.

In disciplinary reflection on the nature of social theorizing in recent times there has been a widespread concern with the active business of the construction of ways of understanding the world. Against the familiar empiricist stress on the accurate description of an independently existing world, which makes enquiry essentially a passive accommodation to the naturally given, theorists in traditions of enquiry such as hermeneutics, critical theory, structuralism, and the lately fashionable postmodernist work, have all argued, one way or the other, not only that the world we inhabit and take for granted is a product of our own cultures, or polities, or discourses, or forms-of-life (or life-styles), but also that social theorizing must be read as an active engagement.

The critical commentaries on orthodox interventionism claim that these strategies are intellectually illegitimate. The crucial objections are that these approaches typically collapse all strategies of enquiry into the one model of authoritative description/explanation, and moreover the model is itself at best implausible.[5] An influential treatment of the different logics of enquiry and action available within the social sciences has been presented in the form of a discussion of three types of argument.[6] The arguments are in outline: (a) the empiricist, where causal explanation is preferred in a scheme which equates explanation with prediction and which looks to authoritative control in practice; (b) the hermeneutic, where understanding patterns of historically occasioned cultural meanings is preferred in a scheme which looks to the elucidation of shared meanings; and (c) the critical, where the

3   P. W. Preston 1994 *Discourses of Development: State, Market and Polity in the Analysis of Complex Change*, Aldershot, Avebury.
4   A. Giddens 1976 *New Rules of Sociological Method*, London, Macmillan.
5   One dazzling critique is offered by A MacIntyre 1981 *After Virtue*, London, Duckworth.
6   B. Fay 1975 *Social Theory and Political Practice*, London, Allen and Unwin.

critical dissolution of received obfuscatory patterns of ideology is the basis for an approach which looks to emancipatory action.

A crucial claim in the analysis is that conceptions of enquiry have necessary relationships with specific strategies of political action in the world. In other words, all social science is in a fundamental sense ethically and politically engaged. The claims of the familiar empiricist orthodoxy to technical neutrality – to the production of work which has only an extrinsic relationship to practice – are false.

Against the simple confidence of the empiricist tradition, which looks to the business of the accurate description of an external realm, theorists adopting positions informed by hermeneutics and critical theory take their work to be lodged within developing intellectual traditions. The acknowledgement of these traditions is a necessary condition of enquiry. In this fashion, more broadly, they take themselves to be lodged within the social world which they are trying to decipher. The business of theorizing the development of the social world is taken to be a part of the overall development of that world: social theorizing thus has a direct internal relationship to the world which it attempts to comprehend.

In sum, the following general points are made against the intervenors (shifting from knowledge, through expertise to ethic): (a) that the strategy of descriptive-explanation, by way of making models, is epistemologically untenable, as the strategy misses precisely what is central to humankind, that is, its characteristic meaning-drenchedness; (b) this being so, the claims that are made to a scientific status modelled on that of the natural sciences cannot be secured; (c) relatedly it can be suggested that the repeated invocation of the status of science is in effect if not design obfuscatory; (d) against the self-understandings of the practitioners it is asserted that what is in fact going on is the deployment of procedures of bureaucratic ordering; (e) such strategies of bureaucratic ordering flow from the information needs and political agendas of dominant agencies of control; (f) this being so, the key issue in respect of this material is not, as is claimed, empirical accuracy but instead political control; and (g) the orientation of such work optimistically regarded is to the model of liberal-democracy, but more pessimistically such work is better read as concerned with the absorption of other cultures within the expanding global capitalist system.

It is clear that there is now a wealth of discussion on this matter of the conception and intent of an interventionist social science. The following points seem to be fairly well agreed: (a) that the broad process of the shift to the modern capitalist world called forth an optimistic rational intellectual package oriented to the political project of the newly established modern state; (b) that this political project of the establishment of a rational society was somehow subverted into the bureaucratic management of a less than perfectly rational society; (c) that an extreme form of the prostitution of the modernist project found expression in the holocaust;[7] (d) that the present-

---

7   Z. Bauman 1989 *Modernity and the Holocaust*, Cambridge, Polity.

day form of this modern world is something of a travesty of the original modernist project in that the pursuit of market-offered consumer life-style has displaced the concern for the pursuit of a rational society of autonomous beings; (e) that the completion of the modernist project requires the reaffirmation of the open dialogic ideal of the early modern period; (f) that the route to such a reaffirmation lies via the critical dissolution of received idea-sets and thereafter political-economic structures; and (g) in brief a political project of democratization is implied by the intellectual supersession of narrow technical-rationality.

Development theory interventions

The set of ideas affirmed by those who operate within the frame of the planners can be uncovered by analysing 'national development planning as a major institution';[8] that is, as a structured social practice now widely distributed throughout the world.[9] The origins of modern forms of planning are located in the inter-war period with the diverse experiences of the Tennessee Valley Authority in the USA, the experience of some US universities with rural development work, the activities of the newly constituted USSR, the theories of J. M. Keynes, and the practical experience of some colonial development planning. In the post-Second World War period a major involvement is made in Third World planning schemes with ideas of modernization and nationbuilding. The late 1970s and 1980s saw something of a crisis of doubt in regard to the package but the complex social-cultural package remains important.

It is clear that planning is usually carried out by the state. In much of the Third World the models offered by foreign expatriate experts have been influential. It is also clearly the case that planning schemes embody ideologies. A national plan has routinely been a part of an attempt to build new nationstates. The discourse of planning reflects this dual function and typically involves partly technical and partly exhortative language.

It is clear that development discourse routinely presents itself as the technical neutral pursuit of the self-evidently desirable. The style of talk is unreflexive and hides a multiplicity of quite specific intellectual, professional and political commitments.[10] The intellectual claims, related institutional structures and organizational practices come together as the vehicle for the imposition of the definitions of one group upon another. The discursive style of development discourse is a 'solution-side utterance, a form of teleological willing. Its statement of the problems is very much determined by the expected nature of their solutions ... Development policy

8 F. Robertson 1980 *An Anthropology of Planned Development*, Cambridge University Press.
9 See also M. Hobart ed. 1993 *An Anthropological Critique of Development*, London, Routledge.
10 R. Apthorpe and A. Krahl eds. 1986 *Development Studies: Critique and Renewal*, Aldershot, Avebury.

practices are about people giving or doing things to others, to other people, countries, cultures'.[11]

These authoritative planners are predisposed to see the resistance of targeted groups as unreasonable and when planning theory is translated into practice there is likely to be a clash of expectations. This is a point made forcefully by actor-oriented theorists[12] who argue that the ideas, interests and self-understandings of the bureaucracies can come into conflict with the ideas and interests of the target populations.[13] In development planning the agencies are various with community councils, communes, cooperatives and the local officials of various state agencies. The scope for confusion and misunderstanding is wide and whilst the technocratic vision of the planners is likely to characterize local communities as unreasonably resisting the rational plan schemes, local communities are complex and the individuals that compose them may have a wide spread of specific interests.

It is clear that planning for the future has come to be seen as the preserve of the expert planners. In this way planning has 'coopted social science'.[14] However, social science must recover its sceptical, critical and moral core. In this way the de-mystificatory role of anthropology, and by implication the other core social sciences, can be reasserted. In this light the efforts of the state planners can be seen clearly as specific political projects and judged accordingly.

In summary we can make the following points: (a) that planning interventions are not technical neutral exercises: they are political projects, and plans emerge from a highly complex bureaucratic context (including cultural, professional and political matters) and their deployment is again a political process of some complexity; (b) it is clear that in the post-Second World War period in the First World planning interventions have typically carried varieties of Keynesian growth and welfare ideas; (c) in the arena of development theory work intervention has been similarly shaped by both Keynesianism and the political agendas of the ruling groups of the First World; and (d) development theory has been constructed around the role of the expert planner and the role is regarded as the social scientific analogue of the natural scientist. In sum, finally, it is clear that the post-Second World War career of development theory can be read as a series of exercises in the construction and deployment of delimited-formal ideologies: arguments on behalf of those in authority and those with power.

The political discourse of planners

The modernist project in Europe cannot be taken to be a natural process but was rather the outcome of definite political projects which required the

11 R. Apthorpe 1986 'Development Policy Discourse', *Public Administration and Development*, 6 p. 386.
12 N. Long et al. eds. 1992 *Battlefields of Knowledge*, London, Routledge.
13 See J. C. Scott 1985 *Weapons of the Weak*, New Haven, Yale University Press.
14 Robertson 1980 op. cit. p. 184.

radical remaking of extant forms of life. We can point to the rise of urban planning (to replace/control slums and their inhabitants), social planning (to discipline the population in line with the requirements of the new ruling political-economic projects), and the cultural invention of the market (which affirmed the centrality in social relations of what Marx dubbed the cash-nexus). In recent years rational Western planning has been the vehicle of an ideology which serves to assist the submission of Third World peoples to the demands of the metropolitan centres.[15] The apparatus of planning has been central to the business of development since the inception of the endeavour in the wake of the Second World War.

Development planning in the post-Second World War period has been engaged in the process of endeavouring to remake the forms-of-life of the peoples of the Third World and commentators have spoken of the process of 'dismantling and reassembling societies'.[16] This metropolitan political project constructs a particular version of the territory with which it is dealing. The underdeveloped are characterized in terms derived from the experience of the metropole and presented as being deficient in many respects and thus in need of planned development. It is clear that this neglects the real history of these areas, acts to block direct consideration of their present circumstances, rules out *a priori* the idea that indigenous cultures have value and preempts the future by affirming the goal of modernity after the style of the West.

Yet it is equally clear that the denizens of the countries of the Third World who are subject to 'development' find many ways of contriving creative responses. Scott has addressed the matter of practical replies to the demands of global structures.[17] In his work on the moral economy of the peasantry and on everyday forms of resistance, he has shown how the local moral resources of the relatively powerless can be invoked and find expression in a range of activities, all of which express the interests of the weak over against the concerns and demands of the strong. The general story is as one might expect with strategies of evasion, avoidance, ignorance, resistance and rebellion. What Scott's work points to quite clearly is the multiplicity of ways in which local cultures can respond to the demands of the encroaching world industrial capitalist system. In Scott's work the peasant communities of the Third World are not the passive victims of an overpowering force; rather they are active in seeking to read and react to the structural forces which increasingly enfold their patterns of life.

The actor-oriented approach

A major concern of actor-orientation has been with the way in which those concerned in the matter of rural development construe and order their various

---

15   A. Escobar 1992 'Planning' in W. Sachs ed. *The Development Dictionary*, London, Zed.
16   Ibid.
17   J. C. Scott 1976 *The Moral Economy of the Peasant*, New Haven, Yale University Press; J. C. Scott 1985 *Weapons of the Weak*, New Haven, Yale University Press.

interactions. The central claim made is that those involved must be seen as agents, as having their own understandings of their situations, their own expectations of change, and their own strategies for securing such objectives. The actor-oriented approach presented by Long[18] derives from an interactionist social anthropology whose injunctions have been buttressed both by the failures of structuralist/interventionist approaches and by the recent rise of postmodernist thought. The central concern of such an approach to development studies will be with the exchange between structures and agents: in particular the ways in which agents make up their social worlds in routine processes of social life. Clearly, much of the theoretical inspiration for these reflections derives from ideas of structuration and the work has a similarly ambiguous relationship to the tradition of political-economy. Yet it is granted that such traditions can help theorists to grasp the dynamics of the wider systems within which particular agent–group interactions are played out.[19]

Overall, against the structural and interventionist orthodoxies of development theory three points are argued: (a) that development studies must pay attention to the micro-scale detail of the social processes of the construction of patterns of life; (b) that development studies must deconstruct the notion of intervention and shift away from untenable rational models of plan-making followed by plan-execution, and grant that intervention is itself a drawn-out and complex social process involving many agents; and (c) that the further theoretical elucidation of these matters requires the supersession of the distinction between structure and agency via the detailed elucidation of these concepts, in particular the notion of agency.[20]

The work of the actor-oriented theorists is concerned to spell out the detail and implications of an approach which centres on the anthropological experience of ethnographic fieldwork. Such fieldwork exercises are taken to be theory-drenched interventions in the ordinary patterns of life of those with whom anthropologists deal. The preparation of a formal academic/scholarly statement in respect of fieldwork exercises represents a subsequent theoretically informed intervention in the discourses of traditions of scholarship. The type of work expounded has clear characteristics. It is interpretive; that is, it is concerned to spell out the detail of the processes whereby ordinary patterns of life are made and remade. It is dialogic; that is, the conduct of fieldwork exercises and their subsequent formal presentation takes place via conversations (with informants and colleagues). The fieldwork exercise is a social process itself and the formal report, the contribution to scholarship, is similarly a specific social process and the final text is thus a complex cultural construct. In orientation the approach may be said to be hermeneutic-critical: it is elucidatory in intention, aiming in a reflexive fashion to spell out the ways in which the agents involved make

18   N. Long et al. eds. 1992 op. cit.
19   Ibid. pp. 37–8.
20   Ibid.

sense of their respective worlds and the various exchanges between these worlds. The hermeneutic-critical elucidation of the detail of the social processes of the construction of the detail of ordinary life is applied in a quite particular context: that of development studies. The patterns of life typically dealt with are those of, to put it very simply, peasant farmers; the various development agencies with whom they deal; and the social anthropologist or development theorist who offers particular reports on these matters to an equally specific audience. The world of rural farming and development is seen by these development theorists to comprise a complex series of exchanges between those who are labelled farmers, peasants, petty-traders, agricultural-extension workers, aid groups, and state-planners. The development theorist is seen by those propounding the actor-oriented approach to be one more agent in the complex exchanges underway.

In the light of such a view of the dynamics of the social world the familiar development theoretic concern with planned intervention comes to look very odd indeed. Out of the wealth of social interactions which constitute the social world the development orthodoxy is overwhelmingly concerned with one pattern of interaction, that of intervention, and this it construes in what upon examination turns out to be a deeply implausible fashion, seeing the business of intervention as one involving active and rational interveenors and passive, and maybe recalcitrant, recipients.

Against this orthodox view the proponents of the actor-oriented approach advocate that this particular social exchange be studied directly, rather than in terms of the familiar ideology of the rational intervenors. In this case it quickly becomes apparent that the exchanges between intervenors and recipient groups are very complex indeed. As Long puts it:

> Intervention is an ongoing transformational process that is constantly reshaped by its own internal organisational and political dynamic and by the specific conditions it encounters or itself creates, including the responses and strategies of local and regional groups who may struggle to define and defend their own social spaces, cultural boundaries and positions within the wider power field.[21]

Overall, one might say that the strength of the work of the actor-oriented approach derives from the detail of fieldwork exercises and the rigour with which these materials are subject to reflexive criticism. In the case of Long the expectation seems to be of a better development studies. However, the actor-oriented approach might prove to be rather more radical because any reflexive criticism entails clarity in respect of the expectations of the development theorists. Elucidations of these particular matters points to the supersession of development studies in a reaffirmation of the central preoccupations of classical social scientific traditions with the business of analysing complex change in pursuit of the modernist project.

21 Ibid. p. 37.

The Contribution of Social Movements

The prime concern of the classical tradition of social theorizing has been with the elucidation of the dynamics of complex change in the process of the shift to the modern world. The most familiar expression of this concern has been within the sphere of political life and has taken the form of the construction and criticism of delimited-formal ideologies. The work of policy analysts which has been oriented to the bureaucratic ordering of change has run alongside the central ideological sphere of debate and the work of scholarship has contributed an overarching critical perspective deployed in pursuit of rational discourse within the public sphere. It is clear that within the classical tradition of social scientific enquiry there is a long-established and profound linkage between political, policy and scholarly concerns. The linkages between these concens can vary as one element (or elements) is stressed. In the core tradition of social theorizing the focus has been on the political sphere and theorists have addressed their remarks to particular social groups or classes. However, in the post-Second World War period two apparently interrelated changes have been noted: (a) the apparent decline in socio-political salience of class groups; and (b) the rise in political prominence of social movements whose members are drawn from many class (or socio-economic) backgrounds and whose political projects focus on non-class single issues.

The emergence of social movements

One way in which the linkages between politics, policy and scholarship find direct expression is through the introduction by social movements of new issues of general intellectual concern.[22] In the post-Second World War period, as class groupings have declined in salience, the social movements concerned with the environment and the situation of women have achieved a widespread practical influence. On the basis of this influence the general intellectual questions they have presented have become the subject of extensive debate.

The character of the new social movements is different from that of earlier social groups. In the work of the classical theorists of the nineteenth century active groups often appeared as class or socio-economic based collectivities self-consciously pursuing their own interests (which may or may not have had wider relevance within the society as a whole). In the case of the new social movements of the post-war period the character of these groups is quite different and the goals to which they commit themselves are also subtly different. In terms of their membership the new social movements draw recruits from accross the socio-economic spectrum of modern society. In terms of their objectives these typically transcend any narrow

22   On social movements, see S. Yearley 1994 'Social Movements and Environmental Change' in M. Redclift and T. Benton eds. *Social Theory and the Global Environment*, London, Routledge.

material concerns in favour of practical issues which are of relevance to the lives of large numbers of people. The two major examples in the post-war period are the environmental movement and the women's movement. In both cases these social movements can be studied in terms of their status as vehicles of political influence. They can also be considered in terms of the contributions which their practical concerns have made to the more abstract intellectual agendas of the world of social science.

The concern for the environment

The debate about development was pursued through the 1960s and 1970s with little practical success. The first United Nations Development Decade of the 1960s was optimistic. The second Development Decade of the 1970s recorded rising poverty and inequality. In the third Development Decade of the 1980s there was simultaneously a sharp turn towards market-based solutions to development problems which, in general, did not work, and a better appreciation of the complexity of the pursuit of development. In the third development decade the problems of global interdependency were affirmed and at the local level the complexity of the pursuit of development was acknowledged. It was from this acknowledgement that an idea of sustainable development began to emerge, for it became clear that it was no use pursuing improvements in one sphere if related spheres were neglected.

The debate about environment dates from the 1960s when a series of First World commentators called attention to the environmental and social costs of industrial forms-of-life. A series of arguments were presented which ranged from the relatively narrowly focused and natural scientifically presented concern with pollution through to the wider anxieties of social critics in respect of the rationalization and dehumanization of the world. At this time the environmentalist movement tended to be an informally organized middle-class concern within the First World. However, the composition of the movement has subsequently broadened and the campaigning has become very well organized. A series of major environmental campaign groups have become both widely known in the public realm and influential in the spheres of policy-making. In the 1960s and 1970s a series of influential texts were produced and gained widespread publicity.[23] They contributed to the groundswell of public concern with environmental issues, which was acknowledged by state governments and international organizations.

In the early period of the presentation of environmentalist arguments an opposition between environment and development was supposed. Indeed much of the early environmentalist work was neo-Malthusian and was

23   D. H. Meadows et al. 1972 *The Limits to Growth*, New York, Basic Books; Paul Ehrlich 1968 *The Population Bomb*, London, Pan; P. and A. Ehrlich 1970 *Population, Resources and Environment*, San Francisco, Freeman. On the early figures see A. Chisholm 1972 *Philosophers of the Earth*, London, Sidgwick and Jackson. See also D. H. Meadows 1992 *Beyond the Limits*, London, Earthscan.

preoccupied with population growth in the Third World. On the other hand the elites of the new nations of the Third World were not well disposed to the environmental movement as economic growth was a high priority. A series of attempts was made to resolve the tensions and draw the two areas of concern into a more positive relationship and in the 1970s the concerns of development and environment began to move together. The two issues began to be brought together under the auspices of the United Nations at the 1972 Conference on the Human Environment held in Stockholm. A linkage between the two areas of concern was forged when it was made clear that environmental problems and poverty were intermingled as the poor suffered the worst conditions and in their search for livelihoods placed great stress on the environment. It was also made clear that environmental and development problems were global in their nature and could only be addressed within the context of the overall global system. The recognition of the linkage of environmental and developmental problems opened up a rich vein of social scientific research and practical activity.

As the link between a concern for the environment and a concern for development began to be made, the linkages of environmental damage to Third World poverty were explored. The marginal position of the Third World poor entailed that they suffered most directly from the degradation of the natural environment. In rural areas the poor would be forced into using the least productive marginal lands and in urban areas there was a similar pressure which generated communities living in informal housing areas and engaged in a myriad of informal economic activities. At the same time the drive for development within the Third World placed pressure upon the natural environment in terms of severe demands upon the natural resource base, both in terms of particular schedules of resource-exploitation and despoliation through pollution. There was a particularly strong concern for Third World population growth as the problems of development and environment were often taken to be exacerbated by the rapid increase in numbers. In particular there were acute problems occasioned by rural–urban migration in the Third World.

The global aspect of the problems of development and environment was also made clear. It was argued that the demands for resources of the industries of the First World placed heavy demands on the environment in both First and Third Worlds. It was argued that the countries of the Third World could not aspire to the levels of material consumption of the First World as there were insufficient global resources to sustain such levels of living. Indeed, it was suggested that the patterns of life of the countries of the First World should be characterized as over-developed. In a similar fashion the problem of pollution was noted as it spilled over national boundaries within the First World and was an identifiable problem in the Third World.

A key breakthrough in linking environment and development was made in 1987 when the Brundtland Commission reported to the UN and argued the case for a strategy of sustainable development. The notion of sustainable development was presented formally as development to meet the needs of today's people without compromising the needs of future generations to meet their needs.[24] The idea of sustainable development has been widely discussed. Indeed the idea has been criticized by some: (a) radical ecologists deny that economic growth and environment are compatible and call for steady state economies; (b) market theorists argue that environmental concerns should be priced and then subject to market ordering; and (c) some marxists have argued that the concern for environment is futile as capitalism is intrinsically exploitative. However the UN mainstream now regards sustainable development as a proper way to reconcile the competing claims of the environmentalist movement and the concerns for growth within the Third World. The mainstream position was affirmed at the 1992 UN Conference on Environment and Development in Rio de Janeiro which was known as the Earth Summit.

It is one thing, however, to identify a desirable goal but another to translate theory into effective practice. The problems in securing sustainable development include: (a) the issue of access for people to resources as present patterns of development often push people to the margins where they have little choice but to degrade the environment in order to survive whilst at the same time the rich in First and Third World enjoy a privileged access to patterns of consumption which have high resource requirements; (b) the problem of the retreat of poverty to the margins as the poor try to utilize ecologically fragile land and perforce adopt environmentally damaging economic practices; and (c) the costs of present patterns of development to people and the environment as evidenced in patterns of ill health, poverty, pollution and environmental degradation. All these problems take on slightly different dimensions in rural and urban areas.

In rural areas sustainable development will involve a series of problems as people try to secure adequate stocks of food and money so as to meet basic needs. A key source of problems will be change in agricultural practices. The shift towards the model of the modern favours market-oriented production over subsistence. This generates new demands on the environment as mechanization and chemical use are increased. At the same time the new patterns of production are likely to generate social dislocation as some farmers become prosperous and others are forced into marginal economic activities or pressured towards migration to the towns. It has become clear that rural development planning is a complex problem that involves much more than introducing new technologies.

In the urban areas sustainable development will confront problems of rapid urban growth as the global population becomes increasingly an urban one. In urban areas the poor face a series of problems: (a) low incomes, underemployment and unemployment; (b) the unregulated nature of much of the informal sector with consequent insecurities; (c) homelessness, low-quality housing and squatter camps; (d) exposure to hazardous conditions

24   See W. Sachs 1992 'Development' in W. Sachs ed. *The Development Dictionary*, London, Zed.

and practices in employment and residential areas; (e) poor infrastructure; and (f) poor health. The drive to secure urban sustainable development requires action across a daunting range of problems and these will require to be acknowledged by international agencies and national governments. A key resource, as with rural sustainable development, will be the skills and energy of the local people.

It is clear that action for sustainable development would be required at a series of levels: (a) international (aid, trade, debt); (b) national (the regulation of patterns of development and economy; and (c) local (NGOs). First, at the international level the global industrial capitalist system is oriented to economic growth and free trade. These goals are evidenced in the behaviour of First World national governments and enshrined in the international machineries which order the global system. A broad area of reform has been identified in the activities of the relevant national governments, in particular with the use of their aid budgets to support home industrial exports, and in the goals and procedures of the institutions of the global system. Here the activities of the IMF, World Bank and World Trade Organization are subject to inspection and criticism. The concerns of sustainable development have to be asserted against their concern to maximize output and trade, but this is not easy.[25] Secondly, in respect of sustainable development national action can be inaugurated by national governments. In the First World regulation of industry and encouragement of recycling have begun. The same ideas will have to be promulgated in the Third World where, in addition, it may well be the case that sustainable patterns of development are more advantageous to the development goals of the governments. Then, thirdly, the role of the broad spread of NGOs will be crucial for education and action at the grassroots level. It is here that problems of poverty and environmental degradation are most acute but it is here also that new patterns of sustainable development might best be encouraged.

The arguments in respect of sustainable development have been widely influential. However there has been a spread of intellectual debates provoked by the social movements concerned with the environment. The exchange offers lessons for both participants. On the one hand, for the environmental movements and government agencies dealing with these issues the lessons of the social sciences relate to the complex ways in which concerns for the environment thread through the routine practices of social groups. It is clear that environmental problems cannot be understood to be amenable to a simple technological or bureaucratic solution. On the other hand the rise of environmentalism offers a series of challenges to received social scientific thinking: the relationship of culture and nature; the relationship of global system and national unit; the issues of time and space where environmental problems are present over wide areas and can persist over long time periods

---

25　A global-level analysis is presented in L. Sklair 1994 'Global Sociology and Global Environmental Change' in Redclift and Benton eds. op. cit.

both of which are awkward to any ahistorical formalistic social science; and the matter of disciplinary boundaries which environmental problems typically transcend.[26] The debates have produced a series of intellectual novelties.[27] One argument of researchers in the influential area of sustainable development is that much of the burden of poverty falls on women and it is also noted that women are often key players in the community organizations which are the heart of NGO activity.[28] The situation of women is often seen as crucial in attempts to deal with the problems of the environment.[29]

The concerns of women

The women's movement in the First World attained its present influence in the post-Second World War period when a combination of factors including unprecedented economic prosperity, social liberalization, the provision of cheap and effective contraception and the presentation of arguments to the effect that the evident widespread systemic discrimination against women was unacceptable, generated a spread of economic, social and legal reforms which had the effect of placing the emancipation of women at the centre of public political agendas. The agendas of reform first advanced by the women's movement in the 1960s have been pursued with mixed practical success in the First World. However, the general intellectual questions which were raised in respect of gender divisions within society have become a significant new area of concern within the social sciences.[30] In turn, these concerns have been pursued within the countries of the Third World where the particular issue of the relationship of development to the patterns of life of women has been centrally important.[31]

The relationship of knowledge and ignorance in development work has been a subject of concern for critical scholars who have pointed out that claims to knowledge can be made in an unconsidered fashion which has the effect of generating significant areas of ignorance.[32] The critics suggest that in the absence of a sceptical and reflexive epistemology the knowledge claims of development theorists are likely to have lodged within them a spread of unconsidered biases. These biases mis-direct enquiry and as a consequence

26   See the introduction to Redclift and Benton eds. op. cit.
27   See Redclift and Benton eds. op. cit.; K. Milton ed. 1993 *Environmentalism: The View from Anthropology*, London, Routledge; R. Eckersley 1992 *Environmentalism and Political Theory: Towards an Ecocentric Approach*, London, UCL.
28   See J. A. Elliot 1994 *An Introduction to Sustainable Development*, London, Routledge.
29   See C. Jackson 1994 'Gender Analysis and Environments' in Redclift and Benton eds. op. cit.
30   An overview of the contemporary social theoretical aspects is offered by S. Hekman 1990 *Gender and Knowledge: Elements of a Postmodern Feminism*, Cambridge, Polity. See also B. L. Marshall 1994 *Engendering Modernity: Feminism, Social Theory and Social Change*, Cambridge, Polity.
31   A related route of influence was via the international agencies of development such as the UN which sponsored work on the situation of women.
32   M. Hobart 1994 *An Anthropological Critique of Development*, London, Routledge.

contribute to the production of ignorance as partial statements in respect of given problem complexes are generated. A familiar complaint within development circles points to the unconsidered use by First World theorists of schedules of concepts and judgements which are appropriate to the metropolitan industrial capitalist countries in the quite different contexts of the countries of the Third World. The effect is to read-out of the analysis the particular experiences of the countries of the Third World. It has become clear that the pattern of life of women has been subject to a similar process of systematic exclusion, of reading-out.[33]

In its early formulations development theory paid no special attention to women. It was supposed that the pursuit of economic growth would automatically attend to the needs of all the population. The implications of the neglect of these issues within development theorizing was that the diversity of the processes involved was simply overlooked. In the economic sphere the patterns of employment and other economic activity between the sexes are very diverse yet the assumptions of the orthodoxy revolved around the cash economy and the contribution of women to the processes of economic and social reproduction was simply ignored.[34]

As research work turned more directly to the patterns of life of people in the countries of the Third World an initial focus of research was the household unit. However, development theorists treated the household as a unitary element of social analysis. It was assumed that the household would operate as a unit and that money and resources would be shared within the household and that any increase in the resources available to a household would have a broad effect upon the members of the household in general. It is now appreciated that the real situation is much more complex and that within the household there are patterns of power which are legitimated by tradition and which can be radically altered by changes in the resources available to household members. It is necessary for development theorists to be familiar with the household dynamics of the areas in which they are working. The provision of new employment opportunities can have direct implications for family patterns as members of the family are drawn into paid work away from the household base.

In a similar way the 1970s ILO concern for patterns of employment initially focused upon the paid employment sector. However, it quickly became clear that the patterns of life of people in the Third World involved economic activity within a broader spread of contexts. The idea of the informal sector was introduced which tried to grasp the activities of all those irregular employment practices. The work of many women falls into this category. However, again, the problem is one of implied exclusion.[35]

33 See T. T. Minh-ha 1989 *Women, Native, Other: Writing Postcoloniality and Feminism*, Bloomington, Indiana University Press.
34 N. Heyzer 1986 *Working Women in Southeast Asia*, Milton Keynes, Open University Press, ch. 1.
35 P. Worsley 1984 *The Three Worlds: Culture and World Development*, London, Weidenfeld.

The informal sector was regarded as distinct from the formal sector and the solution was understood in terms of integration. Yet, commentators have pointed out that the pursuits of the people within the informal sector are not separate from the formal sector but are related to it in a series of ways. What is at issue, the critics say, is not the separation of the sectors but the precise nature of the role of the informal sector, and within it of women.[36]

In a broad perspective it is clear that the shift from traditional to modern societies will entail changes in the pattern of relations between the sexes. A similar pattern of continual reworking of relationships will follow from the shifting demands of the extant global industrial capitalist system. At the present time commentators are not clear that the post-colonial drive for economic development has had a beneficial effect on the situation of women. It can be argued that as the shift towards the modern world progresses it tends to be the men who take up the new opportunities whilst the women are left behind in a contracting traditional sphere.[37] In this case, once again, it is likely to be the women who suffer the most direct experience of poor conditions.[38]

In general it can be said that women are responsible for biological reproduction (child-bearing), social reproduction (child-rearing, household organization, community networks), and are involved in economic production. In the Third World the business of child-bearing is often taken to lie entirely within the sphere of the women. It is women who are the midwives and the carers for infants. In the Third World it is often women who attend to the fabric of the community in the form of domestic duties, kin networks and local community activity. The patterns of women's economic lives in rural and urban areas are very diverse. In the rural areas the closer to the household the activity takes place the more likely it is to fall into the sphere of the women. In the urban areas women must work at a wider spread of activities in order to secure the minimum necessary for their survival and the survival of children.

The impact upon the lives of women of the processes of development can be extensive.[39] In the sphere of small-scale rural life the impact of agricultural change on women can include: a weakening of authority within the household as patterns of activity move away from that centre; an increasing burden of work as women support higher outputs generated by newer technologies controlled by men; limited participation within the bureaucracies created to enhance rural development; and in general a lack of alternative roles within the rural area as development erodes traditional patterns

36 Heyzer 1986 op. cit.
37 See H. Afshar 1985 *Women, Work and Ideology in the Third World*, London, Tavistock.
38 J. H. Momsen 1991 *Women and Development in the Third World*, London, Routledge uses this overall strategy of analysis whereby the situation of the Third World is read in terms redolent of the experience of the First. As an initial statement this may be useful, but thereafter the detail has to be written in so as not to produce one more ideological exercise.
39 Heyzer 1986 op. cit. ch. 7.

of roles. In a similar way the impact upon women of changes in plantation agriculture as men are drawn into newer industrial development can be severe: isolation on the plantations; limited social advancement as estates are run by men; and a struggle between men and women for the control of the money incomes which the women do earn. And there are further problems in the process of development where there is a movement away from rural agricultural life into the industrial and service activities of the towns. The effect of urbanization and industrialization upon women can be negative: there are poor prospects for regular employment and women occupy poorer jobs; and in these jobs they receive poorer wages; and they have poorer health; and the employment situation repeats the traditional pattern of relative female powerlessness.

It is clear that development theory must acknowledge the extensive household- or community-based role played by women. A series of development ideas relating to women has been advanced: (a) welfare focused on child-rearing; (b) anti-poverty programmes designed to draw women equally into the development process; (c) a concern for efficiency in markets such that the contribution of women is utilized; and (d) empowerment which looks to put women in control of their lives.[40] In particular there have been many formal and informal women's organizations over the years and a concern for the situation of women is now a formal element of the development plans of many countries in the Third World. However, commentators take the view that progress has been relatively slow and optimism for the future tends to revolve around the role of grassroots social movements and NGOs.[41] These debates are ongoing and often the situation of women is linked with a concern for the environment. The present situation of women in the Third World is of relative disadvantage and poverty. It is because women experience multiple deprivation that a concern for improving the situation of women often coincides with a concern for sustainable development.[42] As women carry the burden of the ills of development so they are also the active group in local community work in NGOs. It might therefore seem appropriate for development theorists to concentrate on sustainable development and the particular needs of women.[43]

In general, recent analysis has shown that: (a) all societies have gender divisions which are expressed in the domestic sphere, the formal world of work, and the wider social sphere; (b) that to grasp the detail of these relations it is necessary to attend to exchanges within households, between households and the wider economy, and in the social world broadly; (c) that the ways in which gender is read into culture and ideology have to be addressed; and (d) that economic development impacts upon the sexes differently. It has become clear that development theory must acknowledge

40   Momsen 1991 op. cit.
41   Heyzer 1986 op. cit.
42   But see Jackson 1994 op. cit.
43   See Momsen 1991 op. cit.

the issue of gender as these relationships suffuse the practical activities of all societies. An appreciation of the local pattern of life is clearly a necessary condition of effective development planning.[44]

NGOs in the Third World

The reaction against structural explanation oriented towards the needs of the authoritative planners and the newly stated preference for agent-centered analyses, when combined with a continuing commitment to effective action for change, issued in a new concern for the work of the NGOs. The NGOs were taken to embody precisely the grassroots activism oriented to the empowerment of the poor which seemed to be implied by the criticisms made of the orthodoxy.

In the post-war period the sphere of activity of NGOs has grown considerably. Not only are NGO groups involved across a wide range of development activities – in employment-generating activities, provisions for social welfare, political organizing and in groups concerned to protect the cultural legacies of local communities – but they are now routinely acknowledged within the framework of international and national development project work.

The work of NGO groups has typically been small scale, local and concerned to empower the ordinary people of the community. A formal theoretical justification for these activities has been found in the idea of the provision of 'basic needs' which are understood to be the minimum necessities of human social existence – housing, food, medicine, schooling, and welfare – and which, it was argued, might best be provided by development agencies working in close cooperation with the local people through NGOs.

The institutional recognition of the role of NGOs did have a political aspect. The major donor organizations did see NGOs as a way of bypassing Third World state machines which they saw as inefficient or corrupt. The place of NGOs within the overall context of institutionalized development work is consequently somewhat ambiguous so far as recipient states are concerned.

Overall, the burgeoning sphere of NGOs does constitute a distinctive arena of local-level action for change. The sphere has received support from First World governments and in particular from charity-based aid agencies. The record of NGO work is widely regarded as generally good although, as with other development project work, it is as well to recall the advice of Norman Long who noted that all development project work involves a long-drawn-out exchange between those who are providers, those who are recipients and those who would lay claim, however modestly, to relevant expertise.

44 Momsen 1991 op. cit.

Chapter Summary

The matter of agent-centred analysis of development problems may be approached both formally and substantively. In the first place it is possible to review a series of sophisticated critiques of structuralist styles of argument within development theorizing. In the post-Second World War period development theorizing has tended to focus on structural change with a view to informing intervention. In recent years critics have suggested that this approach misses the detail of forms-of-life. In the second place it is possible to review the practical efforts of various social movements which have centred on the efforts of small-scale groups. The key social movements which have had a major impact on development theorizing comprise three broad groups/ concerns: (a) environmentalism; (b) the situation of women; and (c) the activities of NGOs. It is clear that development theorizing will in the future pay more attention to the dynamics of structures and agents in the development process.

17
The Formal Character of a New General Approach to Development

Overview of the New General Approach

It can be argued that development theory is now in process of reconstruction as theorists and practitioners adjust to the lessons learned over time and the impact of recent changes in the global system. The reconstruction of development theory is made more awkward by the related reconstruction of social theory itself, where there has been decline in confidence in respect of simple positive analysis and a rise in interest in interpretive and critical strategies of engagement. A further series of complications revolves around the withdrawal of intellectual and ethical consent amongst theorists and practitioners for any claim to the priority of the model of the First World. The formal reconstruction of what must now be identified as a distinctively First World tradition of development theorizing entails the clear affirmation of the context-bound nature of that tradition of theorizing. The general reconstruction should identify the defensible intellectual and ethical core of the First World tradition of development theorizing, and indicate how this defensible core forms the basis for dialogic engagement with other traditions.[1] In substantive practical terms a new general approach to development will be concerned with the structural analysis of the dynamics of the global industrial-capitalist system and with the elucidation of the ways in which particular local groups read and react to the system's constraints and opportunities.

---

1 A further twist to the tale, which I will not pursue here, relates to the distinctively European nature of the intellectual and ethical core of First World social theory, a matter which may become more important as the global system becomes a tripolar system.

The Decline of First World Theory

By the late 1980s it had become clear that discussions of development theory in the First World had reached an impasse. It was also possible to discern the broad outline of received discourse and to see how familiar ideas would have to be reworked. It became possible to argue that development theory which had been constituted in the post-Second World War period as a technical expert discipline was slowly returning to the mainstream of social theory with its central focus on elucidating the dynamics of complex change.[2] In addition, over the period 1989–91 the political and intellectual world changed radically and the impetus to rework development discourse was reinforced. In practical terms the Second World declared itself part of the Third and submitted requests for development assistance to the West. The intellectual and real world circumstances within which development theorists worked have now changed. A series of theoretical problems must be addressed and the overarching theme will be the requirement that theorists attend to the received intellectual and political positions from which their substantive work flows. In other words, contemporary arguments[3] in regard to the multiplicity of cultures within the global system imply greater reflexivity in development theorizing (see figure 19).

The career of development theory

A series of approaches to Third World development has been considered in this text. It has been argued that post-Second World War development theory both inherits a long tradition of concern on the part of the First World with the Third World and has been shaped by the particular detail of the ongoing dynamic of the global industrial-capitalist system. The theories of development proposed over recent years have to be understood as quite particular interventions within the patterns of social action and argument which eventually constitute and drive the dynamic of the global social system which we inhabit. In this context the contributions of development theorists are both important, as they are the people who make the arguments, and of little real account when set against the scope of the dynamics of complex change which they would grasp. The work of development theorists is one contribution amongst many others.

In the post-Second World War period a sequence of formal theories has been presented. These theories may be analysed in terms of the particular circumstances within the dynamic of the global industrial-capitalist system which generated the concerns they addressed. In this sense social theorizing has an occasion in real world problems. The formal theory can be taken to be offering arguments on behalf of a particular client group. It is also clear that social theories do not gain any effect unless there is some institutional location which can provide the base for the promulgation of the arguments

2   See P. W. Preston 1987 *Rethinking Development*, London, Routledge.
3   Here one might appropriately cite work which has run within the postmodernist frame.

Figure 19 A new formal strategy

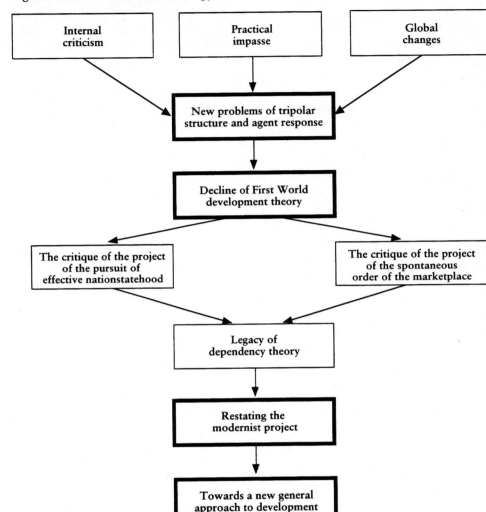

and the provision of relevant resources to pursue theory-informed development project work. It might be said that theories are translated into practice only if there is an institutional base from which they can be serviced and deployed. Thereafter, the impact of theoretically informed action within the global industrial-capitalist system will depend upon a host of local factors, but it might be said in brief that any new line of development will be determined according to the local balance of interests. In contemporary development theory a series of exchanges between real world demands and available theoretical resources can be identified. A series of formal theories has been produced and a series of institutional bases has figured in the work.

At the outset the United Nations-based work of growth theory provided an early post-Second World War statement which subsequently found further expression in the two disparate areas of modernization theory and institutional theory. The former was an influential delimited-formal ideology within the Cold War period and was embraced by the institutions of global industrial-capitalism whereas the latter found a base in the organizations of the United Nations. The United Nations subsequently provided a significant institutional base for the proponents of global development theories. A distinctive approach to development was produced in Latin America in the form of dependency theory. The approach had an early institutional base within the UN agency ECLA and the state machines of the countries of the region. It is fair to say that the United Nations over the post-war period has offered an institutional base to theorists offering approaches to development which tended to stress the social, political and cultural aspects of complex change.

In later years, the preferred First World approach to development within the Third World came to be expressed by the New Right. An influential institutional home for these intellectual and ideological departures was found in the Washington-based IMF and World Bank. These institutions have preferred to work in terms of market solutions to development problems for the entire post-Second World War period. In the early post-war years when the Bretton Woods system was in place these institutions might be taken to have had a positive impact on global development, but in recent years few development theorists would take that view. Over the period of the dominance of the New Right the preference for market solutions has become a damaging dogma.

If the structures of the UN and the World Bank/IMF offer institutional bases for arguments revolving around the respective roles of the state and the market, then it is to the spheres of social movements, NGOs and scholarly research organizations that we have to look to discover arguments which revolve around the role of the polity. The university world within the First and Third Worlds has over the years offered a base for many sceptical approaches to the business of development, yet the efforts of non-mainstream development agencies such as social movements, charities, and NGOs, whose institutional base might be said to lie in the political structures of local communities, have been the key vehicle of alternative thinking and practice.

In the inevitable real world confusion of debate and action it is important that scholarship has a clear idea of its own potential contribution. It is necessary to review in a general fashion the familiar spread of institutionally vehicled development theories. We can identify three very broad approaches. On the basis of this synoptic review we can sketch a plausible role for scholarship. The formal reconstruction of development theory entails the affirmation of the context-bound nature of theorizing and the identification of an intellectual and ethical core. In practical terms a new approach will be concerned with the structural analysis of the dynamics of the interdependent

tripolar global industrial-capitalist system and with the elucidation of the
ways in which groups read the system and order their projects.

The Pursuit of Effective Nationstatehood

The intellectual mainstream of development theory, with its key idea of
modernization, derives from the historical episode of the dissolution of the
mainly European system of formal colonial territories which were admin-
istered from their respective metropolitan centres. At this particular time a
trio of factors came together: the logic of the industrial-capitalist system,
nationalist rhetoric, and available theory.

Very broadly, any review of the historical expansion of the industrial-
capitalist system reveals a system-requirement of access to various territories for resources, trade and markets. In the colonial period this access was
secured via the machineries of the colonial regime. With the collapse of the
colonial system a replacement political form was needed. The available
idea, which was part and parcel of the nationalists' ideology of independence, and which was taken for granted within contemporary social theory,
was that of the nationstate. It is clear that other political forms were available in principle and one could cite for example: UN trusteeship; continued
linkages with the relevant colonial power; and various returns to the pre-
colonial status quo ante. However, none of these were acceptable to the
aspirant power-holders within the countries which were forming within the
territories of the dissolving colonial territories. In addition, the rhetoric of
nationalist developmentalism which had been used by local leaders in pursuit of independence affirmed the model of independent nationstatehood
which was to be the vehicle of the achievement not merely of political freedom for the elite but also growth and welfare for the masses. And finally
it is clear that in its earliest form development theory was influenced by the
success of Keynesianism in taming the vagaries of the capitalist system. The
period of post-Second World War planned growth and welfare coincided
with the experience of decolonization and ideas fashioned in the First World
to tackle specific problems were then shifted to the novel circumstances of
the new nationstates of the Third World. Orthodox development theory has
centred much of its argument on the policy interventionist role of the state.
The whole approach demands the existence of a policy-interventionist state
for it makes no sense without such an agent.

It is clear that for the new replacement elites in the Third World various
demands coincide: the demands of the global capitalist system, the demands
of their own people which flow from the rhetoric deployed by nationalists
in their pursuit of independence, and the intellectual demands of available
theory. The goal of the pursuit of effective nationstatehood is both irresist-
ibly imputed to, and rhetorically embraced by, the new elite. On this view,
ruling elites, having removed by various means the colonial rulers, will face
the complex task of actually building the new nationstate. They must rapidly
engender sentiments of political and cultural coherence as citizens must live

the experience of membership of a single nation, a single community. The elite must secure political and social stability because in place of colonial arrangements there must be new patterns of authority and new political mechanisms to absorb and resolve inter-group conflicts. Finally, the new elite must pursue economic development as this is the base line of claims to legitimacy. Once this goal had been promulgated the whole machinery of the development game came into action, and First World theorists came to lodge claims to relevant knowledge, expertise, and ethic.

The expectations which were held by early theorists were strongly influenced by the experience of the reconstruction of Europe in the post-Second World War period. It came to be thought that the social scientific knowledge necessary to characterize system dynamics authoritatively was indeed available or could be generated. Flowing from this, expert knowledge of social system dynamics was taken to permit the construction of appropriate machineries of intervention. With these two ideas the pursuit of the goal of effective nationstatehood could be presented in terms of planning – at international, national, regional and local levels. Additionally such knowledge and expertise were seen to be the property of First World experts, and their local assistants. An asymmetric relationship was built into the very discourse itself. Positive social scientific knowledge was Western and the recipients of the Third World were taken to be essentially passive. The final element was an appropriate ethic. That the First World ought to help the Third World was taken to be an ethical injunction which flowed from possession of available knowledge and expertise coupled to those broad traditions of European social reformist thinking. In retrospect it seems clear that this ethic was that of the liberal-democratic reformism familiar in the post-Second World War period drive for social reform at home and democracy elsewhere.

Overall it is clear that orthodox development discourse deployed a complex culture-bound package of claims, with the central policy-goal of the pursuit of effective nationstatehood, and the whole panoply of the international development business grew up. But after forty years effort of it is now evident that this clutch of assumptions was not supportable: (a) the requisite knowledge is not there (this has less to do with any failings of research than the unreflective acceptance of essentially positivistic models of the nature of social science and the knowledge it can produce and thus the social roles it can underpin); (b) the expertise in respect of planning was not available (and again this is not so much a matter of specifiable errors and incompetences as it is the affirmation of wildly overconfident models of the planning process); and (c) the ethic was only ever dubiously relevant (and once again it is not a problem of direct error; rather it is a matter of unreflectively deployed ideas). Overall, the imputation of the pursuit of the goal of effective nationstatehood to the replacement elites of the new nations of the post-colonial Third World increasingly looks like an error born out of the requirement to maintain system-access in the Third World coupled with the illegitimate transfer of a context-bound intellectual package.

The resultant intellectual construct now looks increasingly difficult to sustain. In place of the orthodoxy, and drawing upon the lessons it offers, we can posit a return to the classic tradition of social theorizing with its focus on elucidating patterns of complex change. Very broadly, it would seem that we should not speak of the development-expert-assisted pursuit of effective nationstatehood but of the political-cultural projects of specific state-regimes which are characterized using our received traditions in dialogue with local scholars, policy analysts and activists.

The Spontaneous Order of the Marketplace

In the period following the 1971 ending of the Bretton Woods system and the 1973 oil shock the post-war fordist-based class compromise which was intellectually enshrined in the Keynesian liberal-democratic growth and welfare package came under severe intellectual and political pressure from finance-capital and post-fordist productive-capital. It has been argued that within the Atlantic sphere effective power was transferred from productive-capital to finance-capital as the post-Second World War settlement failed.[4] In the 1980s there was a strong resurgence of economic liberalism in the developed world. The intellectual core of the New Right neo-liberal accumulation strategy has been a reaffirmation of economic liberalism. The central and crucial role of the marketplace has been stressed. The New Right have made the material of neo-classical economics the basis of their claims to scientificity and intellectual centrality within the sphere of the social sciences. All this economics work revolves around the model of the pure market economic system.[5] The core elements of this model of a satisfaction-maximizing automatic asocial mechanism involve claims in respect of a fundamental naturally given situation of scarcity, the crucial role of the private ownership of the means of production, and the existence of competition to supply sovereign consumers via the ordering mechanism of the market. The New Right take this model to represent the essential character of all human economic behaviour in society. The core of the social world is constituted by this sort of economic activity. It is the business of economic research to uncover the mechanisms of this given reality so as better to inform the practice of the rule-setting minimum state and other key economic agents such as firms.

In the hands of the New Right the work of the neo-classical economic theorists of the self-regulating market, an approach which was originally designed to replace nineteenth-century political-economy which was seen by its critics as latently socialist,[6] has been the basis of political reaction within the First World[7] and what has been called a counter-revolution in

4   K. van der Pijl 1984 *The Making of an Atlantic Ruling Class*, London, Verso.
5   M. P. Todaro 1982 *Economics for a Developing World*, London, Longman.
6   See A. K. Dasgupta 1985 *Epochs of Economic Theory*, Oxford, Blackwell.
7   See P. W. Preston 1994b *Europe, Democracy and the Dissolution of Britain*, Aldershot, Dartmouth.

Third World development theory.[8] Around the core celebration of the market a series of proposals has been made: (a) the establishment of the minimum state and the related freeing of market-forces with privatization, deregulation, and sharply reduced government spending; (b) the removal of socio-political inhibitions to market functions with repression of trades unions, removal of welfare legislation, and relaxation of government controls on private firms; (c) the encouragement of enterprise with tax breaks for business, the affirmation of the right to manage, and the promulgation of ideas of popular capitalism; and (d) the opening up of the economy to the wider global system with the removal of tariff and non-tariff barriers, and the free movement of capital.[9] In general, the 1980s have seen New Right experiments produce unemployment, reductions in general welfare, declining manufacturing production, and large public and private debt burdens.

Against the familiar claims of the enthusiasts, it is clear that the New Right model of human economic behaviour and the associated pure market system does not describe the simple givens of human existence. The model of the market presented by the New Right is merely an intellectual construct. The major objection to the substantive position of the New Right is not that they favour markets in place of planning (because markets are social institutions and are thus ordered and controlled), rather it is that they adopt a simplistic recipe-interventionism (in favour of markets) in place of the intellectually more plausible task of elucidating the detail of social processes. In place of New Right celebrations of the ordering capacity and benefit-maximizing properties of the free market, an analysis drawing on the classical tradition of social theory would look to offer characterizations of the global system and the actions of powerful agents within this system. The relevant intellectual resources would comprise the strategies of political-economic analysis, social-institutional enquiry and culture-critical interpretation. In substantive terms we have the issue of the emergent tripolar global industrial-capitalist system with its major economic trading blocs of Japan/Asia, the Americas, and Europe. Relatedly, in regard to development, the issue is one of the extension of capitalist modes of production. Any attempt to address this sweeping pattern of complex change in terms of the vocabulary of neo-classical economics would be intellectually ridiculous.

The Legacy of Dependency Theory

As the optimism of the 1960s in respect of the prospects for Third World development slowly declined through the 1970s, culminating in the reaction of the 1980s, the dependency approach was dismissed as intellectually misconceived and politically incorrect. However, we can take from this material a useful concern for linking structural and agent-centred explanations. The key claim of dependency theory was always that the present circumstances

8　J. Toye 1987 *Dilemmas of Development*, Oxford, Blackwell.
9　See K. P. Clements 1980 *From Right to Left in Development Theory*, Singapore, Institute of Southeast Asian Studies.

of the Third World were a product of those political-economic, social-institutional and cultural structures associated with the historical development of the industrial-capitalist global system. The structures which enfold the countries of the Third World and which narrowly circumscribe their actions are taken to have developed over time around the schedules of interests of the metropolitan core countries. It is clear that dependency theory has been presented in diverse guises and that it has generated extensive critical debates. In its initial formulations it was shaped by the particular historical experience of Latin America in the 1940s and 1950s when long-established trading and economic patterns were disturbed by the episode of the Second World War and occasioned a measure of import-substituting industrialization. These circumstances were theorized by a group of economists at ECLA and their work issued in a novel structuralist economics oriented to informing the policy positions of governments concerned specifically with national development. The work of structuralist economics provided the intellectual base upon which the broader schemes of dependency theory were articulated.

Against the schemes of analysis and policy advice derived from the work of First World development theorists who drew on the material of orthodox economics, the proponents of dependency stressed: (a) the importance of considering both the historical experience of peripheral countries and the phases of their involvement within wider encompassing systems; (b) the necessity of identifying the specific political-economic, social-institutional and cultural linkages of centres and peripheries; and (c) the requirement for active state involvement in the pursuit of development.

In contrast to both the aspirations to technical neutral expertise advanced by the orthodox proponents of state-centred development theory and the New Right's preference for putatively technical market mechanisms, the theorists of dependency advanced a prospective, multi-disciplinary and engaged theory oriented to the political practice of elites committed to the pursuit of national strategies of development. However, the initial English-language presentation of the material of this tradition took the form of polemical interventions within intra-First World theoretical debates and this had the unfortunate effect of confusing the reception of the lessons of dependency theory as those ill-disposed on political grounds were able to dismiss the entire approach as left-wing propaganda.[10] In retrospect, it seems clear that the political activism of the early English-language proponents of dependency theory was overoptimistic and underestimated the capacity of the metropolitan centres, in particular the USA, to finance, organize and encourage worldwide reaction.[11] Nonetheless, the basic position of the dependency theorists was sound and the preference for popular political involvement and action has found an echo in a range of development work pursued by social movements, charities, NGOs and scholars.

10   See P. W. Preston 1987 *Rethinking Development*, London, Routledge, chs. 6, 7.
11   See F. Halliday 1989 *Cold War, Third World*, London, Radius.

Restating the Modernist Project

In the material presented above arguments centred respectively on the role of the planning state and the affirmation of the power of the marketplace have been considered. The continuing legacy of dependency theory has been acknowledged. It seems clear that the approaches centred on planning and market were in detail very different but they do have one characteristic in common. It can be suggested that both attempted to secure a measure of certainty in respect of discussions of development. The one looked to discourses of the intervention of experts, where reason secures surety in respect of the future, and the other to the spontaneous order of the market, where individualistic activity generates a structural regularity which offers surety in respect of the future. In both cases it is clear that mechanisms are invoked which are taken to ensure that the future will be in line with present expectations and wishes.

It can be argued that both lines of response could be taken as particular reactions to what critical theorists have called the fundamental insecurity of the modern world.[12] The position is taken that in the wake of the decline in influence of revealed religion, and the parallel rise of a natural science both demonstrably potent in terms of results and fundamentally sceptical in stance, there are no longer any absolute guarantors in respect of our knowledge of either the natural or social worlds to whom citizens, or rulers, or anyone else can appeal. A spread of familiar strategies of dealing with this anxiety can be identified, ranging from social movements claiming priority for their view of the world, or religious groups claiming a privileged access to the truth, through to the more subtle intellectual efforts of social theorists.

In the case of classical social theory we can identify just such a manoeuvre in the shift from analysing progress – which one can argue for as a tendential aspect of the form of life of modernity[13] – to affirming a spurious confidence in respect of bureaucratically ordered social change. This has been critically discussed in terms of a distinction between legislators, who erroneously suppose that they can authoritatively decipher the logic of the social world so as to inform bureaucratically rational strategies of ordering, and interpreters, who operate in a sceptical piecemeal fashion so as to inform debate within the public sphere in the belief that reasoned

12   This theme of the 'insecurity of the modern world' is entirely familiar within certain strands of European social philosophical criticism. The idea has been unpacked in psychological and cognitive terms. The idea has been deployed in the context of various substantive issues. At this time I have in mind the culture-critical work of Zygmund Bauman. See Z. Bauman 1989 *Modernity and the Holocaust*, Cambridge, Polity, Z. Bauman 1992 *Intimations of Modernity*, London, Routledge. Bauman also makes reference to the work of Hannah Arendt; see her 1985 *The Human Condition*, Chicago University Press.
13   This is the cognitive strategy of Jürgen Habermas who lodges a demand for the practical conditions of free communication within the fundamental character of human language itself – in order words a minimum ethic and tendential mechanism point to the idea of progress.

debate, modelled on the broad pattern of the successful natural sciences, will best illuminate routes to the future.[14]

In the case of post-Second World War development theory we can speculate that both the orthodoxy, with their concern for planned change, and the neo-liberals, with their concern for spontaneous order, were deeply concerned to address the insecurity of the social world and to uncover some mechanism which would offer guarantees in respect of future development. In the case of the orthodox the reliance on planning mechanisms is quite familiar and has been routinely criticized. It is also clear that the neo-liberal belief in the spontaneous order of the marketplace plays a similar role for the New Right. It has been suggested[15] that the liberals shift from Leviathan to the Market and in both cases humankind submits to an external authority and is thereafter secure.[16] However, all such strategies fail because the project of modernity is both potent and insecure.[17]

In place of the variously articulated pursuits of certainty, and taking note of the positive lessons of dependency theory in regard to the context-bound specificity of the historical experience of particular countries, it can be suggested that the classical tradition of social theorizing can provide the intellectual resources necessary to the articulation of a new discourse of development which allowed for the vagaries of social life, for the complexities of the dynamics of structures and agents, and which both granted the necessity for the detailed analysis of social processes and centred upon an affirmation of the role of the public sphere in securing patterns of order within the social world generally.

The modernist project is history-specific, which is to say that it is bound up with the rise of European capitalism. It was alliances of intellectuals and commercial groups advancing their respective causes who first brought together the agents, ideas and interests necessary to set the project in motion.[18] Subsequently the bourgeoisie drew back from the radical implications and sought a new status quo, built around the self-regulation of the neo-classical market idea. The modernist project continues to be history-specific and it appears in various guises as agent groups read structural circumstances and promulgate their views. When deployed to read changing structural circumstances the core set of ideas admit of re-interpretation, mis-interpretation and mis-representation. It is a contested tradition.[19]

14   See Z. Bauman 1987 *Legislators and Interpreters*, Cambridge, Polity.
15   F. Jameson 1991 *Postmodernism, Or the Cultural Logic of Late Capitalism*, London, Verso.
16   In regard to the early monetary theorists J. Robinson 1962 *Economic Philosophy*, Harmondsworth, Penguin, remarks that the model of a smoothly working market read in Freudian terms looks expressive of a desire to return to the security of the womb.
17   On this business of the linkage of modernity and natural science, see E. Gellner 1964 *Thought and Change*, London, Weidenfeld; E. Gellner 1988 *Plough, Sword and Book*, London, Paladin.
18   S. Pollard 1971 *The Idea of Progress*, Harmondsworth, Penguin.
19   A fine overview of contemporary debate is offered by Z. Bauman 1988 *Legislators and Interpreters*, Harmondsworth, Penguin.

The modernist project centres on the affirmation of the cognitive power of human reason, and the proposal that reason be deployed in regard to both the natural and the human worlds. The notion of material and ethical progress is affirmed and central to this project is the idea of formal and substantive democracy.[20] These reflections on the nature of the modernist project point to a new way of construing development which may be more adequate to changing world circumstances. The optimistic general expectation is of the possible role of the public sphere in resolving debates/conflicts in regard to matters of responding to societal change. In place of both the authoritative and the spontaneous pursuits of certainty, we can affirm the modernist-project-carried ethic of formal and substantive democracy as offering the outlines of a dialogic strategy whereby political-economic, social-institutional and cultural processes might be understood and their direction made subject to human will.

The shift from this abstract social philosophical point to substantive analyses, and political programmes, is of course more problematic than is usually taken to be the case within the optimistic work of the classical social theorists of the nineteenth century. Our appreciation of the nature of the analytic task undertaken and the problematic nature of the political-economic, social-institutional and cultural processes we would grasp has grown throughout the twentieth century. This scepticism in regard to the extent to which social theorists can authoritatively characterize the social world, coupled to an appreciation of the culture-boundedness of the modernist project, even if it is a world-expansive project given that it is bound-up with the global industrial capitalist system, and given the practical focus on coping with unpredictable and conflict-suffused social processes, leads to a quite distinct view of the nature of any new development discourse. In place of the untenable celebrations of the authoritative interventions of the expert in possession of technical knowledge, and in place also of the suggestions that we can rely on the spontaneous order of the market, those concerned with development must draw on received intellectual tradition to illuminate in a sceptical, piecemeal, tentative and process-centred fashion, via dialogue with locally based scholars, policy analysts and activists, the dynamics of complex change within the interdependent tripolar global industrial-capitalist system.

Towards a New General Approach to Development

In order to advance matters in respect of development theory we need to acknowledge that two inter-related processes of reflection within development theory and social theory are in progress. First, the relative eclipse of interventionist development theory has had the effect of shifting development

20   See C. B. Macpherson 1973 *Democratic Theory: Essays in Retrieval*, Oxford University Press; J. Habermas 1989 *The Structural Transformation of the Public Sphere*, Cambridge, Polity.

theory back towards the mainstream of social theoretic enquiry; centrally, the preoccupation with making sense of complex change.[21] Thereafter, secondly, in regard to social theorizing we can point to the eclipse of naturalistic analyses of industrialism-modernization in favour of the representation of the classical modernist project of the interpretive-critical elucidation of the dynamics of complex change in the global industrial-capitalist system.[22]

The key formal elements of a new position

The key formal elements of the new position revolve around the objective of making a dialogic analysis of the dynamics of complex change within the global industrial capitalist system.

1   In the post-Second World War period it has been thought that the business of the analysis of the development of the countries of the Third World offered a quite distinctive intellectual task, and moreover one which had no particular implications for the developed countries. The analysis of the problem of the development of the countries of the Third World was more or less unthinkingly consigned to a subordinate status within the overall sphere of Western social science. The problem of development retained this status until the emergence of institutional theory in the 1960s. The proponents of this theoretical approach did make a determined effort to upgrade the status of development theorizing. However, the strategy which they adopted was to try to constitute development theory as a separate discipline within the established spread of social science work. The attempt failed and development theory slipped back into its familiar subordinate role. However, against this familiar intellectual positioning of development theory, it is clear that the concerns of development theorists lie very close to the core concerns of the received traditions of classical social theory. It would seem to be the case that development theorists do not need to assert their status against the lack of recognition of the presently influential groups within the social sciences; rather they need simply to be clear about their activities. In this perspective the concerns of theorists of development are close to the central concerns of the classical tradition of social theorizing.

In this context, a key claim is that general development theory is only distinct from the core received social scientific task of analysing complex change by virtue of a typical focus on dependent or peripheral industrial capitalism in the Third World.

2   In the post-Second World War period the proponents of social science in the developed countries were encouraged by a series of factors to adopt a very optimistic positive stance in respect of the nature and possibilities of social scientific work. In the theories which spoke of the convergent logic

21   P. W. Preston 1986 *Making Sense of Development*, London, Routledge.
22   A. Giddens 1979 *Central Problems in Social Theory*, London, Macmillan.

of industrialism there were sets of expectations in respect of the authoritative modelling of social processes which fed a series of exercises in development plan-making. A strong commitment was made to the technical
expertise of development theorists which simply overrode available doubts.
However, in the long period of subsequent development practice and reflection it slowly became clear that the optimistic positive expectations in
respect of the authoritative technical power of social science were badly
mistaken. A slow return to the materials of the classical tradition of social
theorizing has been accomplished, and the implications of that return have
been sharply underscored by recent changes within the global system as the
Cold War bipolar system has given way to an emergent tripolarity, and a
restated sceptical commitment to the modernist project has been made.

It this context, it is clear that analysing instances of dependent or peripheral industrial-capitalism will entail the dialogic deployment of the core
conceptual lexicon of the classical social scientific tradition in an interpretive-
critical fashion (thus the elucidation of the real social processes involved
in complex change rather than the export of intellectual recipes).

3   A significant feature of the post-Second World War concern to make
sense of the situation of the countries of the Third World was the intellectual dominance of First World scholars and policy analysts. The initial
contribution of Third World thinkers tended to be restricted to the spheres
of political theory and action as the members of nationalist independence
movements advanced their arguments in pursuit of political change within
the colonial system. The dominant position of First World theorists was
accompanied by an unremarked optimism in respect of the cognitive power
of the analysis which they deployed. The early theorists of development
were not self-critical. However, in recent years it has become clear amongst
philosophers and theorists of social science that any exercise in social theorizing will be significantly marked by the intellectual and practical context from which it emerges. In other words, all exercises of social theorizing
are shaped by particular cultural contexts. The direct implication of this
view is that reflexive criticism is a necessary condition of the production
of scholarship. It has become clear that it is necessary to review critically the
great body of work which was produced in respect of Third World development in order to identify those ideas which were specific to the culture
of the West and which were deployed uncritically within development theories. The familiar development theory concern for the modernization of the
Third World where this entails the recapitulation of the historical experience of the developed West is no longer intellectually tenable. It is only on
the basis of a critical self-awareness that those ideas which might tentatively be used can be identified and put to work within a sceptical restatement of the classical modernist project, and these ideas in turn are merely
the received basis of dialogic exchanges with scholars, policy analysts and
activists from the Third World.

In this context, it is clear that a reflexive implication of the reconstruction

of development theory is that achieving a process-centred strategy of understanding and engagement will involve a significant element of detoxification
in regard to the sets of assumptions which First World scholars have brought
to the analysis of the Third World and familiar ideas about knowledge, expertise and ethic will have to be examined and revised.

4   The orthodox consensus within post-war development theorizing assumed
that their positive social scientific analyses had a broad range of application
across a similarly broad range of cultures. The work referred back to the
universalizing assumptions of Western science. At the same time, the proponents of the spontaneous order of the marketplace made similar claims
in respect of the unrestrictedly universal character of marketplace rationality and its centrality within human life. The optimistic positive celebration
of the model of the West and its social science reached an apogee in the
modernization theory of the 1960s when the future development of the
planet was assimilated to the model of the contemporary USA. One consequence of this intellectual stance was the more or less automatic disregard
which was shown to the cultural patterns of those people who did not
inhabit the industrial-capitalist countries of the West. It was assumed that
as the logic of industrialism drove the development of the countries of the
world through the grand process of modernization the patterns of thought
of the peoples undergoing these changes would converge upon the cognitive models present in the West. The orthodox theorists found no occasion
to attend to the detail of the forms-of-life of non-Western peoples. However, it has subsequently become clear that processes of development cannot be understood in terms of the Third World's recapitulation of the historical experience of the West but must be dealt with in terms of the subtle
dynamics of structural constraint/opportunity and agent group response.
The forms-of-life of local peoples will carry cultural resources which will be
the basis upon which they read and react to global structural change.
    In this context, as the intellectual task of analysing patterns of complex
change within peripheral industrial-capitalist societies is pursued in terms
of structural change and agent response it is clear that ethnographic work
will assume a significant role. In this case it is clear that analysis can only
proceed via dialogue with local scholars, policy analysts and activists.

5   The post-Second World War orthodox within development theory made
the routine assumption of the cognitive priority of their formulations. It is
clear that the intellectual and real world circumstances which they inhabited disposed them to make this judgement. However, it has become clear
over the subsequent period that the claim to cognitive priority which was
integral to First World theorizing is untenable. As the objective of development theorizing shifts from modelling the process of modernization
towards the task of elucidating the dynamics of complex change, then the
plausibility and relevance of the asymmetry built into the position declines.
It no longer makes sense to prioritize the model of the West and it no longer

makes sense to prioritize the intellectual contribution of the social scientists of the West. A concern with elucidating the dynamics of complex change within the interdependent tripolar global industrial-capitalist system in dia-logic exchange with scholars, policy analysts and activists from many parts of the world implies an equality of contribution. The task of elucidating the dynamics of complex change presents itself as a common problem for social scientists located in different parts of the world and drawing upon particu-lar cultural resources.

In this context, it is clear that the asymmetry in respect of claims to knowledge of social processes which is built into the orthodox position is denied in favour of an equality of contributions to scholarship.

6   The development theory orthodoxy tended to affirm a narrow idea of the nature of social scientific enquiry. It was supposed that the procedures of the natural sciences could be replicated within the sphere of the social sciences. The type of knowledge produced and the use to which it could be put were taken to mirror in essentials the knowledge available within the natural sciences. It is characteristic of the simpler explanations of the nature of natural science that the objective to which research is oriented is taken to be the production of a general model of the natural system in question. On the basis of the general model, predictions about future states of affairs, and the necessary conditions of securing those states, can be made. The knowledge produced by the natural sciences is technical, precise and underpins the familiar role of the expert. This argument has definite consequences for the self-understanding and aspirations of the social sci-ences which were encouraged to aspire to a similarly technical expertise in respect of those spheres of the social world with which they concerned themselves. However, recent work within the philosophy of social science has made it clear that the simple argument by analogy from the nature of the natural sciences to an appropriate strategy for the social sciences is very misleading. The social sciences have their own logics and their own prac-tical application in the broad concern with elucidation the dynamics of complex change. There is no general theory of the social system available. It is also the case that there is no general theory of development available to those who would aspire to an authoritative planning strategy of securing development.

In respect of the cherished core assumptions of the orthodox, the pursuit of a scientific-general model of development for use in the Third World, it is clear that such an authoritative-interventionist scheme is not available.

7   A particularly egregious specimen of positivist mis-analysis has been offered by the proponents of neo-classical economics whose work has been the basis of recently influential theories of spontaneous market order. On the basis of a claim to a scientificity unique within the spread of the social sciences of the West these theorists have looked to a central place within the social sciences. Thereafter, the central place within the social sciences has

underpinned their claims to be offering a positive analysis of the mechanisms of the naturally given system of the marketplace. However, the claim to scientificity can be rejected, and along with it any claim to centrality of orthodox economics within the spread of social sciences. The familiar claims in respect of the marketplace can thereafter be analysed as a particular delimited-formal political ideology. The use of these ideas to inform development policy within the countries of the Third World cannot be seen as the presentation of neutral technical scientific advice; rather they are one way in which the pursuit of metropolitan interests are advanced.

In respect of the market-centred expectation of a spontaneous order which would ensure success it is clear that this is also rejected as it is a social scientific nonsense in the service of the interests of those holding power in the metropolitan capitalist countries.

8   The influential work of the development orthodoxy, and the recently fashionable work of the theorists of spontaneous market order, can now be contextualized – in terms of the political and intellectual occasions of the production of formal theories over the post-war period – and superseded. A sceptical restatement of the modernist project can be affirmed. A new approach to development will draw on the classical tradition of social theory in order to elucidate the dynamics of complex change within the global industrial-capitalist system. These analyses will concern themselves with a series of analyses: (a) the political-economic analysis of global power structures; (b) the related social-institutional analyses of the ways in which particular regions or countries are embedded within global structures; and (c) the culture-critical elucidation of the ways in which groups of agents understand their position within these structures and thereby organize their actions.

In this context, a new general development theory will move from both authoritatively characterized recapitulation and market-focused recipes towards the interpretive-critical elucidation of complex patterns of accommodation to the expansion of the industrial-capitalist global system.

9   The sceptical reaffirmation of the modernist project as a basis for dialogic theorizing in respect of the dynamics of complex change within peripheral industrial-capitalist areas offers a distinctive role for scholarship. The positivistic aspiration to a general model of the dynamics of the system is rejected in favour of a sceptical use of the resources of the classical tradition deployed within the public sphere. The concern to elucidate the dynamics of complex change will be associated with a commitment to the ethics of formal and substantive democracy. The work of scholarship will be prospective, wide-ranging and engaged.

The role of scholarship is characterizing the variety of First/Third World exchanges. The work of scholars, policy analysts and activists in the Third World will be a key resource. Any particular exchange can be characterized and then gain/loss balances drawn up and thereafter arguments for specific patterns of change could be advanced.

10   The theories of development produced within the First World have had it in common that they assumed that they could specify the goals of Third World development projects. In the case of the interventionist ortho-doxy the theories imputed to the replacement elites of the new nations of Third World the goal of the pursuit of effective nationstatehood. In the case of the free market orthodoxy the theories imputed to the elites of the Third World a desire to assimilate their economies rapidly within the global eco-nomy so as to maximize the levels of material consumer satisfactions amongst their populations. It is clear that First World theorists presented general analyses which affirmed sets of ideas particular to the metropolitan coun-tries and neglected the detail of processes of change within the Third World. The intellectual, ethical and practical political resources of the countries of the Third World were read-out of the analyses. However, it is clear that the resources of the peripheral countries must be acknowledged as they are likely to be the basis upon which action at the local level is determined.

In this context, it is clear that what is to count as development will be locally determined.

End-note

In substantive practical terms a new general approach to development will be concerned with the structural analysis of the dynamics of the global industrial-capitalist system and with the elucidation of the ways in which particular local groups read and react to the system's constraints and oppor-tunities. Just as the theorists of the nineteenth century were concerned with the ways people responded to the rise of industrial-capitalism in the Europe, so presently we are concerned with the ways in which people are dealing with the establishment of an interdependent tripolar global industrial-capitalist system.

Gellner has argued that the issue of development as it was presented in the immediate post-Second World War period of decolonization constituted a learning experience for First World theorists in regard to the business of the transition to the modern world.[23] It is clear that the issue of develop-ment lies close to the core of the classical tradition which we presently inherit. The central concern of the classical tradition of social theory is the attempt to make practical sense of complex patterns of political-economic, social-institutional and cultural change. It is upon this basis that a new interpretive-critical dialogue of development within the industrial-capitalist global system could be constituted. It is also clear that the attempt to con-stitute such a general development theory would be a further learning experi-ence for the social theorists of complex change.

23   E. Gellner 1964 *Thought and Change*, London, Weidenfeld.

Chapter Summary

The present situation can be summarized in the following terms: (a) social theorizing is shifting its self-conception of procedure and role from naturalistic modelling to interpretive-critical dialogue, and its attention and object from industrialism and modernization to the expansionary dynamics of global capitalism; and (b) development theorizing is shifting its self-conception of procedure and role from offering technical expertise to facilitating elucidatory dialogue, and its attention and object away from the underdeveloped Third World to the dynamics of complex change in the developing global system.

18

A New Substantive Focus: Elucidating the Dynamics of Complex Change

Overview of the New Substantive Focus

A theoretical preference for the sceptical affirmation of the modernist project implies a particular schedule of substantive enquiry. The opening sections of the chapter will look at the substantive general theory implied by the sceptical affirmation of the modernist project. The later sections of the chapter will look at the dynamics of complex change in the integrated tripolar global system[1] (see figure 20).

---

1 A fuller statement of this argument is made in P. W. Preston 1994 *Discourses of Development: State, Market and Polity in the Analysis of Complex Change*, Aldershot, Avebury.

Changes in Development Discourses

The original impetus to development work in the episode of decolonization has now exhausted itself. A change in the expectations of the proper objects of theorizing might be expected. In simple terms, new circumstances generate new problems and new formulations in respect of the matter of development. In order to survey these issues we can speak of discourses of development. Each discourse offers a way of grasping complex change and suggesting action. The key to these discourses is that they are broad, interpretive and prospective. And these discourses find their vehicles in particular institutional locations. The key discourses centre on the intervention of experts, the mechanisms of spontaneous order, and the role of the public sphere.

The discourse of the intervention of experts expresses certain key elements within received political theoretical traditions. What is characteristic of this strategy of constituting an object sphere and appropriate lines of action is that the social world is taken to be amenable to authoritative characterization by experts in possession of certain bodies of technical knowledge. An asymmetry is built into this discourse with on the one hand those who know, and on the other those subject to expert interventions. The agencies of intervention which use these arguments present them as technical-rational but they are running arguments-on-behalf-of-the-planners, and their engagement with the social world at large is to be seen as a political-type activity. I have criticized such approaches in other work.[2] In brief, a science of the social cannot plausibly take this form. There is no such authoritative knowledge available,[3] notwithstanding that lodging arguments which lay claim to technical expertise is a pervasive feature of contemporary society.

This style of argument and action has been characteristic of the dominant post-Second World War school of development with its expectation of the new nationstates of the Third World recapitulating the nineteenth-century development experience of the metropolitan core capitalist countries. This broad strategy has been the way in which the metropolitan core of the global system assured continuing access to the Third World after the collapse of the colonial empire system. The discourse of state-engendered order revolves around the idea-set of authoritative intervention oriented to the goal of effective nationstatehood, all of which was occasioned by the episode of decolonization and was carried institutionally by the international agencies of the UN and various multi-lateral and bi-lateral aid agencies. However, this mode of social theoretic engagement was in the end intellectually untenable, and acted to mislead theorists, commentators and practitioners by offering an approach (that is, the pursuit of effective nationstatehood ordered by experts), which effectively exhausted available intellectual-institutional space and occasioned the neglect of the business of the elucidation of the detail of real processes.

2   P. W. Preston 1985 *New Trends in Development Theory*, London, Routledge.
3   A. MacIntyre 1981 *After Virtue*, London, Duckworth.

The discourse of spontaneous order refers back to the political project of liberalism with its characterization of the social world as comprising discrete self-moving individuals plus their contractual arrangements, a tradition quite distinct from the democratic tradition. The central claims are for the maximization of economic, social and political benefits. All the claims revolve around the notion of markets (as a natural given amenable to positive scientific analysis). The resultant package is a delimited-formal ideology rather than an exercise in social scientific scholarship. In regard to theorizing development the discourse of spontaneous order has been cashed in quite particular political terms. The adherents of the free market have pressed for deregulation, privatization and welfare reduction in the expectation that the market would spontaneously maximize human benefits.

The political-economic occasion for the representation of these ideas was the collapse of the post-Second World War social-democratic consensus in the First World with oil price shocks, stagflation and the end of the Bretton Woods system. The intellectual occasion was the failure-by-neglect of First World scholars to address the business of the sphere of the economic which had been left to orthodox economists.[4] As the post-Second World War consensus dissolved away the New Right came to dominate the 1980s with notions of marketization and rolling back the state. The discourse of market-engendered spontaneous order centres on the idea-set of liberalism. Through much of the post-Second World War period this position was taken to be moribund but in the wake of the collapse of the Keynesian compromise in the First World the New Right reaffirmed the liberal package. Institutionally this has ever been the view of the World Bank and IMF. Many have argued that this goal is illusory, and indeed the stronger claim is that the ideology is little more than a public relations fig-leaf covering a straightforwardly exploitative stance in regard to the Third World.

In the discourse of spontaneous order the pursuit of effective nation-statehood is replaced with the market system, yet both approaches are external models (and both look to secure surety or certainty for the theorists and their clients). The upshot is that a strategy of analysis is proffered which acts to exhaust available intellectual space thereby squeezing out the more plausible strategy of attending to the detail of real processes via the analytical machineries of the modernist project.

The discourse of the public sphere expresses the optimistic modernist project of the celebration of human reason in the broad sense of the possibility of comprehending and ordering the natural and social worlds. The historical occasion of the modernist project was the shift to the modern world. Thereafter the familiar story is one of the decay of optimistic reason into machineries of control theorized in terms of positive science, all of which issues in the requirement to recover this optimistic core tradition. The discourse of the public sphere affirms an historical project as yet uncompleted.

---

4   See R. Dilley ed. 1992 *Contesting Markets: Analyses of Ideology, Discourse and Practice*, Edinburgh University Press.

Institutionally the position finds expression in the more marginal centres: universities, research centres, the critically minded media and NGOs.

In the sphere of the social sciences the modernist project can be cashed in terms of the deployment of political-economic, social-institutional and culture-critical analyses of the expansion of global industrial-capitalism. In the public sphere such work revolves around the construction and criticism of competing delimited-formal ideologies. The mode of engagement of scholarship is that of the interpretive-critical elucidation of the processes of complex change. After Habermas,[5] we argue on behalf of humankind in pursuit of a reconstructed public sphere. The intimate relationship of the modernist project with the political project of formal and substantive democracy is thereby revealed. The political project rejects both the further advance of bureaucratic rationalization and the disingenuous calls for a return to the neutral mechanisms of the market in favour of an extension of the sphere of public societal decision-making. In regard to the Third World the discourse of the public sphere affirms the notion of dialogue. In place of knowledgeable experts and spontaneous markets, it is proposed to substitute the piecemeal dialogue of equals oriented to the advance of the modernist project.

The Formal Commitments of the Discourse of the Public Sphere

In the discourse of the public sphere, social theorizing is taken to be the generic business of making sense of the social world. It comprises a variety of strategies including social scientific material. In the context of the intellectual and cultural tradition which Europeans inhabit the core strategies of social science express the modernist project: the celebration of human reason, and the expectation of material and moral progress. The historical location of the formulation of the modernist project may be placed in the period of the rise of industrial-capitalism.

Within the broad modernist project is lodged a particular role for scholarship. Broadly this role entails the interpretive-critical elucidation of patterns of complex change. It is thus closely related to, but separate from, the core of the modernist tradition, with its focus on the sphere of political argument and action. Following Habermas/MacIntyre this location and role may be understood as the presentation of arguments on behalf of humankind in pursuit of a reconstructed public sphere (a reanimation via democratization of the classical modernist project).

The concerns of the metropolitan scholar will be with the business of the processes of the extension and deepening of the world capitalist system in exchanges with other groupings (having/inhabiting their own cultural traditions). In regard to the analysis of complex change in peripheral capitalisms the lexicon of the modernist project may be drawn upon in a piecemeal

5 J. Habermas 1989 *The Structural Transformation of the Public Sphere*, Cambridge, Polity.

Figure 20   A new substantive focus

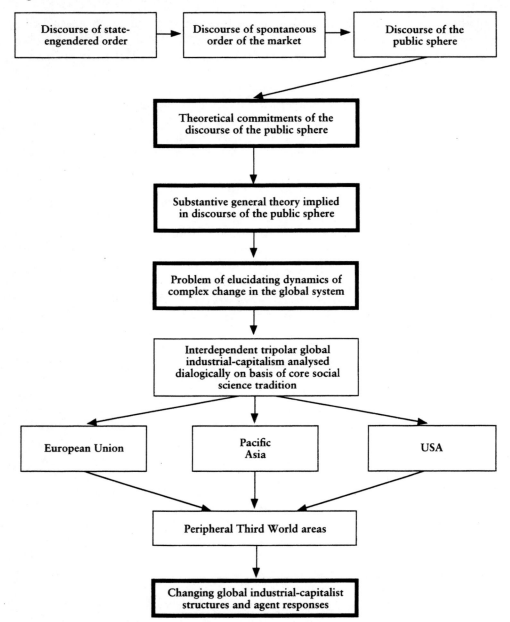

dialogic fashion. A general theory might be constructed in terms of structures and agents. Thereafter smaller-scale enquiries might be made. These could be cast in external/non-dialogic terms but it would be a restricted engagement with the material and further work centred on the detail of processes would involve dialogic exercises.

There is a double line of argument in favour of the notion of dialogue: one flows from the logic of the discourse of the public sphere, which uses ideas of critique; the other flows from the thought that the elucidation of processes underlying/constituting patterns of complex change via political-economic, social-institutional and culture-critical analysis entails amongst other things capturing the understandings of the agents involved, how they read and act within the structures which enfold them. It is not possible to conceive this work as external-descriptive; rather, it is ethnographic and centres on dialogue.

In sum, the main points argued for within the discourse of public sphere, are these: (a) that social theorizing comprises a diversity of loosely related strategies of making sense; (b) that the core strategy of sense-making for the social sciences is the modernist project (within which a role for scholarship is lodged); (c) that in regard to the analysis of complex change in metropolitan capitalism the core analytical strategies are political-economic, social-institutional and culture-critical analysis oriented to the production of delimited-formal ideologies (with scholarship pursuing related interpretive-critical work on behalf of humankind); and (d) that in regard to the analysis of complex change in peripheral capitalism these core analytical strategies are to be drawn on in a piecemeal dialogic fashion.

The Substantive Commitments Implied in the Discourse of the Public Sphere

The sets of intellectual commitments affirmed by theorists working within the discourse of the public sphere entail quite particular strategies of making substantive analyses of the dynamics of complex change within the interdependent tripolar global industrial-capitalist system.

The role of general theory

The notion of general theory is often read within orthodox social science in a way that invokes the natural sciences as they are ordinarily understood. General theory is understood as an exercise in descriptive/explanatory work. A collection of statements which together exhaustively describe/explain the object sphere in question. The intellectual aspiration to the production of a general theory may be articulated, but more usually it is simply assumed and thereafter it prevades enquiry.

In the frame of the discourse of the public sphere the notion of general theory designates a preliminary cashing of a moral stance. It is a limited and restricted set of statements which show in broad terms how the ethic affirmed by the theorist would judge the social world. It represents the simple and direct out-turn of the use of political-economic, social-institutional and culture-critical analyses. It is a substantive statement. It serves its intellectual purpose in this way. It is not to be taken as the basis of an empirical accumulative research project. It structures debate.

The general theory might thereafter be buttressed by empirical material, policy statements might be derived, and explanatory/polemical notes in regard to competing schemes might also be added. At this point the general theory has begun to be developed into a delimited-formal ideological position. The construction of a delimited-formal ideology is a long-drawn-out and collective endeavour, something achieved over time by a group. The general theory is more particular to the work of an individual theorist.

The general theory acts to order enquiry and thereafter more particular substantive analyses can be accomplished. Having rejected the empiricist programme of the exhaustive description/explanation of a discrete object sphere we come to the alternative view carried within the discourse of the public sphere. In Wittgensteinian terms, the discourse of the public sphere affirms in regard to our social scientific interventions in the world an idea of 'finitism'.[6] Enquiry is seen as specific, particular and restricted.

The moral stance carried within the discourse of the public sphere is that of the modernist project: thus, formal and substantive democracy.

It is characteristic of this material that it looks to elucidate the substantive dynamics of structure and agency. The general theory which this all generates in regard to the analysis of complex change is that of the expansionary dynamic of global industrial-capitalism. An example of such an analysis is provided by Worsley[7] who indicates how changes in structures attendant upon the extension of the industrial-capitalist system call forth agent responses. Within the overarching logic of the expansionary system otherwise coherent cultures struggle to read and react to incoming pressures for change.

In the new interdependent tripolar global industrial-capitalis system, the issue for development discourse is the identification and effective characterisation of new areas of possible exchange, that is, who to talk to, about what, in which institutional settings and under the framework of which set of ideas? And in line with the shift of emphasis from legislation to interpretation identified by Bauman,[8] all these analyses are to be arrived at dialogically. It is clear that the way in which such enquiry might translate into practice will be highly localised and complex.[9]

The substantive focus

The substantive focus implied by the discourse of the public sphere is the task of elucidating the dynamics of complex change within the interdependent tripolar global system. In this context, three elements may be noted: (a) a shift in concerns from Third World development to the analysis of complex

6   This idea I take from D. Bloor 1983 *Wittgenstein: A Social Theory of Knowledge*, London, Macmillan.
7   P. Worsley 1984 *The Three Worlds: Culture and World Development*, London, Weidenfeld.
8   Z. Bauman 1987 *Legislators and Interpreters*, Cambridge, Polity.
9   N. Long et al. eds. 1992 *Battlefields of Knowledge*, London, Routledge.

change within the integrated tripolar global industrial-capitalist system; (b) a shift from a focus on nationstates to an analytical level which acknowledges the global system; and (c) a strategy of analysis looking to three interacting levels of political-economic, social-institutional and cultural structures: the global, the regional and the local (national and sub-national).

At the global level, Linklater proposes that a critical international relations theory will look to the development of the notion of a global community,[10] hence: (a) the critical characterization of the record and possibilities of global trans-state organizations, for example the United Nations, where Gott commented that the end of the Cold War meant that the institutional and ideological stasis of the 1970s and 1980s was no longer sustainable – once again real debate would have to be undertaken;[11] (b) similarly, the critical characterization of the record and possibilities of key global trans-state organizations, for example the World Bank and IMF, whose 1980s affirmation of a simplistic marketism will have to be rethought;[12] and (c) in terms of the structure of the global capitalist political-economy a similar critical characterization of the record and possibilities of the development-policy stances of G7 nationstates, and multi-national companies would seem to be a central concern.[13]

At the regional level the critical issues would be the patterns of inter-regional trade, finance, production and consumption, and relatedly the institutional vehicles whereby such economic activity was ordered with formal trans-national organization, bi-lateral linkages and the spread of private economic links. Finally, there would be the issue of the extent to which the peoples of the region self-consciously constituted themselves as a community (as with the USA and increasingly with the European Union).

At the local national and sub-national level the key agent is likely to be a state-regime affirming a particular political-cultural project, a way of reading and reacting to the constraint and opportunity afforded by global and regional structures. The local agent would promulgate an ideology so as to order the population of the relevant territorial unit and legitimate its rule. At the state-level the critical characterization of the political-economic, social-institutional and cultural strategies of state-regimes in the Third World will come into question as established track records and likely futures are evaluated. First World scholars will judge them according to our classical traditions and standards and decide if and how to engage. One implication of this is that any general responsibility towards the Third World is rejected. In regard to the huge spread of local-level NGO work, the position is in principle clear as this is one area where dialogue and empowerment has long been the order of the day.

---

10   A. Linklater 1990 *Beyond Realism and Marxism: Critical Theory and International Relations*, London, Macmillan.
11   R. Gott in *The Guardian* 30/31 December 1991.
12   See J. Toye 1987 *Dilemmas of Development*, Oxford, Blackwell.
13   Think for example of the Rio Summit of 1992.

An overview of changing global structures

In the post-Second World War period the general issue of the nature of the global system had one overarching framework comprising the First World idea of the Free West and the Second World notion of socialism (and for the Third World, development). The key elements of the Cold War ideologies affirmed the distinction between the two realms in terms of the claimed benefits of the respective systems. The delimited-formal ideologies offered political-cultural identities for the masses who were enjoined to support the defence of freedom or socialism. It also offered political-cultural identities for the political elites who were offered roles and a set of slogans to legitimate these roles. However, the ways in which a series of agent-groups understand themselves and their place in the global system is presently undergoing significant change.

The received political wisdom current within the institutions of the global system was destroyed over the period 1985–91. The period sees Gorbachev unilaterally withdrawing from Cold War competition by initiating moves toward disarmament and detente (1985–9) and thereafter the Eastern Bloc simply dissolved itself (1989–91). In this fashion, the central element of the official ideologies of Cold War, the division of the global system into competing blocs, simply disappeared. There has been considerable confusion amongst political elites in the subsequent period as to what to think and what to do with all the institutional apparatus. There seems to be no replacement world view in prospect. It is also true that the end of the Cold War has underscored the importance of existing debates about the constituent elements of the global industrial-capitalist system.

Overall, the familiar post-Second World War situation with its two great powers, a divided Europe and a marginalized Third World was superseded in the period 1989–91 and we have seen the emergence of a tripolar global system. The changes can be grasped in terms of the dynamics of structural change and agent response. We can characterize the general situation of groups in relation to present patterns of structural change within the tripolar global system. In schematic terms we can speak of ascendant, stationary, descendant and non-affected peripheral groupings. In each of these situations the groups in question will read their situations in different ways.

The Presently Discussed Changes in the Global System

In the wake of the end of the short twentieth century and the related collapse of the received certainties of the Cold War which had shaped the understandings of European and American thinkers, it has become clear that a new integrated tripolar global industrial-capitalist system is taking shape. A series of tendencies within the global system can be identified as patterns and styles of production change. First, in the First World the intermingled upgrading and hollowing out of the metropolitan core economies (flexible-specialization and the new international division of labour).

Second, the collapse of the Second World state socialist bloc and its confused shift towards market-based political-economies (a mixture of political collapse and thereafter general reconstruction in the USSR and Eastern Europe, and authoritarian market reforms in China and Indo-China). And third, the further partial dependent integration of certain areas of the Third World in Asia, Latin America and the oil-rich Middle East, and the slow shift of other areas of the Third World into a situation of apparent semi-detachment from the global system (much of Africa south of the Sahara). On Hobsbawm's arguments this is an unstable system which recalls the equally unstable global system of the later years of the long nineteenth century.

At the present the global industrial-capitalist system shows a number of cross-cutting tendencies: (a) to integration on a global scale, with a financial system that is integrated across the globe and extensive increasingly de-nationalized MNC operations; (b) to regionalization within the global system, with three key areas emerging where intra-regional linkages are deepening; and (c) to division on a global scale, with areas of the world apparently falling behind the regionalized global system.

The reconstruction of global industrial-capitalism: the European Union

Western Europe was ordered at the macro-structural level in terms of the ideas, institutions and power relationships established by the Bretton Woods agreement. The USA was the core economy of an open trading region. However in the period of the last third of the short twentieth century this system came under great pressure and has slowly subsided. The following factors have contributed: (a) the oil-price shocks of the early 1970s; (b) the financial implications for the USA of the Vietnam War and the subsequent shift to debtor status in the Reagan years; (c) the rise of the EEC and the Japanese sphere in East Asia; (d) the (partial and uneven) globalization of the industrial-capitalist system; and (e) the abrupt ending of the comfortably familiar bipolar bloc system. The upshot of all these changes over the period 1973–91 has been a movement into an unstable, insecure and novel tripolar global industrial-capitalist system. Confronted with these slow patterns of structural change the countries of western Europe slowly moved towards a closer union. These ideas and institutional mechanisms were in place when the extent of global structural change finally became unequivocally clear with the collapse of the USSR. The countries of western Europe found an available reply in the guise of the European Union, itself a development of the European Economic Community which had been founded back in the early 1950s. The idea of the European Union was pushed to the fore in discussions about the future of the continent.

The core of the European Union lies in northwestern Europe. In Germany the end of the Cold War meant the end of post-Second World War division. It meant an abrupt and uneasy marriage of the two halves of Germany. The citizens of the former German Democratic Republic lost their country altogether and the citizens of the Federal Republic lost their comfortable prosperous country. It meant an unexpected movement to the centre of Europe as the largest country with the strongest economy; this placed new demands on the key alliance with France. However, the commitment of the core countries of the European Union was affirmed in the Maastricht Treaty and Germany, the Netherlands, Belgium and France maintain a pro-union stance. The Scandinavian countries (with the exception of oil-rich Norway) joined the Union, as did Austria; the newly independent countries of middle Europe have announced their intentions of joining as soon as possible.

In Mediterranean Europe there has been a similar strength of commitment. In Spain, Portugal and Greece the European Union has been the institutional space within which post-military liberal-democratic regimes have developed. One of the original EEC members was Italy and here the end of the Cold War meant an end to the corrupt political system dominated by the CDP. A revolt on the part of pro-EU professionals led the attack on the established political-business classes.

In a speculative way we could pick out the key elements of Europeanness: (a) a political-economy in which state and market interact, with the state having a directive role; (b) a social-institutional structure which affirms an idea of the importance of community, and sees economy and polity acknowledging the important role of the community; and (c) a cultural tradition which acknowledges established institutions, a broad humanist social philosophy and a tradition of social-democratic or Christian-democratic welfare politics.

It is on the basis of these political-cultural traits, and the continuing legacies of the European colonial empires, that the countries of Europe engage with the Third World. The experience of the colonial period offers the Europeans both a geographical focus for linkages with the Third World and a body of shared experience (much of which, of course, is deeply ambiguous). The Lomé Convention of 1975 governs the relationships of the countries of the European Union with those territories which were parts of the various colonial empires. The historical linkages are of diminishing relevance but the European political-cultural forms do shape continuing exchanges in areas of Africa, South Asia and the Caribbean.

The reconstruction of global industrial-capitalism: Pacific Asia

The countries of Pacific Asia attained the outline of their present configuration over the period of the expansion of the Japanese empire, the chaos of the Pacific War and the collapse of the Western empires. The Pacific region over the post-Second World War period has been divided by Cold War institutions and rhetoric into a Western-focused group and a socialist bloc. The Western-focused group has been subject to the political-economic and cultural hegemony of the USA. However, the Western-focused group is undergoing considerable change. This may be summarized as the beginnings of a political-economic, social-institutional and cultural emancipation from the hegemony of the USA. At the same time the countries of the socialist bloc which had spent decades following autarkic state-socialist development trajectories are now opening up to the Western-focused group.

The key relationship in the post-Second World War period has been that of the Japanese and the Americans. Thereafter the countries of the inner periphery of East Asia have dealt with a long period of economic development in the political and military shadow of the USA and the economic shadow of Japan. The countries of the outer periphery of Southeast Asia have more recently reoriented themselves towards the economic model of Japan. Relatedly we can note the more recent turn of the countries of Australasia towards the Pacific Asian economies, a turn that is routinely expressed in terms of a commitment to open regionalism, thereby arguably implicitly granting a continued political commitment to the West in general and to the USA in particular. Finally we have the ongoing process of the reorientation of China and Indo-China.

The region has been undergoing considerable structural change since the late 1970s and the 1985 Plaza Accords (which generated a flood of yen-based investment in the region). One key contemporary public issue concerns the arguments to the effect that the pattern of change in Pacific Asia is such that we can talk about a Pacific Asian model of development where this is taken to be a particular variety of industrial-capitalism distinct from the American or European models.

A speculative illustration of the character of the Pacific-Asian model would include these factors: (a) the economy is state-directed; (b) state direction is oriented to the pragmatic pursuit of economic growth (that is, it is not informed by explicit or debated political-ideological positions); (c) state direction is top-down in style and pervasive in its reach throughout the political-economy and culture; (d) society is familial and thereafter communitarian (thus society is non-individualistic); (e) social order is secured by pervasive control machineries (sets of social rules and an extensive bureaucratization of everyday life) and a related hegemonic common culture (which enjoins submission to the demands of community and authority); (f) political debate and power are typically reserved to an elite sphere (and political life centres on the pragmatic pursuit of overarching economic goals); (g) political debate and action amongst the masses is diffuse and demobilized (thus there is no 'public sphere'); (h) culture comprises a mix of officially sanctioned tradition and market sanctioned consumption; and (i) culture stresses consensus, acquiescence and harmony and eschews open conflict.

In respect of the sets of relationships within the region it can be argued that the economic core is Japan and that around this core is a series of concentric spheres. In northeast Asia the countries of South Korea and Taiwan have close links with Japan. In southeast Asia the countries of ASEAN have become increasingly integrated within the Japanese sphere. In the sometime socialist block, China and Indo-China, there is extensive Japanese activity. Finally, in Australia and New Zealand, there is extensive concern to reorganize economies and societies so as to attain a measure of integration with the Pacific Asian countries. In those countries which would until quite recently have been labelled Third World the issues of development are increasingly addressed with reference to the economic influence of Japan within the region, and their key concern with an ordered and cooperative pattern of development.

The reconstruction of global industrial-capitalism: the USA

The episode of the Second World War saw the emergence of the USA as the premier economic, political, diplomatic and military power in the world. The power of the USA was used to establish and underpin the Bretton Woods system within the sphere of the West and the military/diplomatic confrontation with the Second World. The position of the USA was unchallenged until the mid-1970s when the financial burdens of the Vietnam War occasioned the first changes within the Bretton Woods system. The period of the late 1970s saw inflation and economic dislocation within the Western sphere and in the Third World. In the 1980s the military build-up inaugurated by President Reagan led to the USA becoming a debtor nation. In addition the USA was the major sponsor of the doctrines of economic liberalization which have further undermined the order of the global system.

The end of the short twentieth century has seen the USA continuing to press for an open global trading system but arguments are now made within the context of a tripolar system and without the convenience of the existence of the Second World which provided an excuse for US hegemony within the sphere of the West.

The key elements of the American polity might be taken to include a public commitment to an open market economy, a public commitment to republican democracy, a strong preference for individualism, a tradition which celebrates the achievements of ordinary people, and a cultural tradition of liberal individualism. It is on the basis of this commitment to an open business environment that the US engages with the Third World. The influence of the Washington-based IMF and World Bank is extensive in promoting liberalization and free trade, and recent expressions of these concerns have been the establishment of NAFTA and APEC.

The reconstruction of global industrial-capitalism: the Third World

The experience of the countries of the Third World in the post-colonial period has evidenced a diverse mix of advance, drift and stagnation. If we consider the very broad sweep of the countries of Pacific Asia, Latin America and the oil-rich Middle East it is clear that there has been a sharp process of differentiation within what has in the post-war period been called the Third World.

In the case of Pacific Asia it is clear that large areas of what might a few years ago have been called countries in the Third World have experienced relatively rapid development. In the case of Pacific Asia the basis for economic success is elusive. In the 1980s the New Right claimed that the success of the area proved the correctness of market-oriented development policies. However the countries of the area have all pursued state-directed development. The core regional economy has been Japan which industrialized in the late nineteenth century and which has subsequently played a key role in the development of Pacific Asia. In China in the late 1970s the reforms of Deng Xiaoping inaugurated a period of marketization which has seen rapid economic growth in the coastal regions and relative stagnation in the vast rural hinterlands. The country now has pronounced regional inequalities but is increasingly integrated within the Pacific Asian region. The pace of development in the region as a whole over the 1980s has been so rapid that Pacific Asia is now spoken of as one of the three major economic blocs within the global economy.

It is similarly the case for other areas of what would have been called the Third World a few years ago that they have experienced a further round of dependent capitalist development. It is possible to point to the oil-rich states of the Middle East. In the case of the Middle East it is clear that the basis for the economic success of the Middle East is that of primary-product exporting, in particular oil, but these countries have also invested heavily in industrial development. It is also clear that the countries of the Middle East have experienced considerable political dislocation in the shape of war and revolution. At the same time the progress of what has been called westernization, the introduction of modern social patterns, has been deeply problematical.

In the case of Latin America the extent of success is more problematical as social inequalities, environmental problems and political instability work against economic successes. However, Latin America and the Caribbean fall within the ambit of the USA-centred sphere of the global capitalist system. In 1993 the NAFTA agreement was inaugurated which looks to a free trade zone within the Americas.

In contrast to the countries of Pacific Asia, the Middle East and Latin America, the countries of Africa experienced little progress in the 1980s. In Africa the initial legacies of the colonial period included state and administrative machineries, legal systems, educated and mobilized populations, and so on. All these slowly ran down. As the economic changes of the post-colonial period progressed the residual pre-contact and colonial patterns of life began to be reworked. This could include the decay of traditional patterns of family and kin, and problems of tribalism. In Africa there were problems of political corruption, incompetence and instability. The role of the military increased. A series of internal conflicts occurred. These problems were internal to the new countries of the Third World but were particularly acutely felt in Africa.[14] At the same time these countries experienced

14 See B. Davidson 1968 *Africa in History*, London, Weidenfeld; idem 1994 *The Search for Africa*, London, James Currey.

interference from the two great powers as they pursued a series of overt and covert proxy wars. In the case of Africa, development specialists tend to speak of a lost decade. In terms of the African countries' share of world production and world trade it is shrinking and is now very slight. In the case of Africa it seems to be possible to speak of a slow detachment from the mainstream of the global industrial-capitalist system.

If we try to summarize the post-Second World War period as a whole then we can say that by the mid-1970s the orthodox optimism of the immediate post-war period had dissipated and was beginning to be replaced by those fears about debt, instability and failure which were to come to the fore in the 1980s. At the same time the counter-optimism of the critics of the orthodoxy was similarly beginning to decline as unease grew about the further unequal development of the global system. It is also true to say that the unease about the post-Second World War settlement which underpinned the discussion about development also became acute as First World economies suffered economic slow-downs and the societies saw rising problems. In the First World the intellectual and political confusion of the period saw the emergence of the Anglo-Saxon New Right. In the Third World the New Right sponsored a counter-revolution which aimed to sweep away the developmental role of the state in favour of the marketplace. The period of the 1980s was thus one of reduced expectations for both the orthodoxy and their radical critics. However, the position of the radical democrats was further undermined by the ferocious political reaction of the 1980s. The overall impact upon the Third World has been to reinforce the diversity of the area's patterns of integration within the global system, a mixture of dependent development and semi-detachment.

Chapter Summary

The post-Second World War global system with its two great powers, a divided Europe and a marginalized Third World was superseded in the period 1989–91. The 1980s saw the emergence of a tripolar global system. The ways in which a series of agent-groups understand themselves and their place in the global system are presently undergoing significant change. The changes can be grasped in terms of the dynamics of structural change and agent response within the three main areas of the global system. Overall, the substantive tasks of development theorists have shifted *from* the technical social scientific attempt to characterize authoritatively the shift to the modern world of the Western countries in order to order rationally the recapitulation of this experience by the countries of the Third World *towards* the dialogic elucidation of the dynamics of complex change within the integrated tripolar global industrial-capitalist system.

Bibliography

Abrams, P. 1968 *The Origins of British Sociology*, Chicago University Press

Afshar, H. 1985 *Women, Work and Ideology in the Third World*, London, Tavistock

Aglietta, M. 1979 *A Theory of Capitalist Regulation*, London, Verso

Alatas, S. H. 1977 *The Myth of the Lazy Native*, London, Frank Cass

Allen, J., Massey, D. eds. 1988 *The Economy in Question*, London, Sage

Anderson, B. 1983 *Imagined Communities*, London, Verso

Anderson, P. 1976 *Considerations on Western Marxism*, London, New Left Books

Anderson, P. 1983 *In the Tracks of Historical Materialism*, London, Verso

Anderson, R. J., Hughes, J. A., Sharrock, W. W. 1985 *The Sociology Game*, London, Longman

Anderson, R. J., Hughes, J. A., Sharrock, W. W. 1986 *Philosophy and the Human Sciences*, London, Croom Helm

Antoni, C. 1959 *From History to Sociology*, Detroit, Wayne State University Press

Appelbaum, R. P., Henderson, J. eds. 1992 *States and Development in the Asia Pacific Rim*, London, Sage

Apthorpe, R. 1986 'Development Policy Discourse', *Public Administration and Development*, 6

Apthorpe, R., Krahl, A. eds. 1986 *Development Studies: Critique and Renewal*, Aldershot, Avebury

Arendt, A. 1958 *The Human Condition*, Chicago University Press

Aron, R. 1973 *The Imperial Republic: The US and the World 1945–1973*, London, Weidenfeld

Baran, P. 1973 *The Political Economy of Growth*, Harmondsworth, Penguin

Baran, P., Sweezy, P. 1968 *Monopoly Capital*, Harmondsworth, Penguin

Barber, W. J. 1967 *A History of Economic Thought*, Harmondsworth, Penguin

Barraclough, G. 1964 *An Introduction to Contemporary History*, Harmondsworth, Penguin

Barret-Brown, M. 1984 *Models in Political Economy*, Harmondsworth, Penguin

Bartley, R. L. ed. 1993 *Democracy and Capitalism: Asian and American Perspectives*, Singapore, Institute of Southeast Asian Studies

Bauman, Z. 1976 *Towards a Critical Sociology*, London, Routledge

Bauman, Z. 1987 *Legislators and Interpreters*, Cambridge, Polity

Bauman, Z. 1988 *Freedom*, Milton Keynes, Open University Press

Bauman, Z. 1989 *Modernity and the Holocaust*, Cambridge, Polity

Bauman, Z. 1992 *Intimations of Modernity*, London, Routledge

Beattie, J. 1966 *Other Cultures*, London, Routledge

Beetham, D. 1985 *Max Weber and the Theory of Modern Politics*, Cambridge, Polity

Bell, D. 1973 *The Coming of Post Industrial Society*, Harmondsworth, Penguin

Bello, W., Rosenfeld, S 1990 *Dragons in Distress: Asia's Miracle Economies in Crisis*, San Francisco, IFDP

Bennington, G. 1989 *Lyotard Writing the Event*, Manchester University Press

Benton, T. 1977 *The Philosophical Foundations of the Three Sociologies*, London, Routledge

Berlin, I. 1989 *Four Essays on Liberty*, Oxford University Press

Bernstein, H. 1971 'Modernization Theory and the Sociological Study of Development', *Journal of Development Studies*, 7

Bernstein, H. 1979 'Sociology of Underdevelopment Versus Sociology of Development' in Lehman, D. ed. *Development Theory*, London, Frank Cass

Bernstein, R. 1976 *The Restructuring of Social and Political Theory*, London, Methuen

Bienefeld, M. 1980 'Dependency in the Eighties', *Institute for Development Studies Bulletin*, 12

Bienefeld, M., Godfrey, M. eds. 1982 *The Struggle for Development: National Strategies in an International Context*, London, Wiley

Birnbaum, N. 1969 'The Staggering Colossus' in Nagel, G. ed. *Student Power*, London, Merlin

Black, C. E. ed. 1976 *Comparative Modernization*, London, Collier

Block. F. 1990 *Post Industrial Possibilities: A Critique of Economic Discourse*, Berkeley and Los Angeles, University of California Press

Bloch, M. 1983 *Marxism and Anthropology*, Oxford University Press

Blomstrom, M., Hettne, B. 1984 *Development Theory in Transition*, London, Zed

Bloor, D 1983 *Wittgenstein: A Social Theory of Knowledge*, London, Macmillan

Brenner, R. 1977 'The Origins of Capitalist Development: A Critique of Neo-Smithian Marxism', *New Left Review*, 104

Brett, E. A. 1985 *The World Economy Since the War: The Politics of Uneven Development*, London, Macmillan

Brewer, A. 1980 *Marxist Theories of Imperialism*, London, Routledge

Brittan, V. 1988 *Hidden Lives Hidden Deaths*, London, Faber

Brookfield, H. 1975 *Interdependent Development*, London, Methuen

Brown, V. 1994 *Adam Smith's Economic Discourse: Canonicity, Commerce and Conscience*, London, Routledge

Burrow, J. W. 1966 *Evolution and Society*, Cambridge University Press

Callinicos, A. 1989a *Against Postmodernism*, Cambridge, Polity

Callinicos, A. 1989b *The Revenge of History*, Cambridge, Polity

Cardoso, F. H., Faletto, E. H. 1979 *Dependency and Development in Latin America*, Berkeley and Los Angeles, University of California Press

Carver, T. 1975 *Karl Marx: Texts on Method*, Oxford, Blackwell

Carver, T. 1981 *Engels*, Oxford University Press

Caute, D. 1978 *The Great Fear: The Anti-Communist Purges under Truman and Eisenhower*, London, Secker and Warburg

Challiand, G. 1977 *Revolution in the Third World*, Hassocks, Harvester

Chalmers, A. F. 1980 *What Is This Thing Called Science?*, Milton Keynes, Open University Press

Chan, H. C. 1993 'Democracy: Evolution and Implementation – An Asian Perspective' in Bartley, R. L. ed. *Democracy and Capitalism: Asian and American Perspectives*, Singapore, Institute of Southeast Asian Studies

Chisholm, A. 1972 *Philosophers of the Earth*, London, Sidgwick and Jackson

Chitnis, A. C. 1976 *The Scottish Enlightenment: A Social History*, London, Croom Helm

Chomsky, N. 1991 *Deterring Democracy*, London, Verso

Clammer, J. 1985 *Anthropology and Political Economy*, London, Macmillan

Clammer, J. ed. 1978 *The New Economic Anthropology*, London, Macmillan

Clements, K. P. 1980 *From Right to Left in Development Theory*, Singapore, Institute of Southeast Asian Studies

Cole, K. et al. 1991 *Why Economists Disagree*, London, Longman

Colley, L. 1992 *Britons: Forging the Nation 1707–1837*, Yale University Press

Collini, S. 1979 *Liberalism and Sociology*, Cambridge University Press

Culler, J. 1976 *Saussure*, London, Fontana

Daiches, D. ed. 1986 *A Hotbed of Genius: The Scottish Enlightenment 1730–1790*, Edinburgh University Press

Dasgupta, A. K. 1985 *Epochs of Economic Thought*, Oxford, Blackwell

Davidson, B. 1968 *Africa in History*, London, Weidenfeld

Davidson, B. 1978 *Africa in Modern History*, London, Allen Lane

Davidson, B. 1994 *The Search for Africa*, London, James Currey

Denitch, B. 1990 *The End of the Cold War*, London, Verso

Diggins, J. P. 1978 *The Bard of Savagery: Thorstein Veblen and Modern Social Theory*, Hassocks, Harvester

Dilley, R. ed. 1992 *Contesting Markets: Analyses of Ideology, Discourse and Practice*, Edinburgh University Press

DiMarco, L. E. ed. 1972 *International Economics and Development: Essays in Honour of Raul Prebisch*, London, Academic Press

Dobb, M. 1973 *Theories of Value and Distribution Since Adam Smith*, Cambridge University Press

Donaldson, P. 1973 *Economics of the Real World*, Harmondsworth, Penguin

Dore, R. 1986 *Flexible Rigidities*, Stanford University Press

Eagly, R. V. ed. 1968 *Events, Ideology and Economic Theory*, Detroit, Wayne State University Press

Eckersley, R. 1992 *Environmentalism and Political Theory: Towards an Ecocentric Approach*, London, UCL Press

Ehrlich, P. 1968 *The Population Bomb*, London, Pan

Ehrlich, P., Ehrlich, A. 1970 *Population, Resources, and Environment*, San Francisco, Freeman

Eldridge, J. E. T. 1971 *Max Weber: The Interpretation of Social Reality*, London, Michael Joseph

Elliot, J. A. 1994 *An Introduction to Sustainable Development*, London, Routledge

Escobar, A. 1992 'Planning' in Sachs, W. ed. *The Development Dictionary*, London, Zed

Etzioni-Halevy, E. 1981 *Social Change: The Advent and Maturation of Modern Society*, London, Routledge

Fanon, F. 1967 *The Wretched of the Earth*, Harmondsworth, Penguin

Fay, B. 1975 *Social Theory and Political Practice*, London, Allen and Unwin

Featherstone, M. 1991 *Consumer Culture and Postmodernism*, London, Sage

Flemming, D. F. 1961 *The Cold War and Its Origins*, New York, Doubleday

Foster-Carter, A. 1978 'The Modes of Production Controversy', *New Left Review*, 107

Frank, A. G. 1967 *Capitalism and Underdevelopment in Latin America*, New York, Monthly Review Press

Frank, A. G. 1969 *Latin America: Underdevelopment or Revolution?*, New York, Monthly Review Press

Frank, A. G. 1975 *On Capitalist Underdevelopment*, Oxford University Press

Frank, A. G. 1976 *Economic Genocide in Chile*, Nottingham, Spokesman

Frank, A. G. 1972 *Lumpenbourgeoisie–Lumpendevelopment*, New York, Monthly Review Press

Frazer, J. 1922 *The Golden Bough*, London, Macmillan

Friedman, M. 1953 *Essays in Positive Economics*, University of Chicago Press

Friedman, M. 1962 *Capitalism and Freedom*, University of Chicago Press

Friedman, M., Friedman, R. 1980 *Free to Choose*, London, Secker

Frobel, F., Heinrichs, J. 1980 *The New International Division of Labour*, Cambridge University Press

Fukuyama, F. 1992 *The End of History and the Last Man*, London, Hamish Hamilton

Furtado, C. 1964 *Development and Underdevelopment*, Berkeley and Los Angeles, University of California Press

Furtado, C. 1965 *Diagnosis of the Brazilian Crisis*, Berkeley and Los Angeles, University of California Press

Furtado, C. 1976 *Economic Development in Latin America*, 2nd edn, Cambridge University Press

Furtado, C. 1978 *Accumulation and Development*, Oxford, Martin Robertson

Galbraith, J. K. 1958 *The Affluent Society*, Harmondsworth, Penguin

Galbraith, J. K. 1967 *The New Industrial State*, Harmondsworth, Penguin

Garton-Ash, T. 1989 *We The People*, London, Granta

Gellner, E. 1964 *Thought and Change*, London, Weidenfeld

Gellner, E. 1983 *Nations and Nationalism*, Cambridge University Press

Gellner, E. 1988 *Plough, Sword and Book*, London, Paladin

Gellner, E. 1992 *Reason and Culture*, Oxford, Blackwell

George, S. 1984 *Ill Fares the Land*, Washington, Institute for Policy Science

George, S. 1988 *A Fate Worse than Debt*, Harmondsworth, Penguin

Gerth, H. H., Mills, C. W. eds. 1948 *From Max Weber*, London, Routledge

Giddens, A. 1971 *Capitalism and Modern Social Theory*, Cambridge University Press

Giddens, A. 1972a *Emile Durkheim: Selected Writings*, Cambridge University Press

Giddens, A. 1972b *Politics and Sociology in the Thought of Max Weber*, London, Macmillan

Giddens, A. 1976 *New Rules of Sociological Method*, London, Hutchinson

Giddens, A. 1979 *Central Problems in Social Theory*, London, Macmillan

Giddens, A. 1982 *Profiles and Critiques in Social Theory*, London, Macmillan

Girvan, N. 1973 'The Development of Dependency Economics in the Caribbean and Latin America: Review and Comparison', *Social and Economic Studies*, 22

Glenny, M. 1990 *The Rebirth of History*, Harmondsworth, Penguin

Goodman, D., Segal, G. eds. 1994 *China Deconstructs: Politics, Trade and Regionalism*, London, Routledge

Gordon, R. A. 1963 'Institutional Elements in Contemporary Economics' in Dorfman, J. ed. *Institutional Economics: Veblen, Commons and Mitchell Reconsidered*, Berkeley and Los Angeles, University of California Press

Grillo, R. ed. 1985 *Social Anthropology and Development Policy*, London, Tavistock

Grimal, H. 1965 *Decolonization: The British, French, Dutch and Belgian Empires 1919–1963*, London, Routledge

Habermas, J. 1989 *The Structural Transformation of the Public Sphere*, Cambridge, Polity

Hagen, E. 1962 *On the Theory of Social Change*, Homewood, Dorsey

Hall, S., Jaques, M. eds. 1983 *The Politics of Thatcherism*, London, Lawrence and Wishart

Halliday, F. 1979a *Arabia without Sultans*, Harmondsworth, Penguin

Halliday, F. 1979b *Iran: Dictatorship and Development*, Harmondsworth, Penguin

Halliday, F. 1989 *Cold War, Third World*, London, Radius

Hamilton, C. 1983 'Capitalist Industrialization in East Asia's Four Little Tigers', *Journal of Contemporary Asia*, 13

Hancock, G. 1989 *Lords of Poverty*, London, Macmillan

Hankins, T. L. 1985 *Science and the Enlightenment*, Cambridge University Press

Harris, S. 1948 *The European Recovery Programme*, London, Harper and Row

Harrison, A. 1967 *The Framework of Economic Activity*, London, Macmillan

Harrod, R. 1939 'An Essay on Dynamic Theory', *Economic Journal*, 49

Harvey, D. 1989 *The Condition of Postmodernity*, Oxford, Blackwell

Hawthorn, G. 1976 *Enlightenment and Despair*, Cambridge University Press

Hekman, S. 1990 *Gender and Knowledge: Elements of Postmodern Feminism*, Cambridge University Press

Held, D. 1980 *Introduction to Critical Theory*, London, Hutchinson

Herrera, A. O. et al. eds. 1975 *Catastrophe or a New Society*, Ottawa, Barlioche Foundation

Hettne, B. 1990 *Development Theory and the Three Worlds*, London, Longman

Heyzer, N. 1986 *Working Women in Southeast Asia*, Milton Keynes, Open University Press

Higgins, B. 1968 *Economic Development*, London, Constable

Hindess, B. 1977 *Philosophy and Methodology in the Social Sciences*, Hassocks, Harvester

Hobart, M. ed. 1993 *An Anthropological Critique of Development*, London, Routledge

Hobsbawm, E. 1994 *Age of Extremes: The Short Twentieth Century, 1914–1991*, London, Michael Joseph

Hodgson, G. M. 1988 *Economics and Institutions: A Manifesto for a Modern Institutional Economics*, Cambridge, Polity

Holub, R. C. 1991 *Jürgen Habermas: Critic in the Public Sphere*, London, Routledge

Hoogvelt, A. 1982 *The Third World in Global Development*, London, Macmillan

Horne, D. ed. 1992 *The Trouble with Economic Rationalism*, Newham, Scribe

Howell, J. 1993 *China Opens its Doors: The Politics of Economic Transition*, Hemel Hempstead, Harvester

Hughes, R. 1988 *The Fatal Shore*, London, Pan

Hughes, S. 1959 *Consciousness and Society*, London, McGibbon

Huntington, S. P. 1976 'The Change to Change: Modernisation, Development and Politics' in Black, C. E. ed. *Comparative Modernization*, London, Collier

Ignatieff, M. 1994 *Blood and Belonging*, London, Vintage

Jackson, C. 1994 'Gender Analysis and Environments' in Redclift, M., Benton, T., eds. *Social Theory and the Global Environment*, London, Routledge

Jackson, R. H. 1990 *Quasi-States: Sovereignty, International Relations and the Third World*, Cambridge University Press

Jameson, F. *Postmodernism, Or the Cultural Logic of Late Capitalism*, London, Verso

Jay, M. 1973 *The Dialectical Imagination*, Boston, Mass., Little, Brown

Jessop, B. et al. 1988 *Thatcherism: A Tale of Two Nations*, Cambridge, Polity

Johnson, C. 1982 *MITI and the Japanese Miracle*, Stanford University Press

Jones, G. 1980 *Social Darwinism and English Thought*, Brighton, Harvester

Jones, H. 1975 *An Introduction to Modern Theories of Economic Growth*, London, Nelson

Kabbani, R. 1986 *Imperial Fictions: Europe's Myths of Orient*, London, Pandora

Kahl, J. A. 1976 *Modernisation, Exploitation and Dependency in Latin America*, New Brunswick, Transaction

Kay, G. 1975 *Development and Underdevelopment: A Marxist Analysis*, London, Macmillan

Kaye, H. 1984 *The British Marxist Historians*, Cambridge, Polity

Kennedy, P. 1988 *The Rise and Fall of the Great Powers*, London, Fontana

Kerr, C. et al. 1960 *Industrialism and Industrial Man*, Harmondsworth, Penguin

Kiernan, V. G. 1982 *European Empires from Conquest to Collapse*, London, Fontana

King, A. D. 1990 *Urbanism, Colonialism and the World Economy*, London, Routledge

Kitching, G. 1982 *Development and Underdevelopment in Historical Perspective*, London, Methuen

Knakal, J. 1972 'The Centre-Periphery System Twenty Years Later' in DiMarco, L. E. ed. *International Economics and Development: Essays in Honour of Raul Prebisch*, London, Academic Press

Kolko, G. 1968 *The Politics of War: US Foreign Policy 1943–45*, New York, Vintage

Korner, P. et al. 1986 *The IMF and the Debt Crisis*, London, Zed

Krieger, J. 1986 *Reagan, Thatcher and the Politics of Decline*, Cambridge, Polity

Krugman, P. 1994 *Peddling Prosperity: Economic Sense and Nonsense in an Age of Diminished Expectations*, New York, Norton

Laslett, P., Runciman, W. G. eds. 1967 *Philosophy, Politics and Society Third Series*, Oxford, Blackwell

Lehman, D. ed. 1979 *Development Theory*, London, Cass

Lerner, D. 1958 *The Passing of Traditional Society*, New York, Free Press

Leys, C. 1977 'Underdevelopment and Dependency: Critical Notes', *Journal of Contemporary Asia*, 7

Lichtheim, G. 1961 *Marxism: An Historical and Critical Study*, London, Routledge

Linklater, A. 1990 *Beyond Realism and Marxism: Critical Theory and International Relations*, London, Macmillan

Linz, J., Stepan, A. eds. 1978 *The Breakdown of Democratic Regimes*, Johns Hopkins University Press

Long, N. et al. eds. 1992 *Battlefields of Knowledge*, London, Routledge

Lukes, S. 1973 *Emile Durkheim*, London, Macmillan

Lyotard, F. 1979 *The Postmodern Condition*, Manchester University Press

MacIntyre, A. 1967 *A Short History of Ethics*, London, Routledge

MacIntyre, A. 1971 *Against the Self-Images of the Age*, London, Duckworth

MacIntyre, A. 1981 *After Virtue*, London, Duckworth

MacIntyre, A. 1988 *Whose Justice? Which Rationality?*, London, Duckworth

Macpherson, C. B. 1966 *The Real World of Democracy*, Oxford University Press

Macpherson, C. B. 1973 *Democratic Theory: Essays in Retrieval*, Oxford University Press

Marcuse, H. 1969 *An Essay on Liberation*, Harmondsworth, Penguin

Marquand, D. 1988 *The Unprincipled Society*, London, Fontana

Marshall, B. L. 1994 *Engendering Modernity: Feminism, Social Theory and Social Change*, Cambridge, Polity

Martin, K., Knapp, J. eds. 1967 *The Teaching of Development Economics*, London, Frank Cass

Marx, K. 1957 *The Economic and Philosophical Manuscripts*, London, Lawrence and Wishart

Marx, K. 1973 *Grundrisse*, Harmondsworth, Penguin

Marx, K. Engels, F. 1968 *Selected Works*, London, Lawrence and Wishart

McClellan, D. 1973 *Karl Marx His Life and Thought*, London, Macmillan

McClelland, D. C. 1961 *The Achieving Society*, New York, Van Nostrand

McRae, D. G. 1974 *Weber*, London, Fontana

Mead, M. 1928 *Coming of Age in Samoa*, New York, Morrow

Meadows, D. H. 1992 *Beyond the Limits*, London, Earthscan

Meadows, D. H. etal 1972 *The Limits to Growth*, New York, Basic Books

Meek, R. L. 1956 *Studies in the Labour Theory of Value*, London, Lawrence and Wishart

Meier, G., Seers, D. eds. 1984 *Pioneers in Development*, Oxford University Press

Mikesell, R. F. 1968 *The Economics of Foreign Aid*, London, Weidenfeld

Milliband, R. 1977 *Marxism and Politics*, Oxford University Press

Milliband, R., Saville, J. eds. 1965 *The Socialist Register*, London, Merlin

Mills, C. W. 1963 *The Marxists*, Harmondsworth, Penguin

Milton, K. ed. 1993 *Environmentalism: The View from Anthropology*, London, Routledge

Minh-ha, T. T. 1989 *Women, Native, Other: Writing Postcoloniality and Feminism*, Indiana University Press

Mirowski, P. 1988 *Against Mechanism: Protecting Economics From Science*, New Jersey, Rowman and Littlefield

Mitchie J. ed. 1992 *The Ecnomic Legacy 1979–1992*, London, Academic Press

Mommsen, W. J., Osterhammel, J. eds. 1987 *Max Weber and His Contemporaries*, London, Unwin

Momsen, J. H. 1990 *Women and Development in the Third World*, London, Routledge

Moore, B. 1966 *The Social Origins of Dictatorship and Democracy*, Boston, Mass., Beacon

Morgan, L. 1877 *Ancient Society*, London

Myrdal, G. 1958 *Value in Social Theory*, London, Routledge

Myrdal, G. 1970 *The Challenge of World Poverty*, London, Allen Lane

Nairn, T. 1988 *The Enchanted Glass*, London, Radius

Napoleoni, C. 1972 *Economic Thought of the Twentieth Century*, London, Martin Robertson

Nisbet, R. 1966 *The Sociological Tradition*, New York, Basic Books

O'Brien, P. J. 1975 'A Critique of Latin American Theories of Dependency' in Oxaal, I. et al. *Beyond the Sociology of Development*, London, Routledge

Ohmae, K. 1990 *A Borderless World*, Tokyo, Kodansha

Ormerod, P. 1994 *The Death of Economics*, London, Faber

Oxaal, I. et al. 1975 *Beyond the Sociology of Development*, London, Routledge

Palma, G. 1978 'Dependency: A Formal Theory of Underdevelopment or a Methodology for the Analysis of Concrete Situations of Underdevelopment', *World Development*, 6

Pandy, B. N. 1980 *South and Southeast Asia 1945–1979: Problems and Policies*, London, Macmillan

Passmore, J. 1968 *A Hundred Years of Philosophy*, Harmondsworth, Penguin

Passmore, J. 1971 *The Perfectibility of Man*, London, Duckworth

Peet, R. 1991 *Global Capitalism: Theories of Societal Development*, London, Routledge

Petras, J., Zeitlin, M. eds. 1968 *Latin America: Reform or Revolution*, Greenwich, Fawcett

Pheby, J. 1988 *Methodology and Economics: A Critical Introduction*, London, Macmillan

Piore, M., Sabel, C. 1984 *The Second Industrial Divide*, New York, Basic Books

Plant, R. 1991 *Modern Political Thought*, Oxford, Blackwell

Pollard, S. 1971 *The Idea of Progress*, Harmondsworth, Penguin

Postan, M. M. 1967 *An Economic History of Western Europe 1945–1964*, London, Methuen

Prebisch. R. 1950 *The Economic Development of Latin America and its Principal Problems*, New York, United Nations Publications

Preston, P. W. 1982 *Theories of Development*, London, Routledge

Preston, P. W. 1983 'A Critique of Some Elements of the Residual Common Sense of Development Studies', *Cultures et Developpement*, 15

Preston, P. W. 1985 *New Trends in Development Theory*, London, Routledge

Preston, P. 1986 *Making Sense of Development*, London, Routledge

Preston, P. W. 1987 *Rethinking Development*, London, Routledge

Preston, P. W. 1994a *Discourses of Development: State, Market and Polity in the Analysis of Complex Change*, Aldershot, Avebury

Preston, P. W. 1994b *Europe, Democracy and the Dissolution of Britain*, Aldershot, Dartmouth

Preston, P. W. 1995 'The Debate on the Pacific Asian Miracle Considered' in idem ed. *Aspects of Complex Change in Asia*, Occasional Paper 7, Department of Anthropology and Sociology, Universiti Kebangsaan, Malaysia

Pusey, M. 1991 *Economic Rationalism in Canberra: A Nation-Building State Changes its Mind*, Cambridge University Press

Redclift, M., Benton, T. eds. 1994 *Social Theory and the Global Environment*, London, Routledge

Rendall, J. 1978 *The Origins of the Scottish Enlightenment*, London, Macmillan

Reuschemeyer, D. 1986 *Power and the Division of Labour*, Cambridge, Polity

Reuschemeyer, D. et al. 1992 *Capitalist Development and Democracy*, Cambridge, Polity

Reynolds, H. 1982 *The Other Side of the Frontier*, Penguin Australia, Ringwood

Rhodes, R. I. 1968 'The Disguised Conservatism of Evolutionary Development Theory', *Science and Society*, 32

Robertson, F. 1980 *An Anthropology of Planned Development*, Cambridge University Press

Robertson, R. 1992 *Globalization: Social Theory and Global Culture*, London, Sage

Robinson, J. 1962 *Economic Philosophy*, Harmondsworth, Penguin
Rocher, G. 1974 *Talcott Parsons and American Sociology*, London, Nelson
Root, M. 1993 *Philosophy of Social Science*, Oxford, Blackwell
Rosenberg, A. 1938 *Democracy and Socialism*, London
Rostow, W. W. 1956 'The Take-Off into Self-Sustained Growth', *Economic Journal*, 66
Rostow, W. W. 1960 *The Stages of Economic Growth: A Non-Communist Manifesto*, Cambridge University Press
Rostow, W. W. 1990 *Theorists of Economic Growth from David Hume to the Present*, Oxford University Press
Roxborough, I. 1970 *Theories of Underdevelopment*, London, Macmillan
Runciman, G. 1972 *Critique of Weber's Philosophy of Social Science*, Cambridge University Press
Ryle, G. 1949 *The Concept of Mind*, London, Hutchinson
Sachs, I. 1976 *The Discovery of the Third World*, London, MIT Press
Sachs, W. ed. 1992 *The Development Dictionary*, London, Zed
Sahay, A. ed. 1971 *Max Weber and Modern Sociology*, London, Routledge
Sahlins, M. 1972 *Stoneage Economics*, London, Tavistock
Said, E. 1993 *Culture and Imperialism*, London, Chatto
Scammel, W. M. 1980 *The International Economy Since 1945*, London, Macmillan
Schiel, T. 1987 'Wallerstein's Concept of a Modern World System: Another Marxist Critique', *University of Bielefeld Sociology of Development Research Centre Working Papers*, 89
Scholte, A. 1993 *International Relations of Social Change*, Milton Keynes, Open University Press
Scott, J. C. 1976 *The Moral Economy of the Peasant*, Yale University Press
Scott, J. C. 1985 *Weapons of the Weak*, Yale University Press
Seers, D. 1963 'The Limitations of the Special Case', *Oxford Bulletin of Statistics*, 25
Seers, D. 1979 'Patterns of Dependency' in Villamil, J. J. ed. *Transnational Capitalism and National Development: New Perspectives on Dependence*, Hassocks, Harvester
Seers, D. ed. 1981 *Dependency Theory: A Critical Reassesment*, London, Pinter
Skinner, Q. ed. 1985 *The Return of Grand Theory in the Human Sciences*, Cambridge University Press
Sklair, L. 1991 *Sociology of the Global System*, Hemel Hempstead, Harvester Wheatsheaf
Smart, B. 1993 *Postmodernity*, London, Routledge
Smelser, N. 1968 *Essays in Sociological Explanation*, Englewood Cliffs, Prentice-Hall
Smith, A. D. 1973 *The Concept of Social Change*, London, Routledge
Smith, A. D. 1976 *Social Change: Social Theory and Historical Process*, London, Routledge
Smith, D. 1987 *The Rise and Fall of Monetarism*, Harmondsworth, Penguin
Smith, D. 1991 *The Rise of Historical Sociology*, Cambridge, Polity
Solow, R. 1956 'A Contribution to the Theory of Economic Growth', *Quarterly Journal of Economics*, 70
Spybey, T. 1992 *Social Change, Development and Dependency*, Cambridge, Polity
Staniland, M. 1985 *What is Political Economy*, New Haven, Yale University Press
Statera, G. 1975 *Death of a Utopia*, Oxford University Press

Stavehhagen, R. 1968 'Seven Erroneous Theses on Latin America' in Petras, J., Zeitlin, M. eds. *Latin America: Reform or Revolution*, Greenwich, Fawcett

Strange, S. 1988 *States and Markets*, London, Pinter

Streeten, P. 1970 'An Institutional Critique of Development Concepts', *Journal of European Sociology*, 11

Streeten, P. 1972 *The Frontiers of Development Studies*, London, Macmillan

Streeten, P. 1981 *Development Perspectives*, London, Macmillan

Streeten, P. ed. 1970 *Unfashionable Economics: Essays in Honour of Lord Balogh*, London, Weidenfeld

Sturrock, J. 1986 *Structuralism*, London, Paladin

Sunkel, O. 1969 'National Development Policy and External Dependency in Latin America', *Journal of Development Studies*, 6

Sunkel, O., Fuenzalida, E. 1979 'Transnationalization and Its National Consequences', in Villamil, J. J. ed. *Transnational Capitalism and National Development: New Perspectives on Dependence*, Hassocks, Harvester

Swedberg, R. 1987 'Economic Sociology Past and Present', *Current Sociology*, 35

Sweezy, P. 1942 *The Theory of Capitalist Development*, Oxford University Press

Sztompka, P. 1993 *The Sociology of Social Change*, Oxford, Blackwell

Taylor, J. G. 1979 *From Modernization to Modes of Production*, London, Macmillan

Thorne, C. 1986 *The Far Eastern War: States and Societies 1941–45*, London, Unwin

Thurow, L. 1992 *Head to Head: The Coming Economic Battle Amongst Japan, Europe and America*, New York, Morrow

Tipps, D. C. 1976 'Modernisation Theory and the Comparative Study of Societies: A Critical Perspective' in Black. C. E. ed. *Comparative Modernization*, London, Collier

Todaro, M. P. 1982 *Economics for a Developing World*, London, Longman

Toye, J. 1987 *Dilemmas of Development*, Oxford, Blackwell

Tribe, K. 1978 *Land, Labour and Economic Discourse*, London, Routledge

Turner, B. S. 1992 *Max Weber: From History to Modernity*, London, Routledge

United Nations 1951 *Measures for the Economic Development of Underdeveloped Countries*, New York, United Nations Publications

United Nations 1995 *Yearbook of the United Nations: Special Edition UN Fiftieth Anniversary*, The Hague, Kluwer Law International

United Nations Development Programme 1990 *Human Development Report 1990*, Oxford University Press

van der Pijl, K. 1984 *The Making of an Atlantic Ruling Class*, London, Verso

van Wolferen, K. 1993 *The Enigma of Japanese Power*, Tokyo, Tutle

Villamil J. J. ed. 1979 *Transnational Capitalism and National Development: New Perspectives on Dependence*, Hassocks, Harvester

Vogel, E. 1980 *Japan as Number One*, Tokyo, Tutle

Walker, M. 1993 *The Cold War and the Making of the Modern World*, London, Fourth Estate

Wallerstein, I. 1974 *The Modern World System*, New York, Academic

Ward, H. 1995 'Rational Choice Theory' in Marsh, D., Stoker, G. eds. *Theory and Methods in Political Science*, London, Macmillan

White, G. ed. 1988 *Developmental States in East Asia*, London, Macmillan

White, J. 1973 *The Politics of Foreign Aid*, London, Bodley Head

Wilkinson, E. 1990 *Japan versus the West: Image and Reality*, Harmondsworth, Penguin

Willets, P. 1978 *The Non-Aligned Movement*, London, Pinter

Williams, R. 1973 'Base and Superstructure in Marxist Cultural Theory', *New Left Review*, 82

Woodcock, G. 1969 *The British in the Far East*, London, Weidenfeld

Woodiwiss, A. 1993 *Postmodernity USA: The Crisis of Social Modernism in Post-war America*, London, Sage

World Bank 1993 *The East Asian Miracle*, Oxford University Press

Worsley, P. 1964 *The Third World*, London, Weidenfeld

Worsley, P. 1982 *Marx and Marxism*, Milton Keynes, Open University Press

Worsley, P. 1984 *The Three Worlds: Culture and World Development*, London, Weidenfeld

Yearley, S. 1994 'Social Movements and Environmental Change' in Redclift, M., Benton, T., eds. *Social Theory and the Global Environment*, London, Routledge

Zeitlin, I. 1968 *Ideology and the Development of Sociological Theory*, New York, Prentice-Hall

Zeylstra, G. 1977 *Aid or Development*, Leiden, A. W. Sijthoff

Index